Guide to ACE the PMP

Embracing Predictive, Adaptive, and Hybrid Approaches to Project Management

Greta Blash, PgMP, PMP
Steve Blash, PMP

Foreword

Welcome to this comprehensive study guide for the Project Management Professional (PMP) certification exam. Project management professionals are crucial in ensuring successful project outcomes in today's dynamic business environment. This book has been meticulously crafted to equip experienced project managers like yourself with the knowledge, concepts, and techniques necessary to excel on the PMP exam and further enhance your project management skills.

This study guide delves into the actual content aligned with the 2021 Content Outline to assist you on your PMP exam journey. It also references relevant resources, including the *Agile Practice Guide*. The authors of this book are seasoned project management professionals with extensive experience, including contributions to previous editions of the *PMBOK Guide*. As authorized trainers and instructors, they possess the expertise to guide you effectively through the study process.

The study guide is structured into six main chapters, meticulously following a typical project sequence. Each chapter comprehensively covers the domains and tasks included in the Exam Content Outline. From exploring the foundational concepts of the business environment to navigating project closeout, you will gain valuable insights and guidance to navigate the complexities of project management success.

To facilitate your learning and progress, this guide provides additional resources. Key concepts are highlighted, and carefully crafted questions are integrated throughout each section and chapter to assess your understanding. Supplemental information on the Project Management Framework, including process groups and knowledge areas, and an introduction to Agile methodologies, further enrich your knowledge. Additionally, a glossary of terms is provided for quick reference.

As you embark on this study journey, remember that the PMP certification is a testament to your knowledge, dedication to the profession, and commitment to delivering successful projects. Use this study guide as your trusted companion, immerse yourself in the content, and apply the knowledge gained to real-world scenarios.

On behalf of the authors, I commend your decision to pursue the PMP certification and extend my best wishes for success in your endeavors. May this study guide serve as a valuable resource in your preparation, enabling you to excel on the exam and make significant contributions to the ever-evolving field of project management.

Finally, I won't wish you good luck on your PMP exam — luck is for the ill-prepared. If you follow the strategies outlined in this book and apply yourself, you'll certainly pass the exam on your first and only attempt.

Dr. James Lee Haner, PMP

Table of Contents

Introduction

I must admit I was skeptical of getting my PMP after having over 15 years of experience as a project manager. When I was rejected for a consulting project management position because I was not PMP certified, I realized that the certification, and the letters after my name, made a difference. It was then that I studied and obtained the first of many credentials in project management, business analysis, and agile disciplines. Not only did this show prospective employers proof of my diligence in obtaining the certification – but it also added to my knowledge of project management concepts. With those additional "tools" in my toolbox I can better determine the best approach to handle different situations I encounter when managing projects.

This book is meant to serve as a Project Management Professional (PMP) certification study guide for experienced project managers who have on-the-job project management or leadership experience, regardless of whether their formal job role or title is project manager, who are not currently certified project management professionals, and who may or may not have received formal project management training to prepare for the PMP exam from the Project Management Institute, Inc. (PMI).

It provides candidates with additional knowledge of predictive, adaptive, and hybrid concepts, terminology, and techniques addressed on the PMP exam. Additionally, current project management skills can be enhanced by applying a more formalized and standards-based approach to project management while preparing for PMP certification.

Two basic requirements must be met to apply to take the PMP exam. The first is 35 hours of project management training or a Certified Associate Project Management (CAPM) certification, and the second is experience leading projects within the past eight years, depending on your level of education.

The current PMP exam is NOT based solely on any edition of the *PMBOK Guide* but instead on the 2021 PMI Exam Content Outline (ECO) and multiple references, including the *Agile Practice Guide*.

The book includes six main chapters, organized by the typical project sequence, and covers all the domains and tasks identified in the PMP ECO. It also addresses the differences between predictive, adaptive, and hybrid project management approaches.

The chapters include:

- **Business Environment**—foundational project management, organizational, and business concepts integral to the role of the project manager.
- **Project Initiating**—what should be considered at the start of a project, during the preplanning stage, including stakeholders, the team, building a shared understanding of the vision and project objectives, and choosing the approach most appropriate for delivering a successful result.
- **Project Planning**—the steps necessary to plan how various aspects of the project will be managed, including the scope, schedule, budget, resources, risks, quality plans, and differences based on the approaches used.
- **Team Leadership**—the application of the various leadership skills of a project manager.
- **Project Performance**—the tools, techniques, and additional leadership skills to help get the best performance from the project to meet project expectations successfully.
- **Project/Phase Closure**—the activities of closing either a phase, project, or release, including understanding benefits realization and knowledge management.

The book also contains additional supplemental information, including vital foundational concepts and other questions throughout each section to help you check your progress. A review of the Project Management Framework process groups and knowledge areas is included for reference.

Objectives

In this book, as a project manager, you will review how to assemble and manage a team to plan, execute, and complete a project aligned with the business environment. Objectives are related to the following topics:

Business Environment

- Define "project" and how it relates to the more extensive "project management" understanding.
- Understand organizational structures and how they relate to project management.
- Understand the principles of project management.
- Understand the principles of agile and how they relate to managing various types of projects.
- Understand strategic alignment and its elements.

- Determine how projects align with business strategy.
- Identify the types of business value.
- Understand change management theory and its relation to organizational change.
- Define and understand project governance.
- Understand project compliance and its importance.

Project Initiating

- Define and understand stakeholders and the most effective communication methods.
- Understand ways to form a project team.
- Understand how to build the most effective understanding of a project.
- Understand what is needed to execute a project successfully.
- Understand the different predictive, adaptive, and hybrid approaches.

Project Planning

- Understand the importance of a project management plan.
- Provide an overview of scope planning in predictive projects and adaptive environments.
- Provide an overview of schedule planning in predictive and adaptive projects.
- Understand what resources are and how to procure external resources for a project.
- Determine the budgeting structure for a project.
- Identify strategies for dealing with risk planning, and responding to risks when they occur.
- Define quality and how it relates to the outcomes and deliveries for a project.
- Understand artifacts and the strategies for their use.
- Understand the importance of integrating project management plans into the change management process.
- Understand the content of subsidiary project plans.

Team Leadership

- Understand the guidelines for developing leadership competencies and skills.
- Address leadership styles and the components of leading a successful team, either in person or virtually.

- Identify the characteristics and core functions of empowered, self-organized teams.
- Understand strategies for collaborating in a project team environment.
- Learn the value of training, coaching, and mentoring.
- Understand the importance of conflict management.
- Understand the causes and levels of conflict and their outcomes.

Project Performance

- Understand the various methods for implementing improvement.
- Understand the importance of continuously delivering value.
- Understand the various methods for performance measurement.
- Identify the issues and impediments arising during a project.
- Understand the methods for implementing changes during a project.

Project/Phase Closure

- Define the reasons and activities related to the closure of a phase or a project.
- Understand the benefits gained from a project or phase and how they are managed, sustained, etc.
- Examine the reasons for knowledge transfers and how they relate to the closure of a phase or project.

Project Management Framework

- Define the basic Project Management Framework, including process groups, knowledge areas, and processes.
- Identify key concepts and significant deliverables for knowledge areas.

PMP Certification

You are earning your PMP as part of the global PMI community, supporting important project work worldwide. Globally recognized and demanded, the PMP certification marks experience, education, and competency for leading and directing projects. Once you pass the exam, you maintain the credential by obtaining Professional Development Units (PDUs). This is like other certification programs, such as the Certified Public Accountant (CPA) exam, with continuing professional development requirements to maintain certification.

Certification Requirements

No matter where you are, learning the core principles of project management and engaging in continued professional development will help you through guided, lifetime understanding and application of project management concepts.

The requirements to sit for the PMP exam depend on your educational level. In addition to study and academic preparation, your project management experience is essential.

If you have a four-year degree, you will need 36 months of experience leading projects within the past eight years, as well as 35 hours of project management education/ training or a CAPM certification.

Suppose you have a high school diploma or an associate's degree (or a global equivalent). In that case, you will need 60 months of experience leading projects within the past eight years, as well as 35 hours of project management education or a CAPM certification.

The experience should include project management leadership responsibility, rather than simply your involvement working on projects. Your experience should reflect leadership of the team as well as monitoring the project work.

PMP Certification Exam

The PMP certification continues to be a competency-based assessment of the integrated knowledge, skills, and abilities gained from both practical and learned experiences. It is not a test of your ability to read and memorize exam preparation materials. So, think about how the concepts apply to your daily work and explore new ideas while you study and prepare for the exam.

The questions are scenario-based and written by working PMPs and are not based on any single text or supported by any reference. The list of references provided by PMI is part of a more extensive set of educational resources and texts helpful for study and exam preparation. This reference list is provided as a courtesy only, and for the non-PMI publications on this list, PMI does not endorse such publications or warrant the accuracy of the information or opinions contained therein. The references listed on pmi.org include but a few resources to utilize and should not be interpreted as a guaranteed means of passing the exam. PMI does not endorse specific review courses, resources, references, or other materials for certification preparation. PMI does provide an authorized PMP prep course, offered only by Authorized Training Partners (ATPs) and taught by certified instructors.

Note: We at Facilitated Methods are an ATP and are certified, authorized instructors.

The PMI Talent Triangle and the PMP Exam Content Outline (ECO) domains are critical references for the exam. The exam content and questions follow the sides of the PMI Talent Triangle and focus on the following:

- Power Skills of project leadership or the people aspect of projects — 42%
- Ways of Working, or how to do the project — 50%
- Business Acumen, or how projects support the organization's strategic objectives — 8%

The allocations refer to the percentage of exam questions devoted to the triangle side corresponding to the domains in the ECO. The sequence of this book's content reflects how projects are initiated, planned, executed, monitored, controlled, and closed. The content has been mapped to the Triangle and ECO domains, with all domains and enablers addressed.

The 2021 PMP exam includes multiple approaches spanning the value delivery spectrum, including predictive, adaptive, and hybrid. It has been updated to reflect a fuller complement of skills and techniques found and utilized in the dynamic and global project management profession.

The Exam Content Outline (ECO)[1]

An international committee of PMPs revised the exam content. They periodically refine the domains and tasks on the ECO to support current project management practices. The ECO includes a detailed list of the domains, tasks, and enablers relevant to project management work.

- Domains are defined as the high-level knowledge areas essential to project management
- Tasks are the underlying responsibilities of the project manager within each domain area
- Enablers are examples of work associated with the tasks to help explain what the task encompasses
- All exam questions are mapped to tasks identified in the ECO

Exam Tip: The exam is based on the PMP certification ECO, not solely on the PMBOK Guide or other reference books. A Guide to the Project Management Body of Knowledge (PMBOK Guide) — Seventh Edition has been added to develop the exam items. However, a rigorous and thorough review and field test cycle is required before adding any validated exam item. This

---

1   *https://www.pmi.org/certification/project-management-pmp*

process takes multiple months. As a result, it will be a while before any significant changes are made to the exam, and a new ECO is developed.

This book does not explicitly reference the content of the ECO by number. It would be impossible to cover the entire detailed content of the ECO. Use the ECO as a checklist against your knowledge base and as guidance for what you need to learn. This helps guide you in ensuring you have an understanding to answer exam questions.

Exam Tip: You should be familiar with the ECO document as a study aid. Use it to check what you know and determine where you need to spend more time mastering the tasks fully.

The current version of the PMP exam went live in January 2021.

The exam is 230 minutes long, including two 10-minute breaks, and consists of 180 questions. After the first 60 questions, you will be given a chance to take a break. Once you have completed those questions, you will receive the next 60 questions. You will not be able to return to the previous 60 questions.

In addition to multiple-choice questions, it now features new question formats, including multiple responses, matching drag and drop, hotspot, and some fill-in-the-blank.

Steps to Certification

There are three main steps toward PMP certification:

Step 1: Apply to take the exam by completing the online application and submitting your experience and education at pmi.org. Additional aids are available, including the *Certification Handbook*, at pmi.org.

Step 2: Upon acceptance of your application, study and take the PMP exam. Additional aids are available to help you understand what to expect on the exam, what to expect the day of the exam, and how to prepare to pass on pmi.org.

Step 3: Maintain your certification by engaging in continuous professional development activities and events and submitting your Professional Development Units (PDUs).

Business Environment

This chapter addresses the concepts and business areas you should understand before starting a project, including those supporting the understanding related to the "Business Environment" domain in the ECO and the "Business Acumen" side of the PMI Talent Triangle. It also covers foundational project management concepts, elements, and terminology.

The content of this chapter moves above and beyond the typical project management processes to focus on the business environment where the project will be developed to support a change in how the business organization currently operates. It also includes additional elements supporting the strategic alignment between the organization and project results.

Even though this section only represents 8 percent of the exam, we encourage you to spend some time reading and studying this material as it is often overlooked, and there are concepts and questions based on this chapter not included in previous versions of the exam.

Central to this chapter is determining the project's purpose, expectations, and objectives within the business environment. The business documents approving the project will provide the initial information needed. If these are not available, it is necessary to quickly determine the purpose and expectations for the project, regardless of the chosen development approach. Understanding business acumen and a good foundation in modern project practices will enable the successful delivery of results.

In this chapter, you will:

- Learn the definition of a project and the components of project management.
- Understand the principles of project management.
- Understand the principles of agile and how they relate to managing different types of projects.
- Understand the different types of organizational structures and how they relate to the management of projects.
- Understand strategic alignment and its elements.
- Learn how to align projects with business strategy.
- Differentiate between types of business value and how they pertain to projects.

- Describe change management theory and its relation to organizational change.
- Describe project governance.
- Explain project compliance and its importance.

Topics in This Chapter

- Foundation Concepts
- Strategic Alignment
- Project Benefits and Value
- Organizational Culture and Change
- Project Governance
- Project Compliance

Foundation Concepts

The project management discipline continues to evolve and adapt due to changing environments and requirements. Understanding of PMI's primary project management terminology has expanded to include new approaches and "ways of working." Project management principles guide the behavior and actions of project managers, team members, and stakeholders to provide intended outcomes to meet expectations.

The actual Project Management Professional (PMP) certification exam does not explicitly test these concepts, but the content and foundation of the questions are written with an understanding of them.

PMBOK Guide

The *PMBOK Guide* was developed and has evolved based on the best practices by volunteer teams of experienced project management practitioners. It has become a globally recognized standard of best practices for project management professionals. By generally recognized, it means the knowledge and techniques included apply to most projects, most of the time, and are a consensus of their value and usefulness.

In the sixth edition of the *PMBOK Guide,* a new section, Part 2, was added and became the stand-alone ANSI Standard for Project Management. This section presents the processes, as well as the inputs and outputs, considered to be good practices on most projects. "Good practice" means there is general agreement that applying the skills, tools, and techniques included in this guide can enhance the success of many projects.

The seventh edition of the *PMBOK Guide* has two sections, the ANSI Standard for Project Management and the *PMBOK Guide*. Even though the current PMP exam does not cover the seventh edition content specifically, this newer version addresses many of the concepts and principles covered in the exam in a more meaningful way.

Exam Tip: The PMP exam has never been based solely on a specific version of the PMBOK Guide, but rather on a variety of sources. This book covers all the areas that may show up on the exam. We have reviewed all the references listed by PMI in developing this book.

The CAPM exam, on the other hand, is specifically based on the current 7th edition of the PMBOK Guide and latest CAPM ECO.

A common terminology or vocabulary has been referenced in this book. Many of the changes made in the sixth edition of the *PMBOK Guide* result from the standardization of terminology among the various PMI practice guides and certification standards, including those for program and portfolio management. These have become part of the *PMI Lexicon of Project Management Terms*.

Even though this book addresses many of the activities needed to manage a project, each organization and each project team will need to determine what work is appropriate for their assigned project. Not all activities will be necessary for all projects, and it is the responsibility of project management and the performing organization to determine the minimum set of processes required and the level of detail needed.

PMI Talent Triangle

The PMI Talent Triangle is a realistic representation of critical professional skills for project management, and it has also become an essential and well-recognized icon for the PMI brand, encompassing key elements of the project management professional core value proposition.

To help project professionals navigate this changing world of work and embrace more innovative ways of working, the updated PMI Talent Triangle now focuses on the following:

Ways of Working—Formerly Technical Project Management

These competencies are those required to deliver the desired project results and are the skills project managers initially acquire, including:

- – Understanding and delivering the crucial success factors for the project
- – Managing the project schedule
- – Reporting the financial status of the project appropriately
- – Communicating the status of progress and issues through appropriate methods
- – Following quality assurance procedures
- – Implementing lessons learned and continuous improvement activities

Planning key project elements thoroughly, including schedule, cost, resources, and risks, and continually prioritizing them to deliver the most significant value to the customer is essential.

Mastering diverse and creative ways to get any job done by understanding and tailoring the ways of working, where applicable, is often needed for today's projects. This includes traditional and agile tools, design thinking, ideation, or other new practices.

Power Skills—Formerly Leadership

Power skills (often referred to as "soft skills") go beyond typical project management competencies to include the critical people skills of professionals at every level. These enable individuals to apply influence, inspire change, and build relationships. The common thread of all projects is people—and project managers must deal with people at all levels through their behavior, being respectful and culturally sensitive.

As a leader, a project manager must also be a visionary, apply critical thinking, and have a holistic and systemic view of the project while remaining optimistic and positive. This also includes encouraging collaboration and building effective teams, often with a need to manage relationships and conflict. Interpersonal and negotiation skills are required to motivate others.

Communicating is a crucial leadership skill since most of the project manager's time will be spent communicating and engaging with stakeholders and other team members.

Business Acumen—Formerly Strategic and Business Management Skills

Business acumen is an understanding of the business of an organization. It thus enables the ability to make sound judgments and quick decisions while understanding the many influencing factors across an organization or industry. This includes working with project sponsors to implement a strategy maximizing business value in alignment with the organization's mission and strategy. It requires a working knowledge of business functions, products or services provided, and competitors. Regardless of past work, a project manager must understand and explain the essential aspects of a project as they relate to the business.

The Business Acumen side of the Talent Triangle comprises the smallest percentage of the exam questions on the PMP exam. Still, project professionals must understand and support organizations in today's changing and competitive environment.

Project Management

What Is a Project?

A project is defined as a temporary endeavor to create a unique product, service, or result—the key words being temporary and unique.

This definition has been expanded because of the need to adapt to change and create business value. The result of a project effort can be a solution to a problem, enhancement of an opportunity, or conformance to a compliance requirement.

A project always has a beginning and an end. The end may be when the project's objectives have been met, when it is terminated because its objectives will not or cannot be met, or when the need for it no longer exists.

"Temporary" does not mean short duration but refers to the project's engagement and longevity. The resulting product may last for years, as in the case of a building, or involve social, economic, or environmental impacts remaining after the project has been completed.

Delivering the results of a project may involve single or multiple individuals, single or multiple organizations, or multiple individuals from multiple organizations. The structure and impact of these organizations will impact how the project is managed.

Project Management

Applying knowledge, skills, tools, and techniques to project activities to meet the project requirements accomplished through the appropriate application and integration of project management processes appropriately applied to each project.[2]

---

2   *https://www.PMI.org/about/learn-about-pmi/what-is-project-management*

The importance of project management includes helping an organization meet its business objectives while satisfying individual stakeholder expectations.

When project management concepts are utilized, the project results can be more predictable and thus increase the chances for success while better managing change. It can increase satisfaction for all stakeholders, through enabling a customer and quality focus. Project management can also help deliver the right results at the right time, on schedule, within budget, and with acceptable quality, whether resolving problems and issues or promptly responding to risks.

PMI Project Management[3]

The discipline of project management has evolved over thousands of years. PMI, founded in 1969, continues to advance the profession by applying management knowledge, leadership skills, tools, and techniques to project activities to achieve the project and organizations' objectives.

This was supported through the appropriate selection and usage of the components of the Project Management Framework defined in the sixth edition of the *PMBOK Guide* and *Process Groups: A Practice Guide.* This includes processes to help identify requirements, understand and manage stakeholder needs, concerns, and expectations, provide the appropriate level of communication and engagement with all stakeholders, and balance those requirements with project constraints.

The primary artifact created and used by the project manager throughout the project life cycle is the project management plan. This document identifies how the various aspects of the project will be managed. Because changes occur during the project's life, this document uses an iterative approach, continuously improving as more detailed information is available. It may be formally created, often based on the organization's methodology, or may be a checklist of things to consider when managing a project.

The definition of project management and how it is performed is also evolving, as described in the seventh edition of the *PMBOK Guide*. It now takes a "systems view" of value delivery, focusing on the value chain linking project, program, and portfolio outcomes to advance organizational strategy, value, and business objectives.

Exam Tip: "System" refers to a series of interdependent components working together to accomplish the system's aim. Any component of the system contributes to the overall value of the system.

---

3   *https://www.PMI.org/about/learn-about-pmi/history-of-pmi*

"Projects do not simply produce outputs, but more importantly, enable those outputs to drive **outcomes** *that ultimately deliver value to the organization and its stakeholders."*[4]

Project Success

Project success includes understanding project management concepts and adapting and applying them appropriately to individual projects and contexts.

Project success often depends on:

- Maturity of project management within the organization
- Effectiveness and competency of the project manager
- Availability of appropriate funding and resources
- Required skill levels and competencies of team members
- Effective collaboration and communication with team members and key stakeholders
- Understanding concerns and core problems or opportunities, the current situation and impact, and the related needs

Project Methodology

A system of practices, techniques, procedures, and rules identified by an organization where project management is practiced.

The *PMBOK Guide* is not a methodology but a standard-based guide with principles and best practices to tailor for each unique project.

An organization often adopts a methodology for usage by projects. It often impacts the project's life cycle, governance, and deliverables. Most organizational methodologies today support project activities using a predictive approach.

Project Management Process Groups

Project management processes are organized into logical groupings to meet the project needs using a process-based approach. These include:

- Initiating—defines a new project or phase by obtaining authorization to start
- Planning—establishes the project's scope, refines its objectives, and defines the actions required to achieve the objectives the project was undertaken to achieve
- Executing—performing work defined in the project management plan to satisfy requirements

---

4   *PMBOK Guide, 7th ed.*

- Monitoring and controlling — processes to track, review, and regulate the progress and performance of the project, including identifying and initiating the corresponding changes
- Closing — formal completion processes to close the project, phase, or contract

Project Management Knowledge Areas

A set of project management processes associated with a particular topic or specialization. These are described in terms of their component processes, practices, inputs, outputs, tools, and techniques. These include:

- Integration — combines and coordinates activities from other knowledge areas
- Scope — ensures work required to complete the project successfully is included
- Schedule — manages timely completion of the project
- Cost — ensures completion within the approved budget
- Quality — incorporates the organization's quality policy and project quality requirements
- Resources — ensures the availability of resources at the right time
- Communications — dissemination of timely and appropriate project information
- Risk — identifying and monitoring risk on the project
- Procurement — acquisition of resources needed from outside the project team
- Stakeholder — appropriate and effective engagement of stakeholders in project decisions and execution

Project Management Office (PMO)

A management structure standardizes the project-related governance processes and facilitates sharing resources, methodologies, tools, and techniques.

The purpose of the Project Management Office (PMO) is to centralize the management of projects across the organization. PMOs are more common in larger organizations because of the number of projects in progress simultaneously and the need for some standardization across projects within the organization. Having a PMO is not a requirement for project management practices. PMI does not provide official guidelines or standards for a PMO, so large organizations must refer to and utilize PMI principles and best practices to implement a PMO, including tailoring to support the industry and type of projects being performed at any point in time.

A PMO can offer assistance and guidance for all projects in their early phases, as well as ongoing support by providing methods and procedures, templates, and policies for managing projects. They also offer guidance and training on project management concepts and how to manage projects within the organization.

There are several types of PMO (portfolio, program, or project management office) structures, each varying in the degree of control and influence they have on projects within the organization.

Supportive PMO

The supportive PMO's role is to develop and provide best practices for project management by establishing standards and templates for projects. They can also offer coaching, training, and mentoring for project managers and additional support for the project management role in the organization.

Controlling PMO

When the role is controlling, the PMO moves beyond providing support and understanding and fulfills the role of governance and compliance through various activities. This may involve monitoring compliance with project management standards or methodologies; specifying the usage of specific templates, forms, and tools; or ensuring conformance to organizational governance.

Directive PMO

The directive role reflects the PMO organization as the functional or reporting unit for all project managers. In this role, control of projects is taken through the direct management of project managers and shared resources. This type of PMO also assumes responsibility for coordinating communication across all organizational projects.

A relatively small number of PMOs fall into this category, which often includes the controlling aspects in addition to reporting responsibilities for projects.

Centers of Excellence (CoEs)

Organizations may form other groups to support dissemination of skills and knowledge within the organization. These often support projects using an adaptive approach and may be referred to as a Value Delivery Office (VDO). This project delivery support structure focuses on coaching teams through utilization of experts and often provides the organization's best practices, training, and continuous improvement support.

Exam Tip: The term Center of Excellence is also applied similarly to a PMO to support business analysis teams within an organization.

These CoEs enable and support, rather than manage, project efforts, including:

- Coaching teams on adaptive project management and business analysis techniques and usage
- Developing a predictive, adaptive, or hybrid mindset, skills, and capabilities throughout the organization
- Providing training and coaching to team members, sponsors, and product owners

Organizational Project Management (OPM)

A strategy execution framework that coordinates project, program, portfolio, and operations management, enabling organizations to deliver on strategy.

Organizational project management (OPM) is the strategic execution framework at an organizational level where portfolio, program, and project management enable organizations to achieve strategic objectives. These components, working together comprise a system for delivering value aligned with the organization's strategy.

Organizations exist within various environments, working together to provide mutual benefits and value to their stakeholders. External systems, including the economy, technology landscape, marketplace, competition, and local, regional, or country regulations, may impact the organization.

Projects exist as a part of portfolios, or possibly programs, and are part of an organization's internal and external environments. These become vital parts of the system's view of project management.

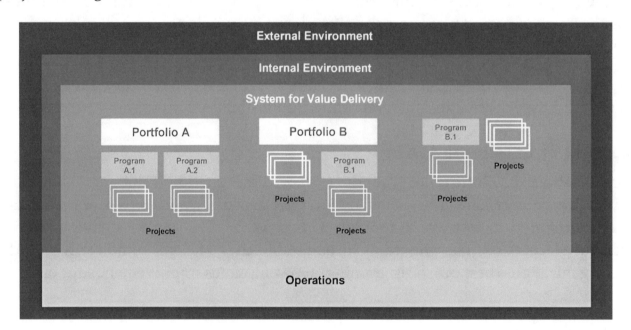

Portfolios-Programs-Projects

These are the key components of the organizational project management (OPM) framework. Projects are part of a broader portfolio, program, or both.

If we look at a portfolio's relationship to programs and projects, we see it at the top of the portfolio for an organization or business unit. The portfolio includes all the work an organization has selected and authorized to be done during a given time frame. The portfolio may consist of programs and projects as well as operations. The programs can be broken down further into multiple projects (and potentially operations), and a project can also include subprojects.

Exam Tip: Remembering this diagram showing the relationships between these components is essential.

Portfolio Management

– *Portfolio*

Projects, programs, component portfolios, and operations that are managed as a group to achieve **strategic objectives***. Programs or projects in the portfolio may not necessarily be interdependent or directly related.*

– *Portfolio Management*

The centralized management method an organization uses to achieve its strategic objectives by authorizing projects or programs.

This is done by making decisions for selecting, approving, and investing efforts to support business strategies and objectives. Business value is realized when the results are transitioned to operations. Over time, the benefits are analyzed to determine whether the business value to support the strategy was achieved.

Each proposal is presented through the portfolio selection process, often including a business case to help justify the investment required. Individual submissions can be accepted, rejected, or deferred for consideration later in a project backlog.

The projects identified through portfolio management may all be interdependent or directly or indirectly related, or they may have been chosen to "maximize return on investment." Often, several independent projects are selected as part of the portfolio management process.

Exam Tip: Remembering the key words for the portfolio are "strategic objectives" will help you select the correct answer for questions referring to this concept on the exam.

Programs

*Related projects, component programs, and program activities are coordinated and managed to obtain **benefits** not available from managing them individually.*

Most people are familiar with the term "projects," but only a few are familiar with the definition of a program.

The definition of a program refers to a group of multiple, individually related projects, subprograms, and program activities managed in a coordinated way to **obtain benefits**. The program activities may include operational activities outside the individual project capability only possible using a program.

If the only commonality between projects includes a shared client, vendor, technology, or resources, the projects should be managed as individual projects within the portfolio and combined into a program.

Exam Tip: The key words to remember for a program are "to provide a benefit."_

– *Program Management*

The application of knowledge, skills, and principles to a program to achieve the program objectives and to obtain projects, subsidiary programs, and program activities, often called components, managed in a coordinated manner to achieve benefits not available if managed individually.

Outcomes from the individual components together provide the anticipated benefits. Program management controls interdependencies between components to ensure the realization of the benefits.

Organizations can use programs and program management to align multiple projects for optimized and updated costs, schedules, efforts, and benefits. Designation of a program allows these related projects to focus on project interdependencies and be managed and executed in an optimal, standard, and controlled manner to realize the desired benefits. These programs may also resolve constraints and issues through sharing resources as well as utilizing a shared governance structure.

Comparison of Projects, Programs, and Portfolios

There are a number of areas where projects, programs, and portfolios differ:

– *Scope*
  - Projects—defined objectives progressively elaborated throughout the project
  - Programs—include scope of components with outcomes and outputs delivered
  - Portfolios—organizational content changing with strategic objectives

- *Change*
  - Projects—expected changes and implement processes to control
  - Programs—adapt to change to optimize the delivery of benefits
  - Portfolios—continuously monitored in broader external and internal environments

- *Planning*
  - Projects—progressively elaborate high-level information into detailed plans
  - Programs—use high-level plans to track progress and interdependencies of components
  - Portfolios—create and maintain processes and communication relative to the aggregate portfolio

- *Management*
  - Projects—manage/lead the team to meet objectives
  - Programs—coordinate component activities to deliver benefits
  - Portfolios—manage or coordinate staff with reporting responsibilities

- *Monitoring*
  - Projects—monitor work of producing results the project was undertaken to produce
  - Programs—monitor progress to ensure overall goals and benefits will be met
  - Portfolios—monitor strategic changes and aggregate resource allocation, performance results, and risk

- *Success*
  - Projects—measured by project and product quality, timeliness, budget compliance, and customer satisfaction
  - Programs—measured by ability to deliver intended benefits efficiently and effectively
  - Portfolios—measured in terms of aggregate investment performance and benefits realization of the portfolio

Projects may be part of a broader program, portfolio, or both, but they also can be executed independently. Program management oversees and controls multiple components and interdependencies to realize benefits, while project management provides the results to achieve organizational goals and objectives.

A project may be part of a program; however, a program will always consist of several projects and potentially additional operational activities.

Exam Tip: Whereas a project delivers results, a program achieves benefits.

Operations Management

This is concerned with managing the ongoing production of goods and services.

In any organization, two types of work are performed. Project work is done to achieve a specific outcome or result, but operational activities are also required to support the day-to-day business.

Operations are ongoing efforts producing repetitive outputs and efficient performance using the optimum resources needed to meet customer demands. Examples may include manufacturing and operations, financial operations, facility maintenance, information technology, or IT support.

This area is outside the scope of formal project management; however, it may intersect with projects and programs at some points.

- *Operations vs. Project Management*

Operations management is responsible for overseeing, directing, and controlling business operations. These especially pertain to the day-to-day support required for the business. They also are necessary to achieve the strategic and tactical goals of the organization.

- Project management is often utilized to enable changes to business operations.
- Projects are temporary and are not concerned with the organization's ongoing operations.
- Projects continually evaluate risks, whereas operational processes are usually designed to minimize or eliminate risk.
- Projects require project management activities and skills, while operations require operation management activities and business process management skill sets.
- Similarities between projects and operations:
- Individuals perform both.
- Both are subject to constraints, including resources, schedule, risks, and others.
- Both are planned, executed, and controlled.
- Both are designed to meet organizational and strategic objectives.

- Differences between projects and operations:
- The project ends at some point, whereas operational processes continue for the life of the functional organization.
- The project may contain several unknown, unpredictable elements, whereas operational details are predictable and repeatable.
- Projects are funded for the project's expected duration, whereas operations are funded annually.
- Project authority varies based on the organizational structure, whereas operations are managed by a functional manager with formal and direct authority over people and processes.

Organizational Structures

An organizational structure reflects the relationships among the various groups and individuals within the organization.

Organizational theory studies formal organizations including their structures and operations and how they interact with their environment. It includes the behavior and performance of groups and individuals within these organizations For projects it includes the understanding of how these groups and individuals are interrelated, the Project Manager's authority, the availability of resources, and how projects are conducted. Depending on whether an organization is designed as a project-based or the more typical functional structure supporting operational needs, the way projects are executed, and especially the authority level of the Project Manager, will vary greatly.

This will often indicate potential organizational silos where functional organizations or employees isolate themselves and refuse to share information or interact with others. These silos prevent the sharing of often critical information.

This includes how organizational groups and individuals are interrelated, the project manager's authority, the availability of resources, and how projects are conducted. Depending on whether an organization is designed as project-based or uses the more typical functional structure supporting operational needs, the way projects are executed, and especially the authority level of the project manager, will vary greatly.

There are organizations whose primary function is to provide project support to other internal or external organizations, including the project manager and the project team members. In those projects involving external organizations, such as business partners or joint ventures, influence on the project may come from multiple organizations.

The organization has a powerful impact on risk management activities and is an area to be assessed early in any project.

Organizations will typically be configured in one of four typical structural implementations.

Functional Organization

One of the most common structures is the functional organization. This is often referred to as the "classic" organizational structure.

Each department is responsible for carrying out a specific organizational set of activities, for example, Finance, Sales, IT, Purchasing, etc., and all work is done by multiple individuals who are part of a specific function, usually the one to which they are assigned. They are grouped by specialties, such as marketing or finance, and possibly further grouped into functional units, such as accounts payable, payroll, and accounts receivable.

These organizational units' management, leadership, and communication styles may differ vastly. Reporting is typically hierarchical, with each reporting to a single functional manager.

Each functional unit will do project work independently, without other departments' involvement. We often refer to these as "silo" organizations.

The functional manager is the individual responsible for directing all the work and managing all the resources required, thus assuming the roles and responsibilities for project-related activities. The functional manager is therefore considered the project manager.

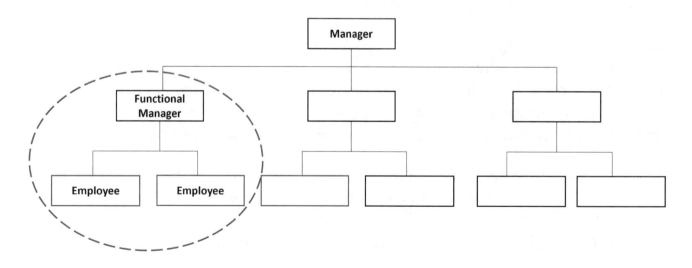

Matrix Organization (Weak, Balanced, and Strong)

The critical aspect of a matrix type of organization is that as a project becomes more involved, team members may be assigned temporarily from other functional areas to provide skills necessary to perform tasks beyond those assigned to functional team members.

The authority and control for project work are shared to some degree between the functional manager and the project manager, depending on the type of matrix structure.

Regardless of their variation, the common factor in matrix organizations is that all team members report to multiple managers. This includes the functional manager of the area where the project is being performed, the resource manager of the organization where they report, and possibly the project manager for the project effort.

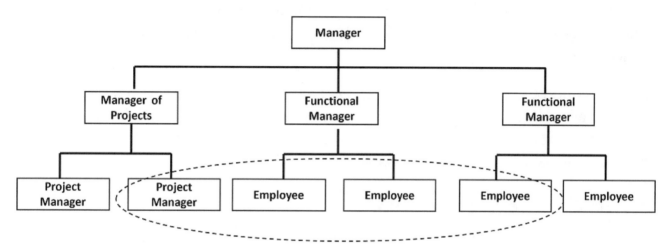

The structure may be weak, balanced, or strong, depending on the authority of the project manager relative to the functional manager.

- *Weak Matrix*

A weak matrix resembles a functional organization with the functional manager still in charge. Still, an individual might be designated as a project coordinator or expediter who often helps with the project's communication aspects. Both the coordinator and expediter have limited authority compared to the functional manager. These roles are very similar to a staff assistant or administrator whose primary function is to handle documentation and administrative tasks.

The project expediter cannot personally make or enforce decisions. Project coordinators have some authority and the power to make some decisions but report to the functional manager.

– *Balanced Matrix*

In the balanced matrix, the need for a project manager is recognized. The project manager shares responsibility with the functional manager but needs to be provided with full authority over the project, especially regarding project funding. Team members report to both functional and resource managers and the project manager.

– *Strong Matrix*

The strong matrix organization more closely resembles a project-oriented organization and often has full-time project managers and possibly even full-time project administrative staff. The project manager often comes from another organization (or the PMO) taking on most project management responsibility, including authority and control over the project team members. However, the resource manager(s) are still involved and have the final say over the assignment and involvement of respective team members from their organizations. Functional managers or executives may be the project sponsor and provide technical/domain knowledge and resources, including project funding, as needed.

The key concept in any matrix organization is that all team members report to at least two managers during the project. And unfortunately, decisions made by the resource manager, responsible for an individual's performance and compensation, will usually take precedence over project involvement.

Project-Oriented Organization

The organizational structure most conducive to project management is a project-oriented organization. The primary purpose of this organizational structure is to deliver projects to internal and external "customers."

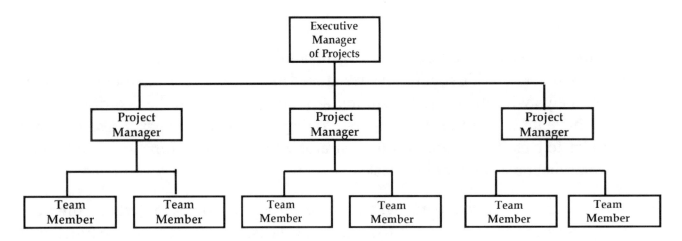

Upon initiating a project, these organizations will assign a project manager with most, if not all, the independence, authority, and control required to deliver a successful project. Core team members are selected to fill the roles needed for the project from a functional area or a pool of resources. The project team resources are usually assigned full-time and preferably collocated within the organization or at a customer location.

In a project-oriented structure, the project manager and a core project team operate as a separate organizational unit within a parent organization. The project manager has significant authority and independence over the team members, including the project schedule, budget, resources, scope, quality, and customer satisfaction.

This type of organization may also be referred to as a project-based organization or PBO when most of the activities done by the organization are projects, and the organization's strategy is based on the success of those efforts. This is the structure utilized by many consulting organizations to provide a project manager and team members for external customer projects. It is also often used for large and complex organizational projects.

Hybrid/Composite Organization

Many modern organizations involve a combination of these structures at various levels. These support projects being delivered purely for usage within a functional organization, external organizations, or "customers."

Small projects can be performed and managed within a functional organization, with the functional manager and the performing organization to determine the minimum set of processes required, or a strong matrix organization. In the latter case, the resources are assigned based on the skills required, regardless of their reporting structure. A full-time, traditional project manager would be responsible for the project effort and have most of the authority for the assigned team members.

They can also support those staffed by multiple individuals for an external organization to support a contract or agreement, where the project structure might look more like a project-oriented structure.

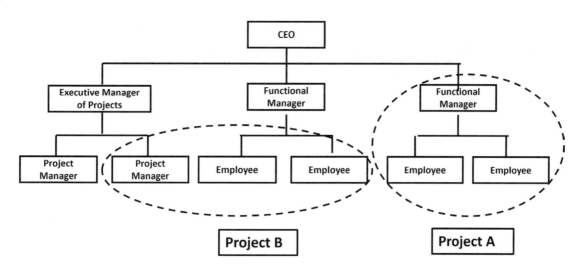

Relative Authority in Organizational Structures

Relative authority refers to the project manager's authority *relative to* the functional manager's authority over the project and the project team, depending on the organizational structure.

- *Team Member Loyalty*
  - Functional—to the functional department and manager
  - Matrix—conflicted loyalty between managers
  - Project-oriented—to the project and project manager

- *Team Member Reporting*
  - Functional—to the functional manager
  - Matrix—to both the functional manager and the project manager
  - Project-oriented—to the project manager

- *Project Manager Role*
  - Functional—seldom or loosely identified as someone other than the functional manager
  - Matrix—coordinator/expediter to an entire project manager
  - Project-oriented—full-time and responsible for project

- *Team Member Role*
  - Functional—part-time on the project among functional responsibilities
  - Matrix—part-time or possibly full-time on individual projects
  - Project-oriented—full-time on the project (preferred)

- *Control of the Project Manager over Team Members*
  - Functional—nonexistent (functional manager controls)
  - Matrix—medium (shared with functional manager/sponsor)
  - Project-oriented—high

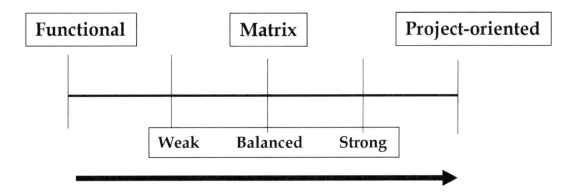

The power and influence of the project manager increases from a functional to a project-oriented structure.

In a purely functional organizational structure, the project manager's authority is low relative to the functional manager. Conversely, in the project-oriented organizational structure, the opposite is true.

Exam Tip: Ensure you understand the various organizational structures and their impact on the project manager's role.

Project Management Principles

In the Standard for Project Management (ANSI/PMI 99-001-2021), the Project Management Institute identified principle statements providing broad parameters for project teams' operation because every project team operates uniquely in alignment with the principles of project management, allowing teams to stay aligned with best practices.

Principles for a profession serve as foundational guidelines for strategy, decision-making, and problem-solving. Professional standards and methodologies are often based on principles. In some professions, principles serve as laws or rules and are, therefore, prescriptive. The principles of project management are not prescriptive in nature. They are intended to guide the behavior of people involved in projects. They are broadly based, so individuals and organizations can maintain alignment with the principles in many ways. Project management principles align with the values identified in the PMI Code of Ethics and Professional Conduct. They do not follow the same format and do not repeat. Instead, the principles and the Code of Ethics complement each other.

Using these principle statements, PMI reflects effective management of projects across the entire value delivery landscape: predictive to adaptive, and everything in between.

Principles include:

- Stewardship—Be a diligent, respectful, and caring steward.
- Team—Create a collaborative project team environment.
- Stakeholders—Effectively engage with stakeholders.
- Value—Focus on value.
- Systems Thinking—Recognize, evaluate, and respond to system interactions.
- Leadership—Demonstrate leadership behaviors.
- Tailoring—Tailor based on context.
- Quality—Build quality into processes and deliverables.
- Complexity—Navigate complexity.
- Risk—Optimize risk responses.
- Adaptability and Resiliency—Embrace adaptability and resiliency.
- Change—Enable change to achieve the envisioned future state.

The introduction of principles-based project management does not negate the conduct of applied project management practices regarding scope, schedule, cost, risk, quality, stakeholders, etc.

Project Performance Domains

The eight identified project performance domains form a group of critical activities for effectively delivering successful project outcomes.

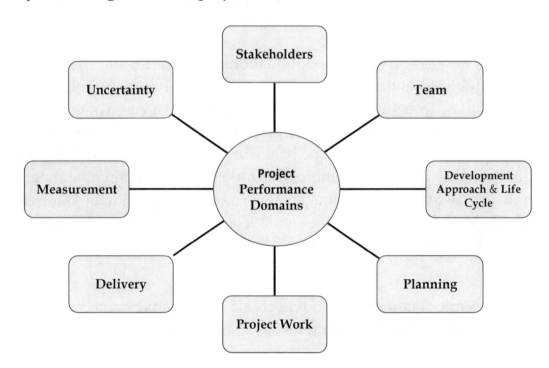

Together the performance domains form a unified whole. In this way, the performance domains operate as an interactive, interrelated, and integrated system, with each performance domain being interdependent on the others to enable the successful delivery of the project and its intended outcomes.

Each domain addresses activities and functions specific to the domain, resulting in specific desired outcomes, including:

1. Stakeholders—addresses activities and functions associated with stakeholders.
   - A productive working relationship where stakeholders derive benefits, and any negative impacts are avoided.
   - Stakeholder agreement with project objectives.

2. Team—addresses activities and functions associated with the people who are responsible for producing project deliverables.
   - Shared ownership.
   - High performance.
   - Everyone has good leadership and interpersonal skills.

3. Development Approach and Life Cycle—addresses activities and functions associated with the development approach, cadence, and life cycle phases of a project.
   - Approaches consistent with deliverables.
   - Life cycle phases deliver value for business and stakeholders from the beginning to the end of the project.
   - Life cycle phases facilitate a delivery cadence and development approach required to produce the project deliverables.

4. Planning—addresses activities and functions associated with the initial, ongoing, and evolving organization and coordination necessary for delivering project deliverables and outcomes.
   - Project progress is organized, coordinated, and deliberate.
   - Holistic approach to delivering project outcomes.
   - Evolving information is elaborated to produce the project's deliverables and outcomes.
   - Planning time is appropriate for the context.
   - Planning information can manage stakeholder expectations.
   - Plans can be adapted in response to change.

5. Project Work—addresses activities and functions associated with establishing project processes, managing physical resources, and fostering a learning environment.

- Performance is efficient and effective.
- Processes are appropriate for the project and context.
- Communications with stakeholders are appropriate.
- Physical resources are efficiently managed.
- Procurements are effectively managed.
- Team capability is improved through continuous learning and process improvement.

6. Delivery—addresses activities and functions associated with delivering the scope and quality that a project was undertaken to achieve.

- Project contributes to business objectives and advancement of strategy.
- Project realizes the outcomes it was initiated to deliver.
- Project benefits are realized in the intended time frame.
- Project team understands requirements clearly.
- Stakeholders accept and are satisfied with project deliverables.

7. Measurement—addresses activities and functions associated with assessing project performance and taking appropriate actions to maintain acceptable performance.

- Project status is reliably understood.
- Actionable data facilitates decision-making.
- Timely and appropriate actions keep project performance on track.
- Goals are achieved and business value is created through informed and timely decisions based on reliable forecasts and evaluations.

8. Uncertainty—addresses activities and functions associated with risk and unpredictability.

- Continue awareness of the economic, social, and political environment and its influence on the project's environment.
- Proactively explore and respond to uncertainty.
- Be aware of the interdependence of project variables.
- Anticipate threats and opportunities and understand the consequences of issues.

- Deliver projects with little or no negative impact from unforeseen events or conditions.

- Realize opportunities to improve project performance and outcomes.

- Utilize cost and schedule reserves effectively to maintain alignment with project objectives.

Performance domains are applied concurrently throughout the project, regardless of how value is delivered (frequently, periodically, or at the project's end). The way performance domains relate differs for each project, but these relationships are present in every project.

The specific activities undertaken within each performance domain are determined by the context of the organization, the project, deliverables, project team, stakeholders, and other factors.

Exam Tip: While memorizing these principles and project performance domains for the current PMP exam isn't essential, they provide a more comprehensive description of project work and PMI's framework in today's environment.

Agile Principles

"Agile" increasingly and frequently is referred to when discussing projects today. Agile has influenced the evolution of project management in recent decades.

It forms the basis for a mindset including the four values from the Agile Manifesto, further described by 12 principles and applied by more than 50 known Agile practices globally. These concepts, though originating in software development, are based on the concept of Lean. They can be applied to any project, with appropriate tailoring to the specific implementation.

Manifesto for Agile Software Development[5]

In 2001 a group of developers released an Agile Manifesto forming the basis for several approaches. The original Agile Manifesto comprises four foundational values mainly applied to software development. Over the years, a few changes have been made to the original wording, and the emphasis has moved from software development to any project effort.

It is not that we do not value the items on the left, but rather prefer the items on the right.

---

5   *https://Agilemanifesto.org*

These include:

Individuals and interactions	Over	Process and tools
Working software/results	Over	Comprehensive documentation
Customer collaboration	Over	Contract negotiation
Responding to change/feedback	Over	Following a plan

Agile Principles[6]

This manifesto was expanded to include 12 principles, often called the Agile mindset.

The key concepts include:

1. Our highest priority is to satisfy the customer through **early and continuous delivery** of valuable software.

2. **Welcome changing** requirements, even late in development. Agile processes harness change for the customer's **competitive advantage**.

3. **Deliver** working software **frequently**, from a couple of weeks to a couple of months, with a preference for a shorter timescale.

4. Businesspeople and developers must **work together daily** throughout the project.

5. Build projects around **motivated individuals**. Give them the environment and support they need and trust them to get the job done.

6. The most efficient and effective method of conveying information to and within a development team is a **face-to-face conversation** (enhanced at a whiteboard).

7. **Working software** is the primary measure of progress. (Measured by results.)

8. Agile processes promote **sustainable development**. The sponsors, developers, and users should be able to maintain a constant pace indefinitely.

9. Continuous attention to **technical excellence** and good design enhances agility.

10. Simplicity—the art of maximizing the work not done—is essential. (Lean concept—eliminate anything not providing value.)

11. The best architecture, requirements, and designs emerge from self-organizing teams.

12. At regular intervals, the team reflects on becoming more effective, then tunes and adjusts its behavior accordingly.

---

6   *https://Agilemanifesto.org/principles*

Hybrid Principles

Agile is often considered too broadly refer to the range of numerous adaptive approaches. In between adaptive and predictive, there is a wide range of tailored hybrid development approaches combining aspects of predictive and adaptive elements. These can be applied to various activities and processes within a project.

The various adaptive approaches are based on the principles of Lean.[7] These include:

- Specify value from the standpoint of the end customer.
- Identify all the steps in the value stream, eliminating whenever possible those steps that do not create value.
- Make the value-creating steps occur in tight sequence so the product will flow smoothly toward the customer.
- As flow is introduced, let customers pull value from the next upstream activity.
- As value is specified, value streams are identified, wasted steps are removed, and flow and pull are introduced, repeating, and continuing this process until a state of perfection is reached and perfect value is created with no waste.

Most adaptive approaches enable iterations to be short in length, with the product continually evolving based on stakeholder feedback, which is encouraged throughout the project—not just at the beginning or the end.

Project practitioners can think about the difference between "doing" Agile, including engaging in fast development cycles with high levels of experimentation and a "fail fast" approach, *versus* "being" Agile. This means adopting the Agile mindset and advocating for its adoption in an organization.

Even though Agile methods are usually applied to software development efforts, Agile principles have been used in other projects and are now most often referred to as the "Agile mindset." These can apply regardless of the development approach selection.

The four characteristics of a hybrid mindset include:

- Adopt a flexible, change-friendly way of thinking and behaving.
- Understand the purpose of these practices.
- Select and implement appropriate practices based on the context of the project.
- Internalize project management and Agile values, mindset, and behavior.

---

7   *The Five Principles of Lean (pmi.org)*

Key Concepts Covered

- Foundational project management concepts
- Organizational project management (OPM)
- Organization structures
- Project management office (PMO)
- Project management principles
- Project performance domains
- Agile principles and mindset

Check Your Progress

1. Which of the following statements is most likely to be true?

   A. The performing organization has a weak matrix structure

   B. The performing organization is doing "management by projects"

   C. The performing organization has a strong matrix structure

   D. The performing organization has a project-oriented structure

2. The primary purpose of the organization's PMO is to ensure that the department receives the guidance needed to deliver successful project outcomes, as well as to coach and train project managers.

   What type of PMO is this?

   A. Supportive PMO

   B. Directive PMO

   C. Controlling PMO

   D. Agile PMO

3. According to the Agile Manifesto, agile values which of the following? (Choose 3)

   A. Individuals and interactions over processes and tools

   B. Customer collaboration over contract negotiation

   C. Responding to change over following a plan

   D. Comprehensive documentation or working software

4. A project may be part of a program; however, a program will always consist of several projects and potentially additional operational activities. True or False?

   A. True

   B. False

5. Which of the following is a characteristic of a project?

    A. It may continue forever

    B. It repeats itself every year

    C. It is not temporary

    D. It creates a unique deliverable

Answers

1. A
2. A
3. A, B, C
4. True
5. D

Project Stewardship

Project Management Principle:

Be a Diligent, Respectful, and Caring Steward[8]

Stewards act responsibly to carry out activities with integrity, care, and trustworthiness while maintaining compliance with internal and external guidelines. They demonstrate a broad commitment to financial, social, and environmental impacts of the projects they support.

Stewardship has different meaning in different contexts. This may include being entrusted with the care of something, responsible planning, usage and management of resources, and upholding values and ethics. This is both internal and external to the organization and includes:

- Integrity
- Care
- Trustworthiness
- Compliance

A holistic view of stewardship includes financial, social, technical, and sustainable environmental awareness. It also requires leadership with transparency and trustworthiness.

---

8   *The Standard for Project Management, Section 3.1 – Project Management Principles*

Strategic Alignment

There are many ways an organization can achieve the objectives identified as part of its strategic plan, but most of these are through initiating projects.

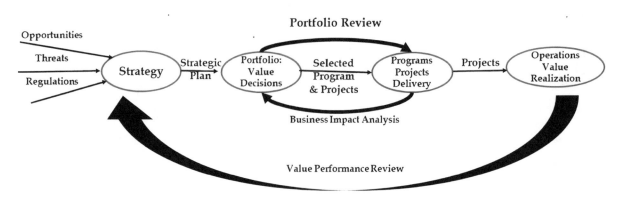

Strategic Planning

The organizational environment for project management starts with the business strategy feeding portfolio management to authorize implementation of the strategic objectives through programs and projects. The results of these efforts are transitioned or delivered to organizations to realize the business benefits.

The projects an organization authorizes can come from any number of strategic considerations. These could be based on market demand or embracing a newly discovered strategic opportunity, especially when developing a new or improved product. They could also arise from the need to support an environmental consideration. Additionally, they could be at the request of a customer to help with one of its initiatives. The organization often embraces new technology to support its internal operations and its products through a project effort.

One of the overriding initiatives for a project often comes from the requirement of conformance to a new legal mandate or regulation. In many cases, these mandate or compliance issues will end up being prioritized ahead of other requested projects — and in many cases, these projects must be done regardless of the prioritization process employed.

Strategic Plan

A high-level business document explaining an organization's vision and mission plus the approach adopted to achieve the vision and mission, including the specific goals and objectives to be completed during the period covered by the document.

Business strategy is often the reason for a project, and all needs are related to the strategy to achieve business value. Professionals at all levels need to understand how their projects align with the big picture of broader organizational strategy and global trends.

The business need, project justification, and business strategy, in addition to benefits and possible agreements, provide the project team with the data to make informed decisions to meet or exceed the intended business value.

Because today's projects demand a broad set of skills and capabilities to meet these needs, PMI continues to focus on providing the tools and insights needed to develop new skills and tackle the next project challenge.

Example: At one organization where we were working, the CEO conducted an "all-hands" meeting presenting what was accomplished in the completed fiscal quarter and the strategic plan for the upcoming quarter. The CEO's vision, mission, and objectives were evident and clear to everyone.

Strategic and Business Management Skills

Strategic and business management skills, also referred to as domain knowledge, involve the ability to see the high-level view of the organization, industry, and products and how the project aligns with the internal and external interests of the business.

Working with business stakeholders, subject matter experts (SMEs), and the sponsor, the project manager must understand the capabilities and capacity of the organization to incorporate the results delivered by the project and develop the appropriate delivery strategy to support the realization of the benefits.

The strategy for both the development and delivery of the project results must be determined to maximize the business value of the result.

Strategic Management Elements and Frameworks

Strategic management includes the following elements

- Vision: where the business wants to go (aspirational).

- Strategic Plan: changes the organization seeks to establish or current conditions that the organization wants to maintain.

- Organizational goals and objectives: defining areas of pursuance, including milestones and resources.

- Organizational needs and opportunities: resources needed to accomplish the organizational goals and objectives.

```
         Vision
           ⇓
      Strategic Plan
           ⇓
   Org. Goals & Objectives
           ⇓
  Org. Needs & Opportunities
           ⇓
  Portfolios. Programs, Projects,
  Operations & Other Initiatives
```

Once the organizational objectives and goals have been established, specific strategies, including milestones, are identified to accomplish them. These strategies will include the authorization of possible resources required and implemented by the combination of portfolios, programs, projects, and ongoing operations.

In addition, operational policies and procedures are established to carry out the strategic elements. This may also include selecting the most appropriate organizational structure to achieve those strategies.

Projects often use Key Performance Indicators (KPIs) as targets to help focus on expected performance, milestones for gauging progress, and insights to help organizations make continuous improvement decisions.

Strategic planning using an adaptive approach can be carried out by KPIs, starting with the organization's objectives and then deciding on the desired key results to achieve through programs or projects.

Organizational Influences

Projects operate in environments with favorable or unfavorable influences. These can include the culture of the organization, the structure of the organization, and the level of maturity of project management.

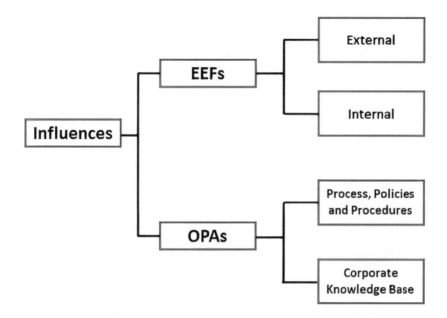

Two major categories often influencing how a project is performed that need to be considered as the project starts are the areas referred to as Enterprise Environmental Factors (EEFs) and Organizational Process Assets (OPAs). EEFs and OPAs are a standard part of every project, and project managers need to understand their role in the strategic alignment of the project.

Enterprise Environmental Factors (EEFs)

Conditions not under the immediate control of the team that influence, constrain, or direct the project, program, or portfolio. These originate from outside the project and often from outside the organization.

– Enterprise Environmental Factors (EEFs)
  • Culture of the organization
  • Established policies and procedures beyond those specifically for projects
  • Government or industry standards
  • Current economic and marketplace conditions
  • Political climate within the organization
  • Stakeholder risk tolerance
  • Current resource availability and capability
  • Established communication channels

– External Business Environment Factors

There are several ways to help us understand the external business environment by applying prompt factors. Brainstorming or discussion with the team and stakeholders can help elicit scenarios that may affect the project.

The three most common external factor frameworks are PESTLE, TECOP, and VUCA.

- PESTLE—Political, Economic, Social, Technical, Legal, and Environmental aspects
- TECOP—Technical, Environmental, Commercial, Operational, and Political aspects
- VUCA—Volatility, Uncertainty, Complexity, and Ambiguity aspects present in the environment where the projects are being performed

These help us understand areas of a project where there is a risk potential, so we can identify potential risks impacting the project.

Exam Tips: These prompt factors are also used when identifying potential risks for the project.

– Internal Business Environment Factors

It is essential to understand the organization and where changes might occur.

Internal EEFs can dramatically impact the scope of the project. The project manager, the sponsor, and the product owner need visibility into business plans, reorganizations, process changes, and other activities. Any such changes by the organization may require modifications before or during the project such as reprioritization of work, including improvement of requirements and deliverables.

Other areas might be reviewed to help understand the internal environment, including:

- Comparative advantage analysis
- Feasibility studies
- Risk alignment with organizational strategy
- Strengths, Weaknesses, Opportunities, and Threats (SWOT) analysis

The EEFs are updated only a few times during the project. They are mostly related to additional information captured regarding newly acquired skills and capabilities of project team members.

Organizational Process Assets (OPAs)

Plans, processes, policies, procedures, and knowledge bases specific to and used by the performing organization. These assets influence the management of the project.

Organizational Process Assets (OPAs)—These are often referred to as "standard operating procedures" (SOPs) and need to be understood and followed. These also provide historical project information to help enable understanding of areas and issues encountered on previous projects.

These often come from the organization itself, or a PMO function outside the project, and may include policies, practices, artifacts, templates, and internal knowledge bases, lessons learned, and historical artifacts from previous projects. These are considered assets to help with the management of projects. They are specific to the organization and used to manage and deliver the project vision. OPAs can significantly assist the project manager through the planning and governing aspects of the project.

OPAs may be modified during the project and added to the historical knowledge base at the end of the project. This may include updates to completed schedules, risks, budget, and earned value data.

Any changes made to either templates or artifacts during the project may be provided to the PMO for potential improvement of the current OPAs.

OPAs fall into two categories:

- *Processes, policies, procedures, and templates developed from previous projects or other records in the organization*
  - Organizational charts
  - Procurement rules
  - Financial controls
  - Staffing and onboarding procedures
  - Product and project life cycles
  - Quality policies and procedures
  - Risks, issues, and defect management procedures
  - Change control and configuration systems
  - Project charter, work breakdown structure (WBS), stakeholder register, and risk register templates
  - Project closure and archiving requirements

- *Organizational Knowledge Bases*
    - Engineering wikis
    - Libraries of archives
    - Lessons learned repositories

Exam Tip: For the exam, PMI assumes OPAs, including policies, templates, and previous project results, are available to the project manager when a project is initiated.

It is also assumed that all relevant project documentation will be captured during the project and become part of the historical knowledge base available for future projects.

Key Concepts Covered

- Strategic alignment
- Talent Triangle
- Strategic management
- Domain knowledge
- Organizational influences (EEFs, OPAs)

Check Your Progress

1. Which of the following statements is not true regarding EEFs and OPAs?

    A. OPAs are external to the organization

    B. EEFs are outside the control of the project team

    C. Resource availability is an example of an internal EEF

    D. Change control processes are an example of an OPA

    E. EEFs may drive compliance requirements on the project

2. Prompts can be used to understand external factors that can introduce risks, uncertainty, or provide opportunities and affect the value and desired outcomes of a project. Which of the following is a prompt? (Choose 3)

    A. PESTLE

    B. CAVU

    C. TECOP

    D. VUCA

    E. TKLSA

3. You have been assigned as project manager for a project to develop an electric battery for bicycles. You understand that the project may require a change in the organization. What is the next thing you should do?

   A. Determine the alignment to the strategic objectives of the organization and the business value of the project

   B. Progressively elaborate the project management plan

   C. Start developing the project charter

   D. Set up a steering committee to engage with the right stakeholders

4. Organizational Process Assets (OPA) are composed of organizational processes, procedures and templates that can influence the way a project is conducted. True or False?

   A. True

   B. False

5. Which of the following are part of EEFs? (Choose 3)

   A. Team member skill inventory

   B. Regulatory requirements

   C. Templates

   D. Technology infrastructure

   E. Lessons learned repositories

Answers

1. A
2. A, C, D
3. C
4. True
5. A, B, D

Project Benefits and Value

Project Management Principle:

Focus on Value[9]

Continuously evaluate and adjust project alignment to business objectives and intended benefit and value.

Projects do not simply produce outputs, but more importantly, they enable those outputs to drive outcomes to deliver value to the organization and its stakeholders ultimately.

One of the critical outcomes for all organizational work, be it accomplished through operations or projects, is to ensure that business value can be obtained for the activities performed.

Project managers need to think more strategically and ensure project results provide the expected benefits and value to the organization. Value is the ultimate indicator of success from the perspective of the organization and the customer or end user.

The benefits and value should be understood at the beginning of the project, reassessed throughout the project effort, and validated at the end of the project (even though in many cases, the actual determination of the benefit will not be apparent until long after the project has been closed).

The *PMBOK Guide* — Seventh Edition represents a shift toward a systems view of value delivery with a perspective change from governing portfolios, programs, and projects to focusing on the value chain and the enablement of organizational strategy, value, and business objectives. It works most effectively when information and feedback are shared consistently among all components. This keeps the system aligned with the organizational strategy while remaining attuned to the environment.

Business Value

The net quantifiable benefit derived from a business endeavor. The benefit may be tangible, intangible, or both.

The goal of a project is to provide business value to the customer. The realization of benefits is based on the value of the results delivered by the project. (This is often referred to as benefits realization.)

---

9   *The Standard for Project Management, Section 3.4 – Project Management Principles*

Business value is the entire value of the business, including both tangible and intangible assets like brand recognition, public benefit, and goodwill.

Comprehensive strategic planning and management must be in place to obtain successful business value. All activities, including operations and projects performed, need to achieve business value for their actions. Establishing new consistent and reliable processes will aid in obtaining greater business value for the overall organization.

These are often identified and included as part of the objectives or description of the project in any initiating agreement(s). They could be either an internal business case or an external contract/statement of work.

Critical thinking, analysis methods, and project management knowledge, processes, skills, and techniques are often used to determine business value. This includes examining actual value through evaluation and confirmation via stakeholder communications, doing personal research, or consulting with experts and utilizing expert judgment.

Types of Business Value

Business value can be gained from multiple areas and activities, often supported by the results of a project. These could include:

- Financial gain
- New customers
- Social benefit
- First to market
- Improvements (technological, processes, etc.)
- Alignment or compliance with standards and regulations

It is essential to think beyond just the initial value identified and understand how each project can provide additional value to the business. Some of the components leading to business value include:

- Shareholder value—for publicly traded companies where the comparison is made between equity and debt, or business growth for private companies
- Customer value—value the customer receives from a product or service
- Employee knowledge—an asset of the business, frequently overlooked
- Channel partner value—the value of business partnerships

Needs Assessment

Analysis of current business problems or opportunities to understand what is necessary to attain the desired future state.

An evaluation and assessment of needs must be conducted to determine how organizational resources should be allocated to projects. This includes understanding the strategic goals and objectives of the organization, existing issues and opportunities, and their current impact on the organization.

A business analyst usually performs this analysis before the business case is developed. Additionally, it helps clarify the business goals, objectives, issues, and opportunities to be supported. This includes a situation statement written by subject matter experts (SMEs) in the domain, often aided by a business analyst. It helps determine whether a solution is required, desired, or optional.

Recommendations are made as part of a proposal to address what should be done and identify any applicable constraints, assumptions, risks, and dependencies. Success measures are identified, as well as a potential implementation approach.

Exam Tip: This area is further described in PMI's Business Analysis for Practitioners: A Practice Guide.

Business Documents

Many of the business documents are developed before the start of the project by a business analyst, key stakeholder, or SME. They must be reviewed periodically to ensure they align with the organizational goals and objectives.

These documents identify the business goals and objectives and provide valuable information on how the project's objectives will contribute to achieving them. They are developed by key stakeholders, including benefit owners, before the project starts, and they are referenced again after the project is completed to determine whether the expectations were met.

Even though these documents are not part of the project management plan, much of the content is included in the project charter and project management plan to help delineate why the project has been approved.

Since an organization's strategic objectives can change, these documents should be reviewed periodically throughout the project, especially before starting a new phase or release.

Business Case

A value proposition for a proposed project, including financial and nonfinancial benefits.

The business case contains the information used to determine whether the project is worth the investment required. It is usually prepared and written by either the requesting organization or a knowledgeable business analyst providing support for the functional area.

The business case includes the business needs and an analysis of the situation prompting the need for the project, including project boundaries. It often uses several project benefit measurement techniques to help sell or justify the selection and authorization of this project.

- *Business Needs*

This describes the justification for the project. It may be a problem needing to be resolved, a potential opportunity, or a compliance requirement.

- *Analysis of the Situation*

A situation statement describes the current environment and impact on the organization, as well as key stakeholders affected. An initial identification of the scope required to satisfy the business need is included.

As part of analyzing the situation, organizational strategies, goals, and objectives may be identified and associated with the need. The root cause of a problem or the contributors to a potential opportunity are usually also identified.

A capability gap analysis is done to determine where gaps currently exist and how those gaps may be addressed, along with high-level known risks, assumptions, and constraints.

Critical success factors and decision criteria to evaluate recommended options are identified. These recommendations may include the most viable option and a suggested implementation approach.

Since most business cases include some calculations to justify the investment and the expected benefits to be realized, a plan to measure those benefits after delivery is also very often included.

- *Economic Feasibility*

Any previous economic feasibility studies conducted may also be documented. This can also include the importance of meeting a specific schedule, cost constraints, and any quality specifications, as well as the results of benefit measurements to support benefits realization.

The project is authorized and funded when this business case is accepted via a portfolio management process.

Benefits Management Plan

A document describing how and when the benefits of a project will be derived and measured.

The Benefits Management Plan defines the processes for creating, maximizing, and sustaining the benefits the project provides. It identifies the tangible and intangible benefits and how the project objectives and goals will be strategically aligned with the business strategies to accomplish the identified benefits. How these benefits will be realized is part of a sustainment plan often developed prior to the completion of the project.

The Benefits Management Plan identifies the expected time frame for realizing benefits, which may be short- and/or long-term. It may also include the benefits owner or the person accountable, along with what metrics will be used to measure the benefits. Any assumptions, constraints, and risks associated with realization of benefits may be provided.

Benefits Realization

Several techniques are often used to calculate how the benefits from a project will be realized.

Benefits realization can be applied in a few ways. Through benefits realization, clearly defined end goals are identified, and the ways to reach them are planned out in advance. This can refer to any organizational change process to improve current business processes.

From a more strategic view, benefits realization includes the processes between the strategic planning efforts and actual implementation to ensure alignment between the project outcomes and business strategies, increasing the success of the project effort. It also can refer to the method for achieving business benefits by utilizing established project management practices.

In addition to the end goals, it is essential to identify milestones to help track progress. For each milestone, clearly defined criteria must be identified, and the achievement of these targets must be reported to the appropriate stakeholders.

Or, in the words of Stephen Covey, *"It is important to always begin with the end in mind"* . . . and in this case, the end provides the benefits realized from this expenditure of organizational resources.

Exam Tip: If you are unfamiliar with this area, refer to the PMI Benefit Realization Practice Guide or review this domain in the Program Standard: Fourth Edition. If you are a member of PMI, these documents are available, in an electronic version, for download at no additional cost.

Project Selection Criteria

Regardless of whether a portfolio process is used within an organization to select projects, different criteria are used to initiate a new project.

This could be because a need has been identified by the business, or an area of the business, to meet a portion of the corporate strategy. The merits of the result or product of this project may be substantial enough to enable the project to be selected. The project could also have specific objectives, such as reducing costs in some areas, meeting a given schedule, or improving or meeting a quality metric. Regardless of why the project was selected, it is important to understand the justification and try to make sure the criteria will be met at the end of the project.

There are also additional economics, finance, managerial, and cost accounting concepts combined as part of the information used to help make the final decisions on project selection. The details regarding these concepts are beyond the scope of the material covered on the exam, even though some are identified as knowledge and skills in the current PMP ECO.

Benefits Measurement Methods

The methods included here range from a very simple calculation to more in-depth financial analysis techniques. These techniques are more appropriate for a project requiring multiple years to deliver and return benefits.

A project manager is only sometimes, if ever, responsible for determining these various calculations. Still, if they have been used to justify the selection of the project, it is important to understand what they are and how they were derived.

There are two main types of benefit measurement methods:

- Business based — including payback period and opportunity cost
- Financial based — including benefit/cost analysis and ratio and time value of money calculations (including present value (PV), future value (FV), net present value (NPV), and internal rate of return (IRR))

Benefit-Cost Analysis

A financial analysis tool used to determine the benefits provided by a project against its cost.

This is one of the most common methods of measuring or evaluating a project's benefit and value. It is often shown as a benefit-cost ratio (BCR) between the expected benefits and anticipated costs.

Benefit-cost analysis is frequently used during portfolio management comparison to determine which projects to authorize and fund, including determination of whether a project's benefits outweigh the cost. The amount of effort required to perform this analysis and the resulting accuracy may vary, impacting the value of this analysis technique.

Exam Tip: This may also be referred to as cost-benefit analysis. Usually at the beginning of the project the focus is on the benefits and the costs of achieving those benefits. Later in the project, the costs are monitored to ensure the benefits outweigh the costs, otherwise the project is in jeopardy of being cancelled.

Value of Future Money

These methods are applied to projects spanning multiple periods when the value of money might change.

– *Present Value (PV)*

The current value of a future sum of money or stream of cash flows, given a specified rate of return.

Present value represents the value for money as it decreases over time. Present value is important to consider when estimating the value of a cash flow for a future time frame. It is determined based on a specific rate of return and the time frames or periods when the value of money would change.

The factors used to determine PV include the future value, the interest rate, and the number of periods being considered. These are combined using a complicated formula (one well beyond the capability of the calculator provided for the exam) to determine the factor.

Exam Tip: In financial formulas, PV represents present value. In earned value management, PV represents planned value.

Year	0	1	2	3	4
Net Cash Flows	-15M	+4M	+5M	+6M	+8M
Factor	1	.91	.83	.75	.68
Net Present Value	-15M	+3.64M	+4.15M	+4.5M	+5.44M

- *Net Present Value (NPV)*

The present value of all cash flows at the required rate of return, compared to the initial investment.

Net present value (NPV) compares the value of a currency unit today to the value of the same currency unit in the future, after considering inflation and discount rate. This information is usually provided to the project manager by the financial organization and provides an understanding of how estimates change for multiyear projects. The NPV adjusts the net cash flow (income minus expenses) for each period by a factor based on the interest rate to determine the net present value. This is also used for capital budgeting and accounts for inflation and macroeconomic changes.

These calculations are not required for the PMP exam but are often used to choose the project with the **largest** NPV during portfolio management activities. It is vital to understand how estimates change for multiyear projects and how they are used to select projects.

*Exam Tip: Remember, projects with **higher** NPV are often selected for investment by the organization.*

- *Internal Rate of Return (IRR)*

The interest rate makes all cash flows' net present value equal zero. This rate is a function of the cost of capital for project implementation.

IRR is an additional financial tool often used in capital budgeting to determine the interest rate to pay for a multiyear project (especially where money is borrowed to finance the project). It is the discount rate resulting in the NPV of the project being zero.

Exam Tip: This calculation is not required for the exam since the calculator doesn't support advanced functionality, but it is essential to understand the concept, its definition, and how it is often used to select multiyear projects.

– *Return on Investment (ROI)*

A financial metric of profitability that measures the gain or loss from an investment relative to the amount of money invested.

This measurement is sometimes called the "rate of return" and is usually expressed as a percentage. It is calculated by comparing the net benefit (benefit – cost) to the cost.

The formula is ROI = (net benefit/cost).

A positive ROI is interpreted as a good investment, while a negative ROI indicates a bad investment.

– *Opportunity Cost*

The value of the project option not chosen.

Another benefit value often identified is the opportunity cost, especially for the project not selected or approved.

Additional mathematical models are used, but they are far beyond the scope of this book and the PMP exam. Project managers are only sometimes responsible for determining these various calculations. If you are unfamiliar with any of these terms, an Internet search is well worth the time to expand your knowledge.

Exam Tip: For the exam, remember when given various options:

- *Business based – "smaller is better."*
  - *Payback period – smallest number (duration) chosen.*

- *Financial based – largest number (profit) chosen – "bigger is better."*
  Time value of money, including:

  - *Net present value (NPV)*
  - *Internal rate of return (IRR)*
  - *Return on investment (ROI)*

Additional terminology:

- Economic value added – Added value produced by the project above the cost of financing or investment in the project.
- Law of diminishing returns – The more you put into it, the less you get out or the greater the likelihood the return will not be as expected.

- Working capital—Amount of money available to invest, or the difference between current assets and current liabilities.
- Sunk cost—Amount of money previously spent on a project or previous activity, not recoverable.

Additional methods of determining potential value:

- Simulation—analysis of uncertainties to evaluate the impact on objectives
- Decision Tree Analysis—used to support selection of best of several options

Incremental Value Delivery

In 1998, The Standish Group published a report showing that many projects fail because value delivery takes too long. Businesses need to show value delivered to please stakeholders and, in many cases, to continue funding the project.

A key value of both adaptive and hybrid approaches can be achieved by using an incremental value delivery approach, where smaller portions of work are delivered more frequently. Breaking down the delivery of features and functions (where possible) allows value to be increased and continuously delivered, enabling:

- Value to be delivered sooner
- Higher customer value and increased market share for the organization to be attained
- Partial delivery (or previews) of functionality to customers
- Early feedback, allowing for adjustments to the customer's directions and priorities and the quality of the product

Key Concepts Covered

- Business value
- Needs assessment
- Business documents
- Project selection criteria
- Incremental value delivery

ECO Coverage

- Execute project with the urgency required to deliver business value (2.1)
  - Assess opportunities to deliver value incrementally (2.1.1)

- Evaluate and deliver project benefits and value (3.2)
  - Investigate that benefits are identified (3.2.1)
  - Evaluate delivery options to deliver value (3.2.4)

Check Your Progress

1. You have been asked to explain the return on investment (ROI) for your project? What was the ROI based on?

   A. The time needed to pay back the investment from a project when future income is discounted

   B. The inherent discount rate or investment yield rate produced by the project's deliverables over a pre-defined period

   C. The rate of negative risk that can be accepted for a project without turning the expected net present value negative

   D. The expected benefit from a project's deliverable calculated as a percentage of the original investment over a specified period

2. You have been provided with a document that contains the market demand and cost-benefit analysis that justifies the go-ahead for the project. What is this document called?

   A. Contract

   B. Statement of work

   C. Business case

   D. Organizational asset

3. To ensure that projects enable business value creation, you must consider tangible and intangible benefits. Which of the following are examples of intangible elements of business value?

   A. Monetary assets

   B. Increase of sales 18%

   C. Market share

   D. Trademarks

4. The Benefits Management Plan defines the processes for creating, maximizing, and sustaining the benefits the project provides. It identifies the tangible and intangible benefits and how the project objectives and goals will be strategically aligned with the business strategies to accomplish the identified benefits. True or False?

   A. True

   B. False

5. The return on investment was calculated for the following 5 projects, however the organization could only select one project. Which one would you recommend?

 A. 2,500,000

 B. 1,200,000

 C. 1,900,000

 D. 2,400,000

 E. 2,000,000

Answers

1. D

2. C

3. D

4. True

5. A

Organizational Culture and Change

Project Management Principle:

Enable change to achieve the envisioned future state[10]

Prepare those impacted for adoption and sustainment of new and different behaviors and processes required for the transition from the current state to the intended future state created by the project outcomes.

A structured approach to change helps individuals, groups, and the organization transition from the current state to a future desired state originating from both internal influences, and external sources. Attempting too much change in a short time can lead to resistance. Stakeholder engagement, increased communications, and sensemaking sessions are important activities to assist in adoption of a change.

Organizational Culture

Organizations have companies or government departments in place to accomplish a specific purpose. Every organization develops a unique culture and style that is representative of its cultural norm and style, based on the beliefs, values, and norms shared by members of the organization and affects project performance. We can think

10 *The Standard for Project Management, Section 3.12 – Project Management Principles*

of this as an internal brand. These organizational cultures strongly influence a project's ability to meet its objectives.

Culture impacts not only the shared visions, values, and beliefs but also the regulations, policies, and procedures implemented within the organization. Often this culture dictates the hierarchy and leadership inherent in the organization and the relationships between authority levels, including diversity, equity, and inclusion (DEI) practices. In addition, an organization's culture often establishes a code of conduct, including the work ethic and the actual hours to be worked.

As a project manager, it is vital to understand the strong influence of culture on a project's ability to meet its objectives and how any change will likely be met with some degree of resistance. Diversity is also a highly variable element in organizational cultures—diversity of people, cultures, thoughts, abilities, and many other kinds of diversity must be factored in when implementing change.

Culture includes an understanding of the organization's:

- View of leadership, hierarchy, and authority
- Shared vision, beliefs, and expectations
- Diversity, equity, and inclusion practices
- Regulations, policies, and procedures
- Code of conduct
- Operating environments
- Motivation and reward systems
- Risk tolerance of both the organization and individual stakeholders

As projects take on more of a global nature, understanding the various cultural aspects and impacts becomes important for successful project management. Interactions with the team and stakeholders may require additional cultural awareness and adjustments to fit within existing cultural norms, regulations, policies, and procedures. Resource management, team working norms, and even project activities must be adjusted to location and culture.

Culture and Risk

An area closely tied to the organization's culture that project managers must be keenly aware of is the risk tolerance of the organization and the individual stakeholders within it. This becomes a key part of the risk strategy identified for a project.

Views about risk differ greatly when working on projects that include global countries and regions with diverse values, such as:

- Countries/regions often differ in how they treat risk, especially in global organizations spanning multiple countries and regions.
- Industry/section—e.g., highly technical sectors value high-risk strategies like experimentation but tolerate little risk in actual production work activities.
- Leadership practices are often dictated by how the organization treats risk.
- Project team composition.

These differences must be understood, as they impact the ability to:

- Establish effective approaches for initiating and planning projects
- Identify acceptable means for getting work done

As a project manager, it is essential to understand how culture strongly influences a project's ability to meet its objectives and that any change will likely be met with some degree of resistance. Beginning with a solid knowledge and consciousness about the organization's style and culture, the appropriate change management practice can then be applied.

Organizational Change

I have noticed that even people who claim everything is predetermined and that we can do nothing to change it, look before they cross the road.

- Stephen Hawking

A comprehensive, cyclic, and structured approach for transitioning individuals, groups, and organizations from a current state to a future state to realize desired benefits.

Exam Tip: This differs from project change control—the process whereby modifications to documents, deliverables, or baselines associated with the project are identified, documented, and approved or rejected.

Change is the single biggest factor when making business decisions. Remaining relevant in today's business environment is a fundamental challenge for all organizations. A strategy of embracing change helps organizations balance investment and risk while being more flexible to help ensure maximum ROI.

Projects create and deliver change, and change is often the catalyst for the authorization of a project. This requires an understanding of change management and how the organization may receive the project's outcome, especially when changes are being introduced. PMI has applied the "changemaker" or "change agent" moniker to project professionals to reinforce the importance of this concept.

Understanding the vision and objectives of the project and the expected results means becoming a key part of the change initiative. This includes adapting the project to remain aligned with changing business objectives.

Change management works hand in hand with continuous improvement and knowledge transfer activities at the PMO level. This includes building and sustaining alignment between projects and organizations with continual updates to processes, enhancements to capabilities, and new skills to support project management. It is important to tailor the strategy to circumstances, people, and timing of delivery through a robust approach.[11]

Change Management Frameworks

Organizational change requires individual change.

PMI has described an iterative model based on common elements across a range of change management models in the *Managing Change in Organizations: A Practice Guide.* The framework has five elements interconnected through a series of feedback loops:

- Formulate change — Focus on building the rationale to help people understanding why change is needed and how the future state will be better
- Plan change — Identify activities to help people prepare for the transition from the current state to the future state
- Implement change — Iteratively focus on demonstrating the future state capabilities and ensuring the capability are having the intended impact, and making necessary improvements or adaptations in response, if necessary
- Manage transition — How to address needs related to the change that may surface once the future state is achieved
- Sustain change — Ensure that the new capabilities continue, and previous processes or behaviors cease

Prosci's ADKAR framework is one of several models supporting change in a new environment. It gives leaders a framework for helping people in their organization embrace and adopt changes.

The ADKAR model names five milestones an individual must achieve to change successfully:

11   *PMBOK 7th ed., X3.3*

A — Awareness of the need for change

D — Desire to support the change

K — Knowledge of how to change

A — Ability to demonstrate new skills and behaviors

R — Reinforcement to make the change stick

Change Impacts on Projects

Understanding and continually assessing organizational culture and the impact of a requested change on both the organization and the project requirements is critical for successful implementation of the project.

This includes:

- Assessing the organizational culture
- Evaluating the impact or organizational changes to the project and determining required actions
- Recommending options for change to the project
- Monitoring continuously the external business environment for impacts on the project scope/backlog

Project managers may require additional activities to understand the change and support the impact on the organization of these types of projects. This often includes an increase in the types and frequency of communications and additional transitional activities.

Some of the common elements of various change management models include five associated elements interconnected through a series of feedback loops including:

- Build rational to understand when change is needed and how the future state will be better.
- Identification of activities to prepare for transition from current state to the future state.
- Iterative focus on demonstrating the future state capability and making necessary improvement or adaptations where needed.
- Consideration of how to address needs related to the change that might happen after the future state is achieved.
- Ensure that new capabilities continue, and previous processes or behaviors cease.

Additional information is contained in *Managing Change in Organizations: A Practice Guide.*[12]

Supporting Change

Supporting change as the organization progresses from one way of doing things or understanding to another level requires changes to the way projects are conducted, including the establishment of a change-centered mindset.

Making the change to a more adaptive approach can be disruptive for team members who are accustomed to a more deliberate style of planning and delivery. The highest-performing teams remain adaptable in the face of dynamic change. The skill sets the project manager and project team members hold or utilize today may need to be updated or expanded tomorrow, especially in a digital world.

Some ways to help enable change include:

- Coaching coworkers to support the business through continual collaboration
- Encouraging team members to adopt an Agile/change-centered mindset
- Continuously improving both processes and knowledge
- Aiming to secure buy-in and understanding of the reason for the change
- Ensure understanding of areas of resistance and concern

Plan for Change

It is important to understand the impact of the change the project is making, especially on the organization, and have an action plan to identify and outline how the transition requirements, including knowledge transfer, training, and production readiness, will be implemented to support the change. Some parts of the organization can adapt quickly while others often take more time to implement change.

Successfully designed and delivered projects can only succeed in execution with proper change management.

An attitudinal survey is often used to determine how individuals feel about the upcoming change. The survey results can help lead to an information campaign, with extensive communications, to help familiarize individuals with the changes. This needs to include being open and transparent about potential impacts and effects of the changes.

---

12   *https://www.pmi.org/pmbok-guide-standards/practice-guides/change*

This is often identified as a Transition, Implementation, or Rollout Plan, and it is usually outside the traditional project management plan. These plans include the planning, management, and delivery of transition requirements before the project is finished. The activities or requirements within these plans are temporary.

Organizational Transformation

PMI's Brightline Initiative[13] was created to support executives who need to know how to bridge the gap between strategy and execution. But Brightline also offers resources on change management relevant to project practitioners who work in environments undergoing transformations.

The Brightline Transformation Compass includes five building blocks:

- A North Star statement to articulate crisply and concisely the vision and strategic objectives of a transformation. Organizational key results (OKRs) are derived from it.

- Understand customer insights and global megatrends, like the factors of the PESTLE framework, but more customer oriented, including understanding what is affecting the business and driving change.

- Use a flat, adaptable cross-functional transformation operating system with rapid response teams and savvy project professionals who can execute transformation strategy and empower the change, rather than a hierarchical structure.

- Use volunteer champions from inside the organization to drive the transformation rather than external consultants, who do not ultimately benefit the organization as much as employees who internalize and advocate for the change.

- Aim for Inside-Out Employee Transformation to transform mindsets and aspirations by changing culture through changing mindsets and empowering individuals.

The Brightline Transformation Compass and its five building blocks are explained fully in the *Organizational Transformation: Foundation* e-learning course. The Organizational Transformation certification (Foundation level) is appropriate for project professionals who want to learn more about how organizations can best approach enterprise-wide change management and their role in those transformations.

---

13 *https://www.brightline.org/resources/transformation-compass/*

Key Concepts Covered

- Organization culture
- Organizational change
- Change management
- Organizational transformation

ECO Coverage

- Support organizational change (3.4)
  - Assess organizational culture (3.4.1)
  - Evaluate the impact of organization change to project and determine required actions (3.4.2)
  - Evaluate impact of the project to the organization and determine required actions (3.4.3)

Check Your Progress

1. A large organization has hired you to apply agile techniques and approaches to a project that involves extensive organizational change. Your job is to move the organization from being internally focused to being focused outwardly on the customer experience. The PMO is a stumbling block. Their lack of support in establishing an organizational change management group is a major concern. The recognition of the change management strategy depends on the PMO and the change management group. Addressing this concern is an example of:

   A. Facilitating communications

   B. Retraining project team members

   C. Identifying change agents

   D. Concentrating on the project baseline

2. What is the most important activity that a project manager should do when implementing a project that creates extensive changes to the way organizational processes are done?

   A. Communicate regularly with all stakeholders to understand their concerns regarding the proposed change

   B. Determine the appropriate rollout plan

   C. Determine the cost of not delivering the change

   D. Delegate the change management responsibility to a certified change manager

3. Organizational culture includes: (Choose 2)

    A. Shared vision, beliefs, and expectations

    B. The organization's I. T. infrastructure

    C. Risk tolerance

    D. Government regulations

4. The Benefits Management Plan defines the processes for creating, maximizing, and sustaining the benefits the project provides. It identifies the tangible and intangible benefits and how the project objectives and goals will be strategically aligned with the business strategies to accomplish the identified benefits. True or False?

    A. True

    B. False

5. The ADKAR model names five milestones an individual must achieve to change successfully. Which of the following are described in the ADKAR model? (Choose 3)

    A. A—Awareness of resisters to change

    B. D—Desire to support the change

    C. K—Knowledge of how to change

    D. A—Ability to follow the command from management

    E. R—Reinforcement to make the change stick

Answers

    1. C

    2. A

    3. A, C

    4. True

    5. B, C, E

Project Governance

"The governance system works alongside the value delivery system to enable smooth workflows, manage issues, and support decision-making."[14]

Project governance is familiar to experienced or senior project managers, but it's essential to know how the organization's governance system supports projects. Many project managers may not be familiar with this concept, depending on the project management maturity or the project approach employed. This is often more visible in projects following a predictive approach rather than a less structured adaptive approach.

The inclusion of these concepts in the exam reflects a slight shift in thinking about project life cycles, from being determined by project governance (*PMBOK Guide* — Fifth Edition) to being parallel, symbiotic systems (*PMBOK Guide* — Seventh Edition).

Organizational Systems

Many structures and frameworks within an organization impact the project manager's responsibility, accountability, and authority.

Organizations determine the power, influence, and political capabilities of their people. These impact the culture and capabilities of the organization. Essential functions include authority and division of work, discipline, fair pay, and unity of command and direction, as well as security and safety in the workplace.

The structure of an organization is unique due to many variables. Factors influencing the structure may include specialization capabilities, the span of control, efficiency, and effectiveness, physical locations, and clear communication.

Some parts of the system may work alone or jointly with other components in a system. Each of these is part of the overall system influencing the project but also being affected by it. Any change in one system most likely will cause a change in other systems.

Note for those in IT: The term "systems" here does not necessarily refer to automated or application systems.

Organizational Governance

In general, organizational governance determines and influences the behavior of the organization's members in many aspects.

---

14   *PMBOK Guide: 7ᵗʰ ed.: Section 2.2 Organizational Governance Systems*

Governance refers to organizational arrangements designed to determine and influence roles, structures, and policies. These rules, policies, procedures, and standards support various aspects of the project to ensure continued alignment with organizational strategy and goals. They influence how the objectives of the organization are achieved, risks are monitored, and performance is optimized.

Project Governance

The framework, functions, and processes guiding project management activities to create a unique product, service, or result to meet organizational, strategic, and operational goals.

Project governance is defined by and required to fit within the larger context of the program or organization sponsoring the project, but it is separate from organizational governance. This is often closely related to the PMO organization and includes the policies, procedures, and established standards. They support various aspects of the project to ensure continued alignment with organizational strategy and goals.

Project governance is an oversight function. It helps achieve project management excellence by providing oversight of the actual deliverables required, the acceptance criteria for those deliverables, the project life cycle approach, and the respective stage gates or phase review requirements. Also, key performance indicators (KPIs) are often established and monitored as part of the project governance activities.

As the project management plan is developed, one of its key aspects will be to ensure an understanding of any identified governance requirements and that a determination has been made as to how they will be met by project activities and documents.

The way project governance is established may be tailored based on the size, complexity, and risks within the individual project, any mandatory compliance requirements, and established responsibilities and authorities within the organization.

It differs among organizations and projects, with key benefits including:

- Single point of accountability, issue management, and resolution
- Encompasses activities and requirements for the entire project life cycle
- Outlines the roles, relationships, and responsibilities among team members and project stakeholders
- Outlines the organizational handling of issue management and resolution
- Enables the appropriate distribution of project information by providing clear communications

Tailoring Project Governance

More governance can become a hindrance to progress, especially annoying stakeholders, while relaxed governance often leads to a lack of appropriate stakeholder and team engagement or accountability.

Project governance is most likely in place before work on the project begins, having been established by the PMO or aligned with the overall governance policies of the organization. The type of governance differs among organizations and projects, especially when using different development approaches.

Governance is essential for managing changes to the business environment, both external and internal, resulting in modifications to the project scope, schedule, budget, resources, or quality.

One key project area most often overseen by a governance function is the budget. This is especially critical when the costs exceed the benefits or defined tolerances in the various subsidiary management plans.

A project manager may need to tailor the governance structure for an individual project based on constraints and other project oversight requirements, including:

- Regulatory environment
- Decision-making hierarchy
- Contractual obligations
- Strategic importance, funding, and risk of failure

Project Governance Components

Project governance provides support for projects in the form of reliable processes to follow and structures or frameworks. Project managers must understand how these are applied within the organization and their potential impact on their project.

Standard project governance components are often provided by a controlling type of PMO and may address:

- Guidelines for aligning project governance and organizational strategy
- Processes for review and approval changes (budget, scope, quality, schedule)
- Communication processes and procedures
- Required project documentation (including the project management plan)
- Processes for project decision-making
- Processes to align internal stakeholders with project process requirements

- Processes for escalation of changes above the project manager's authority
- Processes to identify, escalate, and resolve issues
- Processes for stage gate or phase reviews
- Project life cycle and development approach
- Project organization chart with project roles
- Project success and deliverable acceptance criteria
- Relationships among project team, organizational groups, and external stakeholders

Exam Tip: There is a section in the Governance for Portfolios, Programs, and Projects practice guide from PMI with specific reference to the role of governance on a project. Governance is also identified as a domain within the Program Management Standard – Fourth Edition.

Governance and Life Cycles

"The governance system works alongside the value delivery system to enable smooth workflows, manage issues, and support decision-making."[15]

Project Life Cycles

The series of phases a project passes through from start to completion.

Most projects follow a similar life cycle:

- Need – pre-project phase where ideas are identified based on a problem to solve or an opportunity to pursue
- Business case – justification of the need based on evidence and details to assess the benefits and value it will provide to the stakeholders
- Project charter – authorization of the project by the project sponsor
- Project management plan – activities to complete the project successfully, including both project- and product-related activities
- Execution of the project plan – producing the results to deliver the authorized solution, result, product or service
- Finish the project – closing the project, including administrative closure activities, documenting lessons learned, communicating the project results, and implementing the solution

---

15 *PMBOK Guide, 7th ed.*

Teams can use the appropriate life cycle or method to deliver value in a project. The project life cycle combines the value delivery system and the governance system to:

- Enable smooth workflows
- Manage issues
- Support decision-making

Predictive

- Value is delivered as a product, at the end of the life cycle.
- The deliverable or result is given to customers at the end.
- The benefits can often take a long time to be realized.

Adaptive

- Value delivery is embedded in life cycles.
- The stakeholder, representing the customer, participates in value creation and may receive the benefit of the project incrementally, at the end of iterations or releases.

These together support the project management principle:

Recognize, evaluate, and respond to system interactions.16

Governance Checkpoints

The project's life cycle depends on the organization's governance policies and tolerances for risk, change, and other factors, the importance given to stakeholder or customer inputs, and the type of work being performed. Proper governance enables project managers and teams to make clear decisions about continuing or discontinuing projects. The major difference is when a decision is made — at the end of a phase or work period.

Project Governance: Predictive

Proper governance enables project managers and teams to make clear decisions about continuing or discontinuing projects.

Phase — Refers to a collection of activities within a project. Each project phase is goal-oriented and ends at a milestone.

To manage a project more effectively, the project may be broken up into logically related activities with the delivery of an output, outcome, or deliverable. These usually are grouped into individual phases. The end of a phase is typically the point where decisions can be made as to whether to continue to the next phase, improve the results delivered, or cancel/defer future work. The results from one phase are generally the inputs for the next phase.

Within an organization with a PMO and project governance, these individual phases may have distinct requirements to start, end, or close each phase, along with reviewing and approving the required deliverables, often known as phase or stage gates. These are all part of the project governance activities.

These individual phases are usually given names reflecting the type of work to be performed during the phase—including feasibility, requirements, design, build, test, and deployment.

Regardless of the number or way a phase is identified, each phase has common characteristics.

- The work required for each phase is clearly specified, with activities and deliverable requirements defined by the organization and its methodology.
- Resources perform the work and can involve different organizations in different locations. Because of the nature of the individual activities, the skill set requirements for these resources may vary from one phase to another.
- The completion of a phase includes closure activities, including completion and delivery of various project management documents.

The phases can be sequential or overlap with one another. Sequential relationships contain consecutive phases starting only when the previous phase is complete. This relationship reduces uncertainty, often eliminating the need to shorten a project's schedule.

Overlapping relationships contain phases possibly starting prior to the ending of the previous phase. This relationship increases the level of risk and may cause rework if something from the previous phase directly affects the next phase.

A governance board will review the completed work at the end of each phase, based on the organization's methodology and governance policies and procedures. The approval is often made based on review and acceptance of key phase deliverables and comparison of performance and progress to previously developed documents, including the business case, project charter, project management plan, and benefits management plan. The decision can be to continue to the next phase, continue with modification, or stop the project or program.

These phase end activities often include a review meeting, like an adaptive retrospective, where the team discusses work performance and captures lessons learned.

- *Phase Gate*

A point of review at the end of a phase where a decision is made to continue to the next phase, continue with modification, or end a project or a component of a program.

The term "phase gate" is often used to refer to this review. Steering committee members or a Governance Board review the project's progress, value and business environment. This blocks further progress on the project until some authority "opens" the gate after review of progress made to this point.

Other names, including governance gate, tollgate, phase review, stage gate, kill point, phase entrance, or exit, can refer to phase gate reviews.

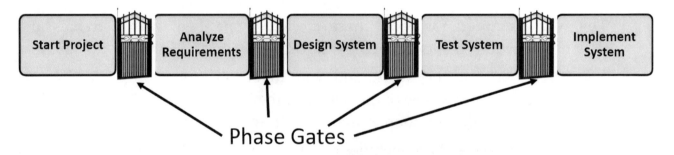

There is a special type of gate, known as a quality gate, located before a phase and dependent on the outcome of the previous phase. It is a formal way of specifying and recording the transition between stages or phases in the project life cycle.

At the beginning of each phase, former assumptions should be verified and validated, risks should be analyzed and reassessed, and a clear and detailed explanation of the phase's deliverables should be understood.

After the phase's key deliverables are produced, a phase-end review, or close-out meeting, ensures completeness and acceptance. If huge risks are identified, deliverables are no longer needed, or requirements change, the phase or entire project may be terminated.

This approach is better suited to large projects where the requirements are well understood and can be planned and managed with little change.

Project Governance: Adaptive

Adaptive approaches offer clear governance benefits to stakeholders through the delivery of outputs meeting expectations. An iterative approach can more quickly identify and deliver value-based outputs than a predictive approach. Adaptive projects split the work into releases and are better suited for projects with complex and ever-changing product and stakeholder requirements.

Results of iterations/sprints are clearly defined, and releases have specific dates, providing a clear road map and view of the project's goals. Work is split into releases, providing smaller portions of functionality and adapting to changing conditions. The customer (or customer representative) participates in value creation and review and may receive the benefit of the project incrementally, at the end of the release.

Reviews are held at the end of each iteration or sprint (like a phase). The customer's acceptance criteria or some statement of expectation meeting the definition of done (DoD) guides this review. The team gathers feedback from the review and uses it to take actions to improve the value of the result in a future iteration.

Combining these individual iterations results in a unit of value delivered to the customer. This could be a minimum viable product (MVP) or a minimum business increment (MBI).

Governance Board

This group, also referred to as a project board or steering committee, very commonly plays a key role in projects utilizing a predictive approach. Within an organization there may be separate or combined committees to provide support to the project manager. These committees may include the project sponsor, senior managers, and PMO resources.

The governance board often provides oversight of the project objectives, performance, and adherence to project policies and procedures. These often include the review of key deliverables as defined by the organization's methodology. They also provide input for key decisions escalated to these bodies.

Some adaptive projects use an intermediary governance board between the project and organizational governance bodies. Such an arrangement is typical for those using scrum or SAFe.

Governance Defined Escalation Procedures

Escalation is the action taken to correct a problem or address an issue beyond the project manager's or team's scope.

Project teams and project managers are given the authority to act on some level of changes and issues. Escalation is required when the change or issue exceeds the approved authority level.

The scope of this authority and the process used is determined by the organization through the PMO or the authority managing programs or portfolios. This level of authority, and the escalation procedure, should be specified in an additional section of the project management plan.

Two key items requiring clear definition during planning include:

- Threshold—a predetermined value of a measurable project variable representing a limit requiring action to be taken if it is reached
- Tolerance—the quantified description of acceptable variation for quality, risk, budget, or other project requirements

These should be defined during the schedule, cost, and risk planning and documented in the individual subsidiary project management plans. They will then be reviewed and used when and if issues are encountered.

When an issue is identified, determine whether it is within the identified threshold. If so, the team should work with the stakeholders to find a resolution. It should also be determined whether it is within tolerance and whether the team or project manager can handle it, or it needs to be escalated.

For a noncompliance issue outside of the project manager's authority, the previously identified stakeholders who are authorized to review the issue should be assigned to manage it.

Key Concepts Covered

- Organizational systems
- Organizational governance
- Project governance

- Governance board
- Governance and life cycle
- Governance checkpoints
- Project approach governance

ECO Coverage

- Establish project governance structure (2.14)
  - Determine appropriate governance for a project (e.g., replicate organization governance) (2.14.1)
  - Define escalation paths and thresholds (2.14.2)

Check Your Progress

1. As a project manager, you are working to make sure that benefits management and stakeholder engagement are carried out according to established policies and plans. Where in the project life cycle do these activities occur?

   A. Pre-project setup

   B. Starting the project

   C. Project planning

   D. Performing the project work

2. Which of the following statements is true?

   A. The project life cycle varies based on the type of deliverables being developed, the industry, and the organization

   B. Organizations generally use one project life cycle and one project management approach for all projects

   C. The project life cycle and project management approach vary based on the types of deliverables being developed, the industry, and the organization

   D. The project management approach varies based on the type of deliverables being developed, the industry, and the organization

3. A major automotive manufacturer is working hard to adjust to recent legislative changes to the fuel mileage ratings on new vehicles. The government has changed the calculation methods to make the determination for gas mileage more realistic. This has caused the distance ratings to decline and resulted in a decline in sales due to consumer expectations to get better fuel economy. When the project was established, which of the following were most likely involved in developing governance for project tracking and updating?

A. Project board

B. Project managers

C. Project office

D. Project management office (PMO)

4. The organization's quality policy identifies the basic principles governing as it implements its approach to quality management in projects?

A. True

B. False

5. All projects need to understand and follow quality, legal, and regulatory requirements. Failure to do so leads to noncompliance, often resulting in serious consequences. Which of the following are regarded to be best practices? (Choose 3)

A. Risk planning

B. Compliance Audit

C. Compliance stewardship

D. Project schedule planning

E. Determining project costs

Answers

1. D
2. C
3. D
4. True
5. A, B, C

Project Compliance

Understanding and prioritization of compliance requirements is of utmost importance to the successful result of a project.

During a project, compliance requirements may change. The project team needs to remain aware of and be proactive about compliance.

Compliance

Compliance is part of the stewardship of a project—and is a responsibility the project manager undertakes to care for the health of the project. Stewardship is a project management principle that is not as well-known and understood as others.

Compliance is related to project quality as well as the political, business, and industry context of the project's product or service. It is important to ensure project activities and outcomes are aligned with applicable internal and external standards, including:

- Government regulations and standards for the context of the project's product or service
- Corporate policies
- Project and product quality
- Project risk

Even though the PMO monitors compliance at the organizational level, the project manager and project team members are responsible for ensuring project activities and outcomes are aligned with legal or regulatory standards, as required.

Project team responsibility for project activity-related compliance includes:

- Quality of processes and activities performed
- Deliverables and products produced
- Work performed by vendors under procurement agreements

Compliance Requirements

Most projects have compliance requirements, in addition to other identified needs. These are often subject to legal or regulatory constraints and identified as aspects of the external EEFs.

Legal or regulatory constraints often become project compliance requirements including:

- Requirements for specific practices
- Standards
- Privacy laws
- Handling of sensitive information

In addition to the project manager, the entire project team is responsible for researching, identifying, tracking, and managing compliance requirements throughout the project.

Project processes must be tailored to the project to provide the relevant amount of rigor and quality control.

Compliance Categories

Because of the number of compliance requirements for a project, it is often necessary to create several compliance categories that impact the project. These categories could vary based on the industry and solution scope and unique legal and regulatory requirements of the product(s) being delivered.

Examples of compliance categories include:

- Environmental risks
- Workplace health and safety
- Ethical/non-corrupt practices
- Social responsibility
- Quality
- Process risks
- Financial

Noncompliance

Noncompliance is one of the most serious risks in projects and organizations. It should be identified as the highest priority on the risk register or on a dedicated compliance register if the organization uses one. Larger organizations, or those in highly regulated industries, typically have a compliance department or officer and provide compliance resources to relevant projects.

As the project proceeds, it is critical to continuously review, track, and validate legal and regulatory compliance requirements and deliverables to help determine whether they can and will be continually and proactively met. It may be necessary to schedule periodic quality audits to ensure compliance requirements are being met. These requirements must be checked before the project is closed to avoid transferring issues relating to compliance requirements to the customer.

Potential noncompliance with identified requirements should be identified on the risk register. In addition to the identified risk, triggers and responses should be addressed and continually reassessed. Additionally, the risk owner, risk responses, and impact of a realized risk may be included on the risk register.

Compliance Threats

In addition to understanding compliance requirements, it is important to understand where compliance-related project threats come from so they can be identified.

Before a project begins, verification should be done regarding external legal or regulatory requirements with an impact on the project, including:

- Where/who in the organization handles compliance? This may be a project stakeholder assigned to the project.
- What specific legal or regulatory requirements impact the organization beyond the project? This could include workplace safety, data protection, or professional association memberships.
- Are the team and stakeholders aware of compliance matters? This is often a simple and effective way to know what level of compliance the team understands.
- What is the organization's quality policy, and how does it support compliance? If the organization does not have such a policy, one will have to be created for the project.

Compliance and Quality Policies

Quality policy — The basic principles governing the organization's actions as it implements its system for quality management.

Remember, the organization's quality policy identifies the basic principles governing its actions as it implements its approach to quality management.

Compliance Best Practices[17]

All projects need to understand and follow quality, legal, and regulatory requirements. Failure to do so leads to noncompliance, often resulting in serious consequences.

Best practices include:

- Documentation—All documentation regarding compliance needs and risks is kept up- to-date and readily available.
- Risk planning—Compliance is the highest-priority risk; therefore, the necessary planning to address these risks is crucial.
- Compliance council/board — A designated stakeholder, or group of stakeholders, should be accountable for each compliance requirement in the project and

---

17   *These were derived from the "5 Pillars," described by Ivan Rincon in his PMI Global Congress paper —*
https://www.pmi.org/learning/library/achieve-compliance-accommodate-constraints-project-6537

authorized to sign off and approve compliance requirements. If the PMO or organization has a compliance council, engaging them early and connecting with them as a project stakeholder would be wise.

- Compliance audit—Includes the formal process established and scheduled, to ensure continued compliance.
- Compliance stewardship—Both the project manager and the team are the project stewards and the last line of defense against noncompliance.

Example: One project I was assigned required implementation of a regulatory report for potential money laundering for all property locations of the organization. There was a very aggressive schedule for completion. Since there were areas where more potential noncompliance would be at risk, a decision was needed by combined property managers as to the implementation sequence of delivering the required government reports. Initially the plan was to start with the properties with the highest risks of nonconformance and then include the remainders as time permitted. Instead, the combined property managers recommended starting with the medium-sized properties as most situations would be discovered and implemented. The larger properties were then addressed with their unique situations. Finally, if time permitted, the smaller properties would be implemented, understanding, and accepting the potential risk of noncompliance in these last properties.

Key Concepts Covered

- Compliance
- Compliance requirements and categories
- Compliance threats
- Compliance and quality policies
- Noncompliance

ECO Coverage

- Plan and manage compliance (3.1)
  - Confirm project compliance requirements (e.g., security, health and safety, regulatory compliance) (3.1.1)
  - Classify compliance categories (3.1.2)
  - Analyze the consequences of noncompliance (3.1.5)

Check Your Progress

1. You are the lead project manager on a government contract, and you are preparing the quality management plan for the project. Given that your project is a part of

a compliance initiative for a government agency, which of the following should you be sure to consider?

A. A. Policy compliance and audit procedures

B. B. Annual nature of government funding

C. C. Multiple civilian and military resources that will be available to you

D. D. How the Federal Reserve decisions may affect interest rate hikes

2. Where should you document areas where you may not be in compliance with the project regulation requirements?

A. Issue Log

B. Risk Register

C. Project Charter

D. Change Request Log

3. Which of the following is a mandatory requirement that must be included in an adaptive project?

A. Daily standup meeting

B. User feedback

C. Update to the product backlog

D. Regulatory compliance

4. Compliance is related to project quality as well as the political, business, and industry context of the project's product or service. It is important to ensure project activities and outcomes are aligned with applicable internal and external standards, including government regulations, corporate policies, project and product quality, project risk. Is this statement true or false?

A. True

B. False

5. All project managers need to understand and follow the quality, legal, and regulatory requirements. Which of the following are considered compliance best practices. (Choose 3)

A. Risk planning—Compliance is the highest-priority risk; therefore, the necessary planning to address these risks is crucial

B. Compliance council/board—A designated stakeholder, or group of stakeholders, should be accountable for each compliance requirement in the project and authorized to sign off and approve compliance requirements. If the PMO or organization has a compliance council, engaging them early and connecting with them as a project stakeholder would be wise

C. Compliance audit—Includes the formal process established and scheduled, to ensure continued compliance

D. Compliance stewardship—The PMO or the compliance council/board are responsible for compliance regulations for a project. Both the project manager and the project team members are not responsible for following compliance regulations

Answers

1. A
2. B
3. D
4. True
5. A, B, C

Project Initiating

There are several important activities to perform when a project is initiated. These include understanding why the project was selected and approved, as well as the stakeholders, who will be vital to provide the understanding of the need and the business requirements to meet those expectations.

In this chapter, you will:

- Understand stakeholders and the most effective communication and engagement methods.
- Learn how teams are formed in predictive and adaptive approaches.
- Learn how to increase the understanding of a project and support successful ways of meeting expectations.
- Explore the different project approaches, including predictive, adaptive, and hybrid.
- Learn which development approach or life cycle may be best suited for the project.

Topics in This Chapter

- Project Stakeholders
- Project Team
- Shared Understanding
- Project Approach

Project Stakeholders

Performance Domain:

Stakeholder[18]

The Stakeholder Performance Domain addresses activities and functions associated with stakeholders.

---

18 *PMBOK Guide, Seventh Edition, Section 2.1 – Project Performance Domains*

The following items defined in the glossary relevant to the Stakeholder Performance Domain:

- *Stakeholder — An individual, group, or organization that may affect, be affected by, or perceive itself to be affected by a decision, activity, or outcome of a project, program, or portfolio*

- *Stakeholder analysis — A method of systematically gathering and analyzing quantitative and qualitative information to determine whose interests should be taken into account throughout the project*

Stakeholders can affect many aspects of a project including:

- Scope/requirements
- Schedule
- Cost
- Project team
- Plans
- Outcomes
- Culture
- Benefits realization
- Risk
- Quality
- Success

Stakeholders are individuals, groups, or organizations who may affect or impact the project, be affected or impacted by the project, or perceive themselves to be affected or impacted by a decision, activity, or outcome of a project, program, or portfolio.

Every project has stakeholders who will either be impacted by the change the project is bringing about — or can impact the project's delivery and result.

Projects start with understanding stakeholders and establishing effective relationships with them. This includes focusing on and understanding what the project means to them and how best to engage with them individually and as part of a group. Even though the relationships and engagement may vary during the project, it is important to continually determine the most appropriate engagement.

Stakeholders are the people and groups best able to help the project succeed, as they are interested in the project and its success. They are valuable sources of information, based on their knowledge of the domain and subject being addressed. It is important to discover, understand, and engage with as many people as possible who are within the project's scope.

Several previously developed project artifacts pertaining to stakeholders are available when starting a project. Additional artifacts are developed and continually updated as the project is performed. Because of the project's unique nature, each of these artifacts will be tailored to the project, and the frequency of updates will be determined. These artifacts include:

- Stakeholder register
- Assessment grids/matrices/models/maps
- Stakeholder engagement plan
- Stakeholder engagement assessment matrix (SEAM) (usually updated to reflect appropriate collaboration throughout the project)
- Communications management plan

Stakeholder Identification

Key stakeholders may be identified before the project starts due to their involvement in the needs assessment and development of the business case used to initiate the project. These stakeholders may continue to be involved well in the project effort. Still, identifying and determining the appropriate level of engagement should begin as soon as the project charter is approved and continue as new stakeholders are recognized throughout the project.

A major change has taken place from previous project approaches, where the stakeholders were only involved at the beginning to capture requirements and then at the end to accept the results. Because of the influence of Agile methods, we now expect some key stakeholders to be fully and continuously engaged throughout the project effort.

Stakeholders take on a variety of roles and responsibilities on a project. An effort should be made to identify as many stakeholders as possible and understand the potential impact they

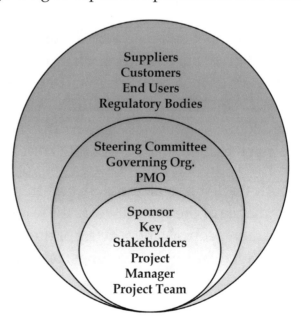

may have on the project. These individuals and groups can be internal or external to the organization and can include:

- – Project Manager and Project Team
- – Stakeholders
- – Sponsor(s)
- – PMO
- – Steering committee and governing organizations
- – Government and regulatory organizations
- – End users and customers
- – Business partners
- – Suppliers and contractors

Stakeholders may or may not be actively involved in project work but still could affect or be affected by a decision, activity, or outcome of a project. Often, stakeholders are unknown to the project manager but may still impact the project. The list of stakeholders may identify and include additional stakeholders who may not realize they are stakeholders.

As early as possible, both internal and external stakeholders should be identified. This includes learning what their needs and interests are and when and how they can be engaged in defining the requirements and success criteria for the project. This helps ensure understanding of their needs and appropriate engagement with them. Key stakeholders have a specific interest in the project objectives and success and are best able to collaborate with the project team to deliver the results needed to satisfy those objectives successfully.

At the beginning of the project, documents like the business case, benefits management plan, and other agreements often provide the names of key stakeholders. As the project progresses, change logs, issue logs, or requirements documents (often referred to as business requirements document(s) (BRD), can assist in the discovery of additional stakeholders. Lists of stakeholders from previous projects may also be very useful and are often included in the corporate knowledge base.

As both the list of stakeholders and their interest in the project may change over the performance of the project work, these identification activities are done throughout the project. Not properly identifying or understanding stakeholders may result in incorrect assumptions, misunderstandings, or missing requirements at the end of the project.

For smaller projects, it is easier to be as thorough as appropriate in the identification and assessment of stakeholders and in developing an effective communications strategy for those stakeholders.

For larger projects, or those with a large, challenging stakeholder environment, try to be as thorough as possible, focusing on key stakeholders and groups. It is helpful to group these stakeholders into categories, especially to ensure that communications and engagement activities are appropriately identified.

There are three main activities to ascertain the project stakeholders and the appropriate engagement.

1. Identify all potential stakeholders, including documentation of relevant information (interest, role, organizational department, and decision-making authority).
2. Identify the impact they may have on the project, either positive or negative, and strategies to deal with issues and concerns.
3. Assess how key stakeholders may respond to specific situations and develop approaches to influence or enhance their support for the project.

Exam Tip: For the exam, the term "stakeholder" could refer to both team members and business or external stakeholders — or only to business or external stakeholders, not including project team members.

Stakeholder Assessment

In addition to identifying these individual stakeholders and groups, the relationship(s) between the individuals and the project should be considered. This becomes part of the stakeholder assessment activities and often results in more confidential information, often not readily shared. The assessment of these relationships includes:

- Specialized knowledge, including areas identified as part of the expert judgment
- Interdependencies among the individual stakeholders and groups
- Their interest in the project or its outcome
- Legal or moral rights of concern or interest to them, such as the ownership or legal title to an asset or property
- Their involvement in the project
- Contribution of funds, other resources, or support provided in more intangible ways, such as advocacy or acting as a buffer between the project and the organization's politics
- Their influence on the project, including the success of the project

Related to understanding the project stakeholders analysis should be done on various aspects of the stakeholder's position and perspective on the project including:

- *Power*
- *Impact*
- *Attitude*
- *Beliefs*
- *Expectations*
- *Degree of influence*
- *Proximity to the project*
- *Interest in the project*
- *Other aspects regarding interaction with the project*

There are several helpful techniques for identifying and analyzing the stakeholders.

Exam Tip: Many of these techniques are the same as those used to help identify requirements.

Data gathering can include finding out more about the stakeholders.

- Questionnaires and surveys (especially for large groups of stakeholders)
- Brainstorming or brainwriting sessions
- Focus groups
- Interviews
- Joint application design (JAD)
- Project meetings
- Facilitated workshops

Data analysis is about taking the data and using it to make decisions. This includes both qualitative and quantitative analysis.

- *Stakeholder analysis* — includes analyzing the result of any data gathered regarding the relevant stakeholders. This includes understanding what each stakeholder needs and wants from the project, their "stake" in the project, and how they perceive the project.
- *Document analysis* — includes review and analysis of the business case and other organizational documents used to establish the project to help understand the key players. These documents may not only lead to identifying additional stakeholders but can also help with the assessment of their role or interest in the project.

Data representation summarizes the results of the data analysis effort and helps determine the most appropriate way of communicating with various stakeholders. These various methods include:

- Two-dimensional grids (interest, power, influence, impact)
- Three-dimensional grids—Stakeholder "cube"
- Salience model
- Directions of influence
- Prioritization of stakeholders

This additional understanding will help formulate the most appropriate way to engage with them during the project.

The first step of analysis helps compare their power, interest, and influence or impact.

- *Power*

The is applied to the person's level of authority but is different from leadership.

Leadership is the position of control given to individuals within an organization to foster overall effective and efficient function. Leadership often carries with it a level of authority.

Authority is the right to exercise power and is usually delegated to a person formally, such as by a charter document or designated title. This person may then have a role or position description indicating their authority. Authority denotes accountability for activities, actions of individuals, or decision-making in certain circumstances.

- *Interest*

Includes their level of concern regarding the outcomes of the project. This might be high if they could be directly affected, especially by a negative outcome. They may be only indirectly affected.

- *Influence*

This concerns their ability to make an impact on the project or the work of the project team. This may include their attitude toward the project (e.g., supporter, neutral, resistant, champion, etc.).

- *Impact*

This includes the level of either contribution or disruption to the project's work.

Data representation takes these terms and applies them to individual stakeholders and are shown in various grids and tailored to meet the project needs. The result will help determine and facilitate the most effective way of communicating and engaging with the various stakeholders.

– *Stakeholder Mapping*

Even though there is no official definition of stakeholder mapping, it usually refers to the various data representation models helping assess project stakeholders. These grids, and the evaluations used to develop them, may change over the project's life—and are a key part of the stakeholder assessment. They are often personal assessments by the project manager and possibly key team members—but should not be made public.

The two-dimensional grids support a grouping of stakeholders according to their level of authority (power); level of concern about the project's outcomes (interest); ability to influence the outcomes of the project (influence); or ability to cause changes to the project's planning or execution activities (impact).

They include:

- Power/Interest grid—groups stakeholders based on their levels of authority/power and interest in the project
- Power/Influence grid—groups stakeholders based on their levels of authority/power and influence/involvement in the project
- Influence/Impact grid—groups stakeholders based on their influence and potential impact on the project

The axis labels on the grid can be changed to better represent the project's need, but the labels within the quadrants stay the same.

To populate these grids, each stakeholder is placed on the grid (making sure no individual names are used, but rather some reference to the stakeholder register). The Power/Interest grid is most often the easiest and is usually done first.

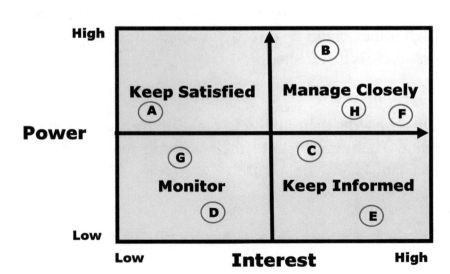

Those stakeholders who fall in the *high power/high*

interest quadrant (Manage Closely) are usually the decision-makers and have the biggest impact on the project's success. It is important to manage their expectations closely and establish good relationships, which includes ensuring the project is proceeding to the stakeholder's satisfaction and addressing issues immediately.

Those stakeholders who fall in the *high power/low interest* quadrant (Keep Satisfied) need to be kept informed and satisfied. Even though they may not exhibit interest, they still wield power. It is important to understand how much information they want and need, as they may use their power to derail the project if they become dissatisfied.

Those stakeholders in the low power/high interest quadrant (Keep Informed) must continue to receive adequate information, especially with open lines of communication and encouragement of feedback. These are often individuals who have knowledge of the current, detailed operational work. They can be key resources for spreading the perceptions regarding both great and bad aspects of the project result.

Stakeholders in the low power/low interest quadrant (Monitor) must be continually observed, especially to determine whether their involvement in the project changes.

The information resulting from this analysis can form the basis for our expectations, future interaction, and determination of appropriate engagement with the various project stakeholders.

Exam Tip: A question on the exam may describe a situation about a stakeholder's power, influence, or interest in the project. You must remember the appropriate way to engage: Manage Closely, Keep Satisfied, Keep Informed, or Monitor.

- *Stakeholder Cube*

The stakeholder cube is a 3-dimensional model combining the grid elements addressing multiple dimensions (power, influence, impact, interest, or attitude). It helps further refine and develop effective communication and engagement strategies for stakeholders.

- *Directions of Influence*

Another way to classify and assess stakeholders is to understand their relationships with other individuals. Influence, or direction of influence, is often dictated by roles or titles, in current as well as previous relationships. These directions include:

- Upward—Relationships within the respective organization of the project, including senior management of the performing organization or the customer organization, sponsor, or steering committee. This often includes business or financial interests.

- – Downward—Team members or other subject matter experts (SMEs) contributing knowledge or skills in a temporary capacity.
- – Outward—External resources outside the organization, including suppliers, government departments, the public, customers, end users, and regulators.
- – Sideward—Peers of the project manager, such as other project managers or middle managers, who compete for scarce project resources or collaborate with the project manager in sharing resources or information.

- – *Salience Model*

The Salience model, developed by Ronald K. Mitchell, Bradley R. Agle, and Donna J. Wood, is another way to assess stakeholders based on their level of authority (power), their immediate needs (urgency), and the appropriateness of their involvement in the project (legitimacy). This model is more appropriate for large complex groups of stakeholders or where there are various networks and relationships of stakeholders.

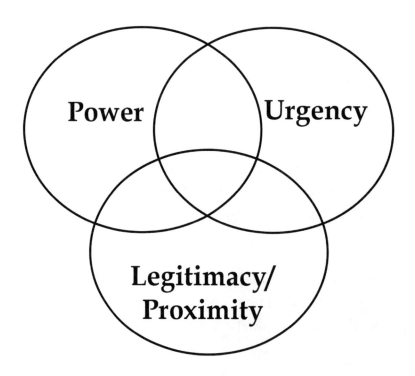

In addition to the stakeholder's *Power* identified on the various grids, this model also looks at the potential *Urgency* required for communications, especially when things go wrong. This includes the level of attention and detail required, any timing considerations or constraints requiring immediate attention, either for time-constrained activities or those with a high stake in the outcome, combined with the importance of communications.

The third component addresses the *Legitimacy* they bring to the project in their role. This is important for key stakeholders and the product owner, especially since they will be the key resource providing an additional understanding of project requirements.

- Do they understand the current situation?
- Can they help move the project forward toward the vision?
- Can they make decisions when changes are required?

There is a variation of the Salience model substituting *Proximity* for *Legitimacy* (also applied to team members) to measure the level of involvement with the work of the project at various times.

- *Prioritization of Stakeholders*

Often the need arises to prioritize the activities and engagement of various stakeholders. This is especially true if the project is very large and there are many stakeholders.

It may also be necessary if the identified stakeholders change frequently. In these cases, the relationship between the stakeholders and the project team is more complex, and additional analysis of individual stakeholders may be required.

By using any or all these models, the project manager is attempting to better understand the individual stakeholder or group and how they may impact the project. These models also help identify more precisely where, or at what point in time, the influence of a stakeholder might be felt.

Most project managers would agree that these classification models are not necessarily something individual stakeholders should see, as the assessments are obviously very subjective. On the other hand, they are the result of analysis efforts and are therefore useful for better understanding the project environment, especially the stakeholders.

Exam Tip: Understand stakeholder interest, importance, and influence, especially for key stakeholders.

Stakeholder Perceptions

Perceptions of the project can be the result of prior situations and potential misunderstandings unknown to either the project manager or the project team. These attitudes must be continually understood and applied to managing the project, especially in product- or customer-centric projects.

Both positive and negative perceptions can impact the project. Some stakeholders may resist the project's intent or purpose and therefore have negative perceptions. These can impede the success of any project.

It is important to identify a strategy for maintaining contact with everyone who can exercise influence or power on the project, regardless of their perceptions. Maintaining open communication and encouraging feedback allows the project manager to become aware of these perceptions and determine appropriate actions to address them.

Stakeholder Register

A project document that includes information about project stakeholders and an assessment and classification.

The stakeholder register is just one of the different types of registers (risk register, lessons learned register, etc.) used to capture and manage project information. It contains valuable information regarding the stakeholders and often includes key information used to develop and continually update the stakeholder engagement plan.

It can contain an extensive amount of information about each individual stakeholder. This register will include a way to identify and classify stakeholders, especially when referring to a group of individuals, for use in eliciting, reviewing, analyzing, and reporting activities. It can also contain the results of the most recent analysis and assessment of individuals or groups.

Because of the sheer number of stakeholders involved in some way with the project, it is best practice to not only try and identify as many of the relevant stakeholders as possible but also to categorize them into groups, such as internal vs. external, by organization, or by role. This aids greatly when identifying the recipients of various project communications.

Exam Tip: An easy way to gather stakeholder profile information is to send each stakeholder an email asking them for their contact information and their role in the organization.

Often it is possible to utilize stakeholder registers from previous projects, an important part of the OPA's historical information. Additional OPAs may include stakeholder register templates and instructions, stakeholder registers from previous projects, and information in the organization's lessons learned repository with information about the preferences, actions, and involvement of stakeholders on previous projects.

In addition to including basic information regarding stakeholders (i.e., their name, department, role, preferred method of contact, email address or telephone number), it's important to understand their potential interest or involvement in the project.

Stakeholder Register Content

The stakeholder register is usually provided to the project manager as a template but often requires tailoring to meet the needs of individual projects. The two main sections include profile (usually public and available to all) and assessment information (including personal opinions of ways to engage with the stakeholder).

Profile – including:

- Name of individual or organization
- Position or role on the project
- Classification based on role or interest
- Internal or external to the organization
- Major requirements of concern
- Expectations of the project and product
- Contact details (both normal as well as escalation – urgent/important)
- Preferred method of contact

Assessment – personal assessment of their potential interest, expectations, influence, or involvement in the project and ways to work with the stakeholder. This additional information will help with the understanding of how best to engage and collaborate with these various stakeholders.

Because some of the information, especially pertaining to the analysis and assessment results, could be considered confidential and subjective, this portion of the stakeholder register often remains private, and only portions of this register are made available and visible to others.

Example: I often ask project managers when they start a new project with previous information available for key stakeholders how they would use this information. Would they review it prior to meeting with the stakeholder(s)? Would they meet with the stakeholder(s) and then review the information?

I personally had a very different opinion of a key stakeholder from previous opinions and worked with him differently based on my own assessment.

Not only are new stakeholders added throughout the life of the project, but additional information regarding the previously identified stakeholders may become apparent, and therefore this stakeholder register is updated continually throughout the project. Rather than removing stakeholders from the stakeholder register, their involvement may be modified to show they are no longer involved.

Stakeholder Engagement

Because engagement with stakeholders changes over the course of the project, this is an iterative activity. This strategy drives connections, collaboration, and engagement with the various project stakeholders and should be continually reviewed at key points in the project.

Stakeholder Engagement Strategy

A strategy for stakeholder engagement drives connections with the project stakeholder.

The strategy for engaging with stakeholders needs to include three aspects:

- Determine how to involve each project stakeholder based on needs, expectations, interests, and potential impact on the project.
- Enable the development of management strategies to engage stakeholders appropriately.
- Create and maintain relationships between the project team and stakeholders.

This strategy is converted into a specific stakeholder engagement plan.

There are two planning artifacts supporting engagement and communication with stakeholders. These plans, the stakeholder communication management plan and the stakeholder engagement plan, are created using information from the stakeholder register and any discovery resulting from further analysis.

- *Stakeholder Engagement Plan*

A component of the project management plan that identifies the strategies and actions required to promote productive involvement of stakeholders in project or program decision-making and execution. It is used to understand stakeholder communication requirements and the level of stakeholder engagement to assess and adapt to the level of stakeholder participation.

Exam Tip: The stakeholder engagement plan has replaced the stakeholder management plan (as we all know we cannot "manage" stakeholders, especially as we have no authority over them).

This plan results from the assessment performed early in the project identifying how individuals will be engaged at various times during the project. It provides details about the people with whom the project needs to maintain communication. It can identify expected processes for engaging with stakeholders throughout the project.

It also details how each project stakeholder, or stakeholder group, will be engaged based on needs, expectations, interests, and potential impact on the project, including:

- Engagement approach for each stakeholder or group of stakeholders
- Interrelationships and potential overlap between stakeholders
- Desired and current engagement levels of key stakeholders
- Scope and impact of change to stakeholders

Stakeholder Communications

To effectively communicate, we must realize that we are all different in the way we perceive the world and use this understanding as a guide to our communication with others.

- Anthony Robbins, Motivational speaker, self-help author

One of the key ways of engaging with stakeholders is through effective and timely communication.

In the project's early days, building open communication channels is essential, especially with stakeholders from the customer organization. This creates the necessary relationships between the stakeholders and project team members and increases the ability of the appropriate stakeholders to participate when required. The number of possible communication paths, or communication channels, on a project increases dramatically as additional stakeholders are added.

Determining the most effective communication method for various groups of stakeholders is vital. Regardless of how feedback and perceptions from stakeholders are captured, it is essential to utilize interpersonal skills, emotional intelligence, active listening, and other communication techniques to determine the most effective methods with specific groups.

All stakeholders need to be appropriately informed (often based on the analysis of the stakeholder grids) to understand the project objectives, vision, and progress—even if only done through a more formalized public relations/marketing campaign. This is often required when major changes will result from the project.

It is important to consider some of the challenges and considerations when determining the method and frequency of communication when developing both plans. These include:

- Urgency for the needed information: Time frame required to send to the appropriate receiver.
- Availability and reliability of technology: access and understanding by everyone.

- Ease of use: by both the sender and the receiver.
- Project environment: including language and formality based on culture and regulations.
- Sensitivity and confidentiality of information: additional security measures and possible encryption requirements.
- Social media policies of the organization: identified protocols and policies in the OPAs.
- Data protection laws and regulations: including privacy concerns in the transmission and storage of information.
- Accessibility requirements: which ones required and for whom.

Some practical guidelines for communicating with different stakeholder groups.

- *All Stakeholders*

All stakeholders need to be informed at appropriate intervals with appropriate levels of detail. This includes an awareness of their need for understanding, as well as the frequency and context of the information provided.

- *Key Stakeholders*

Meet with these people face-to-face as early as possible and start building a relationship. An initial interview can be used to understand their vision, needs or requirements, and preferred communication methods. They are critical to the holistic understanding of the project requirements and vision.

- *Large Groups*

Engaging with a group of identified stakeholders, the public, or other groups is often necessary throughout the project effort. The content and delivery of these communications must be tailored for the audience. These often utilize a mixture and a variety of methods, both written and spoken (verbal), including:

- Email campaigns
- Publicity posters and advertising
- Websites, group chats
- "Town hall" or public meetings—both in-person and virtual

Questionnaires and surveys are a good option, especially for geographically dispersed individuals with a varied audience. In most cases, the results of these surveys will be used to conduct statistical analysis, which will then be used by decision-makers to prioritize, categorize, and determine requirements. The questions must be developed to efficiently support this statistical analysis process. This method often requires time to both develop the questions and then to analyze the responses received.

Facilitated workshops are often used for groups of stakeholders from different organizations or with different roles. An experienced facilitator leads these workshops to enable all participants to not only provide information but also to hear and understand the position of others in the workshop.

Project meetings can also be used either in-person or virtually with stakeholders to generate group decisions. This can include discussion of issues, creation of alternatives, or finalizing suggestions of improvements to project deliverables, goals and expected results. These can also be an effective method of distributing information and communicating with the team and stakeholders.

Regardless of the communication strategies determined for the project, it is essential that they always remain customer centric. This enables the team to monitor the various stakeholder perceptions of the project continually.

Communications Requirements Analysis

Communication can take many forms and convey information along many axes—for example, verbal, nonverbal, written, or visual communication. It can be formal or informal, one-on-one or group based. It can convey information about facts, feelings, or opinions. It can be used to build relationships, solve problems, or create change. This exchange may be intentional or involuntary. It is imperative to understand an individual stakeholder's communication requirements. Often these requirements differ based on the various categories of stakeholder they may be a part of.

Successful communications involve developing an appropriate strategy for communications based on both the needs of the project and the individual needs of the stakeholders. This includes a clear understanding of what information is required. Capturing and analyzing the requirements helps to determine how various groups or categories of stakeholders will be communicated with, including the most effective topics and content, level of detail, frequency, and technology.

Just as stakeholders and risks are continually analyzed during the project—so are the communications requirements of stakeholders.

Areas to consider when analyzing the communication requirements include:

- Organization charts
- Stakeholder responsibilities and relationships

- Departments, specialties, and expertise involved in the project
- Logistics of project stakeholders
- Specific stakeholder information, both internal and external
- Legal requirements

There are several communication areas to consider when identifying and documenting communications.

- *Communications: Dimensions*

There are different elements to consider when defining the ways information will be communicated. These are often referred to as the various dimensions of communications, such as who is the recipient of the communication and how it is composed. These dimensions include:

- Audience—including internal and external stakeholders
- Content and format—formal or informal
- Adjustment due to hierarchy—upward, downward, or horizontal
- Official or unofficial need—annual reports or governance-related vs. project team communication
- Written or verbal—tone, inflection, and nonverbal gestures often influence understanding

Written and verbal often break down into further formats:

- Formal written—including project charter, project baselines, contractual communications, and meeting decisions
- Formal verbal—including presentations and reviews
- Informal written—including memos, emails, and text messages
- Informal verbal—including meetings, workshops, and ad hoc conversations

- *Communications: Technologies*

There are vast and diverse communication methods available for use on projects. In addition to possible technologies, the availability and suitability of their use, sensitivity and confidentiality requirements, and urgency of need for information must also be considered.

- Verbal communications
  - Group meetings
  - Physical (face-to-face)

- Virtual meetings (video and voice conferencing)
- Phone calls

- Digital or electronic media
  - Company or project websites
  - Instant messaging (IM) via computers, phones, or another platform
  - Emails, voice mail, fax
  - Conferencing tools (Zoom, Webex, Teams)
  - Social media
  - Intranet, web-based wikis

- Physical media, including more formal in-person communications
  - Body language, gestures, and tone of voice
  - Presentations
  - Print media and documents
  - Whiteboards

Consideration must be continually given to identify and incorporate any applicable communication constraints based on confidentiality, regulation, or industry preferences in planning communications.

Regardless of the method used to communicate, it is important to remember the five Cs of written communication:

- Correct grammar and spelling
- Concise expression and elimination of excess words
- Clear purpose and expression directed to the reader's needs
- Coherent and logical flow of ideas
- Controlling the flow of words and ideas

As Mark Twain said:

"I didn't have time to write a short letter, so I wrote a long one instead."

- *Communications: Methods*

Another aspect of communication is when and how the information will be delivered and when it is received. This involves procedures, techniques, or processes used to deliver or transfer information among project stakeholders. Communication systems assessment is a technique to help identify the preferred method and content of communication for individual stakeholders.

- Push—This applies to the timing of communications by the sender. This is the typical way project reports are sent to relevant stakeholders based on a predetermined schedule by the sender.

- Pull—The responsibility of receiving information is on the recipient and is based on the time they choose to review it. This often involves providing the information in a location recipients can access on their schedule.

- Interactive communication—This enables both the sender and receiver to interact in real or near-real time. This has become the preferred method and is often referred to as "face-to-face" (enhanced further when done at a whiteboard or a virtual whiteboard), which can include similar types of synchronous discussion with both the sender and receiver involved in and contributing to the discussion simultaneously.

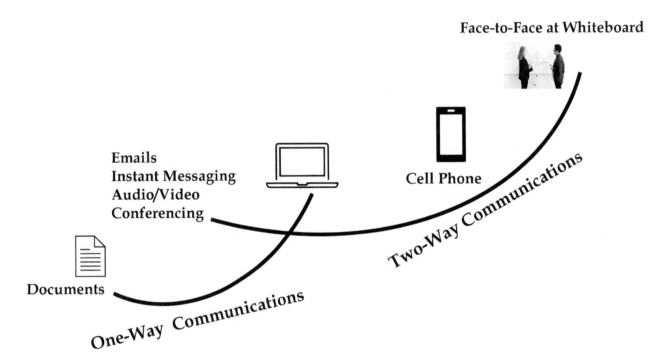

By utilizing colocated teams, as preferred by adaptive models, the interactive method of communication allows the team to work together more collaboratively.

- *Communication Model*

The communication sender-receiver model diagram was coauthored by Clause Elwood Shannon and Warren Weaver in 1948 and has become the most widely adopted communication model to help explain how communication works. This includes the combination of probability and measurement of the uncertainty in a message. It is also sometimes referred to as the cross-cultural communication model.

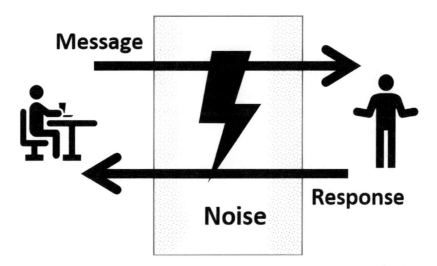

This model includes the process of encoding and decoding a message between a sender and a receiver to be interpreted and understood correctly. The medium is how the message is transmitted, with potential noise, or environmental disruptions, inhibiting the ability to correctly digest and understand the message.

This noise can be the result of poor transmission but could also be due to misunderstanding of terminology or meaning. It can also be impacted by the sender's or receiver's current emotional state. In many ways the transmission choice is as important as the actual encoding and decoding of the message.

Equally as important as the message itself is the acknowledgment that the message was received. This includes ensuring a clear understanding of the message via the feedback response.

Because power skills, such as interpersonal communication and emotional intelligence, are essential in ensuring communications are understood correctly, there are a few elements to consider. These include emotional and cultural factors such as generation, nationality, professional terminology, and gender-acceptable language. Assumptions and personality biases can also factor in a message's encoding and decoding.

Communications Management Plan

A component of the project, program, or portfolio management plan describing how, when, and by whom information about the project will be disseminated.

This plan often takes the form of a grid, questionnaire, or survey documenting each stakeholder's communications preferred delivery method, and technology requirements. Because of the sheer number of communications, a project manager must manage, it is critical to choose a way to enable the ability to focus on the recipients, frequency, etc.

— *Communications Management Plan — Components*

This plan shows identified project communications in a format like the stakeholder and risk register. Most organizations have developed a template for use in documenting project communications, considering the following components:

- Information to be communicated
- Language and terminology to be used
- Reason for the communication
- Time frame and frequency
- Responsible person for content—especially when it regards the release of confidential information
- Sender of the communication
- Receivers/stakeholders of the communication
- Methods, media, or technologies for delivery
- Time and budget allocation for creation of the communications

Additional information may include:

- Escalation process for issues needing visibility
- Updating the method to be used for the plan
- Flowcharts depicting the flow of information, especially regarding approval of communications
- Constraints or assumptions due to regulations or policies—i.e., release of confidential information
- Glossary of common terminology

Key Concepts Covered

- Stakeholder identification
- Stakeholder assessment
- Stakeholder register
- Stakeholder engagement
- Stakeholder communications

ECO Coverage

- Collaborate with stakeholders (1.9)
  - Evaluate engagement needs for stakeholders (1.9.1)

- Manage communications (2.2)
  - Analyze communication needs of all stakeholders (2.2.1)
  - Determine communication methods, channels, frequency, and level of detail for all stakeholders (2.2.2)
- Engage stakeholders (2.4)
  - Analyze stakeholders (power/interest grid, influence, impact) (2.4.1)
  - Categorize stakeholders (2.4.2)
  - Develop, execute, and validate a strategy for stakeholder engagement (2.4.4)

Check Your Progress

1. Several project stakeholders are concerned about the deficiency of communication on the project. They are not receiving regular status reports. What should the project manager do first to address the stakeholders' concerns?

   A. Send the missing reports to the stakeholders

   B. Meet with the stakeholders to address what reports they are looking for, then update the communication management plan

   C. Review the communication management plan to understand their concerns

   D. Update the communication plan to include the stakeholders

2. Which of the following is a form of a push communication method?

   A. Status report emailed to stakeholders

   B. Status meeting with stakeholders

   C. An update to the issue log

   D. A daily standup meeting with team

3. Annalise works in the inventory department and oversees replenishing items in inventory. She is very anxious for the new inventory software system to work as this would mean a reduction of items in backorder. Regarding the Power/Interest grid, which of the following best describes how you, the project manager should assess and engage with her?

   A. A. Manage closely

   B. Keep informed

   C. Keep satisfied

   D. Monitor

   E. Ignore

4. Stakeholders are individuals, groups, or organizations who may affect or impact the project, be affected or impacted by the project, or perceive themselves to be affected or impacted by a decision, activity, or outcome of a project, program, or portfolio. Is this statement true or false?

   A. True

   B. False

5. The Salience model is another way to assess stakeholders. This model is more appropriate for large complex groups of stakeholders or where there are various networks and relationships of stakeholders. What are the three components of the Salience model? (Choose 3)

   A. Power

   B. Collaboration

   C. Urgency

   D. Participation

   E. Legitimacy/Proximity

Answers

   1. C
   2. A
   3. B
   4. True
   5. A, C, E

Project Team

Performance Domain:

Team[19]

Team Performance Domain addresses activities and functions associated with the people who are responsible for producing project deliverables that realize business outcomes.

The following items defined in the glossary relevant to the Team Performance Domain:

---

19 *PMBOK Guide, Seventh Edition, Section 2.2 – Project Performance Domains*

- *Project manager—The person assigned by the performing organization to lead the project team that is responsible for achieving the project objectives*
- *Project management team — The members of the project team who are directly involved in project management activities*
- *Project team—A set of individuals performing the work of the project to achieve its objectives*

Projects are delivered by project teams who work within organizational and professional culture and guidelines. The collaborative team environment facilitates:

- Alignment with other organizational cultures and guidelines
- Individual and team learning and development
- Optimal contributions to deliver desired outcomes

Once a business case is provided and identification and assessment of initial stakeholders have been done, the next step is figuring out the team resources. Resource management refers to the project management area focused on categorizing, allocating, assigning, managing, and releasing all resources. This process is done differently depending on whether a predictive or adaptive approach is used.

For a predictive approach, the team is assembled after the requirements are understood to ensure the needed resources are available at the appropriate time.

For an adaptive approach, the team is assembled initially, with generalizing specialists who support the project requirements collaboratively.

Project teams include individuals with diverse skills, knowledge, and experience required by the project. The goal is to create a high-performing, collaborative team able to execute project objectives well. This can vary based on the organization and project context.

It is essential to ensure that required skills are present in team members or that specialists can be leveraged to coach less-skilled team members. Those project teams working collaboratively can accomplish a shared objective more effectively and efficiently than individuals working independently.

It is important to incorporate team agreements, structures, and processes to enable individuals to work together. These interactions result in increased, synergistic results.

Team Strengths

When forming teams, it is critical to understand the needed competencies and identify individuals with those competencies. These include skills, knowledge, working practices, and any aspect or characteristic to help ensure project success and support a collaborative team culture.

A technique such as SWOT analysis (Strengths, Weaknesses, Opportunities, Threats) can help identify team strengths and weaknesses during the project. Any challenges the team will need to overcome to obtain better performance and opportunities to position the project advantageously should also be identified. This can be handled by leveraging individual team members' skills to develop the team's overall skill level.

Diversity, Equity, and Inclusion (DEI)

Today's teams are often made up of individuals from diverse cultural backgrounds. Every single project has diversity. People come from different backgrounds of gender, language, ability or disability, nationality, etc. It is important to create an environment to take advantage of this diversity and build a team climate of mutual trust.

Diversity, equity, and inclusion, or DEI, is an established human resource component or initiative in most global workplaces. DEI initiatives work toward establishing equitable and "psychologically safe" workplaces.

Team Formation

There are some key concepts from Agile applicable to any project environment. These include the concepts of a self-organizing/cross-functional team and generalizing specialists, often referred to as T-shaped individuals.

Self-Organizing Teams

A cross-functional team where people fluidly assume leadership as needed to achieve the team's objectives.

Cross-functional teams have all the capabilities to deliver the work they've been assigned. Team members can specialize in certain skills, but the team can deliver what it has been called on to build.

The team manages its work activities and the creation of its work product. The entire team, rather than individual members, is accountable for the work produced. Self-management and self-organization concepts apply to everyone serving and supporting the project and the organization.

T-Shaped People

Team members can no longer be experts in one focused area. It is important to develop and include team members with competencies and expertise across a broad range of areas. This allows consideration of both the depth and breadth of team members' knowledge. These individuals are often referred to as generalizing specialists.

Specialized resources who are experts in a single area are often referred to as "I-shaped" individuals, whereas team members with additional knowledge are referred to as "T-shaped" individuals.

From a strategic point of view, there are many benefits to having T-shaped people on cross-functional teams, including value, versatility, and flexibility to both the project team and the organization.

Team members should receive training and coaching to help them become more T-shaped. This also helps avoid critical resource shortages or work stoppages due to the unavailability of those resources.

Team Formation: Predictive

The team is assembled after the requirements are understood to meet the project's specific needs. Project teams consist of individuals with assigned roles and responsibilities.

Major considerations when building a team using a predictive approach include:

- Ensure the team has sufficient relevant skill sets to perform the work and produce the desired results.
- Try to avoid single points of failure, where only one resource has a needed skill to perform a particular type of work.
- Create teams with cross-functional knowledge of both the project domain and the technical aspects.
- Make use of generalizing specialists, who have a core competency along with general skills in other areas and can be leveraged as needed by the team to support its objectives.
- In addition to the team members themselves, other physical resources the team members will require, including equipment, access rights, etc., must be identified.

Additional guidance included in Project Management Principles: Team[20] include

- Team agreements

---

20 *The Standard for Project Management, Section 3.2 – Project Management Principles*

- Organizational structures
- Processes
- Authority
- Accountability
- Responsibility

The activities identified as part of project resource management include the identification, acquisition, and management of resources needed to complete a project successfully. The following are often included in a resource management plan:

- The type, number, and skill levels required for internal and external team resources to fill roles
- Method to acquire the actual team resources to fill the roles
- Management of team members and eventual release from the project (including knowledge transfer before release)
- Resource calendars identifying availability as well as potential lead time to acquire a resource
- Roles and responsibilities associated with the project (possibly including a project organization chart), identifying role, authority, responsibility, necessary qualifications, and required competencies
- Team development activities, including training and improvement to fill gaps in knowledge and skills for individual team members and the team
- Monitoring of team performance to determine where competencies and interactions among team members can be improved to create an effective teaming environment
- Identification of physical resource requirements, including units of measure and techniques to estimate the amount needed
- Acquisition of physical resources aligned with procurement management processes
- Management of physical resources to ensure availability when needed
- Safety methods and procedures based on environmental and equipment aspects of the project, if applicable
- Compliance with regulations, in addition to organizational resource policies and procedures

Exam Tip: The components of the resource management plan pertaining to the team members may also be referred to as the team management plan, or a staffing plan.

The amount of up-front planning in this area is up to the project manager and the team. It will depend on the project manager's leadership, the team's experience level, the project context, and so on. However, the healthy formation of the team is the project manager's responsibility.

Team Formation: Adaptive

The team is assembled initially and self-organizes to support the project requirements. Adaptive project teams are empowered and work collaboratively.

Some Agile practitioners think the role of a project manager or scrum master is not needed due to self-organizing teams taking on those responsibilities. However, pragmatic Agile practitioners and organizations realize that project managers and scrum masters can add significant value in many situations. However, their roles and responsibilities will look somewhat different. The leadership approach often changes depending on the situation. These agile practitioners are often referred to as "agilists".

In some adaptive teams, every team member leads. In other teams, someone assumes the role of team lead. Project management guidance in the PMBOK Guide – Seventh edition team performance domain includes two project team management and leadership models: centralized and distributed. The decision of the most suitable approaches for a project often depends on the team's maturity and the project's complexity.

- *Centralized*

All team members practice leadership activities and accountability, rather than assigning them to one individual such as the project manager or a similar role (team lead). Accountability, or being answerable for an outcome, is usually assigned to an individual such as the project manager or similar role.

- *Distributed*

Project management activities may be shared among the project team with the team members being responsible for completing the work. One project team member at any time may serve as the facilitator to enable communication, collaboration, and engagement on accountable tasks.

Team Formation: Hybrid

The team could be assembled in a combination of predictive and adaptive ways. Still, more often this will depend on the project context, project activities, and approach used at a particular time in the project. A project could start using a predictive approach and switch to an adaptive approach—or start with an adaptive approach, then switch to a predictive one.

In most hybrid team formation activities, the project manager takes on the responsibility of coordinating the team members and being accountable for the completion of the work. In contrast, the team self-organizes to perform the work. This is often true for very large projects with lots of subprojects within them or when projects are individual components of a larger program.

Team formation often includes the initial identification and estimation of needed resources for various sections of the project and then acquiring these resources for the work. The coordination effort of team members at various times during the project depends on the work and approach used. This solution ensures the importance of stakeholders and the organization for accountability and the flexibility needed by team members to provide the best results.

A key concept of team formation from Agile that can be applied to teams in any project environment is servant leadership. Servant leaders allow the team to self-organize when possible and increase levels of authority by passing appropriate decision-making opportunities to project team members.

Servant leaders work to support the needs of their teams, projects, and organizations. The servant leader focuses on paving the way for the team to do its best work and encourages the organization to think differently.

The *Agile Practice Guide* identifies servant leaders who may work with facilities for a team space, work with management to enable the team to focus on one project at a time, or work with the product owner to develop stories with the team. Some servant leaders work with managers in various functional organizations to refine the processes needed to integrate the work of the project with organizational processes and procedures.

Regardless of the approach used, the project manager must continually encourage and support a collaborative team culture.

Team Composition

The team composition refers to the makeup of the team and how the members are brought together. This can vary based on the scope of the project, the organization's culture and location, and the approach used. This can include:

- The assignment of resources to the team
- The assignment of team members to project activities
- The determination of involvement by individual team members (full-time or part-time)

- The knowledge and expertise needed by individual team members (generalists and specialists)

Roles on the project team can include:

- Project management staff members—This role may be supported by a project management office (PMO) and is often referred to as a project coordinator or expediter. This includes supporting activities including budgeting, scheduling, reporting and control, risk management, and project communications.

- Project team members (delivery team)—These individuals perform the work to create the project deliverables. These could also include individuals from other internal functional groups as well as those acquired as the result of external agreements.

- Supporting experts—These individuals or groups support the project manager and team and participate in planning the project and providing additional knowledge and understanding throughout the project. These roles, often referred to as SMEs, can include legal, compliance, technology, engineering, quality assurance, and so on.

- Business partners—These companies and individuals are associated with the project based on previous business partnerships established by the organization.

Supporting Experts

Expert judgment is a technique project managers can use to obtain additional guidance from individuals who are more experienced in various areas needed to be understood for the project.

Experts can help provide the project manager with additional knowledge. They can be utilized to understand what should be included in an agreement, potential solutions, and any additional understanding of the project context. These experts can come from multiple areas, including other areas of the organization, consultants, and stakeholders, as well as professional and technical associations.

Team Norms

A document that enables the team to establish its values, agreements, and practices as it performs its work together.

Team norms are a shared set of mutually agreed standards of conduct and rules to enable teams to handle challenges they may encounter. These norms should be established early in the project to set expectations for the appropriate range of behaviors and actions. They include a means of maintaining a standardized approach to accountability in case of problems by identifying guidelines and techniques for:

- Shared values
- Meetings
- Communications
- Conflict management
- Decision-making

Of course, team norms should always be aligned with the PMI Code of Ethics and Professional Conduct.

PMI Code of Ethics and Professional Conduct21

Project managers can affect the quality of life for all people in our society. As a result, it is vital to conduct work ethically to earn and maintain confidence from all. It is important for project managers to maintain high standards of both personal and professional conduct:

- In their work
- In their relationships with employers and clients
- In fulfilling their responsibilities to the community and the environment

The PMI Code of Ethics and Professional Conduct describes the ethical and professional behavior expectations of any individual working as a project management professional. The Code of Ethics is related to morals and can be adopted to establish expectations for moral conduct. These are also aligned with project management principles and are complementary to each other.

Since PMI is a global organization, this code has been written to help establish a profession-wide understanding of appropriate behavior by project managers, regardless of where they manage projects and especially with global teams. Because of PMI's global nature, the values include mandatory standards that are recognized worldwide as well as aspirational standards, which may conflict with the culture of a particular location.

The Code of Ethics applies to all members of PMI as well as nonmembers who hold a credential from PMI. It also applies to nonmembers who apply for a PMI certification, and agreement to this code is part of the certification application process. In addition, it applies to any member or nonmember who serves in any volunteer capacity for a PMI-sponsored event.

---

21 *The PMI Code of Ethics and Professional Conduct can be found at www.PMI.org/Ethics*

The four values identified as the most important to drive ethical conduct for project management professionals are:

- *Responsibility*—our duty to take ownership for the decisions we make or fail to make, the actions we take or fail to take, and their consequences

- *Respect*—our duty to show high regard for ourselves, others, and the resources entrusted to us. Resources entrusted to us may include people, money, reputation, the safety of others, and natural or environmental resources. An environment of respect engenders trust, confidence, and performance excellence by fostering cooperation—an environment where diverse perspectives and views are encouraged and valued

- *Fairness*—our duty to make decisions and act impartially and objectively. Our conduct must be free from competing self-interest, prejudice, and favoritism

- *Honesty*—our duty to understand the truth and act in a truthful manner, both in our communications and in our conduct

Acceptance of these is required as part of the certification application process and when working or volunteering in any capacity with PMI.

Team Charter and Ground Rules

The project manager and team members often identify how they will work together through establishing team norms. This document is referred to by two different terms depending on the project approach.

- *Team Charter*

A document recording the team values, agreements, and operating guidelines as well as establishing clear expectations regarding acceptable behavior by project team members.

This document is most often used with predictive approaches and developed initially by the project manager. It should include:

- The team's shared values
- Guidelines for appropriate behavior by team members
- Guidelines for team communications and the usage of tools
- Guidelines for team decision-making activities
- Expectations for team performance
- Measures for resolving conflicts when disagreements arise
- Meeting times, frequency, and logistics
- Other team agreements (such as shared hours, improvement activities)

Ideally the team charter should be reviewed and adapted by the team (also referred to as the team ground rules) or at least periodically updated as needed, with the team's active participation.

- *Ground Rules*

Expectations regarding acceptable behavior by project team members.

Ground rules is the term usually used in adaptive approaches to support team norms. These "terms of engagement" are established, modified, and enforced by the team.

Ground rules are clearly stated, written expectations regarding the code of conduct for team members, including clear rules on expectations and communications and how to handle conflicts among the team members when they inevitably occur.

By establishing clear ground rules up front and deciding how violations will be dealt with, the team sets expectations for itself, decreases the risk of confusion, and provides a tool to maintain and normalize its performance.

Team Communication

The team consistently engages in regular communications both internally and with stakeholders outside the team. In many cases, the project team may depend on other external teams, and collaboration will be required to ensure expectations are met.

Project teams become successful by working together to execute work, solve problems, and produce solutions. This is the result of effective communication. It includes understanding how various forms of communication will be used, including verbal, written, behavioral, physical, and virtual methods. It may also include shared work hours for scheduling team meetings and how the team is expected to use and not use tools like threaded discussion groups, shared document repositories, and even webcams.

Part of an effective team charter/ground rules is to make decisions as a team about how, when, and why communications are needed with one another and what the shared expectations are. It may also include communication protocols inside the team (team meetings, shared calendars, etc.) as well as periodic communication with external stakeholders to generate feedback, manage dependencies, and ensure alignment.

In addition to the traditional communications plan developed to ensure the appropriate communications are delivered to stakeholders, the team needs to determine the type, format, frequency, etc. of communications among team members. This includes establishing a team communications plan that covers various categories of communication, including:

- *Internally*
    - Appropriate usage of various communication methods
    - Team meeting times
    - Shared calendars
    - Working hours

- *Externally*
    - Stakeholder information and feedback
    - Internal and external management reporting
    - Conformance to security and confidentiality requirements

The use of retrospectives enables the team to continually discuss, evaluate, experiment, and improve communication, information sharing, and collaborative approaches for the team.

Team Decision-Making

Decision-making is a core function of all teams. They must be empowered to make decisions about activities, risks, estimates, and many other challenges within a safe environment.

These could include:

- Requesting clarification and participating in prioritization of requirements
- Splitting requirements or user stories into smaller tasks, allowing a better estimate of the effort needed
- Classifying and participating in the choice and definition of responses or actions for risks

It is vital for teams to establish their own norms for their way of working (WoW). These decisions are included in the team charter or ground rules. This includes how the team will make decisions together and handle and resolve conflict when disagreements arise. As the project progresses and the team matures, changes may be required, but the team should always try to reach consensus on these areas.

Decision-making techniques are used by a group to reach a decision. This assessment process has multiple alternatives and can lead to many outcomes.

Decision-Making Methods: Predictive

Some of the common consensus methods used in predictive approaches include:

– *Voting*

A way of factoring in much input before arriving at a decision. It is consensus driven and based on presented data. It also gives everyone on the team an equal voice and is therefore preferred in many contexts. Results of voting can include:

- Unanimity—Everyone agrees on a single course of action. This is useful in project teams requiring greater cohesion.
- Majority—Decision reached by greater than 50% of the group.
- Plurality—Decision reached with the largest block of the group, even if a majority is not achieved.

– *Multi-Criteria Decision Analysis*

Another way to arrive at a decision involves the use of systematic and analytical approaches to evaluate and rank many ideas or options toward a solution. The criteria may be weighted based on the relative importance of the criteria. It is commonly used to select the accepted proposal resulting from a request for proposal (RFP). It may also be used to evaluate and select team members with criteria including availability, cost, experience, ability, knowledge, skills, attitude, and global factors (time zone coverage).

– *Autocratic Decision-Making*

A leadership-driven approach, where one team member makes the decision for the group. Sometimes, such a method is necessary in cases of straightforward decisions requiring a limited amount of input. Or when the team cannot decide, causing a delay moving forward.

Exam Tip: This was previously referred to as dictatorship but has since been replaced by the term autocratic.

Decision-Making Methods: Adaptive

Most agreements using an adaptive approach are less structured and more informal—with the entire team participating in the decision-making activities. Some of the consensus methods used in adaptive approaches include:

– Thumbs up/down/sideways (Roman voting)—indicating agreement, disagreement, or unsure

- Fist of/to five—indicates the range of agreement, from a fist indicating no support or agreement to all five fingers indicating full support or agreement, and everything in between

- Planning poker—used mainly to determine agreement on the effort required to deliver a user story, often with Fibonacci sequence numbers indicating the perceived degree of difficulty

- Dot voting—where everyone is given several "dots" to use to indicate their preference from several options

- Polling—number of responses to previously identified options, often to determine preferences by a group

Decision-Making Methods: Hybrid

Consensus is a group decision technique where the group agrees to support an outcome even if the individuals do not agree with the decision.

Team Work Environment

Project Management Principle:

Create a collaborative project team environment[22]

Project teams are made up of individuals who wield diverse skills, knowledge, and experience. Project teams that work collaboratively can accomplish a shared objective more effectively and efficiently than individuals working on their own.

There are multiple ways the team can be organized depending on the location of the various team members. These apply to predictive, adaptive, and hybrid approaches. Each method has both advantages and disadvantages.

- *Colocated Teams*
- Colocated team members work from the same office or work location. Interaction is easier, which facilitates greater team bonding.
- Multiple tools, including physical tools, collaboration, and boards, as well as virtual versions of these, are still available to colocated team members.

- *Virtual Teams*

A group of people with a shared goal who fulfill their roles with little or no time spent meeting face-to-face.

---

22 *The Standard for Project Management, Section 3.2 – Project Management Principles*

Many project teams now have many team members virtually and not colocated. Addressing the individual needs of virtual team members often requires different skills and activities.

Virtual teams create opportunities for engaging team members with greater skills at lower costs and allow a project to avoid relocation expenses. These virtual team members can experience a better work/life balance.

Bonding and team identity can be hard to create when team members are geographically dispersed because finding ways to provide a sense of team spirit and cooperation may take time and effort. Individual contributions may be overlooked because roles, reporting, and performance can be harder to track on a dispersed team.

Virtual Team Challenges

There are obviously some challenges for a virtual team to be successful and problem solve. As a project manager, it is important to understand how to set up a successful virtual team and address problem-solving in this environment.

Overcoming these challenges includes:

- Enabling individual performance tracking through visibility of electronic collaboration and individual contributions on work activities.
- Managing communications through leveraging technology solutions to facilitate face-to-face communications, the storage and continuously updating of share files, and threaded conversations.
- Diversity of team members, including language and gaps in technical skills, can require additional translation software and coaching and training on gaps in skills.
- When individual team members are working on their own, this can inhibit the sharing and working together that form a bond among team members. There may be a lack of opportunities to provide a sense of team spirit and cooperation.

Virtual teams also encounter challenges with communications technology. These challenges can be overcome through the leveraging of technology solutions to facilitate face-to-face communications, store and share files, create threaded discussions and wikis, and manage the team's calendar. However, managing electronic collaboration so everyone on the team can reliably transmit and access information from one another can remain challenging.

Knowledge Sharing

Knowledge sharing consists of connecting individuals, in person or virtually, to share knowledge and collaborate.

It is important to keep the team excited about learning, especially from each other. Knowledge transfer opportunities can be among the most exciting moments at work.

Different ways that may be considered to acquire and share knowledge, especially external to the actual project, include:

- Networking
- Meetings, seminars, or other in-person and virtual events
- Training
- Work shadowing—an on-the-job technique that enables sharing of knowledge through learning about and performing a job while observing and working with another, more experienced person
- Special interest groups, often referred to as communities of practice

Communities of Practice (CoPs)

E. Wenger, in his book, *Cultivating Communities of Practice*, describes the establishment of local forums of "experts" with the specific mandate to create an environment in which project managers would feel comfortable sharing their findings and learnings from their projects. These Communities of Practice (CoP)s are often organized groups, both internal and external to many organizations, including PMI chapters, to provide learning, share common interests and coexist with the more formally established CoPs within an organization.

Team Communication

Both colocated and virtual teams need collaboration tools and technology to support their members' appropriate and effective communications requirements. It is critical to plan how the team will communicate and collaborate. This plan needs to consider team members' working hours, geographic dispersion, and security requirements.

Team location choices will have substantial implications for collaboration technology, not only the technologies the team uses but also how they use them. This is especially important when transparency, visibility, and collaboration among team members is required.

Examples of various types of communication tools include:

- Shared task boards to promote visibility
- Messaging and chat boards to enable effective communication
- Shared access to calendars to promote visibility of team members and stakeholder availability
- Document storage and access for shared artifacts
- Knowledge repositories to store and provide access to historical artifacts
- Videoconferencing tools to enable face-to-face communication including both colocated and virtual team members
- Fishbowl windows to allow stakeholders to observe and provide feedback during an iteration review, while allowing the team to maintain focus on the project

Fishbowl windows are set up to provide long-lived video conferencing links between various locations when team members are dispersed. It allows stakeholders to observe and provide feedback spontaneously to each other, reducing the collaboration lag otherwise inherent in geographical separation. It can also be a physical space where everyone can see what others are discussing, allowing additional collaboration and communication.

Any combination of these types of tools can be useful to help the team promote visibility and enable collaboration.

- While these technologies can certainly support the team's endeavors, continually monitoring how the team uses the tools and how well the tools reflect the team's values and priorities is critical. The usage and effectiveness of these tools can be discussed as topics in retrospectives, and improvements can be identified and implemented in the next iteration or phase.

Key Concepts Covered

- Team formation
- Team composition
- Team charter
- Team communication plan
- Team work environment
- Virtual teams
- Knowledge sharing

ECO Coverage

- Empower team members and stakeholders (1.4)
  - Organize around team strengths (1.4.1)
  - Determine and bestow level(s) of decision-making authority (1.4.4)
- Engage and support virtual teams (1.11)
  - Examine virtual team member needs (e.g., environment, geography, culture, global, etc.) (1.11.1)
  - Investigate alternatives (e.g., communication tools, colocation) for virtual team member engagement (1.11.2)
- Ensure knowledge transfer for project continuity (2.16)
  - Discuss project responsibilities within the team (2.16.1)
  - Outline expectations for working environment (2.16.2)

Check Your Progress

1. The resource management plan includes which of the following? (Choose three)
   A. Roles and responsibilities
   B. Project organization chart
   C. Competence and skills required for the project
   D. The amount of contingency permitted in the project schedule

2. A key benefit of the team charter is?
   A. Requires subject matter experts to create sustainable solutions
   B. Selects team members who can deal with high rates of change
   C. Implements a zero-sum reward and recognition system for the team
   D. Influences team behavior to optimize project performance

3. PMI has established a code of ethics that guides ethical conduct for project management professionals. Which of the following are the four core values? (Choose 4)
   A. Collaboration
   B. Respect
   C. Responsibility
   D. Honesty
   E. Fairness

4. The team values and operating guidelines are included in three artifacts, including the team charter, ground rules and the team communication plan. Is this statement true or false?

   A. True

   B. False

5. Team members are no longer expected to be an expert in just one focused area. It is important to develop and include team members with competencies and expertise across a broad range of areas. Which of the following best identifies the type of person that best fits within a project.

   A. I-shaped people

   B. T-shaped people

   C. S-shaped people

   D. A-shaped people

   E. B-shaped people

Answers

1. A, B, C
2. D
3. B, C, D, E
4. False
5. B

Project Understanding

Building a shared understanding of the project depends a great deal on the project context, the team, the stakeholders, and the project manager.

One of the first goals in starting a project is to ensure all team members and stakeholders have a common understanding of the project's objectives and any agreements, such as contracts or statements of work, used to initiate the project. It also includes enabling the team to understand the importance of the project and its alignment to the organization's strategic objectives.

Before work starts, it is important to make sure everyone is aligned and focused on creating a collaborative team environment, as the stakes are highest in this period. If the team can start from a good place, keeping them motivated and inspired to do their best will be easier in the weeks ahead.

First, perform due diligence to learn what the project is about and ensure the project vision and project charter are clearly articulated. Be able to talk about the details and the spirit of the project as part of sharing a holistic understanding of the project with the team and stakeholders. Remember, this is the value of stewardship.

Next, ensure buy-in to the project agreements, including those used to initiate the project as well as the vision statement and project charter. Without this buy-in, especially from key stakeholders, the management of the project may be difficult. Whether a key stakeholder lacks enthusiasm or openly voices a clear objection, it needs to be dealt with. Continually work to reach consensus about the project from all key stakeholders.

Every team will make decisions regarding roles and responsibilities, priorities, assignments, and deliverables differently, but establishing a way of working to suit them and deliver the best value for the project is fundamental to success.

The last step in achieving a shared understanding requires fulfilling the role of steward once again. Ensure the project agreements are upheld by the stakeholders and the team for the duration of the project.

Open and reliable communication methods and leadership "power skills" will help enable this shared understanding by all.

Project Initiating Agreements

As the project is initiated, project managers and project sponsors or product owners who need a better initial understanding of a project can benefit from looking at existing agreements. These agreements describe what is needed or wanted, schedule and budgetary requirements or constraints, etc. and are often legally binding documents, possibly subject to remediation in courts of law.

There are various types of agreements that often provide an initial understanding of the objectives and expectations for a project, which may be referred to by different names:

- Contracts — used for external customers.
- Memorandums of understanding (MOUs) — often tied to a previous contractual agreement.
- Statement of work (SOW) — including specifics on deliverables, roles, and responsibilities.
- Service level agreements (SLAs) — including service performance standards.
- Letters of agreement or intent — less formal, usually tied to a previous contractual agreement.

- Email—written verification of agreement, usually tied to a previous understanding or contractual agreement between key stakeholders.
- Verbal agreements—often used when previous work has been performed under a more formal agreement and a strong relationship exists between parties. (Not acceptable in all situations and organizations.)

In these documents, the organization describes various aspects of what is needed or wanted, schedule requirements or constraints, budgetary sources and amounts, stakeholder names, and possibly:

- Deliverables
- Schedule milestones
- Performance reporting
- Period of performance
- Roles and responsibilities
- Pricing, payment terms, fees, and retainers
- Inspection and acceptance criteria
- Warranty and limitation of liability
- Penalties and incentives
- Change request handling
- Termination clauses and alternative dispute resolution mechanisms

Business Documents

When a project has been selected as part of a portfolio management process, a business case and additional documents previously created by the business team, with the help of a business analyst, may be available for review at the beginning of the project. The project manager and the project sponsor or product owners can benefit from reviewing existing business documents and agreements to better understand a project.

The goals for this review include:

- The boundaries of negotiation for the project agreement—what, if anything, is eligible for discussion or troubleshooting?
- Assessment of organizational priorities and determination of the ultimate objectives. This includes applying critical thinking skills and business acumen to help identify how the project fits in with the current organizational landscape.

These documents contain the understanding of "why" the project is needed—to solve a problem, support an opportunity, or meet a compliance requirement.

The business case includes not only the objectives and a potential solution(s) but also the financial justification based on a documented economic feasibility study. This establishes the benefits of the project and becomes the basis to support the authorization and funding for the project effort.

Other business documents may also be available, such as those used in the creation of the business case, identifying and providing an understanding of the high-level requirements and deliverables. The requesting organization often collects and analyzes these as part of the needs assessment activities.

Systems Thinking

Project Management Principle:

Recognize, Evaluate, and Respond to System Interactions23

Recognize, evaluate, and respond to the dynamic circumstances within and surrounding the project in a holistic way to positively affect project performance.

A project is a system of interdependent and interacting domains of activities. It is essential to take a holistic view when considering projects. They are multi-faceted entities that exist in dynamic circumstances. A project is typically a piece of a whole, possibly a program, which is in turn a part of a portfolio. This is called a "system of systems."

Skills needed to support systems thinking include:

- Empathy with the business areas
- Critical thinking with a big picture focus
- Challenging of assumptions and existing processes
- Seeking external review and advice
- Use of integrated methods, artifacts, and practice so there is a common understanding of project work, deliverables, and outcomes
- Use of modeling and scenarios to envision how system dynamics may interact and react
- Proactive management of the integration to help achieve business outcomes

23   *The Standard for Project Management, Section 3.5 – Project Management Principles*

Critical Thinking

Critical thinking includes a disciplined, rational, logical, and evidence-based thinking. It requires an open mind and ability to objectively analyze any situation. It can include conceptual awareness and imagination, insight, and intuition as well as reflective thinking and being aware of one's own perceptions.

Project Vision

When a new project begins, it is critical to have a clear vision of the desired objectives and alignment with the organization's strategic goals for the project. Time is of the essence prior to the start of project work, so it is important to move quickly to ensure everyone's buy-in to the vision. If additional understanding of the project is needed, the sponsor and key stakeholders can always elaborate on and clarify their vision.

This includes creating a vision statement from the product owner, sponsor, or key stakeholders and continually reinforced by the project manager or product owner to the team throughout the project. There are many ways this vision statement can be expressed and understood.

The vision statement often includes a description of the product or solution and the alignment with the organization's strategic goals. It may also identify the intended users or consumers of the solutions and the key features, benefits, and objectives desired, in addition to the differentiators from competitors' products or approaches.

This vision statement becomes part of the approved project charter and project statement, is presented during the project kickoff activities, and is referred to throughout the project.

Using project management interpersonal and leadership power skills provides a way to give an overview of the business case and show people how the project brings value to the organization. It is important to influence and motivate the team members to provide their best work and care about the project as much as the sponsor and key stakeholders.

In addition, it might be appropriate to use some creative techniques to share the project vision with stakeholders and team members. Even though these Agile techniques are considered "collaborative games" and typically used to communicate during product development, they are great techniques to help increase understanding about the project.

Collaborative Games

- *Product Box*

This is a typical collaboration game in Agile projects, to help team members understand and internalize the vision and value of the product or result from a customer's point of view.

Creating the product box helps move the team to more of a marketing mindset for the project—describing the solution's features, functions, and benefits in customer terms. It also replaces the initial inclination to describe the technical aspects of a project rather than the value provided to the customer.

The team, in a collaborative meeting, designs and constructs a blank product box (just like a box you pick off a shelf to view the product). This includes the features, benefits, value, and any additional graphics or artwork to represent the product the project will develop and deliver to the customer.

Example: On a project where we were to implement a customer relationship management (CRM) software solution. The delivery team was very familiar with the software product, having implemented it previously for other customers. When asked by others about their current project, they always would describe the technical infrastructure of the software solution, including the web browser, data base and version of the operating system – rather than explaining "why" the solution was being implemented.

- *XP Metaphor*

The way a vision statement is usually presented within an eXtreme programming (XP) software development effort is using an XP metaphor. This includes the high level as well as the detailed explanations of the software development work. These are usually written using simple, common vocabulary and language and nontechnical terminology. It helps explain a complex item in simple terms by comparing what is not yet known or understood to something well known.

Project Charter

A document issued by the project initiator or sponsor formally authorizing the existence of a project and providing the project manager with the authority to apply organizational resources to project activities.

Once stakeholders and team members have accepted and can begin to internalize the project vision and agreements, it's time to ensure the project charter is finalized.

If there is no formal project selection process in an organization, a project professional may draft the project charter and review it with the executive sponsor (and possibly key stakeholders) for approval and distribution. The project charter is written as coming from the project sponsor, not the project manager.

There is no single way to create a project charter, but it is imperative a project has one.

For any project there is an organization requesting the work to be done, as well as an organization responsible for the actual performance or delivery of the work. The project charter in this case is the official document establishing and formalizing the partnership between those two organizations. Regardless of how the decision to begin the project was made, this process creates a document showing formal acceptance and commitment to the project from the organization and the formal authorization of the project.

The project charter provides the direct link between the project and the organization's strategic objectives, including information contained in previous business documents (business case and benefits management plan). It often defines the project start date and any established boundaries for the project effort.

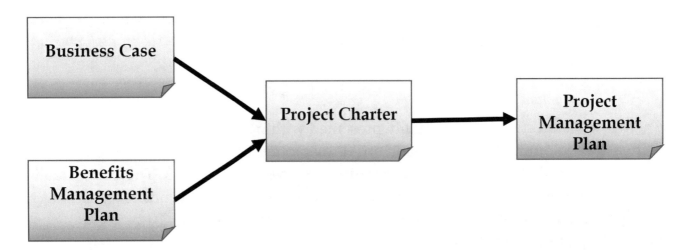

An effective project charter conveys the "why" or rationale for the project being initiated, describes its expected outcomes, and helps ensure support for the project. In addition to formally authorizing the project, the project charter assigns and authorizes the project manager to apply resources to project activities.

It should be created, or at least be distributed, by a member of senior management, often the project initiator or sponsor, who provides the resources and support for the project and is accountable for enabling the project's success. Because it states a business need approved at the executive level, it verifies alignment with strategic goals.

In many cases, the management responsible for the project and the defining charter have also provided the funding for the project.

Finally, and very importantly, it keeps everyone on the team and the stakeholders focused on a clear project vision. Later, everyone can refer to it for a high-level vision of the project.

When a project is the result of a contract or procurement SOW, the content may serve as the project charter.

This project charter development is usually only performed once, with no need for updating during the project. In the rare case when a project has run into substantial difficulties, a new charter may have to be written to specify the new direction needed.

Project Charter Contents

The project charter may look different depending on the organization, the project context, and how well-developed the ideas are. Most practitioners recommend a simple one-page document.

Based on the definition of the project charter, two key items must be included:

- The assigned project manager and their responsibility and authority level for the project
- The sponsor, including their name and authority

If a business case has been used to select and approve the initiation of a project, information from the document can be copied or pasted into the project charter, including:

- Names of the project sponsor, project manager, and key stakeholders
- Business strategic alignment
- Project objectives and success criteria
- High-level project description
- Business need, purpose, or justification
- Preliminary high-level requirements with measurable objectives
- Project boundaries and key deliverables
- Key stakeholders
- Overall project risks, assumptions, and constraints
- Required milestone schedules

- Preapproved financial resources and budget targets
- Project approval and success requirements
- Project exit criteria

Care must be taken to refrain from gathering additional information which is not part of the initial project agreement at this time. Additional information becomes more of a preliminary scope statement—and no longer meets the purpose of this initiating document.

Exam Tip: The project charter always will refer to high-level items, such as high-level objectives, requirements and risks. If you see high-level items included, the question is referring to the project charter.

Project Success Criteria

An important part of a project agreement is clarity on how the respective parties will report on and verify the project objectives are met. This requires customer, client, and stakeholder input to understand how "success" is defined. This can be done through interviews with the key stakeholders and domain or subject matter experts (SMEs).

This also includes any technical success criteria as well as OPAs identifying what is needed to meet the organizational quality policy. Performance criteria and expectations may include organizational key performance indicators (KPIs) and organizational key results (OKRs).

- *Key Performance Indicators (KPIs)*

KPIs help measure performance against strategic, financial, and operational achievements. These can be financial, customer-focused, or process-focused. Projects use KPIs as targets to help focus on expected performance, milestones for gauging progress, and insights to help organizations make continuous improvement decisions.

Most effective KPIs are written utilizing effective metrics as part of SMART objectives:

- Specific—clear and concise—no ambiguity
- Measurable—quantifiable indicators of progress
- Assignable—individual must be responsible
- Realistic—achievable within constraints
- Timely—specific durations and target dates

- *Organizational Key Results (OKRs)*[24]

Individuals, teams, and organizations often use objectives and key results (OKRs) as a goal-setting framework to define measurable goals and track their outcomes. This was derived from Peter Drucker's Management by Objectives.

Objectives are the goals and intents of expected results. Key results are time-bound and measurable milestones under the goals and intents. They help clarify investment ideas as well as specifying the metrics used to measure success.

The three components include:

- Objectives set qualitative, inspiring goals to guide work
- Key results quantify progress with measureable outcomes to gauge success
- Initiatives outline actionable steps to achieve the OKRs

> *"The key results have to be measurable. But at the end you can look, and without any arguments: Did I do that, or did I not do it? Yes, or No? Simple. No judgements in it."*
>
> *— John Doerr*

OKR best practices include:

- Supporting each objective with 3–5 measurable key results
- Aiming for a 70% success rate to encourage competitive goal-making
- Writing action-oriented, inspirational OKRs with concrete, measurable outcomes

Additional information can be found in lessons learned repositories or other historical data. Requirements may also be specified for the verification of success obtained through user acceptance testing (UAT) activities.

Team members need to know the goals for individual work items, including the acceptance criteria for the individual pieces of work.

Predictive—Each deliverable is identified, and objective acceptance criteria for each are specified. Additional reporting of the verification of performance of individuals is identified.

---

24   *More information on OKRs can be found at:*
https://www.pmi.org/disciplined-Agile/da-flex-toc/strategic-planning-and-lean-portfolio-management

Adaptive—Since the actual deliverables will vary as the product backlog is added to, reprioritized, and so forth, each story needs to have clearly defined acceptance criteria approved by the customer.

The project may also specify a definition of done (DoD) for the project in addition to the DoDs for releases, phases, iterations, and user stories/requirements.

Assumptions and Constraints

- *Assumptions*

A fact or statement accepted as true or certain, without proof.

Assumptions initially identified in the business case, benefits management plan, or agreements are placed on an assumption log. These may be moved into the project charter, along with any additional assumptions as they are identified.

This log will continue to be updated as the project continues, both with the addition of new assumptions and constraints and the removal of assumptions that are determined to be no longer valid.

- *Constraints*

A limiting factor that affects the execution of a project, program, portfolio, or process.

Projects are usually executed under several constraints, and project management must be able to balance the influence of those constraints on the project efforts. Constraints are limiting factors that may be necessary for the successful completion of the project. Sometimes the constraints severely impact the way in which the project must be performed, as well as customer satisfaction.

In previous versions of the *PMBOK Guide*, reference was made to a "triple constraint," also known as the "iron triangle." The depiction was that of an equilateral triangle showing that if any one leg of the triangle changed, the other two legs were impacted. It supports the understanding that a change to one factor (scope, schedule, or cost) will impact the other two. For example, if the schedule is shortened, the budget may need to be increased to complete the same amount of work in a shorter period.

The triple constraint has been replaced with additional factors that have the potential to severely impact the execution and optimization of a project effort. These additional constraints include risks, quality, and resources. These constraints will involve making trade-offs and will have an impact on the development of the scope, schedule, and cost baselines.

Different constraints may come into play at different times, and each needs to be evaluated in terms of ultimate customer satisfaction and the needs of the project. Since stakeholders have differing ideas about the most important factors, it is critical to understand these various constraints and how they might affect the project's outcome. Since these often have an impact on customer satisfaction, the project manager must balance all the constraints and still deliver the highest level of customer satisfaction.

Kickoff Meeting

After the project has been formally initiated with the distribution of the approved project charter, kickoff meetings may be held to further explain the project and establish its context. These may include a meeting with the organization to announce the initiation of the effort, as well as a separate meeting with the actual delivery team (depending on the approach being used).

Organizational kickoff: This meeting announces the start of the project and provides a common understanding of the high-level vision, purpose, and value of the project. The sponsor, key stakeholders, and project manager are introduced, and high-level items from the project charter are presented.

Team kickoff: This meeting is commonly used to help establish the team, including alignment of both the team and stakeholders with the project. The project charter and the product road map, if applicable, are reviewed during this meeting. Depending on the approach, the team charter, roles and responsibilities, and additional information may also be shared with the team members.

Predictive approach—information regarding initial planning efforts is presented. This may also be repeated at the beginning of a new phase if new stakeholders or team members are added, including presentation of a responsibility matrix for team members.

Adaptive approach—the initial product backlog may be presented or developed to support the product road map. The team ground rules can be provided, updated, or initially developed at this time.

Hybrid approach—the product road map is provided to enhance understanding of the delivery of components of the vision. Expectations of participation in the project by key stakeholders are often addressed, including roles, activities, and time commitments.

Role of the Sponsor

The sponsor plays a key role in both kickoff meetings. In the organizational kickoff, the sponsor reinforces the project's importance and helps ensure that everyone is aligned on the project goals. In the team kickoff, the sponsor provides support and guidance to the team and helps ensure that the team is set up for success.

Here are some additional tips for conducting effective kickoff meetings:

- Keep the meetings short and to the point. People's attention spans are limited, so it's important to get to the key points quickly.
- Use visuals to help people understand the project. Charts, graphs, and diagrams can be helpful for communicating complex information.
- Get input from the team. Ask team members for their feedback and suggestions. This will help ensure that everyone is invested in the project.
- Follow up after the meeting. Send out a summary of the meeting and any identified action items. This will help keep everyone on the same page.

Example: For one project which was going to change the way employee paychecks were to be distributed, from paper checks being handed out to electronic funds transfer, it was imperative that the kickoff meeting was conducted by a top-level executive. Not only was the purpose of his involvement to explain the reason for the change, but also to reinforce the importance of the team's effort in facilitating this change.

Project Consensus

A few project management principles to guide this very important point in a project include:

- Demonstrate leadership behaviors—Listening is key, so demonstrate the ability to listen, understand, and communicate with emotional intelligence.
- Focus on value—Value for the organization is the reason for the project.
- Be a diligent, respectful, and caring steward—Genuinely caring about the outcomes while being respectful of everyone's opinion and input.
- Navigate complexity—Especially at the start of a project, when the stakeholders may not be well known, or the vision is not crystal clear.
- Embrace adaptability and resiliency—Helps toward thriving in the project ecosystem.

Often the project manager will not be handed a clear, prescriptive mandate for the project with instructions on how to succeed. Initiating a project is often fast-paced and filled with the complexity of many voices, opinions, and expectations—both realistic and unrealistic. It is important to understand the path ahead as quickly as possible and then drive consensus-building from the start.

This effort results in an understanding and agreement on the project vision statement and approval of the project charter. Both are vital artifacts to help guide the team and stakeholders for the entire project.

Key Concepts Covered

- Initiating agreements
- Project vision
- Project charter
- Project success criteria
- Kickoff meeting
- Project consensus

ECO Coverage

- Lead a team (1.2)
  - Set a clear vision and mission (1.2.1)

- Negotiate project agreements (1.8)
  - Analyze the bounds of the negotiation for agreement (1.8.1)
  - Assess priorities and determine ultimate objective(s) (1.8.2)
  - Participate in agreement negotiations (1.8.4)
  - Determine a negotiation strategy (1.8.5)

- Build shared understanding (1.10)
  - Survey all necessary parties to reach consensus (1.10.2)
  - Support outcomes of parties' agreement (1.10.3)

- Define team ground rules (1.12)
  - Communicate organizational principles with team and external stakeholders (1.12.1)
  - Establish an environment that fosters adherence to ground rules (1.12.2)

Check Your Progress

1. The project team has established a mutual agreement on the vision of what the product should look like when it is complete. This is an example of:
   A. Shared vision
   B. Product scope statement

    C. Rolling wave agreement

    D. Business Case

2. There are various types of agreements that often provide an initial understanding of the objectives and expectations for a project. Which of the following can be a project agreement? (Choose 3)

    A. Contract

    B. MOU

    C. SOW

    D. Change Request

    E. Approved change request

3. Which business documents can be developed and used to create the project charter? (Choose 2)

    A. Business case

    B. Benefits management plan

    C. Project management plan

    D. Project scope statement

4. The development of a product box is a typical agile collaboration game to help team members understand the vision and value of the product from the customer's point of view. Is this statement true or false?

    A. True

    B. False

5. The development of a product box is a typical agile collaboration game to help team members understand the vision and value of the product from the customer's point of view. Is this statement true or false?

    A. True

    B. False

6. Which of the following are part of SMART objectives? (Choose 3)

    A. Specific—clear and concise—no ambiguity

    B. Measurable—quantifiable indicators of progress

    C. Assignable—the team and not the individual must be responsible

    D. Realistic—achievable within constraints

    E. Timely—each activity must be completed within 2 weeks

Answers

1. A
2. A, B, C
3. A, B
4. True
5. A, B, D

Project Approach

Once the purpose, objective, stakeholders, and team resources required for the project are understood, it is time to determine the approach or methodology that would be best suited to deliver a successful result. No two projects are the same, so it is important to understand the project's unique context. Project managers must be knowledgeable and competent in different life cycles and approaches to best address and support the context of various projects.

Project Purpose

While the predictive life cycle has been effective in supporting good practice, process-based project management standards for many years, project management is evolving more rapidly than ever before. The process flow-based orientation of the predictive development approach is prescriptive and therefore cannot support the amount and complexity of dynamic and perpetual change inherent in today's global business landscape. This also includes the changing perception of value (e.g., sustainability, customer-centricity).

More and better ways are needed to solve problems, provide solutions, and offer businesses and organizations a wider range of value options, especially as complexity and risk increase.

Project teams are increasingly asked to innovate and be dynamic while focusing more on intended outcomes rather than predefined deliverables. As a result, project management approaches have also changed and diversified.

In addition to what PMI offers, there are many other Agile frameworks and methods to manage projects. Some of the more well-known ones might be mentioned on the exam, so it is important to be aware of them.

These include many branded Agile approaches including:

- Scrum™—emphasizes small increments of work, driven by prioritization, productivity and simplicity
- Kanban—visual approach to work management, typically employed in conjunction with other methodologies with project tasks monitored through tracking of work
- eXtreme Programming—focus on speed and continuously commonly used for software improvements
- Crystal family of methodologies—prioritizes communication and team reflection to identify what worked and what didn't
- DSDM—concentrates on delivering the prioritization of 80% of value in 20% of the time
- Test-driven development (TDD) and Acceptance test-driven development (ATDD)—tests designed and then code is developed to pass the test and then revised until code meets the test
- Feature-driven development (FDD)—iterations based on feature-based list of requirements through iterations for development
- Behavior-driven development (BDD)—focus on utilization of the system by users
- Disciplined Agile—context sensitive, rather than prescribing a collection of "best practices," to allow choice for what is best based on the situation
- SAFe—organization and workflow patterns intended to guide enterprises in scaling lean and agile practices.
- Lean Six Sigma—process improvement approach using a collaborative team effort to improve performance by systematically removing operational waste and reducing process variations
- PRINCE2 Agile—blends the flexibility and responsiveness of agile with the defined governance of PRINCE2

And many, many others

Project Outcome

The outcome of a project can result in a unique product, service, or result. It can also be a solution to a problem or support for an organizational change initiative.

Product

Artifact that is produced, is quantifiable, and is either an end item or a component item. Products may also be called materials or goods.

A product could be an enhancement to an existing product or a component of a final product. It can also result in the delivery of the service or merely a result such as a completed document.

The result of a project may be tangible or intangible. Although repetitive processes and similar deliverables may be employed as part of the project effort, the result will be unique with different circumstances and situations, stakeholders, etc. The result can also be a service or capability to improve or provide support for a business function. It could also be an outcome or document, especially in the case of research projects.

Product Management

The integration of people, data, processes, and business systems to create, maintain, and evolve a product or service throughout its life cycle.

Product management is different from project management, as each has its own life cycles and management approaches, but some areas overlap. Product management is usually a management role within the organization identified as the product manager.

Tailoring

Project Management Principle:

Tailor Based on Context[25]

Design the project development approach based on the context of the project, its objectives, stakeholders, governance, and the environment using "just enough" process to achieve the desired outcome while maximizing value, managing cost, and enhancing speed.

Tailoring an approach is iteratively captured and continuously done throughout the project life cycle. Feedback is received from all stakeholders on various methods and processes to help evaluate the effective and value-added to the organization.

A tailored project can produce direct and indirect benefits by:

- Deeper commitment from project team members because they took part in defining the approach

---

25 *The Standard for Project Management, Section 3.7 – Project Management Principles*

- Reduction in waste in terms of actions or resources
- Customer-oriented focus, as the needs of the customer and other stakeholders are an important factor influencing the tailoring of the project
- More efficient use of project resource, as project teams are conscious of project processes

Tailor Projects

Tailoring is the deliberate adaptation of the project management approach, governance, and processes to make them more suitable for the given environment and the work at hand.

Because of the way projects and project management have evolved, it is important to emphasize that no two projects are the same. It is even more important to understand the unique context of the project. With an understanding of the various contexts methods can be adapted and applied in the most appropriate way of working to produce the desired outcomes.

This applies to all aspects of project management including tools, techniques, processes, and ways of performing project activities.

Tailoring is needed to balance potentially competing demands including:

- Delivering as quickly as possible
- Minimizing project costs
- Optimizing value delivered
- Creating high-quality outcomes and deliverables
- Complying with regulatory requirements
- Satisfying diverse stakeholder's expectations
- Adapting to change

This tailoring of project methods to determine what is most appropriate is iterative; it is a continuous process throughout the project. Adapting to the environment's unique objectives, stakeholders, and complexity contributes to project success.

In a project environment, tailoring considers the development approach, processes, project life cycle, deliverables, and choice of people with whom to engage. The guiding project management principles in *The ANSI Standard for Project Management* drive the tailoring process.

Together with the PMO, project teams discuss and decide on the delivery approach and resources required for producing outcomes on a project-by-project basis. This includes the selection of the processes to use, development approach, methods, and artifacts needed to deliver the project outcomes.

Project teams collect feedback from all stakeholders on how the methods and tailored processes are working for them as the project progresses to evaluate their effectiveness and add value to the organization.

This tailoring advances project management into utilization of a more hybrid approach with the appropriate choice of processes, practices, and methods for each individual project.

Development Approaches

There may not be an ideal approach to manage any project, but experienced project managers can choose the best approach, depending on the resources, timelines, stakeholders, industry, project work, and many other factors. Every project and situation require an assessment of what method, or way of working, will be best.

Complexity

Project Management Principle:

Navigate Complexity[26]

Continually evaluate and navigate project complexity so that approaches and plans enable the project team to successfully navigate the project life cycle.

The more complex the project and the variations from various stakeholders, the more important the integration of project work and elements becomes. It can emerge and impact the project in any area and at any point in the project life cycle.

Complexity can be the result of uncertainty including:

- Human behavior—conduct, between diverse individuals and groups of stakeholders
- System behavior—dynamic interdependencies within and among project elements
- Uncertainty and ambiguity—lack of understanding and awareness of issues, events, paths to follow, or solutions to pursue, including "unknown unknowns"

---

26 *The Standard for Project Management, Section 3.9 – Project Management Principles*

- Technological innovation—causing disruption to products, services, ways of working, processes, tools, techniques, procedures, and more

- Interdependencies—among and between the various components and systems of the organization

Most complex projects contain multiple parts with several connections between them. Adding to the complexity is the dynamic interactions between the parts. Often emergent behavior is present, including behavior not equal to the "sum of the parts."

Understanding and recognizing these areas is critical for managing and delivering expected results on complex projects.

Exam Tip: If you need to become more familiar with this area, review the Managing Complexity Practice Guide from PMI.

The Stacey Complexity Model

One of the most often used tools to help decide on the appropriate approach for a project is Ralph Stacey's complexity model. It can be used in all kinds of contexts to help us understand the complexity of a situation in terms of the degree of uncertainty/certainty about requirements and the technology and knowledge (capability) available to complete the work.

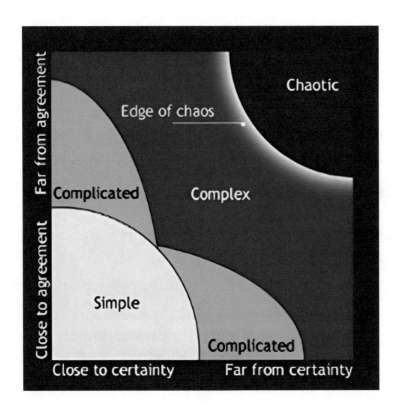

PMI has adapted the model to show where predictive (linear) and adaptive (responsive) approaches work well according to the complexity of the subject being analyzed.[27]

Suitability Filter

A suitability filter tool helps project teams consider whether a project has characteristics lending themselves toward a predictive, hybrid, or adaptive development approach. It is an informational tool combining its assessment with other data, decision-making activities, and the Stacey complexity model, so an appropriately tailored approach can be determined for a project.

The suitability assessment looks at organizational and project elements under three main categories. The team sends a questionnaire to the appropriate audience and then assesses the results. Questions asked are:

- Culture—Is there a supportive environment with buy-in for the approach and trust in the team? Have we utilized cultural awareness to understand differences and adapt strategies to support these?

- Team—Is the team of a suitable size to be successful in adopting Agile? Do its members have the necessary experience and access to business representatives to be successful?

- Project—Are there high rates of change? Is incremental delivery possible? How critical is the project?

The answers to these questions are plotted on a radar chart.

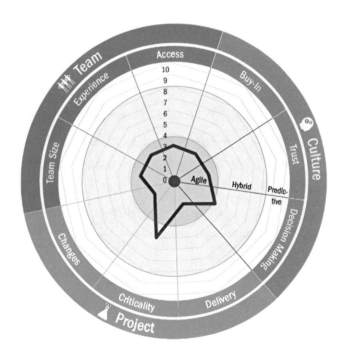

---

27 *Agile Practice Guide, p. 14*

Clusters of values around the chart's center section indicate a good fit for an adaptive approach. Results around the outside indicate a predictive approach may be more suitable. Values in the middle portion (between adaptive and predictive) indicate that a hybrid approach could work well.[28]

Tailoring the approach to support today's dynamic work environment is important. This includes discovering the value expectations of the requirements providing value to the organization. To ensure this understanding, it is important to continually promote close collaboration between the project team and the stakeholders.

By using a tailored approach, continuous improvement and quality can be provided by increased assessment of desired features or capability.

Servant leaders influence the delivery of projects while encouraging the organization and team members to think differently. This involvement helps improve and increase the organization's tolerance for change.

Project Management Development Approaches

Performance Domain:

Development Approach and Life Cycle Performance[29]

Development Approach and Life Cycle Performance Domain addresses activities and functions associated with the development approach, cadence, and life cycle phases of the project.

The following items defined in the glossary relevant to the Development Approach and Life Cycle Performance Domain:

- *Deliverable—Any unique and verifiable product, result, or capability to perform a service that is required to be produced to complete a process, phase, or project*

- *Development approach—A method used to create and evolve the product, service, or result during the project life cycle, such as a predictive, iterative, incremental, adaptive, or hybrid method*

- *Cadence—A rhythm of activities conducted throughout the project*

- *Project phase—A collection of logically related project activities that culminates in the completion of one or more deliverables*

---

28 *For more information on how to use this tool: Agile Practice Guide, p. 127+*

29 *PMBOK Guide, Seventh Edition, Section 2.3 – Project Performance Domains*

- *Project life cycle — The series of phases that a project passes through from its start to its completion*

As projects are initiated to meet the changing demands in today's environments, project managers must be knowledgeable and competent in different life cycles, and development approaches must adapt to the context of each project.

Development Approach Choice

While it is true that organizational governance and EEFs will be a major determining factor in the life cycle the project follows, other aspects need to be considered, especially to ensure successful project outcomes.

As the project starts and the team forms, the pros and cons of various development approaches should be considered. Understanding the diverse options will help the team focus on the work to deliver the result. If a phased approach is used, additional decisions need to be made as to whether the work will be batched and timeboxed or if a continuous flow approach would be better.

The development approach and delivery cadence choice determine the project life cycle and its phases or releases. It is always possible to switch between approaches, but normally this should be done at the beginning of a phase or release, not midstream.

Some questions helpful in determining the appropriate approach include:

- Product, service or result
  - Degree of innovation
  - Requirements certainty
  - Scope stability
  - Ease of change
  - Delivery options
  - Risk
  - Safety requirements
  - Regulations

- Project
  - Stakeholders
  - Schedule constraints
  - Funding availability

- Organization
  - Organizational structure
  - Culture
  - Organizational capability
  - Project team size and location

The three main project approaches include predictive, adaptive and hybrid.

Predictive/Plan-Driven Approach

A more traditional, established, and highly reliable approach wherein, as much as possible, the project needs, requirements, and constraints are understood at the beginning of the project, and plans are developed accordingly. The certainty of requirements is high from the beginning since most are known from previous project efforts. The more well planned, the more predictive and controlled the project.

This is often referred to as a plan-based approach, and like the traditional waterfall approach:

- The activities are completed in a linear or sequential manner, broken into phases.
- Most activities are understood, as they are based on previous projects or experience.
- A new phase of the project is authorized to begin when the previous phase is completed.
- Governance is often done by governance reviews or phase gates to meet requirements as specified in an organization's methodology.

Key roles include the:

- Project sponsor, who authorizes the project
- Key stakeholders, who provide direction for the expectations of the project objectives to be achieved
- Project manager, who leads the project team

Value delivery is provided by:

- Deliverables transitioned to the customer at the completion of the project
- Value realized after project completion in both the short and long term

Change is always possible but is considered and controlled through a process ensuring the project's continued viability.

Risks are continually reviewed and methodically managed.

Adaptive/Agile/Change-Driven Approach

This is a more modern approach wherein the team works collaboratively with the customer to determine the project needs, quickly building outputs based on those assumptions, getting feedback, and continuing forward or adapting as needed. It includes a range of iterative, incremental, or adaptive approaches as appropriate. This can also include a timeboxed cadence (referred to as iterations or sprints) or continuous flow.

The aim is to deliver value early by regularly confirming and incorporating feedback from key stakeholders. This collaboration between the project team and the stakeholder(s) is needed to clarify requirements, which are often unclear initially. In addition to continual discovery, the involvement and input from the customer helps drive the project forward to providing the vision.

Adaptive methods are built on the assumption of a high degree of change, and therefore continual reprioritization and understanding of requirements is a typical activity.

- The key concept is the ability to respond to change.
- Often used when previous experience or knowledge is not available.
- Can be conducted using a timeboxed cadence with iterations or sprints or through a continuous flow of activities.

Key roles include the:

- Product owner, who controls the value proposition through continual prioritization of requirements.
- Project team, who delivers the work.
- Additional roles can include a team lead, scrum master, Agile coach, or facilitator (depending on the framework followed).

Value delivery is provided by:

- Iterative or incremental delivery to the customer during the life cycle of the project.
- Regular customer feedback cycles enable the continuous development of value toward a "final" product or release.

Risk, or uncertainty, is high and as a result, risk management guardrails must be established to understand when a risk needs to be escalated to determine whether the risk is acceptable. Risks are still identified and managed, especially within a release.

Adaptive approaches acknowledge that risk and change are a natural part of innovation.

- *Cadence*

Delivery cadence refers to the timing and frequency of project deliverables. Projects can have a single delivery, multiple deliveries, or periodic deliveries.

- Single delivery — Project has a single delivery at the project's end.
- Multiple deliveries — Project may have multiple components delivered at various times throughout the project.
- Periodic — Similar to projects with multiple deliveries, but on a fixed schedule — e.g., monthly or bimonthly.

Adaptive development can use one of two cadences: timeboxed into iterations/sprints or continuous flow.

- *Timeboxed*

Requirements (user stories) are batched into releases, and chosen releases are then developed and delivered within a set time frame. Essentially, this means repeating the development process of individual user stories or requirements during sprints/ iterations until the work meets the definition of done and the customer is happy.

- *Continuous Flow*

Requirements are prioritized on the product backlog, and the team works on them individually until they are completed and handed to the customer. This approach is usually more appropriate for organizations such as call centers or support teams handling individual requests as they arrive.

Hybrid Approach

A third option incorporates components of both approaches. This combination of predictive and adaptive approaches is referred to as a hybrid approach and is often done through tailoring by the project manager. It incorporates both iterative and incremental development concepts, depending on the various project activities to be performed. This allows for the reliability of a plan-based approach with the flexibility of an adaptive approach.

In many cases a portion of the project, such as the initial planning, may utilize a predictive approach, while the development or delivery activities utilize a more adaptive approach.

A more predictive approach can be used for those portions that have fixed requirements or are well understood. Different project teams developing deliverables can be modularized, or when elements change and evolve, a more adaptive approach can be used.

An organization may formalize these approaches into a methodology, but often these approaches include various methods, techniques, and practices to select from that are then tailored to meet the needs of the project.

Life Cycles

The series of phases a project passes through from start to completion.

The development approach describes how the project work is conducted.

It is how the work of the project is organized, including the logical breakdown of what is needed to create project deliverables. Just as different approaches are used in the development effort of a project, there are corresponding life cycles to support these various approaches. These include agile life cycles, iterative life cycles, incremental life cycles, and predictive life cycles.

Product Life Cycle

The product life cycle is a series of phases representing the evolution of a product, from introduction through growth, maturity, and to retirement.

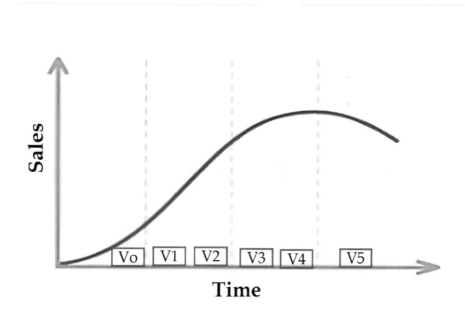

Product management may initiate programs or projects at any point in the product life cycle to create or enhance specific components, functions, or capabilities. The projects related to product enhancements include product requirements as part of the overall project scope and requirements, either as an end item itself or a component item.

Because the project supports the development or enhancement of a product, the key stakeholder is referred to as the product owner. Being accountable for the result of the project, the product owner works closely with the team to provide the product details and maximize the product's value to the end user or customer.

Exam Tip: As a product is released to the customer through different versions, a project life cycle was used to manage the work necessary to create or deliver each release or version of the product.

Project Life Cycle

The series of phases a project passes through from its initiation to its closure.

The project life cycle is based on the industry, the organization's preferences, and the development approach, whether predictive, adaptive, or hybrid. The project manager is responsible for managing and successfully delivering the project objectives and vision.

The phases may be sequential, iterative, or overlapping. Project life cycles are used to deliver new releases or versions of a product throughout the product life cycle. These include determining what needs to be done, organizing and preparing how it will be done, performing the work to create the result, and then completing or closing the project.

The names of each phase, as well as the requirements to move from one phase to another, are defined by the organization's methodology. Depending on the project approach used, these phases may not be clearly defined, but all efforts will go through the activities — often without clear distinctions between them.

Predictive Life Cycle

The predictive life cycle determines the project scope, time, and cost in the early phases of this life cycle.

The overall project is broken down into predefined phases, based on the organization's methodology.

In a predictive life cycle, the project scope, schedule, and budget are determined as early in the project as possible and used to plan the work to be done. Once those determinations have been made, changes, especially in scope, must be carefully managed.

Each phase includes a subset of the overall project activities, while the work performed is different from other phases, allowing for different resources and skills to be included only in the phases where needed.

This approach is preferred when the scope and project outcomes are well understood and known, and a substantial base of industry practice exists.

Once the planning has been completed, there is little chance of change. This approach is often used for enhancements to an established product.

This predictive approach can utilize rolling wave planning to concentrate on the required tasks in the immediate phases, while postponing the specification of the actual detail work required in later phases.

Using a predictive life cycle delivers an outcome or output, identified as a deliverable, for the result. The complete product is required to be delivered in full, at the end of the project, to provide value to the stakeholders.

The project management life cycle is applied to each phase when using a predictive approach — and often includes governance, or oversight, through reviews at the end of each phase. These life cycles are often formalized into an organization's methodology. This enables the project team to stay focused on the work required for each phase of the project.

As the name suggests, predictive life cycles are very good when fixed requirements and fixed expectations exist. There is a high element of control, and thus predictability, in projects using a predictive life cycle.

Adaptive Life Cycle

An adaptive project life cycle is iterative or incremental, also referred to as change-driven. It works well in environments with high levels of change and ongoing stakeholder involvement in a project.

The Standish Group in 1998 showed that many projects failed because they took too long to deliver any value. This idea is also a key feature of the Lean method to deliver smaller chunks more frequently. Breaking down the delivery of features and functions enables the results to provide value sooner and gives early feedback to the project team, allowing for adjustments to the direction, priorities, and quality of the product.

Because we live in an age of high complexity and change, it is very difficult to determine the requirements needed for the result at the beginning of the project. Changes in business needs and conditions, as well as external environmental factors, require a project to readily adapt. As a result, there may be fewer and fewer cases where projects can adopt a purely predictive life cycle.

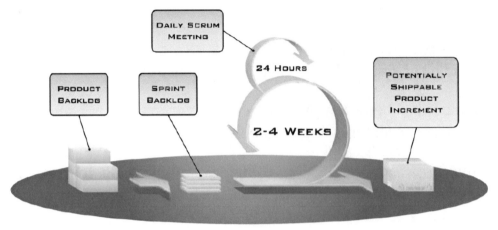

A project using an adaptive approach begins with an initial vision for the product and is developed iteratively or incrementally with the customer's input until the customer is happy. The detailed scope for each cycle is defined, prioritized, and approved before the start of the work on those requirements, usually written as user stories and then further decomposed into actual tasks.

The project effort is often released to the customer through potentially different versions, with the project life cycle being used to manage the work necessary to create or deliver each release or version of the product.

Adaptive life cycles or approaches are also known as change-driven cycles and are incorporated into most Agile methods. These can be done using either an iterative or an incremental approach.

Adaptive life cycles fall into several categories utilized individually or combined by a project to deliver the result. All of these are often used when the requirements are dynamic or subject to change. They work well in environments with high levels of change and continual stakeholder involvement in the project. Because they break the overall scope into smaller components, they can move more quickly and deliver results in a shorter time frame.

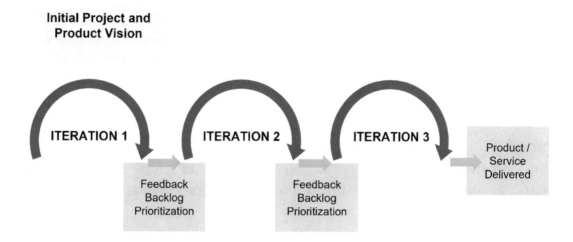

Iterative and Incremental Approaches

Iterative and incremental development approaches are similar and are used in both adaptive and hybrid life cycles. They enable teams to release value to the customer before the end of the project.

– *Iterative Approach*

Time frames allowing teams to develop a product through a series of repeated cycles, or iterations. The final project scope is identified, while increments successively add to the functionality and final scope of the product.

In most iterative life cycles, a high-level vision is developed for the entire effort, but the detail scope is determined one iteration at a time. It focuses on an initial, simplified implementation of a release and is progressively elaborated, adding to the feature set until the final iterative deliverable is complete. This allows feedback for unfinished work to improve and modify it.

By breaking the work into smaller chunks or repeated cycles, the result will be decomposed into smaller groups, allowing additional feedback from stakeholders, incorporating team insight, and delivering small benefits in a shorter period.

Employing an iterative approach helps in identifying and reducing uncertainty. It is used when complexity and uncertainty are high and frequent changes are expected.

Planning for the following iteration may be done while the work on the current iteration's requirements and deliverables is in progress. The work required for individual iterations may change, as may the project team composition. Changes to the project scope must be carefully managed, though, once work has begun on an individual iteration.

- *Incremental Approach*

Incremental approaches are used to deliver value over a shorter time by delivering the result through subsets of the result, with each increment adding additional value to the result. This approach optimizes the speed and delivery of value to the customer through more frequent completion of deliverable subsets. It is often used with an existing product, with each release adding features and functions to the previous version.

This approach works best if the overall scope can be decomposed into smaller portions, often using user stories to define the requirements for either releases or smaller iterations. The size and complexity of those requirements determine what can be completed in each portion.

In many adaptive approaches the results of these smaller portions, or increments, are referred to as minimal marketable features (MMFs). They identify what can be delivered and approved at the completion of each increment.

Iterative and incremental developmental approaches are best thought of together, rather than trying to make a distinction between them. These ideas work together to describe how work can be developed in a way that accrues value through the process of involving the customer. The team continually innovates and solves problems until all stakeholders are happy with the product or service, and it meets the standards set for "done" or completion.

An adaptive life cycle often incorporates either or both above life cycles but may additionally use a continuous flow or timeboxed approach for the delivery. This cycle is often used in highly flexible, interactive, and adaptive organizations where project outcomes are realized while the project work is being completed, not at the beginning of the project. This is especially important when dealing with a rapidly changing environment, in which scope and requirements are difficult to define in advance and small incremental deliverables have value to stakeholders.

- *Continuous Flow*

This method is based on kanban and Lean and allows requests to be addressed individually rather than batching several requests into an iteration. It works best in a project with complex dependencies and relationships, when the work can be subdivided and performed by different individuals or groups.

Requests are prioritized upon receipt to determine the start time, and then the request will be moved through different stages as required until completion. As a team member has availability, they pull a request from the queue, work on it, and upon completion move it into the next queue to wait for availability to continue the work. Managing the prioritization and assignment of work to resources allows the work to be leveled out.

There is not a schedule identified for actual completion of the request and delivery to the requester unless a service level agreement (SLA) is in place or work is within the limits specified for each category/column on the kanban chart. The requests are *individually* prioritized and worked on until completion.

Usage of this approach provides incremental business value based on the prioritization of individual requests or requirements received.

- *Timeboxed Approach*

Requirements are collected into a backlog. Individual items are then pulled and combined to become part of a release and then later, individual iterations.

Specific time frames include the release of new functionality and are usually determined by the customer or business. The length of the iterations is usually determined by the delivery team, typically in one-to-four-week intervals. (This time frame can be changed, usually for a new release, when deemed necessary by the team.)

The iteration planning session reviews the prioritized user stories from the product owner and determines the *group* of user stories or work successfully provided by the team during the iteration. Stories not selected for an iteration are moved to the release backlog and continually refined and reprioritized by the product owner.

A sense of urgency can be established by using a set "timebox" and consistent cadence, which allows the team to focus on a smaller set of stories within any single iteration. Over time more predictable measures can be established to help identify the amount of work to be successfully completed in an iteration (referred to as the velocity). This also enables an earlier and incremental delivery of business value.

Hybrid Life Cycle

Obviously, multiple approaches must be considered when determining the appropriate method to deliver a successful result. Many projects utilize a combination of approaches.

The term "hybrid" indicates a combination or blend of life cycles and development approaches. Often projects can plan to use a predictive approach, but the actual development requires more adaptability, and therefore, a more adaptive approach is adopted.

Typical examples include:

- A mostly predictive life cycle with an adaptive development approach—for example, use of an adaptive approach to develop a product with significant uncertainty associated with the requirements. However, the deployment of the product can be done using a predictive approach.
- Mostly adaptive with some sequential activities—for example, use of adaptive for software development but then a predictive approach to support the sequential installation of equipment.
- Incorporating business analysis techniques to assist with management of requirements.
- Incorporating a mixture of predictive and adaptive tools for complex elements in a project.
- Incorporating organizational change management methods and resources to help prepare the transition of project outputs into the organization.

Examples of these hybrid approaches are shown and described in PMI's *Agile Practice Guide*.

Project Tailoring

Project Management Principle:

Tailor Based on Context[30]

Design the project development approach based on the context of the project, its objectives, stakeholders, governance, and the environment using "just enough" process to achieve the desired outcome while maximizing value, managing cost, and enhancing speed.

Each project is unique, and tailoring allows a project to make approaches, governance, and processes more suitable for the given environment and work of the project. Tailoring factors include the business environment, team size, degree of uncertainty, and complexity of the project.

Tailoring the approach is iterative, and therefore is a continuous process throughout the project. It is necessary to produce the desired outcomes necessary to adapt to the unique context of the project and determine the most appropriate methods to employ.

---

30 *The Standard for Project Management, Section 3.7 – Project Management Principles*

The areas of a project tailored to take advantage of the combination of adaptive and predictive approaches include:

- Project life cycle—Type and phases used.
- Development life cycle components—How will the work be performed? Does the team need a lot of or continuous customer feedback to develop the product? Needed planning topics?
- Way of working—How will the people on the project work together? What kind of management approaches and team relationships should evolve or be set?
- Knowledge management—How can the team be ensured a collaborative work environment and manage the knowledge assets from the project?
- Change management—How will the team approach changes to project work, requirements, and so on? Strategy and processes are needed, no matter how "Agile" the team.
- Governance—Where will project governance be located—inside the project? Is the project management office (PMO) involved? Will the team establish a governance board? Should committees or stakeholders be involved?
- Benefits management—Who is responsible, how is it measured, and how and when is all of this decided?

Scrum Terminology

Agile is an umbrella term referring to a family of approaches sharing common values and principles. Agile focuses on the entire organization, including the leadership and company culture.

Scrum is one of the best known and most often utilized Agile frameworks. It offers suggestions on how work can be organized to maximize value to the end user. These are applied to developing and sustaining complex products with specific roles, events, and artifacts. Scrum uses timeboxed iterations referred to as sprints.

Scrum is most often implemented at the product development team level. The leader of the team is referred to as a scrum master, who is responsible for facilitating ceremonies. The key stakeholder is referred to as the product owner and is knowledgeable of what needs to be accomplished. The role is also empowered to make any necessary decisions, especially when change is needed.

During a sprint planning meeting, the team collaborates with the product owner to plan work for the upcoming sprint.

Scrum Ceremonies

Scrum identifies project activities as ceremonies. These include sprint planning, daily scrum, sprint review or demo, and sprint retrospective.

The sprint planning meeting is held before the team begins work on the user stories delivered during the sprint. The scrum master facilitates this meeting, while the team collaborates with the product owner to understand the prioritized user stories, breaking them down into tasks.

The daily stand-ups (also referred to as the daily scrum) are short meetings, usually for 10-15 minutes, allowing team members to communicate with each other. This includes the work they are doing as well as identifying and asking for help with any potential obstacles. This is NOT considered a daily status report but rather a focused time when team members can understand what others are working on. The scrum master may facilitate this, but only team members are involved in the discussion, which may not necessarily be held daily.

At the end of each sprint, the team holds a sprint review with the product owner and other customer stakeholders to review progress and receive feedback for the work done during the sprint. This may also be referred to as a sprint demo, because of the work demonstrated.

At the end of each sprint, the scrum master also facilitates a sprint retrospective for the team to review its processes and practices and identify ways to improve performance and collaboration. This retrospective concept has now influenced PMI's lessons learned activity—from being done at the end of the project to being conducted more frequently throughout the project.

A sprint may also be referred to as an iteration.

Additional Agile Ceremonies

There are additional ceremonies associated with Agile approaches and teams.

Product strategy meeting—where the product owner includes the future vision of the product.

Release planning meeting—where the user stories from the product backlog associated with the upcoming release are selected and the story map is developed.

Backlog refinement—often considered a behind-the-scenes activity where the product owner continually refines and prioritizes the items on the backlog before the sprint planning meeting with the team.

Project or release retrospective—held at the end of the release or project (depending on the project approach) and used to review the work and processes used and areas of improvement identified. This is like the traditional lessons learned activity.

Key Concepts Covered

- Project result
- Development approaches
- Life cycles
- Project tailoring

ECO Coverage

- Determine appropriate project methodology/methods and practices (2.13)
    - Assess project needs, complexity, and magnitude (2.13.1)
    - Recommend project execution strategy (e.g., contracting, financing) (2.13.2)
    - Recommend a project methodology/approach (i.e., predictive, adaptive, hybrid) (2.13.3)

Check Your Progress

1. An organization has decided to move from a traditional project management approach to more of a hybrid/agile method. The project will start with a traditional approach then switch to an agile approach and end with a hybrid method. Where would the artifacts or deliverables be reviewed by the key stakeholders during the project? (Choose 2)

    A. Validate project scope

    B. Monitor and control the baselines

    C. Integrate project management plans

    D. Conduct a sprint demo review

2. What is the difference between project management and product management?

    A. Project management oversees the scope of the project while product management oversees the development and life of a product

    B. Product management oversees the scope of the project while project management oversees the development and life of a product

    C. There is no difference between project management and product management, they are the same

D. Project managers have the same role as product managers

3. The Stacey matrix model is based upon the degree of certainty and level of agreement that help managers and leaders choose between the different decision-making and management approaches to use in different situations. Which of the following is best for an agile approach? (Choose 2)

A. Simple

B. Complicated

C. Complex

D. Edge of chaos

E. Chaos

4. Backlog refinement is an activity where the product owner continually refines and reprioritizes the items in the backlog before the sprint planning meeting with the team. Is this statement true or false?

A. True

B. False

5. Which of the following are scrum ceremonies? (Choose 3)

A. Conduct daily standups

B. Conduct sprint planning meeting

C. Review product by demo-ing it at the end of a sprint

D. Prepare project scope statement

E. Conduct a quality audit

Answers

1. A, D
2. A
3. B, C
4. True
5. A, B, C

Project Planning

Alice: "Would you tell me, please, which way I ought to go from here?"
The Cheshire Cat: "That depends a good deal on where you want to get to."
Alice: "I don't much care where."
The Cheshire Cat: "Then it doesn't matter which way you go."

— from Alice in Wonderland

This section includes all aspects of planning the project, including scope, schedule, resources, and budget, and the impact of quality and risk on the project's ability to successfully deliver the expected results.

These activities will be performed differently depending on the project approach being used.

In this chapter, you will:

- Understand the importance and content of a project management plan
- Understand the content of subsidiary project plans
- Learn aspects of scope planning in both predictive projects and adaptive environments
- Learn aspects of schedule planning in both predictive projects and adaptive environments
- Understand resources and potential procurement of external resources for a project
- Learn the budgeting structure for a project
- Learn strategies for dealing with risks, risk planning, and responses to risk
- Understand how quality relates to the outcomes and deliveries for a project
- Understand the importance of integrating project management

Topics in This Chapter
- Plan the Project
- Plan Project Scope
- Plan Project Schedule

- Plan Project Resources
- Plan Project Procurement
- Plan Project Budget
- Plan Project Risks
- Plan Project Quality
- Integrate Project Plans

Plan the Project

Performance Domain:

Planning[31]

The Planning Performance Domain addresses activities and functions associated with the initial, ongoing, and evolving organizations and coordination necessary for delivering project deliverables and outcomes.

The following items defined in the glossary relevant to the Planning Performance Domain:

- *Estimate—A quantitative assessment of the likely amount or outcome of a variable, such as project costs, resources, effort, or durations*

- *Accuracy—Within the quality management system, accuracy is an assessment of correctness*

- *Precision—Within the quality management system, precision is an assessment of exactness*

- *Crashing—A method used to shorten the schedule duration for the least incremental cost by adding resources*

- *Fast-Tracking—A schedule compression method in which activities or phases normally done in sequence are performed in parallel for at least a portion of their duration*

- *Budget—The approved estimate for the project or any work breakdown structure (WBS) component or any schedule activity*

All projects need project planning regardless of the life cycle or methodologies adopted. The purpose of planning is to proactively develop the approach used to create the project deliverables. Planning variables include:

- Development approach

---

31 *PMBOK Guide, Seventh Edition, Section 2.4 – Project Performance Domains*

- Project deliverables
- Organizational requirements
- Market conditions
- Legal or regulatory restrictions

Various circumstances determine the time spent planning a project, both initially and throughout the project. There is little value in planning more than necessary. The result of planning should enable the team to move forward appropriately but with no more detail than needed at the time.

Adaptability and Resilience

Project Management Principle:

Embrace Adaptability and Resiliency[32]

Build adaptability and resiliency into the organization's and project team's approaches to help the project accommodate change, recover from setbacks, and advance the work of the project.

Adaptability is the ability to respond to changing conditions, challenges or obstacles encountered. Resiliency consists of two complementary traits: the ability to absorb impacts and the ability to recover quickly from a setback or failure.

To adapt to changes, even in a predictive project with a fixed scope, the planning is not all done at the beginning of the project but rather divided over a few time periods. Rolling wave planning and progressive elaboration are used to continue understanding the various requirements placed on the backlog.

- *Rolling Wave Planning*

An iterative planning technique where the work to be accomplished in the near term is planned in detail, while the work in the future is planned at a higher level.

Planning rarely happens all at once at the beginning of the project for the entire project. Rolling wave planning enables work to begin, even if terms and conditions are uncertain and subject to change.

When using rolling wave planning, the focus is on the activities needing to be addressed soon. Activities scheduled for later are only planned at a high level, waiting until the time is closer to include any additional details. Planning for any activities later in the future is delayed, especially since priorities may change by then.

---

32 *The Standard for Project Management, Section 3.11 – Project Management Principles*

As rolling wave planning is thought of as planning "throughout," progressive elaboration is planning "downward" and adds more detail as requirements are understood and as the time grows closer to when those requirements are needed.

Rolling wave planning is used regardless of the development approach being employed. It enables the work to start without having all the details or a full understanding of the project requirements. The high-level requirements are decomposed into smaller activities or tasks as work progresses. Deciding at the last responsible moment to take advantage of additional understanding or technology advanced for competitive advantage supports the Lean concept of "Decide as late as possible."

    – *Progressive Elaboration*

The iterative process of increasing the level of detail in a project management plan as greater amounts of information and more accurate estimates become available.

This supports the needs of the current "wave" and allows the capture of additional information and detail, closer to the actual time the activities will be addressed. This is sometimes referred to as "drill down" into the details and is critical for understanding the most recent detail required for any project component.

As projects support more and more change-oriented organizations, it is critical to delay any detailed analysis or planning until closer to the time when work would start—especially since things could change by the expected start time.

These planning processes, including both progressive elaboration and rolling wave planning techniques, are used as more and more is understood about the project's specific requirements and potential constraints.

In predictive approaches, rolling wave planning and progressive elaboration techniques are applied to work packages and planning packages.

In adaptive approaches, rolling wave planning and progressive elaboration techniques are applied to both release and iteration planning.

Complexity

Project Management Principle:

Complexity[33]

Continuously evaluate and navigate project complexity so that approaches and plans enable the project team to successfully navigate the project life cycle.

Additional factors that interact with each other and make managing difficult at any time during the project including:

- Multiple parts and interdependency between components
- Dynamic and changing interactions between components
- Emergent behavior (not sum of parts)

Some ways to work with systems-based complexity include:

System-Based Methods

- Decouple or disconnect part of the system to simply and reduce the number of connected variables. This often reduces the size of the complexity and helps focus on smaller pieces rather than being overwhelmed by a larger portion.
- Simulations allow the use of similar or unrelated scenarios to try to understand the complexity by seeing how a similar system operates.

Reframing the Problem

- Use different approaches, including brainstorming or brainwriting with the team, to view the problem from different perspectives and provide divergent ways of seeing it. Or use Delphi-like processes to move from divergent to convergent thinking.
- Balance thinking by looking at diverse types of data, including competing data models to see where similarities exist. Also, balance forecasting with looking at and comparing similar past data.

Process-Based

- Agile modeling helps the team review the workflow of a process or system before implementing it in code. There are various process-based models including

---

33   *The Standard for Project Management, Section 3.9 – Project Management Principles*

sequence, activity, value stream maps, and data flow diagrams which represent processes in various ways.

- Value stream mapping is often used in lean approaches to document, analyze, and improve the flow of value to customers through the delivery of specific products or services. It identifies where value is delivered and where waste occurs, providing visibility where improvements can be made.

- Iterations allow a focus on smaller pieces, and rather than trying to achieve the goal in one process plan, utilizes incremental improvements toward the goal. This includes focusing on one feature or function at a time rather than everything together.

- After each iteration, identify what worked, what did not work, customer reaction, and what the project team learned, and determine how improvements might be made in the next iterations.

- Engagement with stakeholders on a continual bases reduces the number of assumptions and builds learning and engagement into the process. This includes adopting a collaborative mindset and continually allowing feedback and suggestions for improvement throughout the project.

- Fail safe by planning for failure. Einstein famously said, "Failure is success in progress." For critical system elements, build in redundancy or "graceful degradation of functionality" in case of critical component failure. Also, do not expect that every decision made will "work," but by adopting a continuous improvement mindset, we can see that a failure just helps us move closer to success.

Responding to uncertainty includes several options:

- Gather additional information.
- Prepare for multiple outcomes.
- Investigate and explore multiple designs or alternatives.
- Build in resilience to adapt and respond quickly to unexpected changes.

Complex Situations

Sometimes the project plan, context, or problem needs to be more detailed to properly plan and manage.

Tailoring the plans and incorporating adaptability and resilience are better ways to handle complex situations. This may also include adopting a mindset and framework prioritizing collaboration over following procedures and plans and concentrating on controlling various aspects of the project. It is important to incorporate the ability to change into the project planning effort and self-correct when necessary.

It is always important to start with a plan and then remain open to making modifications or changes when necessary. Plans are based on what is known at the time they are developed. As more information becomes known, the plan must be flexible enough to allow modifications.

Planning across Life Cycles

The planning process can be done differently depending on the life cycle being used.

- *Requirements Specification*—How much needs to be known about the desired outcome?
  - Predictive—defined in specific terms before development
  - Adaptive—elaborated frequently during delivery
  - Hybrid—elaborated periodically during delivery

- *Outcome(s)*—When are these delivered to the customer?
  - Predictive—delivered at the end of the project
  - Adaptive—delivered after each iteration or release according to the stakeholder desired value
  - Hybrid—divided into pieces (iteratively or incrementally)

- *Change*—How is change handled?
  - Predictive—constrained as much as possible after baseline is agreed upon
  - Adaptive—incorporated real-time during delivery
  - Hybrid—incorporated at periodic intervals

- *Stakeholders*—What is the typical involvement?
  - Predictive—involved in specific activities and milestones
  - Adaptive—involved continuously
  - Hybrid—involved regularly

- *Risk and Cost*—How are these applied to different life cycles?
  - Predictive—controlled by detailed planning and consideration of mostly known items
  - Adaptive—controlled as requirements and constraints emerge
  - Hybrid—controlled by progressively elaborating plans with new information

Project Planning: Predictive

Project Management Plan

A project management plan describes how the project will be executed, monitored and controlled, and closed.

All projects, regardless of the context, industry, life cycle, or development approach supporting their activities, need a plan. This is referred to as the **project management plan**, which helps the project manager manage the work required for the project. These planning artifacts provide stakeholders with the information to make decisions, and act, while managing expectations and maintaining alignment between the project and the stakeholders.

Additional plans and explanations covering specific needed areas regarding project management may be included. These are standard for predictive projects, but adaptive and hybrid projects often find many of them useful and can tailor any component to meet the needs of the project.

Deeper analysis and understanding of various aspects impacting the project produces subsidiary plans specific to the area of focus. These are often referred to as knowledge areas and are consolidated into an overall project management plan.

In addition to the subsidiary plans, baselines are established when using a predictive approach as guardrails for the project scope, schedule, and budget. Adaptive projects also have subjective baselines, even though they are not referred to by those terms and are established on much shorter time frames (releases or iterations) rather than the whole project.

- *Project Management Plan Components*

The components of the project management plan include subsidiary plans for each project management knowledge area, in addition to the scope, schedule, and cost baselines.

Subsidiary management plans include:

- Scope management plan
- Requirements management plan
- Schedule management plan
- Cost management plan
- Quality management plan
- Resource management plan

- Communications management plan
- Risk management plan
- Procurement management plan
- Stakeholder engagement plan

Baselines include:

- Scope baseline
- Schedule baseline
- Cost baseline

Additional components may include:

- Change management plan
- Configuration management plan
- Performance measurement baseline
- Project life cycle
- Project governance plan
- Development approach
- Compliance management plan
- Process improvement plan
- Rollout-implementation plan
- Transition plan
- Benefits transition plan
- Management reviews

Except for the baselines, these are plans, and as a result, will need to be monitored and possibly changed as actual project results are reviewed. Any changes to the baselines will need to go through the defined change control system.

Project Planning: Adaptive

The team, utilizing a self-organizing approach, is the principal leadership element, rather than the project manager making most of the decisions for the team. They determine how work will be planned and completed during iterations.

A product owner decides the priority for the team's work based on the desired objectives and needs/wants of the customer/stakeholders. The product owner plans *what* work should be done, but the team further plans the tasks, or *how* the actual work presented for them to perform will be done. The product owner and project team collaborate as to what can be accomplished in an iteration.

Everyone on the team contributes, but someone may be responsible for ensuring a psychologically safe environment for the team. This person is sometimes called a team lead, scrum master, or coach, rather than always being referred to as a project manager. This individual helps focus the team to execute the work planned.

Project Planning: Hybrid

This could include portions of the project being planned and managed using either predictive or adaptive approaches. Often the planning of a project may use a predictive approach, while the development or delivery activities use an adaptive approach.

Areas identified where several changes may occur will often be addressed using more of an adaptive approach. These could be supported by different individuals or groups or identified as subprojects within the context of a larger project or even a program.

Product Road Maps

A high-level, visual summary of the product or products of the project, including goals, milestones, and potential deliverables. It may also depict such things as significant events, reviews, and decision points.

Even though these originated in Agile approaches, they are applicable to predictive, adaptive, or hybrid approaches and are a way to show the potential delivery time frame and various features and functions. They often utilize various ways of presenting this information but focus on the strategy and direction of the product and the value it will deliver.

This often becomes a visual chronological depiction of the project work with an initial vision and plan for the "big picture." It often utilizes themes, features, or goals to provide structure and association to previous project documents, depicting both short-term and long-term visualization of the product.

The components shown on the road map may refer to project themes or high-level requirements, features, or functions. They may be associated to other diagrams and progressively elaborated to add detail for the work in progress as identified, including maybe a high-level master schedule, work inputs, and refinement of the vision.

Key Concepts Covered

- Rolling wave planning
- Progressive elaboration
- Adaptability and resiliency

- Complexity
- Project planning: predictive
- Project planning: adaptive
- Project planning: hybrid

Check Your Progress

1. The project management plan describes how the project will be planned, executed, measured and closed. Which of the following are included in the project management plan? (Choose 3)

    A. Subsidiary plans (10)

    B. Baselines (3)

    C. Additional components such as configuration management plan

    D. Business case

2. Choose which statement below is correct.

    A. In a predictive project, the outcomes are usually delivered at the end of the project

    B. In a predictive project, the outcomes are usually delivered after each iteration or scrum

    C. In an adaptive project, the outcomes are usually delivered at the end of the project

    D. In a hybrid project, the stakeholders are not engaged because the scrum master and team can determine what is best for the customer

3. Which of the following is most important during the planning of an agile sprint for a project?

    A. Significant contributions by the project sponsor

    B. Significant contributions by the product owner

    C. Significant contributions by the quality assurance manager

    D. Significant contributions by the risk management manager

4. Which of the following are principles of agile planning? (Choose 3)

    A. Conduct planning throughout the entire project

    B. Engage the project team

    C. Engage stakeholders throughout the project

D. Plan the project mostly at the beginning of the project since agile projects do not need any more planning during the project

E. Agile projects don't need to do planning since they use sprints with short durations

5. Agile projects conduct planning sessions at multiple points in time. The plan that is identified for a grouping of epics or user stories from the product backlog are known as?

A. Progressive plan

B. Transition plan

C. Release plan

D. Project scope plan

E. Progressive elaboration

Answers

1. A, B, C
2. A
3. B
4. A, B, C
5. C

In order to help you identify all the areas that you should consider as part of planning your project, we have developed a Project Planning Checksheet and it is available for you to download at <u>PMP® Certification Opportunities – Facilitated Methods</u>. https://facilitatedmethods.com/pmp-landing-page/

Performance Domain:

Delivery[34]

The Delivery Performance Domain addresses activities and functions associated with delivering the scope and quality that the project was undertaken to achieve.

The following items defined in the glossary relevant to the Delivery Performance Domain:

- *Requirement—A condition or capacity that is necessary to be present in a product, service, or result to satisfy a business need*

---

34 *PMBOK Guide, Seventh Edition, Section 2.6 – Project Performance Domains*

- *Work Breakdown Structure (WBS) — A hierarchical, decomposition of the total scope of work to be carried out by the project team to accomplish the project objectives and create the required deliverables*
- *Definition of Done (DoD) — A checklist of all the criteria required to be met so that a deliverable can be considered ready for the customer use*
- *Quality — The degree to which of set of inherent characteristics fulfills requirements*
- *Cost of Quality (CoQ) — All costs incurred over the life of the product by investment in preventing nonconformance to requirements, appraisal of the product or service, or conformance to requirements, and failure to meet requirements*

After the project management plan has been developed, the project manager and project team can focus on ensuring that the project activities are running smoothly including:

- Managing the flow of existing work, new work, and changes to work
- Keeping the project team focused
- Establishing efficient project systems and processes
- Communicating with stakeholders'
- Managing material, equipment, supplies, and logistics
- Working with contracting professionals and vendors to plan and manage procurements and contracts
- Monitoring changes that can affect the project
- Enabling project learning and knowledge transfer

Plan Project Scope

Planning the scope includes planning how to determine what is going to be included in the project and how the work is to be done.

The planning of the project scope varies not only in the planning process itself but also in the development approach used by the project and the involvement of those participating.

Project Scope

The features, functions, and work characterizing the delivery of a product, service, and/or result.

Project scope specifically refers to the work required to deliver the project and varies greatly depending on the approach used. It is the sum of the products, services, and results to be provided through a project effort.

It will include deliverables identified in initiating agreements or procurement statement(s) of work (SOWs). The product scope may also be included within a project scope but can be defined and documented separately.

Product Scope

The functions and features characterizing a product or a service.

This includes the high-level features and functions to be included in the delivered product. Additional requirements and details are added as identified and approved. It is a description of the expected output of the work.

This is often referred to as the solution scope and includes the capabilities a solution must deliver to meet the business need. It will include both functional and non-functional requirements.

Fixed vs. Flexible Scope

Both project and product scopes may be fixed or flexible and will determine the appropriate development approach.

When a scope is fixed, the product is built, and the way the project is performed uses a more detailed, plan-based approach.

For areas where flexibility is required, the fixed scope may not be appropriate. This can be the result of changing circumstances, uncertainty, complexity, innovation, or within a customer-driven environment where stakeholders change their minds.

These are the key considerations to help determine the most appropriate project approach (predictive, adaptive, or hybrid).

Requirements

Conditions or capabilities that must be present in a product, service, or result to satisfy a business need.

A requirement is a single measurable statement and tells how the result of the project will satisfy a business need, often identified in the business case. To determine whether these needs are met, the requirements must be:

- Completely and fully defined and understood
- Consistent
- Unambiguous (measurable and can be evaluated or tested)

- Traceable
- Acceptable to key stakeholders

Types of Requirements

There are different types of requirements to consider.

- *Business requirements* are higher-level organizational needs, usually identified in the business case or project charter and aligned with business objectives—e.g., business issues or opportunities and reasons why a project has been approved.

- *Stakeholder requirements* are necessary for individual or groups of stakeholders, including reporting requirements for external stakeholders.

- *Quality requirements* are usually tied to product quality aspects and include the conditions or criteria needed to validate the successful completion of a project deliverable or fulfillment of other project requirements—e.g., compliance, test results, certifications, inspections, or validations.

- *Compliance requirements* are often aligned with legal or regulatory standards and must always be prioritized as the mandatory, must, or highest. The way these requirements are identified and the necessary approach and actions to address them are identified in an optional project compliance plan.

- *Project requirements* are actions, processes, or other conditions the project needs to meet to be completed. These are usually included in contracts or SOWs—e.g., milestone dates, contractual obligations, and constraints.

- *Product or solution requirements* are more focused on the features and characteristics of the product, service, or results to meet the business and stakeholder requirements, including:

  - *Functional requirements* identify the expected features and functions of the product or solution.

  - *Nonfunctional requirements* pertain to the performance of the product and may include supplemental environmental conditions or qualities for the product to be effective. They may be identified through the contract/procurement SOW, a service level agreement (SLA), or as the product development proceeds. They often are organizational requirements for products and quality attributes in general, including:
    - *Availability and continuity – operability and accessibility when required for use*
    - *Certification – constraints needed to meet standard or industry conventions*
    - *Compatibility – need to operate effectively and either coexist or interact with other solutions in the same environment*

- o *Compliance — regulatory, financial, or legal constraints*
- o *Extensibility — ability to incorporate new functionality*
- o *Functionality — measures the extent stakeholders can recognize whether needs are met*
- o *Localization — modifications needed for regional differences*
- o *Maintainability — how easy it will be to change a component without affecting other components (including reuse, diagnosing problems and ability to implement changes without causing unexpected failures)*
- o *Performance efficiency — how long it takes to perform activities and the resource utilization levels for the solution*
- o *Portability and compatibility — ability to migrate to, or be installed in, and uninstalled from different environments when needed*
- o *Reliability — focuses on availability when needed and recovery from errors or failures*
- o *Scalability — degree with which a solution can grow or evolve to handle more work*
- o *Security — storage and protection of information from authorized use, and authorization of users and auditing reporting*
- o *Usability — evaluates the ease of learning to use the new solutions, its capabilities, and how usable is the solution*

Transition or readiness requirements are temporary requirements needed to transition the result successfully to meet the desired future state and ensure the result can be used effectively by the customer — e.g., training, documentation, or data conversion.

Well-defined Requirements

Well-defined requirements meet the following criteria:

- – Clear — only one way to interpret the requirement
- – Concise — stated in as few words as possible
- – Verifiable — verification can determine that the requirement meets specifications
- – Consistent — no contradictory requirements
- – Complete — represents the entirety of the current project or product needs
- – Traceable — the development status of each requirement can be recognized

Delivering Results

How the result is made available to the customer/end user is often tied to the project approach. This needs to consider many aspects including stakeholders, schedules, risks, budgets, and required quality standards.

Several terms describe various ways of organizing and delivering the value of work incrementally to the customer. These are the outcomes of the work done during a release.

- *Minimum Viable Product (MVP)*

The smallest collection of features that can be included in a product for customers to consider the result functional ("bare-bones" or "no-frills" functionality in Lean).

The term "MVP" came from agile and refers to the bare bones or minimum for the initial/prototype release. In traditional approaches, it often refers to the results of a feasibility study or prototype — where early feedback can be obtained before delivering the full production result by seeing and experiencing project outcomes.

It facilitates feedback and generation of additional ideas and concepts. The team sees results, providing inspiration and contributing to the sense of urgency.

- *Minimum Business Increment (MBI)*

In Disciplined Agile (DA), the smallest amount of value that can be added to a product or service benefiting the business.

MBIs emerged from Disciplined Agile to portray the smallest amount of value attached to a product or service that benefits the customer. The MBI ensures the product delivered as part of a release is the minimum "consumable" to the customer/end user.

MBIs are determined by the product owner, and the team decides what work is required to be completed for the next release.

The advantages to either of these include:

- Enabling the project team to deliver value sooner
- Helping the team validate improvements
- Enabling the team to incrementally build on success or pivot as needed

– *Additional Terms*

Additional terms regarding small delivery portions:

Each iteration develops an MMF (from scrum) or an MRF (from Disciplined Agile) representing a component of the overall outcome.

- MMF—Minimum Marketable Features
- MRF—Minimum Releasable Feature
- MMR—Minimum Marketable Release (includes the MRFs)

The activities to support the handoff to the customer, previously identified as transition requirements, are part of the scope of work and need to be planned and managed like other project work. This may be referred to as an implementation or rollout plan and included as an optional item in the project management plan.

When using adaptive or hybrid approaches, since there are multiple releases rather than one at the end of the project, this transition must be addressed for each release, including:

- Activities and deliverables identified as part of transition and implementation plans in the scope of work.
- Determination as to how the result is made available to the customer/end user based on the approach used.
- Questions to consider include:
  - Is the result new, or an update to an existing functionality?
  - Does the update need to be transitioned in a live environment?
  - Are there activities required to decommission or remove old systems, processes, equipment, or materials?
  - Have training and knowledge transfer been satisfied or completed?

Scope Planning: Predictive

The planning is often started before all the team is assembled, since the actual need for team members is tied to the scope and work of the project. Usually this means the project manager and maybe a few team leads, including possibly a business analyst, help create the initial scope management plan.

Scope Management Plan

A project or program management plan component that describes how the scope will be defined, developed, monitored, controlled, and validated.

The scope management plan defines the activities for developing, maintaining, and approving the various scope artifacts (including the detailed scope statement, scope baseline, and creation of the WBS, derived from the scope statement) at the appropriate level of detail for the project. It also specifies what is excluded from the scope of the project, how required changes will be incorporated, and how the final acceptance and approval for the project deliverables will be achieved.

The details included will reflect the approach and processes used to elicit and document the scope of the project and the product.

Information previously captured in either the business case or the project charter regarding the scope of the project can be copied and included here. This often includes the consideration of assumptions, constraints, and other influences (EEFs and OPAs) impacting the way the scope is developed.

This plan addresses how requests for changes to the scope will be handled within an established change control process, as part of the overall organizational and project change control system, to minimize or eliminate scope creep. It helps identify gold plating where additional scope items beyond the customer requests have been added. This includes the determination of what level of authority and types of changes to the scope can be made by the project manager or key team members, as well as the way requests must be processed through the change control system.

Contents include:

- How scope will be defined, developed, monitored, controlled, verified, and validated
- How requirements collection or elicitation activities are conducted and techniques and guidelines for preferred usage
- How requirements are documented
- Additional artifacts required
- The format and content of the detailed scope statement
- Identification of in-scope and out-of-scope items
- How project deliverables will be decomposed into a WBS, including the format used (chronological or product components)
- How changes to the WBS will be managed
- How the scope baseline will be managed
- How to minimize or eliminate scope creep and gold plating

- Escalation path in case of disagreement on required scope elements, especially between stakeholders
- How acceptance for deliverables will be done
- Assumptions and constraints

Collect Requirements

In predictive projects, clear and specific requirements are essential to effective planning. They also provide the foundation for creating the scope baseline.

In predictive projects, requirements are collected, elicited, and agreed upon as part of the scope baseline at the beginning of the project. There are different types of requirements, and they can be identified, understood, and incorporated into a project in different ways. This is often the realm of a business analyst, domain expert, or someone else with those competencies.

Even though project management often refers to these as part of a "collect requirements" activity, it may be better referred to as "elicit requirements," since many times it is not possible to find and collect requirements, but rather we need to facilitate the elicitation, or "drawing out," of those requirements.

Elicitation can be very challenging and may require understanding the language of individual stakeholders. You are not always told everything the first time around. Utilizing different elicitation techniques can help gather as much relevant information as quickly as possible. This often provides tacit knowledge otherwise not available to the team.

Contracts, agreements, business cases, and the project charter should include high-level project and product requirements. Additional effort is required to research, analyze, communicate, and document the requirements for the project. Requirements will need continual refinement, often using progressive elaboration techniques.

Using the most effective communication and engagement techniques to gather or elicit requirements is important. Most of these utilize interpersonal skills and can be used with any project development approach. Techniques to help identify scope and requirements usually fall into several categories: data gathering, data analysis, and data representation.

- *Data Gathering*
  - Brainstorming or brainwriting
  - Interviews

- Focus groups
- Questionnaires and surveys
- Benchmarking
- Facilitation
- Observation

- *Data Analysis*
  - Document analysis
  - Diagramming techniques (including data, process, rule, organizational models)
  - Alternatives analysis
  - Expert judgment
  - Product analysis (if the result is a product)

- *Data Representation*
  - Affinity diagram
  - Mind mapping
  - Context diagram
  - Prototyping—including ideation
  - Storyboarding

Data Gathering Methods

These techniques are commonly used at various times in a project to collect different types of data. By understanding the purpose of the individual techniques, you can determine when and how to use them. This is most often done when using a predictive approach but can be applied to an adaptive approach, with less detail.

- *Brainstorming or Brain Writing*

Brainstorming is a group technique to encourage spontaneous contribution of ideas from a broad or diverse group, drawing from the experience and creativity of members of the group. Includes focus on a topic or problem and then identification of many possible solutions.

Brainwriting is an idea generation technique where participants write down their ideas on a piece of paper, then, each person in the group passes their ideas to the next person who uses them to add their ideas or enhance the ideas that are passed around.

- *Interviews*

Interviews obtain information directly from one or more participants by directly talking, asking relevant questions, and documenting responses. These can also be used for establishing relationships and building trust and increase stakeholder involvement.

- *Focus groups*

Focus groups consist of small, pre-selected group of people who provide their options about the subject matter in a moderated, interactive group environment.

- *Questionnaires or surveys*

A survey or questionnaire is used to elicit information from a group of people in a structured way and in a relatively short period of time. It presents a set of questions to stakeholders and SMEs, whose responses are then collected and analyzed to formulate knowledge about the subject matter of interest.

The questions can be either closed end (with selection from a list of predefined responses), or open-ended (with answers in a free form).

- *Benchmarking*

Benchmarking studies compare or measure organizational practices against best-in-class practices. This can be applied as part of market analysis to compare a new product or service to a standard or best practice in an industry or a competitor's product.

- *Facilitation*

Facilitation utilizes a moderator, or facilitator, to enable all participants within a group to articulate their views and collaborate in an open discussion about a topic. These sessions may be small focus groups or larger groups using brainstorming techniques.

- *Observation*

Two basic approaches for observation include active/noticeable (where questions are asked during the observation), and passive/unnoticeable (where the observer does not interrupt the work but may seek clarification after the observation is completed).

Data Analysis Methods

Once the requirements have been gathered, further analysis should be performed to gain a deeper understanding. This is most often done when using a predictive approach but can be applied to an adaptive approach, with less detail.

- *Document Analysis*

A technique used to gather project requirements from current documentation evaluation.

The document analysis method can be used to gather information from existing documentation including business plans, contracts, service agreements, marketing materials, current procedures, process and engineering diagrams, and application software documentation. This can provide contextual understanding of the subject matter.

Care should be taken to ensure the analysis is applied to the most recent version of these documents—and that they have been kept current.

- *Diagramming techniques*

There are various types of models that can be used to help with the future understanding of requirements with the use of combined visual and textual representations. These visual diagrams may take multiple forms to represent relationships between processes, data, business rules and organizations.

- *Alternatives Analysis*

Several potential options and approaches are identified to choose between various solutions, product functionality and requirements, or how to execute and perform the work of the project.

- *Expert Judgment*

Analyzing information, usually from SMEs or other experts, along with previous experience and knowledge to develop the scope or other requirements.

Product Analysis Methods

For projects with a product as a deliverable, product analysis asks questions about a product to describe its use, characteristics, and other relevant aspects.

Depending on the product the project is delivering, several analysis methods exist to create a working understanding of the product and develop the scope. This includes the use of a methodical, multidisciplinary approach for the design, realization, technical management, operations, and retirement of a system. (In this context, a "system" is defined as the combination of elements functioning together to produce the capability required to meet a need.)

- *Product Breakdown*

Splits a product into visual components to help illustrate the work required. This is like the project WBS, but specific to the components of a product.

- *Requirements Analysis*

Additional analysis on identified requirements to verify, validate, and document the specification for the work required.

- *Systems Analysis*

Includes the analysis of product/service goals and purpose to create systems and/or procedures to achieve them efficiently.

- *Systems Engineering*

A multidisciplinary way of integrating design, integration, and management as part of the life cycle of complex systems.

- *Value Analysis*

Value analysis is a systematic method of remediating product deficiencies to enhance an item's value, utility, and cost efficiency. It analyzes the functionality of a product or process regarding its cost. It then identifies and eliminates unnecessary costs in the development of a product, business process, or function. This systematic and interdisciplinary analysis focuses on cost reduction. This in turn results in product requirements with the lowest cost that still meet the required quality and reliability standards.

- *Value Engineering*

When applied to projects, value engineering uses a systematic and organized approach to help provide necessary aspects of a project at the lowest cost. It promotes less expensive alternative materials and methods, without sacrificing functionality. This allows projects to improve cost-effectiveness without negatively impacting quality, reliability, or performance.

Data Representation Methods

There are several data representation methods to help visually illustrate ideas, concepts, and progress.

Some are used for gathering requirements, whereas many other techniques are used later to show progress or evaluate quality aspects of the project.

- *Affinity Diagrams*

These are often used to group ideas generated through group gathering sessions, like brainstorming, brainwriting, or facilitated workshops. These may also be referred to as affinity maps where similar features are grouped together to identify related or similar features.

– *Mind Maps*

These group the various results from an affinity diagram, brainstorming, or brainwriting session into a single diagram. They can also be developed during a brainstorming, brainwriting, or ideation session.

– *Context Diagrams*

The visual depiction of product scope shows a business system (process, equipment, computer system, etc.) and how people and other systems interact.

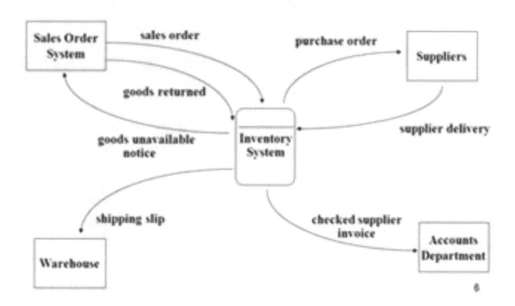

This diagram is often used to visually show the boundaries of the system and the interfaces with it, including what is in scope and what is out of scope for a project.

The center box or circle represents the boundaries of the scope with external business units, organizations, or other groups providing information to the project and receiving information from the project.

When used in a hybrid approach, the center may also include the high-level features/ functions that would be in scope.

– *Prototyping*

Assists in the process of obtaining early feedback on requirements by providing a working model of the expected product before building.

Project stakeholders and other team members can use a prototype for evaluation and experimentation. It is essentially a working model of the expected product before it is built. The results of the evaluation can then be analyzed and assembled into a prioritized list of redesign ideas for the prototype or a detailed list of project requirements.

It can be a throwaway model to explore options or enhanced over time to become a final product.

This process can be cyclical, with many revisions until the final requirements are determined, and may be part of a release to earn value for the organization, often included in the MVP version of the product. In Disciplined Agile, this is part of an exploratory life cycle before moving into a production mode.

- *Storyboarding*

A prototyping method using visuals or images to illustrate a process or represent a project outcome.

Storyboards are useful visuals to illustrate how a product, service, or result will function and move from one state to another.

This is a common tool used in the entertainment industry to depict various scenes and the flow and sequence of those scenes.

Requirements Management Plan

A project or program management plan component that describes how requirements will be analyzed, documented, and managed.

This plan is like other project management subsidiary plans and helps identify how requirements will be captured, analyzed, verified, traced, and ultimately delivered to the customer, including:

- Identification of requirements, including source and definition
- Analysis of requirements, including impact to the product or project approach
- Requirements categories
- Requirements documentation and attributes
- Planning, tracking, and reporting information regarding requirements activities (often with a version of a traceability matrix)
- Levels of authorization required to approve changes to requirements
- Process and criteria used to prioritize requirements
- Possible metrics and rationale for product requirements
- Traceability structure, attributes, usage, and maintenance
- Configuration management, including version control rules for requirements
- Impact analysis activities as part of tracing, tracking, and reporting of requirement changes

– Validation and acceptance of requirements

Requirements Traceability Matrix (RTM)[35]

A grid linking product requirements from their origin to the deliverable satisfying them.

During planning, the RTM is used to control the evolution of the functionality to fulfill each requirement. The core idea is that this matrix should have one row for each requirement and one column for each work category or stage of development within the project, corresponding to a stage of the product evolution.

The requirements traceability matrix helps ensure that each requirement adds business value by linking it to the strategic and business objectives. It is most often used by business analysts on projects to trace the progress of requirements to ensure they meet specifications, are completed, approved, and delivered at the end of the project.

ID	Objective	Requirement	Status	In Progress	Tested	Accepted	Delivered
1							
2							
3							
4							
5							
6							
7							
8							
9							

The detail contained in the matrix is dependent on the project approach and the criticality of individual requirements. This can include the tracing of requirements to WBS deliverables, product design, product development, testing activities.

---

35   *https://www.pmi.org/learning/library/requirement-traceability-tool-quality-results-8873*

A spreadsheet is often utilized to enable incorporation of hyperlinks to other documents related to each requirement (including analysis and design specifications, test cases and test results, and approval documents).

Exam Tip: The RTM is used in predictive approaches where it is important to ensure delivery of baselined requirements. It is similar to adaptive task board, or kanban board, tracing the "in progress" status of a requirement at a more detailed level.

Project Scope Statement

The description of the project scope, major deliverables, assumptions, and constraints.

This is the textual description of what is included, and not included in the project (as well as the product) scope. More often associated with a predictive approach, it includes all the requirements specified to define the scope of the project.

Even though projects may include different components in this scope statement, most include:

- Project objectives
- Project scope description (project and product)
- Project requirements
- Project boundaries (including in-scope and out-of-scope items for clarification)
- Project deliverables and artifacts
- Product acceptance criteria
- Project assumptions and constraints (known at this time)
- Initially defined risks
- Scheduled milestones
- Funding limitations
- Cost estimates
- Project configuration management requirements
- Product specifications and metrics, if applicable
- Approval requirements, including process and possible templates

Work Breakdown Structure (WBS)

A hierarchical decomposition of the total scope of work to be carried out by the project team to accomplish the project objectives and create the required deliverables.

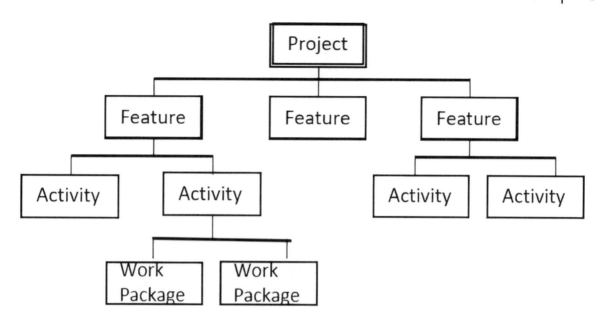

A WBS is a graphical representation of the deliverables representing the total scope of work required to complete the project using a predictive approach. It can also be represented in the form of a textual outline or contents for a book. The 100% rule applies, with every aspect of the scope included—nothing extra or missing.

The deliverables are decomposed into sub-deliverables and are represented on the WBS in descending levels. The project is usually represented at the highest level, with the deliverables identified at the next levels. The lowest level is referred to as the work package and is the item of greatest interest to the project manager. It represents the work needing to be delivered.

The WBS often includes both project and product components.

Decomposition of the WBS

A technique of dividing and subdividing the project scope and deliverables into smaller, more manageable parts.

This allows the high-level requirements and deliverables to be broken into smaller parts, enabling better focus to deliver the results.

The decomposition process includes:

- Identify the deliverables and the work activities necessary to accomplish key deliverables.
- Structure and organize into an outline format and/or a diagram similar to an organization chart.

- Decompose high-level WBS scope components into low-level components.
- Develop and assign a unique identification code (referred to as the code of accounts) to each component.
- Review the decomposition of work packages and verify that they align with the project requirements.

The level of decomposition is based on specific project needs and the level of granularity needed to manage the project effectively.

WBS Components

The WBS structure can be grouped in different ways depending on the resources and methods used to deliver the project requirements. Some of the methods include top-down approach, use of organization-specific guidelines, and templates. It can represent:

- Phases of the project life cycle (often shown chronologically)
- Major deliverables (including both project and product deliverables)
- Organizational-specific functions

- *Work Package*

The work is defined at the lowest level of the WBS, and cost and duration are estimated and managed at that level.

The work package is the lowest level shown in the WBS representing a unit of work and is used for both planning and managing project work. It will form the basis for identifying and estimating the cost and duration of the necessary activities. Each work package may be assigned to an individual or a group responsible for completion of the work.

It will be moved to the schedule, where further decomposition is done to include the activities required to deliver the work package. Individual work packages integrate additional information on schedule duration, estimated cost, resources, risks, etc. as continued planning is conducted.

The 8/80 guideline is often applied when determining the size of work packages for typical projects. This suggests that a work package require at least 8 but not more than 80 hours to complete. Obviously, this would not apply if the work package was being given to a group, maybe as part of a contract, where the receiving team would further break it down into smaller work packages.

－ *Code of Accounts*

Numbering system uniquely identifying each component of the WBS.

The code of accounts is associated with the individual "boxes" on the WBS and represents the numbering used for textual outlines, especially in the scope statement. This allows the project manager to track individual WBS components using this unique identification code. It is especially helpful in the areas of performance, reporting, and cost.

－ *Control Account*

A management control point where scope, budget, actual cost, and schedule are integrated and compared to earned value for performance measurement.

Work packages may also be assigned a control account to enable the management of portions of the work throughout the project, especially when different groups either deliver portions of the project, are financially responsible for portions of the project, or work is covered under different agreements or contracts.

These accounts associated with different work packages within the WBS can then be tracked using performance measurements to verify that actuals costs remain within budget.

Control accounts may contain more than one work package, but each work package should be assigned to only one control account. These work packages are then combined into a planning package.

－ *Planning Package*

The planning package represents the combination of the individual work packages with the same assigned control account. Often the WBS work packages are grouped into planning packages, with one organization or group responsible for the delivery of a package.

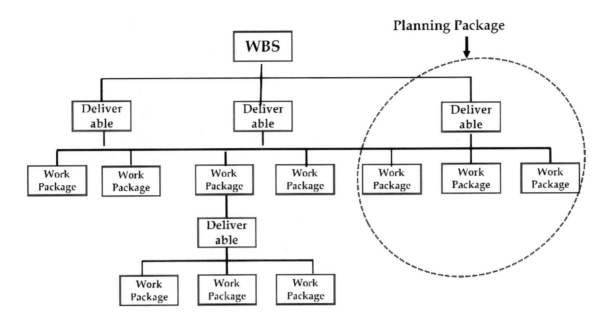

The WBS could be structured to show all the work packages associated with a control account, thus depicting individual planning packages. The control account identifiers provide a structure for hierarchical summation of costs, schedule, and resource information. These are especially useful when monitoring the performance of the project using earned value management (EVM) techniques.

The planning package is optional and will only be identified if control accounts are assigned to individual work packages.

Exam Tip:

– *A planning package may or may not be used, depending on how performance monitoring will be conducted (usually for contracts).*
– *A control account is assigned to two or more work packages.*
– *A work package is only assigned to a single control account.*

WBS Dictionary

Provides detailed deliverable, activity, and scheduling information about each component in the WBS.

Since the WBS often has only a single noun to identify a deliverable, the detailed understanding regarding the requirements for individual work packages is contained in the WBS dictionary. This often includes the information needed to convey the results of planning this portion of the project to an individual or team to deliver the result.

It can be done for multiple levels of the WBS, but most often it is created for the work package level.

As additional planning activities are completed, the WBS dictionary can incorporate additional information for each work package, including:

- Code of account identifier
- Description of work
- Assumptions and constraints
- Responsible organization
- Schedule milestones
- Associated schedule activities
- Resources required to complete the work
- Cost estimations
- Quality requirements
- Acceptance criteria
- Technical references
- Agreement information

Scope Baseline

Approved version of a scope statement, WBS, and its associated WBS dictionary. Changed only using formal change control procedures.

This is the first of three baselines developed using a predictive approach.

Scope is more thoroughly defined in a predictive approach—because requirements must be specified in detail and therefore can be easily identified and planned. The project scope documentation is used to determine the schedule and costs needed to deliver the project results.

Traditional scope artifacts using a predictive approach include the textual documentation of the scope statement, the graphical WBS structure, and additional explanations in the WBS dictionary.

Even though we do a preliminary scope baseline, until the schedule and cost baselines are completed and integrated, changes may be needed in the scope to meet the other constraints or assumptions. Once all three baselines have been completed, they are simultaneously baselined and then fall under change control if additional changes are requested. The sponsor and/or key stakeholders usually review and approve the three combined baselines.

Scope Planning: Adaptive

In traditional approaches the scope is identified, and then the schedule and budget are determined to deliver the scope. In adaptive approaches the time, and the resulting cost, are set, and the scope items are prioritized to fit within the time constraints.

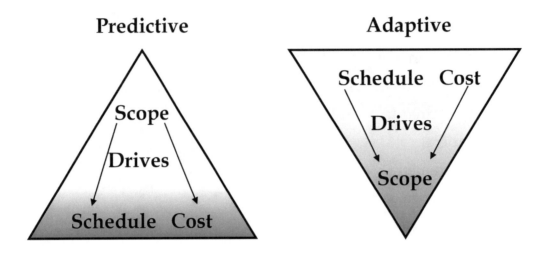

In adaptive projects, user stories are used to represent a kind of requirement. Depending on the approach, these may be captured and refined for inclusion in a release or iteration or continually gathered throughout the project. They represent a different way of thinking about the requirements process.

The product owner and project team members create user stories. The product owner continually refines the user stories based on the business value, as part of the backlog refinement process.

Adaptive methods build, review, and release prototypes and initial versions to help refine the requirements. As a result, the scope is defined and redefined throughout the project. In adaptive approaches, the evolving requirements make up the backlog(s).

Backlogs

There are multiple backlogs when using a timeboxed adaptive approach. These include a preliminary group of requirements, often written in a user story format. The product owner continually updates, refines, and prioritizes these in collaboration with the end users and the project team.

The name, content, and detail in the backlogs highly depend on the approach used. Rolling wave planning and progressive evaluation techniques support the Lean concept of "*Decide as late as possible.*" The detail is usually delayed, so analysis effort and time is not spent on items not chosen for delivery based on prioritization of value. This can include estimates of work, duration, or other details eventually needed by the project team to deliver the results to satisfy the user story.

A good product backlog has four characteristics referred to as DEEP.

- **D**etailed appropriately — more detail is added for higher priority items closer to work starting
- **E**stimated — from an initial guess based on relative sizing to more specific story points
- **E**mergent — ability to improve and revise as additional information is known
- **P**rioritized — based on needs and delivery of value for each item

- *Product Backlog*

A list of customer-centric identified needs or requirements for a product.

The product backlog includes all the epics and user stories or requirements identified for the product. The stories in the product backlog are analyzed and related to the features or functions needed for a release. Those selected becomes the release backlog.

- *Release Backlog*

The associated epics, user stories, or requirements from the product backlog pertaining to the release.

The release backlog includes the stories from the product backlog pertaining to the functionality or features for the release. The product owner will continually prioritize these items, including refining the individual stories, breaking the epics into smaller user stories, removing unnecessary stories, adding missing requirements, and adding more understanding for the team to successfully deliver the expected result. The stories in the release backlog are prioritized, analyzed, and provided by the product owner to the delivery team for potential inclusion in an individual iteration. The selected user stories by the team become the iteration backlog.

- *Iteration/Sprint Backlog*

A list of user stories agreed upon by the delivery team to be completed during the iteration.

The iteration or sprint backlog is the set of stories the product owner and the team select and agree will be developed and approved by either the product owner or stakeholder. This is done during the iteration or sprint planning meeting prior to the start of the iteration or sprint. The team can also add some technical user stories as needed. The team decides whether these stories are considered part of the iteration's velocity.

The adaptive project scope planning activities include:

- Creating and maintaining a product road map to identify the release milestones based upon product features to be delivered
- Selecting user stories from the product backlog and incorporating them into a release backlog to support the identified features and function for the identified release
- Utilizing a story map to sequence and prioritize the user stories in the release backlog
- Continually reviewing user stories in the product backlog

The product owner:

- Refines the release and iteration backlogs to prepare for the release and iteration planning meeting
- Refines, prioritizes, and splits many of the original user stories into a size that can be delivered in an individual iteration
- Explains each prioritized user story in detail to the team (often based on the Definition of Ready (DoR))

The team estimates the effort and negotiates the final stories to be included in the iteration, creating the iteration baseline or backlog. The selection of the stories is also based on the expected velocity of the iteration.

Project teams using adaptive life cycles may take different approaches to planning project work. Incremental or iterative development is common in most adaptive life cycles.

Though user stories are similar in concept to requirements, they propose an alternative way of looking at the requirements process.

Release and Iteration Planning

Adaptive approaches include many planning meetings throughout the project, whereas predictive planning is concentrated in the early part of the project.

These various planning meetings are collaborative sessions with key stakeholders/ product owner and appropriate team members. They continually decompose the requirements to focus on those for a particular release or iteration as follows:

– *Release Planning*

During release planning meetings, verification of the release dates is received. These release dates are determined by the organization or product management function.

The team then agrees on the number and length of iterations or sprints needed to complete each release and sets the cadence for the individual iterations. This can be modified from one release to the next depending on the velocity and complexity of the release.

The features for the release, which may be shown on the product road map, are reviewed for understanding and clarification where necessary. The corresponding user stories that pertain to the release functions are selected from the product backlog and added to the release backlog.

A story map may be developed to show the sequence of features/epics for the release and the associated user stories for each feature/epic. The user stories are often prioritized under the associated features/epics to aid in prioritization during the iterations.

Exam Tip: Not all agile methods identify the activities of release planning and development of a release backlog.

– *Iteration Planning (or Sprint Planning)*

Prior to the iteration planning meeting, the product owner continues to refine and prioritize the potential user stories as part of the backlog refinement effort.

The product owner presents the team with the user stories prioritized based on the potential business value to the organization. For each of the user stories, additional information is provided to the team, including answers to any questions they may have regarding the story.

The team then takes each of the presented stories and "disaggregates" it into the tasks required (like breaking a work package from the WBS into activities on the schedule when using a predictive approach). The team then estimates the effort required to complete the tasks for the selected user stories.

Based on the team's velocity, the combined estimate for the tasks needed for the identified stories will determine the final selection of stories for the iteration and become the iteration baseline or backlog.

Those user stories not selected for the iteration are returned to the release backlog for additional reprioritization and "grooming" by the product owner in preparation for the next iteration planning meeting.

Daily Collaboration

The need for additional planning and refinement can be discovered during the daily stand-up meeting. Areas requiring further discussion on work progress, including identified obstacles, are identified, placed in a "parking lot," and scheduled with the appropriate individuals after the daily meeting and not during the time-limited, focused meeting.

Road Maps and Story Maps

There are additional techniques used to determine not only the scope of the work for a release or iteration but also when those requirements might be delivered.

- *Product Road Map*

The product road map provides a "big picture" and includes a sequence of the features and functions at a high level, showing the anticipated delivery time frame and releases for those items.

2023	Mar	May	July	Sept	Oct	Dec
Product Development	Member Portal	Payroll Capabilities	Retail & Inventory Tracking	Affiliate Marketing via email Promotions	Device Integration (Key Cards, CC Processors)	Mobile App

It is often initially developed prior to the start of the project but may be modified as additional information becomes available. This is normal for items on the road map far out in the future. There are many influences acting upon the sequence of items shown on the product road map.

- *Story Map*

A story map is a helpful tool to visualize a release's functionality, the potential sequence to deliver functionality, and the associated user stories for each feature or epic.

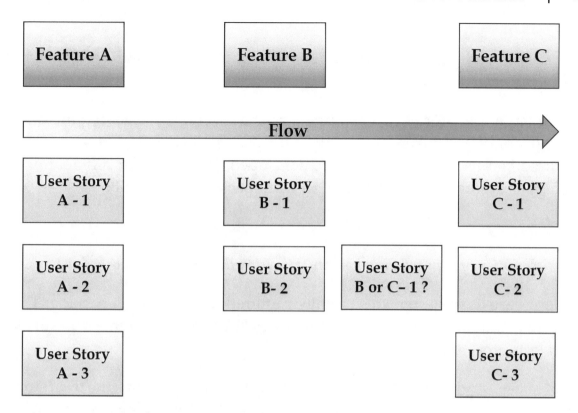

User stories are often associated and prioritized under the various features or epics to aid in prioritization during the iterations. This prioritization helps with the determination of work for individual iterations. In this way not only is the prioritization and value of the story considered but also the most efficient and effective way to develop and deliver functionality, without requiring rework.

Features/Functions, Epics, User Stories

The hierarchy of these items, especially features and epics, is dependent on the agile approach used.

Exam Tip: The product owner, product manager, or stakeholder management usually identifies features and functions of the product first, and the epics or user stories are derived as the detail requirements for those features or functions.

– *Features/Functions*

A set of related requirements allowing the user to satisfy a business objective or need.

Features relate to the functionality identified as required to deliver business value. These are usually identified as deliverables for a release or broken into smaller pieces and delivered over several releases.

Features have associated epics and user stories to define the requirements needed to deliver the value.

– *Epic*

A large body of work that can be broken down into smaller pieces — features and user stories. Epics can take months to complete.

Epics are large user stories representing larger deliverables. They require additional detail and are often broken down into multiple associated user stories. This could be required because the story could be developed differently for different end users (personas) or decomposed to determine a work package on the WBS.

– *User Story*

A short description of required functionality; told from the end user's point of view.

User stories are the requirements initially captured in the product backlog. This term is most frequently used in adaptive approaches but is becoming more useful even for predictive approaches.

Individual user stories are often written on an individual card, thus the term story card, representing a single unit of delivery of requirements. These are usually written using a format to help identify the user or persona, the requirement, and the benefit of the requirement.

An example of a user story format:

As a *stakeholder/persona*

I want to *requirement*

So that *benefit*

These usually represent functional or stakeholder requirements using business language, but they can also be used to identify technical or nonfunctional requirements included in the iteration planning meeting. Some Agile methods only deal with business user stories and will break out technical items using tasks from the user story. Technical user stories can be used to identify and manage any discovered defects or repairs needing to be addressed during an iteration.

The quality of a user story is assessed using the following INVEST criteria.[36]

– **Independent** — of other stories
– **Negotiable** — flexible statement of intent

---

36   *User Stories for Agile Software Development* , Cohn, Mike, Addison-Wesley, NY, 2004.

- Valuable — providing value to the customer
- Estimable — to a good approximation
- Small — fits within an iteration
- Testable — ability to test

These user stories are then selected and associated with the functionality they support during the various releases.

Prioritize and Refine the Backlog

While the team is working on the agreed-upon content of the iteration, the product owner works with end users to incorporate changes and reprioritize the stories in the release backlog in preparation for the next iteration planning meeting. This continual reprioritization and reorganization of the backlog items allows the high-priority items to be completed and deliver value first. The product owner also answers questions from team members about the user stories they are working on.

This refinement often looks at large user stories, or epics, and starts to break them down into smaller user stories, helping enable the completion of the smaller items within the cadence of the iteration.

Additional refinement to the user stories is often done during the iteration planning meeting as the team asks additional questions regarding the user story presented.

There are several techniques used to help prioritize requirements. Not only is it impossible to deliver ALL requirements, but obviously, some requirements deliver more value than others.

Simple Scheme

Prioritization can be done using a simple scheme where stakeholder rank items by using simple numbers. Even though this sounds easy it may be challenging since the user might want to rank many, or even all the items as priority one. These rankings help to determine which items are addressed first and which are held to the next iteration or even the next release.

This is like "stack ranking" where the team ranks the user stories by comparing them directly with each other and then "stacking" the most important story on top. These could also include weighting factors such as value added by the feature, the urgency, the amount of effort to implement, or the implementation risk.

MoSCoW Analysis (Developed by Dai Clegg)

The MoSCoW analysis method is widely used to reach a common understanding based on the importance placed on each requirement. This enables comparison of several points of view to help with prioritization of requirements.

It is often used for prioritization of user stories when using an adaptive approach to enable focus on the most important requirements.

It is also commonly used in predictive projects, though not often referred to by this name, when developing RFPs or evaluating proposals submitted by potential sellers. The prioritization factors include:

- M — Must have
- S — Should have
- C — Could have
- W — Won't have (for now)

Before this technique became widely known and practiced, most projects used a priority system of 1, 2, 3, or 4.

Kano Model (Developed by Noriaki Kano)

This model is typically used in product management to understand, prioritize, and classify potential product features and requirements from a customer's perspective. This framework categorizes customer preferences for various product elements, helping businesses prioritize which features to focus on based on their impact on customer satisfaction.

A marketing approach is used to determine the features, value, and cost to help determine potential new functionality provided in upcoming releases of the product. Development efforts can be prioritized based on the ones with the most influence on customer satisfaction and loyalty.

The horizontal, or x-axis is functionality from poorly executing on the left to well executed on the right. The vertical, or y-axis, is customer satisfaction.

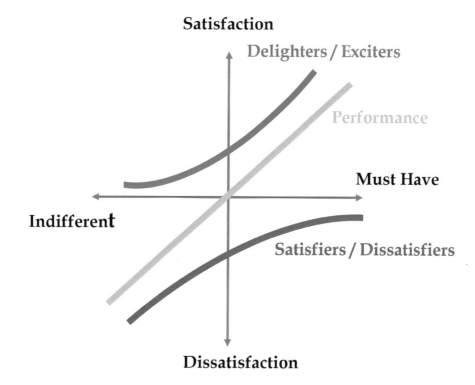

Customer preferences for product features are grouped into four main categories. These help businesses understand how different features impact customer satisfaction and prioritize their development efforts accordingly. The categories include:

- *Delighters/Exciters*

These features or elements go beyond customer expectations and create a positive surprise. Delighters are often unanticipated by customers and can generate a significant increase in customer satisfaction. They have the potential to differentiate a product or service from competitors and create a memorable user experience. Customers do not typically explicitly express delighters since they are unexpected, but they have the power to wow and delight users when experienced. *Example: three cameras on a smartphone.*

- *Satisfiers*

Satisfiers are features that meet customer expectations and are considered essential or necessary. They are the basic features that customers anticipate and require for a product to function adequately. Satisfiers do not necessarily lead to increased customer satisfaction, but failing to provide them can result in customer dissatisfaction. Meeting these basic expectations helps prevent dissatisfaction but does not create a significant competitive advantage. *Example: enhanced battery saver capabilities on a device.*

– *Dissatisfiers*

Dissatisfiers are features that lead to customer dissatisfaction when present or poorly implemented. If dissatisfiers are present, customers are likely to have negative experiences and may even abandon the product or service. However, improving dissatisfiers alone does not necessarily result in increased satisfaction. *Example: MS Project compared to MS Excel, where extensive knowledge to use MS Project effectively is required, rather than providing both basic and advanced functionality as in MS Excel.*

– *Indifferent*

Indifferent features are neither satisfying nor dissatisfying to customers. These features do not significantly impact customer satisfaction or influence their purchase decisions. Customers are generally indifferent to whether these features are included or not. *Example: prompt responses to customer service requests, requiring additional technology and representatives.*

Paired Comparison Analysis (Developed by L. L. Thurstone)

This method, also known as pairwise comparison, helps determine the relative importance of several different options. It allows the choice of the most important item by rating and ranking alternatives by comparing one against another.

It is primarily used when there are only a few requirements and only subjective data is available. All items are placed in the rows and columns of a matrix and then compared as to importance.

100 Points or Dot Voting Method (Developed by Dean Leffingwell and Don Widrig)

This method is often used for large groups of stakeholders when considering prioritization of various aspects. It is a simple and effective way to prioritize or indicate the value of several small items quickly.

When using the 100-point method, each stakeholder receives 100 points with which to vote for their preference and importance of requirements. The points can be distributed in any way, and not necessarily equally.

This results in a weighted distribution to reflect the high-priority items preferred by the group. It is also referred to as "Monopoly money," "fixed sum," or "fixed allocation method" and often used after a brainstorming session to prioritize results gathered.

Exam Tip: There is a baseline using an adaptive approach, but it is referred to as the iteration baseline and applies only to the work on a single iteration. Several iterations will be identified and used to deliver the MVP or MBI for a release baseline.

Scope Planning: Hybrid

Many organizations with emerging requirements find there is often a gap between the real business requirements and the business requirements originally stated.

There may be artifacts required by the organization and PMO, especially regarding requirements in a Business Requirements Document (BRD), for predictive portions of the project and user stories documentation for adaptive portions.

This is the benefit of hybrid project models, as requirements elicitation and prioritization combines these approaches to suit the project.

Key Concepts Covered

- Project and product scope
- Requirements
- Requirements management plan
- Requirements traceability matrix
- Project scope statement
- Work breakdown structure (WBS) and WBS dictionary
- Planning package
- Backlogs
- Release and iteration planning
- Backlog prioritization

ECO Coverage

- Execute project with the urgency required to deliver business value (2.1)
  - Support the team to subdivide project tasks as necessary to find the minimum viable product (2.1.3)

- Plan and manage scope (2.8)
  - Determine and prioritize requirements (2.8.1)
  - Break down scope (e.g., WBS, backlog) (2.8.2)

- Plan and manage project/phase closure or transitions (2.17)
  - Determine criteria to successfully close the project or phase (2.17.1)

Check Your Progress

1. Product scope is measured against product requirements, while project scope is measured against:

    A. The WBS and WBS dictionary

    B. The acceptance criteria

    C. The project scope statement, WBS, and WBS dictionary

    D. The project requirements and the WBS

2. What should be included in a Requirements Management Plan?

    A. The tracing requirements to the project scope and WBS deliverables

    B. The description of how requirement activities will be planned, tracked, and reported

    C. The tracing of high-level requirements to more detailed requirements

    D. The tracing of requirements to business needs, opportunities, goals, and objectives

3. Which artifact is created by decomposing the project scope into smaller, more manageable elements?

    A. Scope statement

    B. Network diagram

    C. WBS

    D. Change request

4. Which of the following is true regarding the code of accounts?

    A. It allows a project manager to easily identify the breakdown level of the item in the resource structure

    B. It describes the coding structure used by the performing organization to report financial information in its general ledger

    C. It is the collection of unique identifiers generally assigned to WBS items

    D. It defines ethical behavior in the project and the responsibilities to the customer and the profession

5. Your company has a new CEO, and she believes in "Go Green!" As part of a paperless initiative, you have been chosen to manage a project to replace the document management system. Requirements have been elicited, captured, and documented. What should be your next step?

   A. Call a meeting with the transition team

   B. Reassign contractors to other phases in your project

   C. Schedule a review meeting with the key stakeholders

   D. Request a preliminary design review

Answers

1. C
2. B
3. C
4. C
5. C

Plan Project Schedule

To meet changing customer and market demands, organizations need scheduling solutions they can tailor to fit product development or project needs. This often includes:

- Ability to tailor the schedule, combining flexibility of scheduled work with consistency and management oversight

- Better product/deliverable quality, with incremental value delivery and feedback with changes incorporated at defined points (including improvements and fixes)

The way the project schedule is determined and monitored will vary depending on the development approach used. It should be flexible enough to adjust for additional knowledge and understanding gained through project activities, especially those adding value. It must also be able to adapt as contingencies and risks are identified, as well as required changes when risk events occur.

Using a predictive approach, once the scope work packages have been identified, then the activities required to complete them are identified as part of the schedule.

Using a timeboxed adaptive approach, the scope is prioritized, and user stories are assigned to pre-established iteration time periods.

Exam Tip: For more detail, see PMI's Scheduling Practice Guide.

Overview of Schedule Planning Processes

Schedule planning takes many forms, in alignment with the project type, team, and life cycle. The project manager takes the lead for scheduling when using a predictive approach, whereas the team is responsible for the scheduling aspects using an adaptive approach.

Adaptive

Adaptive projects can either use a timeboxed approach or a continuous flow method.

The steps when using the timebox method include:

- Adopt the release time frames for the organization.
- Collect user stories pertaining to the release to create the release backlog.
- Determine the cadence for the iterations within the release time frame to successfully complete prioritized stories.
- Prioritize, estimate, and disaggregate or "slice" user stories into tasks.
- Estimate user stories to determine velocity for the iteration.
- Refine and reprioritize the backlog in preparation for the next iteration planning meeting.

The steps when using a continuous flow method include:

- Prioritize individual incoming user stories.
- Place the user story in the appropriate queue to be worked on by the appropriate resource.
- When work on a portion of the story is completed, move the user story in the queue for the resource to do the next step.
- The team member for the next step pulls the story from the queue and starts working.
- Continue moving the story through the columns until it is complete.

Schedule Planning: Predictive

Characteristics of predictive schedules include:

- Predictable with deadlines or milestones for deliverables.
- Focus more on the importance of quality rather than quick delivery.
- Schedule and work focused on single delivery at the end.
- Change is constrained and controlled.

The steps for planning the activities using a predictive approach include:

- Decompose a work package into required activities to complete the deliverable.
- Obtain historical information from past projects.
- Estimate the duration of activities based on average resources.
- Determine dependencies and precedence relationships between activities.
- Determine the critical path(s).
- Identify the need and timing for critical resources (if applicable).
- Resolve any resource overallocations.
- Review estimates with resources performing the activities.
- Compress the schedule, if needed, to meet constraints.

The schedule management plan for the project shows how and when products, services, or results will be delivered. This serves as an important communication tool to help manage stakeholder expectations as well as the basis for reporting performance.

It also provides guidance and direction on how the project schedule will be developed and managed, as well as appropriate control thresholds and schedule contingencies.

Schedule Management Plan

A component of the project or program management plan establishing the criteria and activities for developing, monitoring, and controlling the schedule.

The schedule management plan will vary according to the project approach as well as the complexity of the project, including:

- How the activities or tasks to deliver the project requirements will be defined and progressively elaborated
- The scheduling method and scheduling tool used
- The format used to report schedule information
- The criteria for monitoring and controlling the schedule
- How the status and progress will be reported during execution
- How schedule contingencies will be reported and assessed

Schedule Management Plan Components

Additional areas addressed regarding the project schedule include:

- Scheduling methodology—The methodology and tool used to develop the project schedule, including the maintenance and updates of the schedule, as well as status and progress reporting.

- Release and iteration length for time-bound approaches.

- Accuracy of estimates—Acceptable range used to determine realistic activity duration estimates, including a possible amount to cover risk contingency.

- Units of measure—Individual resource staff hours, days, or weeks.

- Organizational links—Processes to convert WBS and the work packages to the schedule activities to ensure consistency with the estimates and resulting schedules.

- Control thresholds—Defined variance thresholds for monitoring schedule performance before action is taken, including when additional review and possible escalation is needed. These are often expressed as percentage deviations from the baseline plan. This may also include estimated standard deviations (plus or minus amounts), based on the organizational requirements.

- Rules of performance measurement—Includes the rules used for control accounts, establishing

- earned value management (EVM) techniques (discrete, apportioned, level of effort, percent complete), and measurements (SV, SPI).

- Reporting formats—Defined frequency, format, and content for schedule-related reports.

Project Schedule

The purpose of the project schedule is to coordinate activities into a master plan to complete the project objectives on time. The project schedule is an output of a schedule model presenting linked activities with planned dates, durations, milestones, and resources. It is normally created by a software tool included as part of the project management information system (PMIS), such as Microsoft Project, MS Excel, MS Teams Planner, Smartsheet, or another calendar tool.

The project manager develops the initial project schedule, possibly with help from team leads. It is then progressively elaborated with team members after they have been assigned to the project.

The time and effort to develop the project schedule can be greatly reduced by comparing it to similar past projects. This initial estimate will help assess the feasibility of the project, especially in meeting any date constraints.

- *Historical Data*

Additional historical data from other projects completed within the organization, where detailed information is available. Often this would be found in a lessons learned repository.

Exam Tip: Be aware that PMI uses the term "activity" in the predictive approach but uses the term "task" in adaptive approaches. Regardless of the term used, these are foundational to provide estimates for schedules, budget, and the monitoring and controlling of project work.

- *Benchmarking*

Schedules can be developed by referring to any available benchmarks from external sources. These will aid in the comparison to another similar product/service schedule and estimation before detailed analysis is started.

Work Package Activities

A distinct, scheduled portion of work performed during a project.

Individual work packages are broken down to identify the activities needed to complete the work. While work packages represent deliverables and are nouns as part of the project scope, activities use a verb-noun format and are identified on an activity list.

Activities have a distinct beginning and end with start and end dates included for every activity. They may involve several smaller steps. When these are completed, the whole activity is considered complete. Several related activities can be combined to form a summary activity.

The amount of detail included for each activity will vary as to the project context and planning and estimating needs at various times in the project.

Activity Dependencies

A logical relationship between two project activities.

Dependencies and precedencies will also need to be considered as activities are added to the project schedule. Understanding potential dependencies between activities is important, as they will influence the order in which activities are performed.

There are four main types of activity dependencies having an impact on the sequence of individual activities.

Mandatory — These activities MUST be done in a specific sequence. These are referred to as hard logic or hard dependencies. They may be contractually required or inherent in the nature of the work. The project manager must schedule them in the specific sequence required.

Discretionary — These activities may often be done in a different sequence from best practices, especially when the schedule needs to be condensed or resource modifications are required. These are often called soft logic.

External — These represent relationships between project activities and non-project activities, especially where the project manager has little or no control. They must be closely monitored for potential impact to the project schedule.

Internal — A relationship between project activities, usually under the control of the project manager and team.

Precedence Relationships

In addition to dependency between individual activities, there are precedence relationships, with the first activity being the predecessor (or driving activity), and the subsequent activity being the successor (activity being driven).

Precedence relationships are always assigned to activities based on the dependencies of each activity and are shown on a network diagram using a precedence diagramming method (PDM). This visually depicts the order in which activities must be done.

There are four precedence relationship types.

- *Finish-to-Start (FS)* — a logical relationship where a predecessor activity finishes, and the successor activity can start
- *Finish-to-Finish (FF)* — a logical relationship where two or more activities finish before a successor activity can start
- *Start-to-Start (SS)* — a logical relationship where two or more successor activity start after a predecessor activity has finished
- *Start-to-Finish (SF)* — a logical relationship where a successor activity cannot finish until a predecessor has started

Exam Tip: The default and majority of relationships in a network diagram utilize finish-to-start (FS). Next most common are start-to-start (SS) or finish-to-finish (FF). Start-to-finish (SF) is rarely used.

– *Precedence Diagramming Method*

A technique used to create the network diagram. It constructs a schedule model with activities represented by nodes that are graphically linked by one or more logical relationships to show the sequence of the activities to be performed.

- Precedence relationships consider appropriate logic while connecting these points to another activity.
- Precedence relationships are always assigned to activities based on the dependencies of each activity.
- Each activity has both a start and a finish.
- Precedence indicates the activity driving the relationship (the predecessor activity) and the one driven by it (the successor activity).
- In most situations, predecessors occur earlier in time than successors.

Leads and Lags

Leads and lags are another method used to further modify the dependencies between two activities.

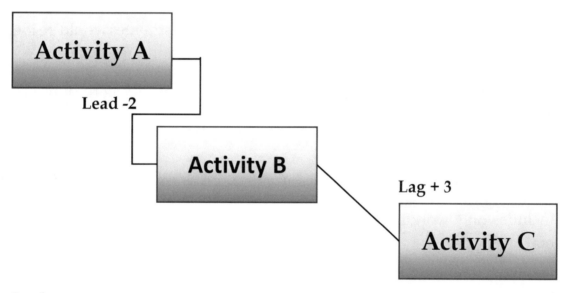

– *Lead*

The amount of time whereby a successor activity can be advanced with respect to predecessor activity.

Leads only apply to finish-to-start relationships. This creates a head start for one of the activities or an overlap in the two activities and is normally shown as a negative amount of time in scheduling software.

   – *Lag*

The amount of time whereby a successor activity will be delayed with respect to a preceding activity.

A lag is the opposite of the lead. This can be internally or externally imposed and is normally shown as a positive number of days in scheduling software.

Exam Tip:

- *The use of leads and lags should not replace schedule logic.*
- *Duration estimates do not include any leads or lags.*
- *Leads and lags do not have a value, so do not include them in duration estimates.*
- *Activities and their related assumptions should be documented, especially when using discretionary dependencies, leads, and lags.*
- *If a lag time must be included between two activities, it is often replaced by an activity with the required duration. (Example: Mandatory time for concrete to cure between pouring the foundation and framing the structure.)*

Activity Duration

The unit of measure (e.g., months, days, or hours) for these estimates would be identified in the schedule management plan and can vary by activity and resource.

Estimates can be effort driven, with the duration reduced by adding resources, or fixed duration.

   – *Duration*

The quantitative assessment of the likely number of time periods required to complete an activity.

- Includes only working time and not nonworking periods such as weekends or holidays
- Is often the estimate shown on the project schedule
- Does not include lags between activities

   – *Elapsed Time*

The actual calendar time required for an activity from start to finish.

- Actual calendar time required for an activity's completion
- Includes nonworking periods such as weekends or holidays

- *Effort*

The number of units required to complete a scheduled activity or WBS component.

- Often expressed in the unit of measure used to estimate and manage the activity progress.
- The estimates of effort provide the basis for cost estimating and resource allocation.

- *Ideal time*

The time to complete a certain activity or task assuming there are no unplanned problems or zero interruptions.

- Often used as a benchmark for measuring efficiency or productivity of a process or a person.

Estimating Technique: Predictive

Estimates are quantifiable assessment of a variable, including project costs, resources, effort or duration. As the project work is performed, the estimates can change based on current information and circumstances. The phase of the life cycle for the project impacts four estimating aspects:

- Range— including a broad range at the beginning when little information is known, to more precise as the project continues
- Accuracy—correctness linked to the range of values
- Precision—degree of correctness associated with the estimate and based on the desired accuracy
- Confidence—level increases with experience from previous, similar projects, while for new, evolving technology, the confidence may be very low

Estimating of time, effort, and cost is done at a minimum of two points in the project life cycle. In the early stages of the project a comprehensive order-of-magnitude is usually provided to obtain approvals. These early estimates are considered top-down estimates. As additional information is obtained a more definitive estimate can be provided and rolled-up using a bottom-up approach.

Several techniques are used for estimating the time needed for an activity as well as the cost.

- Deterministic estimating, also known as point estimates, provide a single number or amount.

- Probabilistic estimates include the dispersion of data within a range of estimates along with probabilities within the ranges.

- Absolute estimates are specific, while relative estimates are shown in comparison to other estimates. Relative estimates only have meaning within a given context (e.g., planning poker)

- Adjusting estimates for uncertainty including a range of certainty for the estimate

Analogous Estimating

Uses historical data from a previous project with a similar scope or activities to estimate the duration or cost of similar activities. It is a form of expert judgment, also known as "top-down estimating."

- *Pros*
  - Less costly and less time-consuming, providing an early estimate when requested
  - Used when historical information is available from similar efforts
  - Can be done quickly

- *Cons*
  - May be inaccurate, depending on the integrity of the historical information available and how it relates to the current project

Parametric Estimating

Relies on the statistical relationship existing between historical information and variables using an algorithm to calculate an estimate for parameters such as duration and cost. Also considered a "high-level" approach.

- *Pros*
  - Can produce higher levels of accuracy depending on the model and historical data applied
  - Can be quicker than bottom-up
  - Scalable and linear

- *Cons*
  - Doesn't account for a learning curve if applied to people.
  - Historical information may not be available.
  - Uniform units of work are only applicable to some types of work activities, including estimates regarding equipment and supplies.

Bottom-Up Estimating

Estimates the cost of individual activities, then aggregates or "rolls up" to higher levels, especially within the components of the WBS. Based on detailed, reliable historical data.

- *Pros*
    - Very accurate
    - Gives more estimating responsibility to those performing the work

- *Cons*
    - Time-consuming and costly
    - Subject to padding by team members
    - Only as accurate as the WBS
    - Requires detailed knowledge to determine the individual estimates

Delphi Estimates

An interactive estimating and forecasting method that uses a panel of independent experts, with all participants providing anonymous input.

- *Pros*
    - Prevents influence from others
    - Allows free expression of personal opinions

- *Cons*
    - Prevents discussion to help clarify situations
    - Discourages open critique

A variation of this is the wideband delphi estimating technique where the individual experts together discuss the area to be estimated before independently providing their consensus-based estimate. This method often negates the "cons" of the traditional delphi estimating technique.

Three-Point Estimating

Includes input from multiple points of view, including the team members assigned to an activity who understand the potential risks and level of effort required. These can be used for estimating both time and cost. This method uses approximate range estimates including optimistic, pessimistic, and most likely.

- *Triangular Distribution* — (or three-point, straight average) includes the most likely (M), the optimistic or best (O), and the pessimistic or worst (P) time or cost. This is then divided by 3 to get the average. $E = (O + M + P) / 3$.

- *BETA or PERT Distribution* — like the triangular distribution but weighs the most likely (M) four times higher and then divides by 6. $E = (O + 4M + P) / 6$.

- *Pros*

  - May improve accuracy of single-point estimates.
  - The estimates include risk and uncertainty factors.

- *Cons*

  - Requires estimates based on previous knowledge, usually by the individuals who will be responsible for performing the work.

Exam Tip: The results can be close depending on the range between the optimistic (O) and the pessimistic (P).

Heuristic

A rule of thumb often determined by previous experimental and trial-and-error methods.

Variance

Rather than just getting a single estimate, a variance can be determined by calculating the standard deviation $((P - O) / 6)$ and including this as the plus or minus variance to the estimate.

- *Standard Deviation*

This refers to the measurement of precision identified in a normal distribution or bell curve. It is often used when setting the control limits within the specification limits on a control chart.

A range of one standard deviation above or below the mean equals 68% of the population.

A range of two standard deviations above or below the mean equals 95% of the population.

A range of three standard deviations above or below the mean equals 99% of the population.

Accuracy measures conformance to target values.

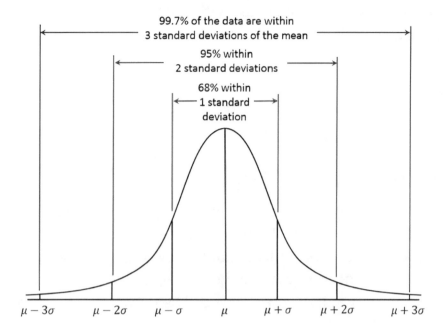

Exam Tip: You will not need to calculate standard deviation, but you need to understand the concepts of accuracy, precision, and standard deviation.

Probability Distributions

Common probability distributions include:

Cumulative distribution – (S-curve)

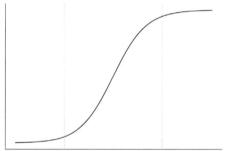

- Represents the probability of achieving any particular outcome or less.
- Used in earned value management to represent the Plan Value (PV) for the project.

Continuous distribution – (Bell curve)

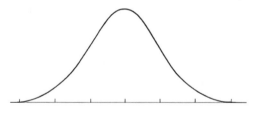

- Represents the expected distribution of random variables.
- Used in triangular, beta or pert estimations.

Discrete distribution – (Decision Tree)

- − Represents several uncertain events with tests on an attribute with branches representing the test outcomes.
- − Used in risk management to help determine Expected Monetary Value (EMV) of various potential results.

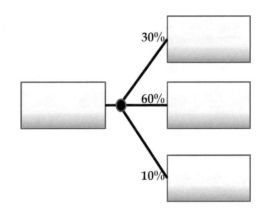

Project Schedule Network Diagram

The network diagram is the most common way to display the scheduled activities with their dependencies. Network diagrams have clear advantages over other project scheduling methods because they additionally show the interrelationship of activities. This enables a clear view of progress and workflow, including where activities may be affected if another activity starts to be delayed. The network diagram also shows:

- − Clear visual of progress and workflow to enable collaboration and sharing
- − Justification of time estimates for project activities and the project as a whole
- − Assistance in planning and organization of activities and resources
- − Improved analysis and determination of schedule compression and resource utilization

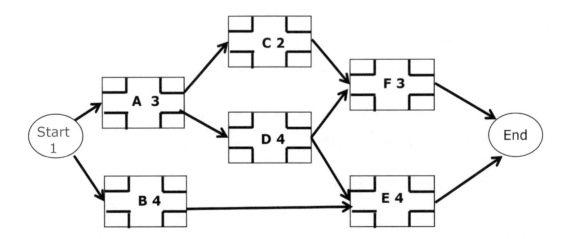

To draw the diagram:

- − Sequence and connect the activities based on predecessors or successors creating paths from Start to End.
- − Identify the duration of each activity.
- − For each path, sum the duration of each activity on the path.
- − Identify the path(s) with the longest duration as the critical path(s).

- For each activity, determine the early start, early finish, late start, and late finish dates using a forward and backward pass. (If scheduling software is used, these dates will be automatically calculated.)

Exam Tip: It is most likely that you will not have to perform a forward or backward pass, but rather understand the concepts, especially as regards the critical path.

There are a couple of key terms to be aware of:

- *Early start date (ES)* – the earliest possible point in time when the uncompleted portions of a schedule activity can start based on the schedule network logic, the data date, and any schedule constraints

- *Early finish/end date (EF)* – the earliest possible point in time when the uncompleted portions of a schedule activity can finish based on the schedule network logic, the data date, and any schedule constraints

- *Late start date (LS)* – the latest possible point in time when the uncompleted portions of a schedule activity can start based on the schedule network logic, the project completion date, and any schedule constraints

- *Late finish date (LF)* – the latest possible point in time when the uncompleted portions of a schedule activity can finish based on the schedule network logic, the project completion date, and any schedule constraints

The difference between critical activities' early and late start dates should be zero. For noncritical activities, the difference in days between the early and late start dates and the difference in days between the early and late finish dates should be different, indicating the float or slack time for the activity; in other words, the activity has some "wiggle" room.

Critical Path Method

A technique of schedule analysis with schedule activities evaluated to determine the float or slack for each activity and the overall schedule. To calculate the critical path, use the forward and backward pass along with float analysis to identify all network paths, including the critical path.

The critical path method is the most common project schedule management method. It helps to identify the most important work to ensure the project is completed on time.

Activities are sequenced, and the length of each path in the diagram is determined. The longest path(s) are considered the critical path(s) and will represent the shortest possible project duration. The activities on the critical path are referred to as critical activities.

It is important to determine all the paths, and then determine the longest (critical path). Remember, there can be multiple critical paths. If the length of other paths is very close to that of the critical path, those are identified as "near" critical paths and will require monitoring by the project manager, so as not to also become critical paths.

It is important to manage the critical activities and the critical path to ensure the project isn't delayed. Other paths can be used to add flexibility to the schedule where needed.

Critical Path Activity

Any activity on the critical path in a project schedule.

Activities on the critical path(s) have no flexibility in the start time or finish time, including no total float or slack. Any delay in any critical path activity will delay the overall project and thus must be monitored closely by the project manager.

Float or Slack

Two different terms are applied to the variances between any activity's early and late start or end dates. These are known as float or slack. They are shown as the nodes on a network diagram and can refer to work packages or activities/tasks. Activities on the critical path will have a float or slack of zero.

This float/slack (or "wiggle" room) enables noncritical path activities to be delayed, helping manage overallocated resources.

- *Float or Slack*

This is the difference between an activity's early and late dates or between activities. Understanding these concepts is helpful when developing and managing a schedule to accommodate resource availability.

- *Total Float (or Slack)*

The amount of time a schedule activity can be delayed or extended from its early start date without delaying the project finish date or violating a schedule constraint.

Total float is within an activity. If the total float is zero, the activity is a critical activity, and if the total float is not zero, then there is float, slack, or "wiggle" room. The activity can be delayed without affecting the project schedule.

- *Free Float (or Slack)*

The amount of time a scheduled activity can be delayed without delaying the early start date of any successor or violating a schedule constraint.

Free float is between activities and is important when needing to modify the schedule to accommodate resource availability.

 – *Project Float (or Slack)*

The amount of time the project can be delayed or extended without delaying another project.

 – *Negative Float*

The amount of time that must be saved to bring the project to completion on time.

Exam Tip: Total float is within an activity.

Free float is between two activities.

Activities on the critical path will have no float or slack.

Additional key terms include:

 – *Path divergence*—any point in a schedule network diagram where a single predecessor activity has more than one unrelated successor activity, forming multiple "paths"
 – *Path convergence*—any point in a schedule network diagram where more than one path has a shared successor activity with another path or paths

Critical Chain

The critical chain method is based on Eliyahu Goldratt's Theory of Constraints (TOC) and described in some detail in the book *Critical Chain Project Management* by Lawrence P. Leach.

The theory of constraints is a management philosophy that focuses on identifying and improving the constraints or bottlenecks in a system to optimize overall performance. The critical chain method, an application of TOC, is a project management technique that emphasizes the efficient allocation of resources and the management of project dependencies to improve project completion time.

It is an additional method of planning and managing projects that emphasizes the resources, referred to as the chain resources, required to execute project activities. In contrast to the critical path and PERT methods, which emphasize activity order and rigid scheduling, a critical chain project network will tend to keep the resources loaded but will require them to be flexible in their start times and to quickly switch between activities and activity chains to keep the whole project on schedule.

Tasks are expected to start as soon as the previous task has been completed and immediately passed on to the next activity. The work will be done 100%, with no multitasking.

This includes feeding buffers when activities converge. This is used on noncritical path activities or on parallel path activities to protect the critical chain from slippage. The idea is that if any of the activities on the parallel path are delayed, only part of the feeding buffer will be expended without pushing out the project's end date.[37]

For a better understanding of Critical Chain, refer to book *The Goal*, by Eliyahu M. Goldratt and Jeff Cox.

Exam Tip: Critical chain accounts for limited resources, adds duration buffers, and focuses on managing the time buffer and resources. It is often abbreviated as CCM.

With critical chain, the focus is on managing the buffers and critical resources. With critical path, the focus is on managing the dependencies and critical activities.

Schedule Formats

A visual representation of the schedule can include the project team's plan for starting and finishing activities on specific dates and in a certain sequence. It often specifies planned dates for meeting project milestones. It can also display schedule information at either a high-level milestone level or with additional detail when needed.

Project progress can be tracked and reported to upper management and stakeholders based on the schedule performance.

The project schedule can be presented in different formats, depending on the audience as well as the approach and circumstances, including:

- *Road map*—with high-level functions and features and expected delivery time frames (applicable for both predictive and adaptive).

- *Milestone chart or list*—including high-level information when a detailed schedule is not required.

- *Gantt chart*—showing activities between the milestones, with start and end dates and duration (including a modified Gantt chart with dependencies shown). Also called a horizontal bar chart.

- *Project schedule network diagram*—a graphical representation technique used in precedence diagramming methods (PDM) to model and analyze the logical

37   http://facilitatedmethods.com/critical-chain-project-management-estimating-and-scheduling-by-greta-blash-pmp-2/

relationships between project activities. The diagram uses nodes or boxes to represent activities and arrows to depict their dependencies or relationships. (A less frequent method of depicting these relationships is with an activity on arrow diagram, rather than the activity on node method supported by most scheduling software.)

Milestones

A specific point within a project life cycle that is used to measure progress toward the goal. A milestone marks a specific point along a project timeline. The point may signal anchors such as a project start and end date or a need for external review, input, or a budget check. It is represented as a task of zero duration and displayed as an important achievement in a project.

Milestones serve as markers and are defined by the project manager, customer, or both. These can indicate big events, where reviews are held and decisions made, or merely be important points of time during a project. They may be based on contractual requirements, government regulations, historical information, or required by the organization's methodology or governance processes.

Milestones have no duration and often trigger a reporting requirement or require sponsor or customer approval before the project proceeds. Milestones represent the completion of a key deliverable, work package, or phase. In the case of work performed under a contract, this may result in predetermined funds being released as a partial payment.

Milestone List

Identifies all the project milestones, including whether they are mandatory (required by contract or other agreement) or optional (based on organizational governance or other historical information). This is often included in the project management plan, the project scope statement, and the WBS dictionary.

Milestone Chart

Milestone charts are often shown on the summary level of the project schedule. This is a graphic representation of the project milestones and project road map used to communicate schedule progress to various audiences. Milestone charts provide a high-level view of the timeline for a project. Often this is the view provided to upper management who only require an overview of the project schedule.

Gantt Chart

A bar chart of schedule information where activities are listed on the vertical axis, dates are shown on the horizontal axis, and the activity durations are shown as horizontal bars placed according to start and finish dates.

Gantt charts, created years ago by Henry Gantt, are pure bar charts with no dependencies shown. This is often the default schedule format to present and report the schedule progress for a project. Durations are indicated by the length of the horizontal bars based on start and end dates. Its horizontal depiction of activities provides a visual method to see how work is scheduled.

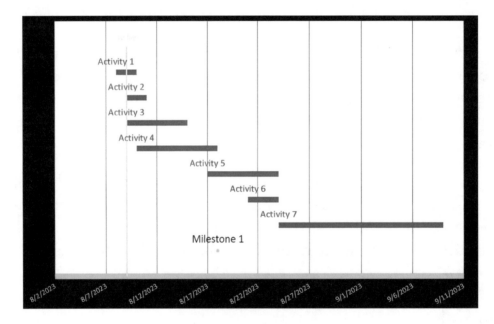

This chart can also be modified to show both the planned duration and the percentage complete or actual progress of each activity. This is referred to as a Tracking Gantt chart.

Most scheduling software allows a modification to include the dependencies between activities. In this way it becomes a simple version of a network diagram.

Resource Optimization

After resources have been assigned to schedule activities, it often becomes obvious that some resources have been assigned to more work than can be completed in the given time. This resource histogram is often indicated by a vertical bar chart showing when a resource will be needed in the project.

Resource optimization is needed to adjust work assignments to meet resource availability. These adjustments are made during development of the project schedule.

The two methods used are smoothing and leveling.

Resource Smoothing

A resource optimization technique using free and total float without affecting the critical path.

This method is often used to reallocate resources and adjust the schedule and resources to remain within limits for assigned activities. It does not change the critical path or delay the completion of the project. This can only be done within the free and/or total float amounts of activities. Even though resource smoothing modifies overallocation of resources, it can only sometimes optimize all resources.

Resource Leveling

A resource optimization technique where adjustments are made to the project schedule to optimize the allocation of resources. This often impacts the critical path.

Leveling expands the duration of activities to accommodate overscheduling—and thus can GREATLY impact the final date of the project. It attempts to balance the resources assigned by adjusting the start and finish dates on activities with overallocation. This changes the critical path and thus the final date.

Exam Tip: Many scheduling software packages support this leveling method but be aware of the negative impact on the project finish date before using.

Schedule Compression

After the initial schedule is developed, it often requires adjustments to meet any date constraints.

There are two techniques to compress the schedule. One is usually done during planning, and the other is more often done toward the end of the project, especially when it becomes clear the end date will not be met. These can be used to compress the schedule and handle negative float.

Fast-Tracking

A schedule compression technique where activities or phases normally done in sequence are performed in parallel for at least a portion of their duration.

This includes performing finish-start activities in parallel or starting the successor before the predecessor activity is completed. This technique reduces the time for activities in the schedule.

This process may result in rework, increased risk, and increased cost, but it allows potential shortening of the schedule.

Crashing

Applying additional resources to one or more tasks/activities to complete the work more quickly. Crashing usually increases costs more than risks. In comparison, fast-tracking increases risks.

This method shortens the schedule duration for the least incremental cost by adding resources (e.g., working overtime, scheduling additional resources) to critical path activities. Crashing only activities on the critical path will result in a reduction of the schedule.

This is not a planned method, but rather a way to potentially get the final work completed before a milestone or end of the project. Because of the increased risk and cost, it does not always produce a viable alternative.

Exam Tip: Fast-tracking is usually applied during planning, whereas crashing is usually applied toward the end of the project to ensure the end date is met.

Schedule Baseline

The approved version of a schedule model can be changed using formal change control procedures and is used to compare results. It is one of the main project documents created before the project starts.

A schedule baseline can be identified after completion of schedule planning activities using a predictive approach. Ideally, this is done before the project starts, even though the entire schedule may not include all the details for future activities until additional planning and progressive elaboration have occurred.

Even though the baseline for the schedule could be determined at this time, best practice delays the final schedule baseline until the resource and cost factors have been added. In this way the constraints and requirements for scope, schedule, and budget can all be baselined at the same time. This schedule baseline can then be added to the project management plan.

During the project, continual comparison of actual progress to the baseline helps ensure timely completion of work. Since schedule baselines will require approval along with the scope and cost baselines, formal change control processes will be required to make changes to any of these baselines.

Schedule Planning—Adaptive Approach

Adaptive schedule planning is different for either an adaptive timeboxed or continuous flow approach. The adaptive approach uses short cycles and smaller units for work, review, and adaptations or adjustments, with the focus on the following:

- Value provided more frequently instead of only at the end of the project
- Frequent delivery of product, driven by cadence
- Change incorporated in real time during the delivery

In all adaptive methods, the schedule is planned at different levels with involvement from different individuals or roles. It is also closer to scope and requirements than when using a predictive approach. Rapid feedback about the approach and deliverables received becomes the basis for both iterative and on-demand, pull-based scheduling.

Schedule Management

Although a final completion date may be scheduled in an adaptive approach, activities throughout the project use iterative scheduling, with a backlog or on-demand scheduling to adjust priorities as the product and project evolve. This includes the development of the project road map to show release functionality and time frames while allowing priorities to be adjusted as the project environment evolves.

The specific scheduling method depends on the context and complexity of the project, the team composition, and the organization methodology and life cycle. This is often determined jointly by the project team and product owner.

If the on-demand method is appropriate because of continuous requests, the prioritization and separation of work between groups would be determined at this time.

For a timeboxed approach to scheduling, the project continues to deliver results based a high-level road map showing release functionality and time frames, often driven by the product owner or manager. The release time frames are then broken down into similar time frames or iterations by the team to identify when actual work is performed. Timeboxed iterations are useful for creating a cadence or rhythm for regular delivery and feedback cycles.

The activities done during an iteration or sprint are determined just before the beginning of the iteration, as part of the iteration planning meeting.

Exam Tip: Understand the difference between the schedule and a time estimate.

The schedule is calendar-based, including weekends, holidays, resource availability, and non-working times. A time estimate is for an activity and indicates how many hours or days it may take to complete the activity. It is also called the work effort or level of effort.

Schedule Planning

Adaptive schedule planning helps the team focus on what is most important and provides the most value to the customer at any time. It can include iterative, incremental, timebox, or continuous flow methods.

The definition of the work to be done in a specific iteration usually concentrates on the solution requirements, especially those prioritized functional requirements from the product owner, with possible nonfunctional or technical requirements added where needed. The "what" is needed is usually provided to the team, as opposed to the "how" the result is to perform.

Time-boxed Method

Timeboxed scheduling steps include:

- Releases

Releases represent the time periods that were specified by the customer or business to deliver results, usually in 3-to-6-month intervals. The functionality and time frames for these releases are usually shown on the product road map.

Features or Functions — Features or functions are the high-level requirements or capabilities identified initially and associated with various release time frames on the product road map. This allows business and end users to understand when blocks of functionality are planned to be released.

- Release Plan

Adaptive scheduling starts with the features or functions and decomposes those into epics, smaller user stories. The user stories from the product backlog are selected based on the identified features and functions of the release and added to the release backlog.

Story Map — One very helpful technique when starting to understand and analyze the stories about a release is using a story map. This graphical technique allows the features/functions and epics planned for delivery during a release to be sequenced. The individual user stories are then associated and prioritized with the features/functions.

This also enables the determination of the stories to be addressed in each iteration. This is not only by the priority and value of individual stories but also by the combination of sequence and priority identified on the story map. It also helps identify the potential sequence of user stories in each iteration, especially when prioritization of the stories has been done.

- Iterations

The release time frames are broken into small periods of equal length, defined by the team, usually 1-4 weeks in length. This is when the prioritized user stories are developed.

- Iteration Plan

Prior to each iteration, the product owner provides the team members with the prioritized stories for the iteration. During the iteration planning meeting, the team clarifies and identifies the tasks needed to support the prioritized user stories. The estimated story points of these stories and tasks are used to determine how many user stories can realistically be completed in the iteration. The total number of story points selected for an iteration is based upon the team's velocity, or capacity to complete the work.

- Iteration Backlog

The work committed to be performed during a given iteration and expected to burn down the duration. The work does not carry over to the next iteration.

During the iteration planning meeting, the product owner presents previously prioritized and selected user stories to the team members. Those user stories agreed upon to be delivered in the upcoming iteration or sprint then become the iteration backlog. The user stories are disaggregated or "sliced" into tasks for inclusion in a single iteration.

Depending on the framework used, if a user story is not successfully completed at the end of the iteration, it is moved to the release backlog for reprioritization and possible inclusion in a future iteration.

- Sprint Velocity

A descriptive metric used by adaptive and hybrid teams.

This describes the volume of work a team performs during a sprint. Initially, the teams choose a number and then refine the metric at the end of the iteration based on discussions during the retrospective meeting.

Teams use this metric to understand the rate of work during an average sprint based on previous performance. It is purely based on the project's complexity and the team members' capabilities and cannot be compared to other teams.

Continuous Flow Method

Continuous flow is an agile approach based on lean that emphasizes the importance of moving a single item or request through every step of the process instead of grouping items into batches. The goal is to reduce waste by balancing the work and minimizing the wait time for individual items.

Each individual story is individually received and prioritized as it arrives and placed into the appropriate queue to be worked on when the appropriate resource is available. As a portion of the work is completed, it is moved into a queue to await availability of the resource for the next portion of work. This is similar to an assembly line where different work is done in different sections of the line.

As work is moved from one "station" to the next, it is put into a queue, and when the team member is available, they pull the story from the queue and start working. The story is continuously moved through the "stations" until it is complete.

A Kanban board is often used to show the various "stations" and queues, and as work is completed in a column it continuously moves until it is completed.

Estimating Techniques: Adaptive

There are several adaptive techniques to estimate the work to be accomplished during a given cycle or timebox.

Regardless of the approach used, it is highly recommended to address relative effort required rather than absolute time estimates. These adaptive estimating techniques include:

- *Relative Sizing*

Compares effort required by multiple user stories and assigns a relative value, often using t-shirt sizes (XS, S, M, L, XL) or another grouping. This is also referred to as affinity estimating.

- *Story Points*

Relative point values (e.g., numbers in the Fibonacci sequence: 1, 2, 3, 5, 8, 13, etc.), **not** hours, days, or weeks, are used to estimate the difficulty of implementing a user story. It's an abstract measure of effort required to implement work.

- *Planning Poker*

Uses iterative estimates by team members, often using story points, to determine user stories' relative size or effort.

Definition of Ready and Definition of Done

These definitions are closely related but only sometimes understood or implemented in adaptive approaches. They often include checklists to help the team be prepared to commit to and deliver work.

Definition of Ready (DoR)—identifies what understanding should be provided to the delivery team during iteration planning to ensure they can deliver the expected result. It is highly dependent on the complexity of the requirements and the environment. This often includes the type of information gathered and presented to the development team by a business analysis function for a predictive approach, including:

- Identification of different scenarios based on different users (personas) or situations
- Processing sequence required
- Information needed and calculations defined
- Business rules that might apply to different scenarios

Definition of Done (DoD) – describes the target result or stakeholder's expectation. It is like the acceptance criteria but may also include intermediate stages of "doneness." All team members must determine, understand, and accept this definition.

Reprioritize Sprint/Iteration Backlog

While the team is working on the current iteration, and prior to the iteration planning meeting, the product owner continually reviews stories, often breaking them down into smaller ones. As new stories are received, they are reprioritized within existing stories on the product or release backlog.

This assumes a product road map with features and functions has been initially identified for each release.

During the individual iteration/sprint planning meeting, those user stories prioritized highest are presented to the team. The team then estimates the effort required to deliver a story and determines, based on estimation, the velocity for the iteration. Those become the stories they will commit to as part of the iteration. Stories not accepted by the team are replaced on the release backlog for reprioritization by the product owner.

The product owner continues to "groom" the stories in the release backlog by adding new stories, removing stories, enhancing the information regarding the user stories for the team, and reprioritizing stories while the project team works on the stories selected for the current iteration.

Hybrid Scheduling Model

There is not a generally agreed-upon hybrid scheduling model. The hybrid model usually combines the high-level planning components common in predictive methods with more adaptive processes to deliver the work, including:

- Tailored plans combining consistency with flexibility in scheduling of work
- Quality increased with incremental or short-term value delivery
- Product delivery divided into predefined subsets (milestones, releases, cadence)
- Change incorporated at intervals based on the cadences (e.g., release/iterations, or continuous flow)

The project manager usually plans the high-level phases or releases with features and milestones. These are then decomposed into smaller "chunks" of work with requirements associated to each.

Just as the project schedule and project management plan may be reviewed prior to starting a new phase using a predictive approach, so are planning meetings conducted for both releases and iterations. The work should be prioritized to be done within a project phase or to achieve a milestone.

Those requirements well understood or requiring sequential activities are managed using more of a hybrid approach. In areas with uncertainty or potential change, a more adaptive scheduling approach is appropriate.

Regardless of the approach, continual refinement and prioritization of requirements should be addressed to deliver the highest value more frequently. This includes estimating the effort required of any work, reviewing the results at the end of the phase or iteration, and determining whether adjustments are needed to the estimation process.

Also, retrospectives should be scheduled and held at the end of phases or releases, milestones, completion of major deliverables, or iterations. This enables the team to reflect on the work just completed and identify areas for improvement.

When using a hybrid approach, management or the PMO may require schedule reporting and therefore should be identified as part of the schedule management plan.

Special Intervals

There may be some downtime, or time when the team produces no value. Negotiation and agreement may be needed as to when these intervals may take place to avoid work disruptions or conflict.

– *Predictive*

Predictive approaches often include blackout times prior to deliverables being handed over for implementation. During these times, no additional functionality or changes are added, but final test results are completed. This is often part of the organization's methodology or governance procedures and is included in the project schedule.

The "Go Live" occurs at the end of the project timeline and is usually specified by the organizational procedures, including the decisions and resources involved in making the final determination to release the project to the customer or end user.

– *Adaptive*

Another interval like the blackout or go-live times used in adaptive projects is referred to as Iteration H, or Hardening Iteration, where the team ties up loose ends, as well as other organizational functions, prior to releasing to the customer. It is primarily used for refactoring and/or reducing technical debt. Regardless of the need, no additional functionality is added during these times.

There may be a special interval at the beginning of the project using an adaptive approach, referred to as Iteration Zero. This is like a staging or preparation time before the actual work is started on the release or project.

Key Concepts Covered

- Schedule management plan
- Project schedule
- Dependencies and precedence relationships
- Estimating techniques
- Critical path method
- Critical chain method
- Resource optimization
- Schedule compression
- Schedule baseline
- Adaptive schedule planning
- Definition of Ready (DoR) and Definition of Done (DoD)

ECO Coverage

- Plan and manage schedule (2.6)
  - Estimate project tasks (milestones, dependencies, story points) (2.6.1)
  - Utilize benchmarks and historical data (2.6.2)
  - Prepare schedule based on methodology (2.6.3)

Check Your Progress

1. You are reviewing your project schedule with your team, and you realize that your team must set up the software program development server and test it for 3 days and then programmers can start to write their programs and save it to the server. What is this an example of?

   A. Lag

   B. Lead

   C. Smoothing

   D. Crashing

2. The sponsor has asked you to shorten the project schedule by two months to beat a competitor's product launch date. To achieve this target, you will need to add two additional team members and receive overtime approval for the team. This will add more risk to the project and possible potential conflicts, additional time, and cost of the project. What schedule technique are you using?

   A. Fast tracking the project schedule

   B. Crashing the project schedule

   C. Critical path method

   D. Critical chain method

3. A new manager of testing has joined your project and she asked you, the project manager, about the scheduling methodology and tools that were used to develop the project schedule. She would also like to know about the schedule change control procedures and reporting requirements. Which documents would you refer her to?

   A. Project schedule baseline

   B. Project charter

   C. Stakeholder register

   D. Schedule management plan

   E. Business case

4. Which of the following are time-boxed approaches used in agile projects? (Choose 2)

   A. Backlog

   B. Iteration

   C. Phase

   D. Sprint

   E. Story map

5. An agile project team has completed their first iteration planning meeting. Which scrum ceremony did they perform?

   A. Progressive planning

   B. Rolling wave planning

   C. Project scope planning

   D. Progressive elaboration

   E. Sprint planning

Answers

1. A
2. B
3. D
4. B, D
5. E

Plan Project Resources

Resources include both people and physical resources such as equipment, materials, facilities, and infrastructure needed to conduct the project activities. These resources needed to complete individual activities are identified as the activity resource estimates and are often expressed as a probability or range.

Resources: People and Equipment[38]

Even with an amazing core project team, it is important to continue valuing and empowering those people.

---

38 *"People Management" resource from PMI's Disciplined Agile framework – https://www.pmi.org/disciplined-Agile/process/people-management*

Having the best team and equipment available is important to make the project successful. Yet sometimes it is necessary to move beyond the organization to secure external human resources, such as contractors, consultants, and SMEs who can play development or leadership roles on the team.

Resource Planning: Predictive

Resource Management Plan

A project document that identifies resources and how to acquire, allocate, monitor, and control them.

The plan identifies what resources are needed and how those resources will be managed, both people/work resources and physical resources. The plan includes:

- How to acquire needed resources
- Controls for physical resources
- Skills, competencies, capabilities and capacities required for individual work and physical resources
- Project organization chart—with resource categories and reporting relationships
- Roles, responsibilities, and authority levels of team members
- Training strategies and requirements
- Team development methods
- Reward and recognition plan

This plan will vary based on organizational requirements as well as the project approach being used.

Resource Assignment

Using a predictive approach, the team resources are identified, acquired, and assigned to various activities by the project manager or team leads. This assignment includes specifying their individual roles and responsibilities for work activities.

These roles and responsibilities can be shown with a project organization chart or team directory. Individual resource schedules or the overall project schedule with resources identified also show team member roles and responsibilities.

Because of the dependencies and impact on the project, resources should be assigned to activities on the schedule, including the length of their participation and therefore their cost to each project activity. This creates a resource-loaded schedule with associated resource costs. These are combined to determine the overall budget for the project.

A work authorization system may be utilized to identify, acquire, and manage the usage of critical resources, at the right time.

Pre-assignment of team members may occur as a result of a competitive proposal, or if the project is dependent upon an individual's specialized knowledge or skill set.

Resource Calendars

Identify working days, shifts, and when specific resources are made available to the project.

To schedule resources using a predictive approach, knowing the working schedules and availability for individuals and group members during a planned activity is important. Resource calendars are used to identify when certain team members and physical resources will be available during the project.

Understanding availability, skills, and experience level, especially of key or critical resources, is important when assignments are made to activities. Their availability, or lack thereof, may need to be taken into consideration and scheduled activities modified.

Just as the schedule is progressively elaborated to include additional detail regarding activities, so should the resource calendar be continually updated to provide the most recent and accurate information regarding availability.

Pre-Assignment Tools

It is often beneficial to assess potential team members for various roles on the project. Some tools that can be used to help determine resource viability for the project — as well as assessment during the project — include:

- Attitudinal surveys
- Specific assessments
- Structured interviews
- Ability tests

Responsibilities Assignment

The assignment of responsibilities to team members must be tailored based on the team, the needs, and the project approach. This includes considering both technical and interpersonal skills.

When a predictive approach is used, the work is assigned to various team members. Assignments may be based on:

- Experience – Does the team member have the relevant experience to carry out the activity?
- Knowledge – Does the team member have appropriate information about the customer's need, prior implementations, and the nuances of this project?
- Skills – Does the team member have the pertinent skills?
- Attitude – Can the team member collaborate with other team members?
- Location or geographic factors – Are there specifics to consider regarding team member location, time zone, and communication needs?

Responsibility Assignment Tools

A responsibility assignment matrix (or RAM) is a grid showing the project resources assigned to each work package or work activity.

The RAM shows a check mark to signify involvement, without specifying the role played by individual resources. This creates a visible representation of task accountability.

- *RACI Chart*

A common type of responsibility assignment matrix (RAM) where Responsible, Accountable, Consulted, and Informed statuses define the involvement of team members and stakeholders in project activities.

	Product Owner	Project Manager	Business Analyst	Developer
Activity A	A	I		R
Activity B		R	A	
Activity C		A		R
Activity D		C	R	A
Activity E		R	A	

The RACI expands the RAM to include the role of the individuals assigned and is the most used method. RACI charts are often used to document the role and accountability of individuals working on activities in a predictive approach. Created and maintained by the project manager, a RACI chart can be done early in the project as part of pre-assignment and may only "assign" a resource type. It is further refined as individual team members are assigned to individual work activities and tasks.

It can also be extended to identify stakeholders involved in activities, especially to note those who should be consulted and informed of decisions—as well as identifying who will approve the result of the work.

The degree of involvement is defined by the following indicators:

Responsible (R)—indicates the resource involved in doing the work on a task or activity to create a deliverable. There is at least one responsible person per task, typically a team member.

Accountable (A)—indicates the individual who delegates, ensures understanding of the expectations, and reviews the project work, often also approving the result. There should be only one accountable person, who is in a leadership or management role within the project team for each task or activity.

Consulted (C)—usually a stakeholder or expert providing input and feedback on the project work. Not every task needs this role, but it should be reviewed carefully.

Informed (I)—usually a stakeholder, not necessarily in a decision-making role, who needs to be aware of the work to ensure there is not a negative impact to existing work.

Resource Planning: Adaptive

Because adaptive teams are organized and formed before the project requirements are identified, many of the items in the resource management plan for a predictive approach do not apply. It differs especially when it comes to determining the resources needed for various activities. For projects using an adaptive approach, this process is reversed.

Resource Assignment

Adaptive teams treat and assign resources in quite a different way. Adaptive approaches utilize self-organization and self-assignment for work by team members rather than assignment by a project manager. Teams are the focus, not the individual. So, teams are assembled, and they then determine how best to self-organize and distribute the work among the team members.

Team members are often a combination of generalists and specialists. The preference is for more generalists, as the team composition very seldom changes to meet individual project requirements. Such teams can have the ability to cover more areas and be more flexible in delivering the results.

Resource Planning: Hybrid

In hybrid projects the project manager or team lead works with the team to make decisions about roles and responsibilities. Since adaptive teams are self-organizing and seldom identify roles and responsibilities or assignment to individual work activities, the portion of a hybrid project using an adaptive approach would not be shown on either a RAM or RACI matrix.

Regardless of the approach used, the team and individuals who have been assigned tasks must understand that they are accountable for completing the committed work. In adaptive projects this is a key component of the iteration planning meeting. The entire team makes commitments to tasks, rather than individuals being assigned.

Key Concepts Covered

- Resource management plan
- Resource requirements
- Resource assignment

ECO Coverage

- Build a team (1.6)
  - Deduce project resource requirements (1.6.2)

Check Your Progress

1. As a project manager, you can assess potential team members for various roles on the project. Some tools and techniques can be used to help determine each potential team member's capability for the project. Which of the following are a tool or technique you could use? (Choose 3)

   A. Attitudinal surveys

   B. RACI chart

   C. Structured interviews

   D. Ability tests

   E. Stakeholder Engagement Assessment Matrix (SEAM)

2. While working on a housing project you need to find out if any of your team members are available to work during the upcoming weekend. Which of the following will help you in this situation?

   A. RAM chart

B. RACI chart

C. H.R. Resource directory

D. Resource breakdown structure (RBS)

E. Resource calendar

3. RACI charts are often used to document the role and accountability of individuals working on activities in a predictive approach. Which of the following terms are used to identify a person's role in an activity? (Choose 4}

A. Responsible

B. Accountable

C. Consult

D. Inform

E. Advise

4. Resources include both people and physical resources such as equipment, materials, facilities, and infrastructure needed to conduct the project activities. These needed resources are identified as activity resource estimates and are often expressed as a probability or range. Is this statement true or false?

A. True

B. False

5. Which of the following are scrum ceremonies? (Choose 3)

A. Conduct daily standups

B. Conduct sprint planning meeting

C. Review product by demonstrating it at the end of a sprint

D. Prepare project scope statement

E. Conduct a quality audit

Answers

1. A, C, D

2. E

3. A, B, C, D

4. True

5. A, B, C

Plan Project Procurements

The processes regarding procurements do not differ between the various development approaches, but the contracts used are different. This is mainly due to whether the deliverables are identified in the contract, as they are for predictive approaches, or are closer to staff augmentation support for adaptive projects.

Exam Tip: Most procurement questions will be related to traditional procurement activities and documents used with predictive approaches. The actual activities performed by the project manager in this area are defined specifically by the organization.

External Resource Requirements

Sometimes the individuals or equipment required to complete the project are not part of the team. In those cases, it is necessary to look beyond the team to get the needed people or equipment. Many of these processes are identified in the enterprise environmental factors (EEFs) and pertain to the way the project manager will work with the procurement department to obtain resources. This also addresses the authority of the procurement manager in executing a contract.

In a centralized environment, a procurement manager manages many contracts with standardized company practices, but procurement expertise is in the procurement organization, rather than in the project.

In a decentralized environment, the procurement resource may be assigned specifically to a contract and report directly to the project manager. This allows direct access to contracting expertise and closer working relationships with the project manager and team. This can lead to duplication of effort with similar contracts, or sellers, across multiple projects.

Make-or-buy decisions are made regarding the external purchase versus internal manufacture of a product. This, along with other options, has become part of the procurement strategy. The make-or-buy analysis helps determine the best option for the project and team. This process includes gathering and organizing data about product/service requirements and analyzing data against available alternatives, including the purchase or internal development of the product.

When considering resource requirements against the budget and timeline, questions about how a required product or service can be obtained might include:

- Do we buy it? Or should we try to make it in-house?
- How do the budget or quality metrics impact the schedule?
- Is the skill or capability of the resource needed beyond the project?

- Do these resources exist somewhere else in the organization?
- Will they be available at the time needed by the project?
- How steep is the learning curve, for both project requirements and the activity supported?
- Would outsourcing to an external source allow the team to focus on other activities?

Trade-offs include:

Reasons to "Make"	Reasons to "Buy"
Cost	Cost
Integration of operations	Supplier expertise
Idle existing capacity	Small volume costs too high
Direction control/customization	Limited capacity/time
Proprietary design	Augment labor force
Poor supplier experiences	Maintain multiple sources/reduce risk
Stabilize workforce	Indirect control is acceptable

Another option not often considered is borrowing a resource from another team or temporarily outsourcing a product or service, rather than taking longer to perform the work.

Procurement Strategy

Once the make-or-buy analysis is complete and the decision is made to acquire from outside the project, a procurement strategy should be identified.

It is important to decide on the approach used to acquire resources, the type of legally binding agreement(s) to use, and how the process will be completed in phases. The organization's governance usually guides these decisions but may require tailoring to meet the project's specific needs.

There are four areas to take into consideration:

- Prerequisite OPAs—The organizational procurement strategy within which the work must be performed. This includes the organization's finance or procurement departments.
- Acquisition method—This refers to the processes required to obtain external resources and often is based on predefined purchase limits. This may require

defined bidding processes and templates, preapproved vendors, and approved contract types.

- Contract types — The definition and usage of different types of contracts identified by the organization to meet different needs.

- Delivery method: professional services — Delivery including buyer/services provider with no subcontracting, buyer/services provider with subcontracting allowed, joint ventures between buyers and services provider, and buyer/services provider acting as the representative.

- Delivery method: industrial or commercial construction — Delivery including turnkey, design-build (DB), design bid build (DBB), design-build-operate (DBO), build-own operate transfer (BOOT), etc.

- Procurement phases — The processes involved, from requesting an external need to identifying and selecting a seller under a contract and then working to ensure the contract terms and conditions are met and allowing the contract to be closed.

Procurement Management Plan

A component of the project or program management plan that describes how a project team will acquire goods and services outside the performing organization.

This plan is usually tied to the organization's procurement function and helps identify:

- Types of contracts to be used
- The process for obtaining and evaluating bids
- Standardized procurement documents to be mandated
- How providers and contracts will be managed

Procurement SOW

Describes the procurement item in sufficient detail to allow prospective sellers to determine whether they can provide the products, services, or results.

The project manager or lead team members develop the statement of work (SOW). The project develops this SOW to request an organization, external to the team, to provide a product, service, or result through a procurement effort. It is considered a legal agreement like other legal agreements, legally binding on both buyer and seller.

Just as a set of requirements and an approved scope statement are needed for a project, so is a statement of work needed to provide a potential seller with a clear understanding of what is expected to be delivered. These are found more often in contracts for services or results, rather than for material. Specifications for the latter still must be provided, but this is usually not referred to as a SOW.

The SOW includes the requirements and the parts of the scope baseline pertaining to this procurement and should identify those items provided through a procurement agreement. These must be written in a clear, complete, and concise manner with the detail necessary for a seller to estimate the time and cost required to deliver the result.

The buyer provides many different types of information to the seller, mostly pertaining to the specifications and quality elements required. This information can also identify when and where the performance of this contract is to be conducted.

Procurement Documents

Documents used in bid and proposal activities, including the buyer's invitation for bid, expression of interest (EOI), invitation for negotiations, request for information (RFI), request for quotation (RFQ), request for proposal (RFP), and seller's responses.

Many procurement documents are tied to legal contracts and follow specific procedures of the organization.

Request for Quotation (RFQ) – Request for the amount charged to provide the result, often with no additional detail as to how the amount was determined. This can also be called a bid, tender, or quote. It does not constitute an agreement but allows the buyer to determine the best response to meet the requested need.

Invitation for Bid (IFB) – Usually part of a more formal procurement process. The IFB is sent or published to a wide range of potential sellers to determine those specifically interested in the next step of the procurement process.

Request for Information (RFI) – If the seller or their products or services are not well known to the organization, an RFI can be sent to gather additional information, which is then used to pare down the list of potential sellers.

Request for Proposal (RFP) – Usually a very formal and time-consuming document to develop. As a result, it is normally reserved for critical or high-price items. This should specifically define what is being requested, but it often also includes questions regarding the result and how it will be delivered, including management philosophy and the types of resources included. There can also be questions regarding the seller organization in general, and references are often requested. Usually, the answers to these questions are requested to be returned separately from the proposed cost. In this way, an initial decision can be made based on the merits of the seller and the way they would deliver the results, separate from the final proposed cost.

Expression of Interest (EOI) – A nonbinding formal offer made by one party to another to ensure the latter is aware of the former's level of interest in collaborating to achieve a common goal or provide a product. Used more often before a formal request has been distributed.

Bid and Proposal Activities

Formal RFP Process

A type of procurement document used to request proposals from prospective sellers of products or services. It may have a narrower or more specific meaning in some application areas.

An RFP is used by many organizations to acquire resources, goods, or services from outside organizations. These take time to develop the questions, submit to prospective bidders, receive and evaluate the proposals, finalize the selection of the seller, and complete the legal contract. The procurement officer or department can provide any procedures or regulations to be followed in these processes.

Bidder Conferences

Meetings with prospective sellers prior to the preparation of a bid or proposal to ensure all prospective vendors have a clear and common understanding of the procurement. Also called vendor conferences, pre-bid conferences, or contractor conferences.

Where prospective bidders have additional questions regarding the content of the RFP, a bidder conference is held to collect and answer all questions. This is done to ensure all bidders have a clear understanding of the requirements of the contract. These may be done in person and on-site or virtually. These involve collecting questions from all and then distributing the answers to all questions to all bidders. **All** communications must be given to **all** bidders, and no additional information is provided only to a select few, thus avoiding preferential treatment. Not utilizing this single point of contact is usually grounds for disqualification as a potential conflict of interest.

Source Selection Criteria

A set of attributes or elements, desired by the buyer, that a seller is required to meet or exceed to be selected for a contract.

Additional documents are developed concurrently with the RFP, or shortly afterward, to identify the various ways the responses or proposals from the potential seller will be evaluated. These criteria may be objective and/or subjective. There may also be criteria required by the purchasing department or other departments within the organization to be included in the selection process, as defined by regulations or policies of the buyer's organization. Criteria may include:

- Weighting systems — A grid listing all the criteria and assigning a numeric weight to each. Each seller is then scored against each criterion, with the seller having the highest score being selected.

- Independent estimates — The buyer hires an external resource, usually having previous experience with the required effort but not qualified to bid, to help estimate the various proposals. Helps ensure that the bids are realistic for the work requested.

- Screening systems — A prequalification tool used to screen out nonqualified vendors, often including a list of "showstopper" criteria the seller must achieve to be considered for the contract.

- Sellers' rating systems — A repository of past performance evaluations of the sellers to give the buyer an idea of how the seller may perform on the current proposal if selected.

- Expert judgment — Utilizing one or more multidisciplinary teams to review specific parts of the proposals, including cost, technology, security, and legal review teams.

Criteria often include a determination as to whether the seller understands the requirements and capabilities specified in the RFP. The way the seller proposes to provide both the management oversight and the technical approach to be used should be understood.

Additional items considered as part of the source selection criteria include:

- Overall or life cycle cost (LCC)
- Understanding of need
- Technical capability
- Management approach
- Warranty of product or service
- Financial capacity
- Production capacity and interest
- Business size and type
- Past performance of sellers
- References
- Intellectual property rights
- Proprietary rights

The seller organization is reviewed to ensure it can provide the financial and production capacity requirements of the effort. This can include review of previous performance as well as follow-up with provided references.

Another area of great concern to some projects is the intellectual property of both the seller and the buyer and the proprietary rights to the result of the agreement. Since many projects include highly sensitive areas producing results utilizing specific components requiring protection by the buyer and/or seller, these should have been identified in the RFP, and the proposal or response should indicate how they will be maintained.

The source selection criteria should be of the same importance as the development of the RFP.

Noncompetitive Selection

There are certain noncompetitive types of procurement. These include:

- Sole source provider—the only provider available for the requested work, previously identified, evaluated, and given that designation by the organization
- Single source provider—choice of only one provider, even though others are possible, often because of previous relationships, high quality, low cost, or short turnaround times

Qualified Vendors

Most organizations have a working list of qualified vendors. These have been reviewed based on past performance by the procurement organization. They are often considered "preferred" because they have already been in the system and are proven to deliver successful results. This saves a lot of time in finalizing any procurement request.

One source of qualified vendors, beyond the purchasing group, is within the lessons learned repository, with potential historical data regarding their usage and results.

This does not mean another vendor can't be used, but it will often take a lot of time and paperwork to get a new vendor set up with the organization.

Benefits to the buyer include:

- Familiarity with the seller's management structure, technical capabilities, methods, procedures, and standards.
- The quality of previous deliverables is well known and understood, often serving as a yardstick to measure other potential vendors.
- Establishment of (or existence of) a "master services agreement" with basic contractual "rules of engagement" defined.

Contracts

A contract is a mutually binding and often legal agreement obligating the seller to provide the specified project or service or result and obligating the buyer to pay for it.

There are multiple types of contracts, and it is important to understand both the details included in a contract and the risks associated with the various contract types. These different contracts result in different benefits to the buyer, the seller, or both.

Because of the legal nature of a contract, a strong relationship is established between both parties. Often a positive result of an initial contract will lead to future collaboration efforts. These associations may even become established, long-term partnerships between the two organizations.

Project professionals actively participate in providing requirements for contracts, often reviewing the proposals submitted and building successful relationships with vendors and suppliers after the contract has been finalized. Negotiating contracts in good faith is important to help ensure a positive working relationship between the parties.

Adaptive projects go a step further by valuing customer collaboration over contract negotiation, pursuing a shared risk-reward relationship where all sides, including the project, benefit.

Components of Contracts

The contract is a legally binding document that includes a description of what is being purchased and the terms and conditions, or Ts & Cs, agreed upon by both the seller and the buyer.

The required elements of a contract include:

- Offer—Description of work, including both the deliverables and the scope.
- Acceptance—Describes the explicit criteria under which the buyer will accept the product or service delivered by the seller.
- Capacity—The seller's physical and/or financial capability to deliver the product or service according to the specifications in the contract.
- Consideration—What the seller will receive for performing the work of producing the product or service for the buyer, in the form of direct monetary compensation to the seller or some other form of compensation.
- Legal purpose—The contract must be legal under federal, state, or local laws.

Additional contract information normally includes:

- Any delivery dates and schedule information associated with the work
- Identification of authority, where appropriate, especially regarding the authority to sign or administer the contract
- How changes to the contract are to be handled
- Roles and responsibilities of both parties
- Management of technical and business aspects, including reporting requirements
- Price and payment terms, related to the "obligation" aspect referring to the seller providing and the buyer paying for the specific product, service, or result
- Provisions for termination, including premature closure obligations
- Applicable guarantees and warranties
- Intellectual property
- Security, confidentiality, data privacy

Additional Contract Terms

There are some additional terms often included in a contract, and the project manager needs to understand their meaning, if included:

- *Agent*—Authorized representatives from both the buyer's and seller's organizations.
- *Assignment*—One party can assign the contracted rights or obligations to another party.
- *Confidentiality*—Certain information relating to the contract must be kept confidential, and failure to do so may result in a breach or default of the contract.
- *Force majeure*—A standard disclaimer that refers to Acts of God, describing a situation where neither the seller nor the buyer can be held accountable or responsible for an event.
- *Indemnification or liability*—Defines who is responsible for injury, damage, or accidents.
- *Intellectual property*—Defines who owns any patents, designs, trademarks, copyrights, or product that was developed or used during the contract.
- *Privity*—The prime contractor can use subcontractors, with the buyer having no contractual control over the sub, since the sub is contracted to the prime contractor.
- *Retainage*—Specific amounts withheld from each payment to ensure delivery of the final product—usually in the 5%–10% range.

- *Teaming agreements*—Legal contractual agreements between two or more parties that define the buyer–seller relationship. These are usually arranged to pursue a new business opportunity or to optimize the strength of each organization to produce a better product, but they are only valid for the duration of the agreement.

- *Time is of the essence*—Means the delivery dates are contractually binding, and the procurement activity is time constrained, with any delay being considered a cardinal breach of contract.

- *Waivers*—Contract statements specifying that rights under the contract may not be waived, either intentionally or unintentionally, unless agreed to by both parties.

- *Work made for hire*—The buyer owns all contracted work.

Traditional Contract Types

There are three basic types of contracts: fixed-price, cost-reimbursable, and time-and-material.

Fixed-Price

Sets a fixed total price for a defined product, service, or result; used when requirements are well defined and no significant scope changes are expected.

These are especially applicable when there are well-defined requirements, and no changes are expected. Clearly written statements of work should be made available to allow the seller to understand what is being requested and determine the cost to provide the result as well as an acceptable profit margin.

If change orders to these types of contracts are requested, they will most likely increase price. This often happens when the initial cost was lowballed to win the contract. Additionally, a bait-and-switch tactic may be used to meet the agreed-upon price with substitutions of lower quality resources.

There are several variations of fixed-price contracts:

- *Firm fixed-price contracts (FFPS)* set the fixed price at the beginning with no changes or adjustments included. This is the most common type of contract and the one most preferred by organizations, as the price is set at the outset and not subject to change unless the scope of the work changes.

- *Fixed-price with an incentive fee (FPIF)* contracts can include an additional amount or percentage earned by the seller if a specified incentive is met. This is often used when additional effort may result in an early delivery or higher quality beyond the amount specified in the contract. Performance targets are established at the outset, and the final contract price is determined after completion of all work, based on the performance of the seller. Under these types of contracts, a ceiling price is set, and the seller is obligated to complete the work and assume all costs above the ceiling. This is known as the point of total assumption.

- *Fixed-price with economic price adjustments (FPEPA)* contracts are used on multiyear projects to handle the impact of inflation on a fixed price determined at the beginning of the contract. A reliable financial index is used to precisely adjust the final price. These contracts often are used with preapproved vendors or when international payments are required.

Cost-Plus

Contracts used for projects with expected, significant scope changes.

These contracts are often used for project work when less is known at the beginning of the contract or when significant scope changes are expected.

When cost-plus contracts are used, the seller is not required to determine what the costs will be ahead of schedule but rather is reimbursed for all legitimate, actual costs, including an amount to cover the profit margin for the seller. These may also include financial incentive clauses for when the seller exceeds or falls below a defined objective, such as cost, schedule, or technical performance targets.

Since the repayments are made based on the actual costs, there must be an open relationship between the buyer and the seller allowing the seller's "books" to be examined if requested. The invoices for these costs need to be audited to ensure the charges are applicable to the contract, and no additional charges above those agreed upon are included.

Variations of these cost-plus contracts include:

- *Cost-plus fixed fee (CPFF)* contracts reimburse the seller for all allowable costs and include an additional fixed fee amount calculated as a percentage of the initial estimated project costs. The fee is paid for the completed work regardless of the performance of the seller at the end of the contract.
- *Cost-plus incentive fee (CPIF)* contracts include an additional amount above the reimbursement for the actual cost, which is based on some identified incentive. Both the seller and the buyer share costs from any difference between the target and actual cost, based upon a predefined target cost.
- *Cost-plus award fee (CPAF)* contracts include an award fee to cover the seller's profit. The seller is reimbursed for all legitimate costs, but most of the fee earned is based upon the satisfaction of certain broad-based, subjective performance

criteria specified at the time of the contract. The buyer determines the amount of the fee the seller receives, which is not subject to appeal by the seller.

Exam Tip: These Cost-Plus contracts may also be referred to as Cost-Reimbursable.

Time-and-Material (T&M)

Time-and-material contracts are used when the buyer reimburses the seller for the time spent working on contract activities as well as any expenses incurred. This type of contract is often used for staff augmentation, especially where labor resources are required with skills and expertise not available internally. Unless not-to-exceed limits on schedule and costs are included, these contracts often end up involving open-ended and unknown total costs.

Invoices for both time and expenses should be closely reviewed to ensure hours were not padded or expenses included that were not in the agreement. To adhere to a predetermined time frame, you need to clearly define deliverables and specific milestones for the work.

Term Contract

A variation of the time and material contract is a term contract. It only addresses the time spent delivering a set amount of work over a set period and is measured in staff-hours or a similar unit.

Contract Risk

Contracts are often used as a response to an identified risk. In each type of contract there are risks to either the buyer or the seller.

In a fixed-price contract, the risk lies with the seller. The seller must fully understand the requested requirements and then determine the cost to deliver those requirements, as well as some additional profit. If the requirements are not well defined, there is a risk that the seller will require additional costs beyond the stated amount to fulfill the contract requirements.

The opposite risk occurs in a time-and-material contract. The seller is assured that all work and expenses will be paid by the buyer. The buyer, on the other hand, does not know the final cost of the work. To mitigate this risk, the buyer will often place a ceiling on the cost or identify specifically what costs will be covered.

When a cost-plus contract is used, the risk is shared by both the seller and the buyer. This type of contract does require collaboration and trust between the two parties.

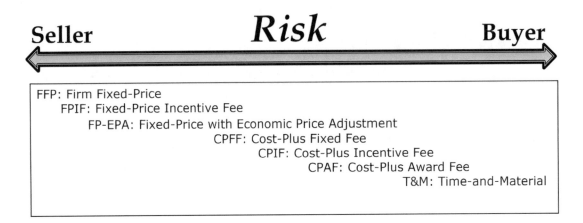

Adaptive/Agile Contract Types

The main difference between traditional and adaptive contracts is that adaptive contracts don't include identification of deliverables to be created, but rather emphasize the working agreements and collaboration between the parties.

- *Multi-Tiered Structure*—Achieves flexibility by including different content related to the contract in different documents. This could include establishing a master service agreement for fixed items. Variable items could be identified in a schedule of services or possibly a work order. A SOW could also be attached to provide additional specific project information.

- *Emphasize Value Delivered*—Envisions incremental value delivery in milestones or phase gates. Both the milestones and payment terms are based on the value delivered at the milestone. This focuses on encouraging feedback during product development.

- *Fixed Price Increments*—Break the scope into smaller pieces. Micro-deliverables provide more control over cost and budget while limiting the supplier's financial risk.

- *Not-to-Exceed Time-and-Materials*—Like the traditional time-and-material contract with additional limits on potential risk. The budget is limited to a fixed amount, while allowing the customer to add or remove items. The work must be monitored to avoid overage, or contingency hours should be added.

- *Graduated Time-and-Materials*—A time-and-material contract that shares financial risk by connecting quality and timely delivery of work to the financial award. This utilizes the DoD and provides a reward for early delivery or reduction for late delivery.

- *Early Cancellation Option* — Focuses on value delivery rather than scope by enabling a flexible delivery of scope, including early completion with a cancellation fee paid. This is often referred to as "payment for nothing, change is free."

- *Dynamic Scope Option* — For contracts with a fixed budget, enabling innovation while limiting risk. This allows the option to vary scope and fund innovation at specific points, including adjusting features, while limiting risk to the supplier.

- *Team Augmentation* — Like the traditional staff augmentation contract, with a focus on collaboration to enable flexible scope by embedding the supplier resource directly into the customer organization. Funding is based on the team resource(s) rather than the scope.

Hybrid Contracts

In addition to the various predictive or adaptive contracts, a Completion Contract may represent the completion of the product delivered from the seller/vendor to the buyer and the buyer accepts the product.

Key Concepts Covered

- Procurement strategy
- Procurement management plan
- Procurement documents
- Contracts

ECO Coverage

- Build a team (1.6)
  - Deduce project resource requirements (1.6.2)

- Plan and management procurement (resources) (2.11)
  - Define resource requirements and needs (2.11.2)
  - Manage suppliers/contracts (2.11.3)
  - Plan and manage procurement strategy (2.11.4)
  - Develop a delivery solution (2.11.5)

Check Your Progress

1. A contract is a formal agreement between two parties, and as a project manager, you should have a copy of it so you can refer to the terms and conditions of the contract. Which of the following statements are true about contracts? (Choose 3)

    A. A contract cannot be cancelled at any time by the buyer for a convenience

    B. A contract can help reduce project risk

    C. A contract is legally binding unless it is in violation of applicable law

    D. Contracts are legally binding and backed by the judicial court system in most countries

2. You recently completed a detailed SOW for an expensive item you need to purchase for your project. You have identified the source selection criteria, terms and conditions, and the type of contract you want to use. You are required to send a proposal to at least three vendors, but you have decided to send the SOW to five venders to get a more competitive bid. What tools and techniques will you use in the next project management process?

    A. Market research, make or buy analysis, and expert judgment

    B. Bidder conference

    C. Procurement audits

    D. Procurement negotiations

    E. Contract change control system

3. The main difference between traditional and adaptive contracts is that adaptive contracts don't include identification of deliverables to be created, but rather emphasize the working agreements and collaboration between the parties. Which of the following are types of contracts that agile projects can use? (Choose 2}

    A. Fixed price increments

    B. Firm fixed price

    C. Not-to-exceed time-and-materials

    D. Cost Plus Incentive fee

    E. Fixed price with economic price adjustments

4. For a Firm Fixed Price, the risk is greater for the seller. Is this statement true or false?

    A. True

    B. False

5. You've just finished negotiating the terms and conditions of a contract and reached an agreement with a vendor. You sent the contract that was signed by the authorized executive of the vendor to your purchasing department for signature and approval. What should the project manager do next?

    A. Identify required external project resources

    B. Estimate cost of contract

    C. Inform sponsor of the need for external resources

    D. Monitor and control work under the contract

Answers

1. B, C, D
2. B
3. A, C
4. True
5. D

Plan Project Budget

Budget and cost are primarily concerned with the costs of both the people doing the work and the physical resources, such as equipment, vehicles, computers, etc., needed to meet the scope, schedule, and quality requirements to complete project activities. It may also consider the subsequent recurring costs to use, maintain, and support the project results after completion of the project.

It is important to recognize that stakeholders measure project costs differently and at different times; therefore, reporting needs in this area may vary widely.

Even though the project may have been selected based on expected financial performance of the product or result, both the prediction and analysis of the performance are beyond the project scope, although it is important for project managers to understand these performance expectations.

Budget Planning

When putting together the project's budget, consider the cost of activities and resources and the quality and value requirements, as well as the importance of the investment, cost, and project budget to the organization.

Resource costs for project resources are determined at different times during the project and in different ways, depending on the approach used.

The budget creation process is highly dependent on the predictive, adaptive, or hybrid approach selected and the project life cycle.

In predictive projects, a budget is set during project planning when the cost baseline is approved and only changes if a change request is approved.

In adaptive approaches, the budget is based on the number and cost of the combined resources and the amount of time worked. This budget could be set for a portion of the work, maybe for each release rather than the entire project. This provides flexibility to deliver the greatest value within fixed time and costs over shorter periods.

In hybrid projects, the predictive portion of the work can be budgeted based on the scope and resources, while the adaptive portions are based on the number of team members and the combined resource cost. Changes inherent in these types of projects must be considered and determination made as to how they might affect the budget. This allows for adaptability while still including some confidence and understanding in the project's overall cost.

Budget Challenges

Changes will occur, even in the best-planned project. There could be new or changing project requirements, new risks, changes to probability/impact of existing risks, or an array of other external impacts. These will all need to be identified and considered as potential risks, regardless of the project approach and budgeting activities.

While the organization's approach to budgeting will be a major factor in the design of the project budget, it shouldn't be the only factor.

The organization and individual stakeholders have different priorities regarding the need for speed of delivery, agility, value, and high quality. The determination of the importance of these, needs to be balanced when determining the budget for the project.

Because projects may often be delivered differently than in the past, project managers need to utilize their interpersonal skills to communicate, influence, and collaborate with internal stakeholders, including key financial stakeholders, to consider new possibilities for project budgeting and funding.

Cost Management Plan

A project or program management plan component that describes how costs will be planned, structured, and controlled.

Cost Management Plan Components

This plan establishes the criteria for several areas including:

- Units of measure to indicate how staff time, currency, weights, and measures will be specified for each resource.

- Level of precision or accuracy identifying whether estimated activity costs will be rounded up or down, based on the activity scope and magnitude of the project and the acceptable range, or allowable percentage variation, used to determine realistic cost estimates, including possible amounts for contingencies.

- Organizational procedures for cost including possible control accounts identified for a WBS work package to link the accounting for the work directly to the accounting system.

- Identified variance, tolerance, and control thresholds indicating the agreed-upon variation allowed before some action needs to be taken. These provide insight into how much leeway a project manager has during the project, especially regarding costs. These cost thresholds are like the schedule thresholds and are typically expressed as a percentage variation from the cost baseline, or as individual items when determining human work or physical resource costs.

- Rules for earned value performance measurement for cost to define the WBS work package activities where the measurement of control accounts will be performed using earned value techniques, including weighted milestones, fixed formula, percent complete to be used, tracking methodologies, cost-related earned value equations (CV, CPI), and calculation of projected estimate at completion (EAC) forecasts.

- Various financial reports, including their frequency and formats, specified in conjunction with the communication plan.

Additional details unique to cost management activities include:

- Descriptions of strategic funding choices
- Procedures to account for currency exchange rate changes
- Procedures for reporting and recording organizational project costs.

The cost management processes, how they will be applied for this project, and any associated tools and techniques are identified at this time. This includes how the cost factors, and the final budget will be estimated, budgeted, monitored, and controlled. This enables effective and efficient performance and coordination with other cost-related activities.

It also identifies any specific organizational policies, procedures, and required documentation related to managing project costs.

Exam Tip: An additional cost concept is the life cycle cost, or "total cost of ownership." This includes not only the cost to develop the result or product but also the cost to maintain the product over its usable lifetime.

Historical Information

Experience from previous projects is another important component of the budgeting process. Historical project information contains valuable data about cost-estimating successes and shortcomings and can be used to develop cost estimates for activities and work packages in similar projects.

It always makes sense to review previous activity cost estimates from similar projects. This is valuable cost-estimating information, including both successes and shortcomings. Both analogous and parametric estimates based on historical information can be used. The actual numbers may have to be adjusted based on when the project was performed and how much change may have occurred since then, especially regarding cost.

Budget Planning: Predictive

Budget at Completion: The sum of all budgets established for the work to be performed.

Budget planning is based on the decisions identified in the cost management plan, including the estimating techniques used to assign costs to individual activities. Cost aggregation is used to combine the individual lower-level estimates associated with the various work packages or cost control accounts resulting in the budget at completion (BAC) or cost baseline. Additional contingencies may be needed to address identified high-level risks and can be added to activities, work packages, or the overall budget.

This cost baseline will be used to monitor, measure, and control cost performance throughout the project, comparing actual costs to those budgeted for specific times during the project. As one of the approved baselines, it can only be changed through a formal change control process.

The individual activity costs need to be estimated to determine the overall cost for a predictive project. These estimates can be at the activity level and/or summarized at the work package level. They include:

- Direct labor
- Direct cost

- Materials
- Equipment
- Facilities
- Services
- Information technology
- Contingency reserves

There is always a certain amount of uncertainty that exists at the beginning of a project. This can be reduced as more information is understood and a better estimate of time or cost can be made. This is often depicted by the cone of uncertainty.

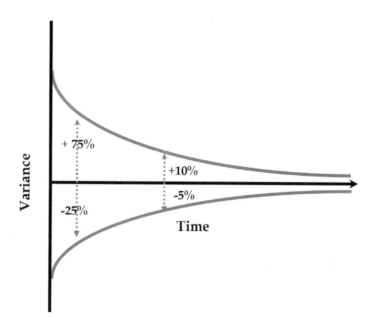

There are a number of terms that refer to estimates at different times in the project, including the accuracy:

- *Rough Order of Magnitude (ROM)*

  Identified early in the project and developed without analysis or availability of detailed data. It is often based on high-level historical data, expert judgment, or a costing model.

  Accuracy: -25% to +75%

- *Definitive (or "Control" or "Detailed") Estimate*

  Based on additional detailed information about the project work and developed by estimating the cost for each WBS work package and its associated activities.

  Accuracy: –5% to +10%

- *Phased (or "Rolling Wave" or "Moving Window") Estimate*

  While the current phase can be estimated more accurately (perhaps at a definitive level), future phases use a less-detailed estimate (using rolling wave and perhaps a ROM) for some later parts of the work.

Resource Costs

The scope, schedule, and their activities identify the resources needed to perform the work. The organization's initial resource cost is usually based on a blended rate for identified resources according to an average skill or capability. For external workers as part of a contract, their actual rate (hourly or daily) is used in the development of the budget.

Actual selection and assignment of resources often is determined based on criteria regarding their availability, experience, and attitude. The actual skill levels or capabilities of the final resources will often require modification of the cost of both individual activities and the overall budget.

Cost Baseline

The cost baseline is the approved version of the time-phased project budget, excluding any management reserves.

This is often referred to as BAC—budget at completion and used during project execution for comparison to actual results.

Project Budget	Management Reserve			
	Cost Baseline	Control Accounts	Contingency Reserve	
			Work Package Cost Estimates	Activity Contingency Reserve
				Activity Cost Estimates

A bottom-up approach is usually used to aggregate the components of the cost baseline:

- Activity costs (plus contingency) — allocated to the time when the cost would be incurred
- Work package cost (plus contingency) — now referred to as work cost estimates
- Cost baselines (potentially with additional contingency)

The cost baseline is the number the project manager monitors and measures cost performance against for the project. It can only be changed through formal change control procedures.

Exam Tip: Cost baseline is the cost of all activities, work packages, project estimates, and contingency reserves. The total project budget includes the cost baseline along with the management reserve.

Project Budget Planning: Adaptive[39]

The adaptive budget is usually estimated based on the project's length of time and assigned resources. It is controlled by the product owner or by higher-level organizational management.

Resource Costs

Adaptive project costs are based on the number of workers, their blended cost, and the time worked. The cost of the resources during a period is referred to as the burn rate and includes:

- Number of team members
- Blended or actual team member rates
- Time of involvement by the team members

Adaptive approaches usually include a blended rate for the team members involved rather than individual rates for different team members. The blended rate for the entire team is then multiplied by the time scheduled to determine the overall budget or burn rate.

If the approach used identifies the cost or point value, and the number of items to be completed during a period is known, then the cost per point can be determined. This would be done by dividing the loaded cost of the resources for a period by the points completed.

---

39   *Agile Practice Guide and Michelle Sliger "Agile estimation techniques." Paper presented at PMI Global Congress 2012* https://www.pmi.org/learning/library/Agile-project-estimation-techniques-6110

Additionally, by knowing the value of the work and the cost per point—a budget can be determined by multiplying the cost per point by the total point value of the items to be completed (plus any additional expenses).

There is an assumption the time involvement will be full-time. Also, most adaptive projects include only the cost of the resources (internal team members and possible contractors). The estimation of the project costs becomes specific as additional information becomes available, like predictive projects.

Cost Baseline

The organization may require a high-level estimation for the entire year but remain open to change as individual releases are approved. Because adaptive projects are broken into smaller parts or releases, the budget is usually done for individual releases, with only a high-level budget identified for the entire anticipated project.

The budget should be based on either current information or a forecast algorithm utilizing historical data or expert guidance—e.g., Lean, Scrum or Kanban historical experience.

Budget revision can be done at various times, depending on how the cost is determined and the velocity achieved by the project team. If additional software or equipment is needed, then those additional costs would be added to the overall project cost.

If the organization is very cost conscious, then the burn rate is continually monitored and adjusted, which often requires changing the budget at various times.

Project Budget Planning: Hybrid

Since the resources and costs will vary when using a hybrid approach, the budget is often separated and then managed according to the portions of the project using either a predictive or adaptive approach.

Key Concepts Covered

- Cost management plan
- Budget planning
- Resource costs
- Cost baseline

ECO Coverage

- Plan and manage budget and resources (2.5)
- Estimate budgetary needs based on the scope of the project and lessons learned from past projects (2.5.1)
- Anticipate future budget challenges (2.5.2)
- Plan and manage resources (2.5.4)

Check Your Progress

1. There is always uncertainty in the beginning of most projects. The cone of uncertainty identifies two levels of uncertainty. What are the two levels of uncertainty?

   A. Rough order of magnitude (ROM)

   B. Definitive estimate

   C. Basis of estimate

   D. Ballpark estimate

2. The project manager is in the final steps of determining the cost baseline for the project and has utilized the cost aggregation method by which activities are summed up to the work package cost and the control accounts and finally to the project cost baseline for the project. What is not included in the project cost baseline?

   A. Activity contingency

   B. Management reserves

   C. Work package contingency

   D. Planning packages

3. The project manager has presented the preliminary project cost estimates to the sponsor, and he is upset about the inexactness of the estimate since it was based upon a previous project conducted 5 years ago. He suggests that the project manager use a more accurate estimating technique. Which of the following techniques will help to provide a more accurate estimate?

   A. Bottom-up estimate

   B. ROM

   C. Heuristic estimates

   D. Parametric estimates

   E. Top-down estimates

4. The cost baseline will be used to monitor, measure, and control the schedule throughout the project, comparing the planned activities to the actual completed activities. Is this statement true or false?

   A. True

   B. False

5. The cost baseline is referred to as the Budget At Completion (BAC) and is what the project team uses to manage and control the expenditures for the project. Which of the items below are part of the cost baseline? (Choose 3)

   A. Activity estimates

   B. Management reserve

   C. Activity contingency

   D. Project budget

   E. Work package cost estimates

Answers

1. A. B
2. B
3. A
4. True
5. A, C, E

Plan Project Risks

Performance Domain:

Uncertainty[40]

The Uncertainty Performance Domain addresses activities and functions with risk and uncertainty.

The following items defined in the glossary relevant to the Uncertainty Performance Domain:

- *Uncertainty—A lack of understanding and awareness of issues, events, paths to follow, or solutions to pursue*

---

40 *PMBOK Guide, Seventh Edition, Section 2.8 – Project Performance Domains*

- *Ambiguity—A state of being unclear, having difficulty in identifying the cause of events, or having multiple options from which to choose*
- *Complexity—A characteristic of a program or project or its environment that is difficult to manage due to human behavior, system behavior, and ambiguity*
- *Volatility—The possibility for rapid and unpredictable change*
- *Risk—A uncertain event or condition that, if it occurs, has a positive or negative effect on one or more project objectives*

Risk

Risk is an uncertain event or condition that, if it occurs, has a positive or negative effect on one or more project objectives.

Project managers must accept things will go wrong on the project. Each project has varying degrees of complexity and takes on unique objectives, therefore introducing different types and severities of risk. With any group of stakeholders there will be conflicting and changing expectations, often resulting in an increased risk of not meeting their expectations.

Risk must be undertaken in a controlled and intentional manner to ensure the value expectations are met. There is always a need to balance risk and reward, including understanding trade-offs for different risk responses. Rather than being reactive to those situations, it is important to understand the source of these risks, as well as their potential impact on the project.

Risk assessment often starts early in the project, including the review of risks identified in the business case and the project charter. Risks are uncertainties that might occur— and if so, they may have different impacts on the project.

Project Risk Strategy

To create the risk strategy for a project, it is important to understand and consider the risk parameters for the organization, stakeholders, and project early in the project. These exist at two levels within every project—individual and overall project risks.

Individual project risks can affect one or more project objectives in a negative or positive way.

Overall project risk is the combination of all sources of uncertainty, including individual risks. This represents the exposure of potential variations in project outcomes to stakeholders.

It is important to understand factors that apply to individuals as well as to the organization and their potential impact on the project, including:

- *Risk Appetite*

The degree of uncertainty an organization or individual is willing to accept in anticipation of a reward.

Risk appetite is the assessment of the organization's or individual's willingness to accept and deal with risks. The various attitudes toward risks are usually classified as:

- Risk seeking—adaptable, resourceful, and unafraid to take action, and likely to identify few threats and overestimate the importance of possible opportunities
- Risk neutral—reasonably comfortable with most uncertainty, resulting in lack of proactive actions and missed opportunities
- Risk averse—feels uncomfortable with uncertainty and ambiguity, seeking security and resolution in the face of risk, tending to overreact to threats and underreact to opportunities

- *Risk Threshold*

The measure of the level of risk exposure above which actions must be taken to address risks proactively, and below which risks may be accepted.

This determines risks too high to accept and low enough to be accepted. It is tied to individual (people) and organizational risk appetites.

- *Risk Tolerance*

The degree, amount or volume of uncertainty an organization or individual can withstand.

Defines the risk exposure level to determine the risks included in the risk register. This also identifies the qualitative (high, medium, low, etc.) and/or quantitative (numerical) definitions of risk rating. It also identifies the maximum level of risk exposure within the project before escalation is required.

Probability and Impact Measures

As part of the risk strategy, definitions of risk probability and impact levels are determined. Quantitative measures are identified, usually based on the risk tolerance of the organization and of key stakeholders. These measures are identified in the risk management plan.

The designated measures include the probability and the potential impact on time, cost, and quality. This may include a separate document with further definitions of the probability and impact levels tied to specific measures. The measures can be simple — just low, medium, and high — or include additional measures, depending on the project needs. This often also includes the threshold for identifying what qualifies a risk as too high or too low to consider within the project.

These definitions need to be used as each risk is identified, especially to help determine the potential risk exposure. Depending on the organization's guidelines, further quantitative analysis may be needed before identifying the appropriate risk responses.

Additional Risk Assessment Factors

In addition to probability and impact, additional characteristics may be considered including:

- *Urgency* — the period of time in which action needs to be taken
- *Proximity* — the period before the risk might have an impact
- *Dormancy* — the period that may elapse after a risk has occurred before it is discovered
- *Manageability* — the relative ease of managing the risk
- *Controllability* — the ability to control the impact of the risk
- *Detectability* — the ease of detecting that the risk is about to or has occurred
- *Connectivity* — the extent to which the risk is related to other risks
- *Strategic impact* — the potential for the risk to influence the organization's strategic objectives
- *Propinquity* — the degree to which the risk is perceived in importance to one or more stakeholders

More information on risk management may be found in *The Standard for Risk Management in Portfolios, Programs, and Projects.*

Project Risk Management: Predictive

Project risk management includes the processes of conducting risk management planning, identification, analysis, response planning, response implementation, and monitoring risk on a project.

Risk management is a systematic process maximizing the probability of positive events and minimizing the probability and consequences of negative events.

Once the initial risk strategy is defined and set, continual refinement is often required. Factors to consider include the size and complexity of the project, its importance, the selection of the appropriate development approach, and the risk appetite and tolerance of the organization and stakeholders. These then lead to the development of the risk management plan.

Risk Management Plan

A component of the project, program, or portfolio management plan describing how risk management activities will be structured and performed.

The risk management plan addresses how risk management activities will be done on the project using both predictive and hybrid approaches, and should include:

- Risk strategy
- Methodology
- Roles and responsibilities
- Funding requirements
- Timing and frequency of reassessment
- Risk identification techniques
- Risk categories
- Stakeholder risk appetite, tolerance, and thresholds
- Definition of risk probability and impact
- Probability and impact matrix
- Analysis using both a subjective and an objective approach
- Appropriate risk responses and plans
- Reporting formats
- Tracking documents including reassessment of risk

Key risk terms include:

- *Opportunity*

A risk that, if developed, would positively affect one or more project objectives.

Positive risks, or opportunities, produce a positive project outcome, and project managers should maximize the probability and consequences of these occurrences.

- *Threat*

A risk that would have a negative effect on one or more project objectives.

Negative risks, or threats, have a negative impact on the project, and project managers should minimize the probability and consequences of these occurring.

- *Issue*

A current condition or situation that may have an impact on the project objectives.

Once a potential risk is identified as having occurred, it now becomes an issue and must be addressed immediately. It is recorded in the issue log.

- *Trigger*

An event or situation indicating a risk is about to occur.

Rather than waiting until a risk happens, it is important to identify a trigger and monitor the trigger situation indicating that the risk is about to happen or has happened.

Because of their uncertainty, both opportunities (positive risks) and threats (negative risks) must be identified.

Risk Types

For predictive projects, there are three main types of risks:

- Pure risks—representing a threat or loss only
- Business risks—representing an opportunity at the organizational level for gain or loss
- Project risks—identified risks with the impact determined and handled at the project level for both opportunities and threats
- Emergent risks—"unknown unknowns" only recognized once they have occurred
- Event risks—uncertain future events that may or may not occur
- Non-event risks—uncertainty related to critical characteristics of a planned activity or decision (also referred to as a variability or ambiguity risk)

The different types of risks are handled differently depending on the project approach. Regardless of the approach, the two factors to consider for each identified risk include:

- Probability the risk will occur
- Impact if it occurs

Risk Identification Techniques

The identification of risks should be done as soon as the project is initiated. Some risks are identified on initiating documents, including the business case and other agreements, such as a statement of work for the project.

Another common method includes utilizing a risk workshop. This special meeting might include in addition to the project team members, the project sponsor, SMEs, customer representatives, and other stakeholders. The audience and frequency of the meeting is dependent on the size and criticality of the project.

Several techniques are used to identify risks. They are very similar to those used to identify and analyze requirements, and include:

- Data gathering and analysis
- Risk breakdown structure (RBS)
- Brainstorming or brainwriting
- Nominal group technique
- SWOT analysis
- Affinity diagrams/maps (to help classify and group types of risks)
- Assumption and constraint analysis
- Document review
- Delphi method
- Monte Carlo simulation (especially for larger organizations)
- Interpersonal and team skills

Prompt lists, previously identified as external factors, are also used to evaluate the external environment that could potentially impact the project.

Risk Categories

Risks are organized using various categories including by their source (using a risk breakdown structure (RBS)), the portion of the project affected (using the WBS), or other categories to help determine areas of the project most exposed to the effects of uncertainty.

Typical categories include:

- Effect-based — impact on success (scope, schedule, cost, and quality)
- Scope and requirements — scope creep, unclear requirements, lack of feedback

- Schedule—unrealistic schedule, availability of resources, weather
- Financial—funding, economy
- Technical—new technology, skills available, standards
- Management—commitment, governance, alignment
- External market or competitors—customers, vendors, credit
- Source-based—origin of the risk

Risk Breakdown Structure (RBS)

A hierarchical representation of potential sources of risk.

The RBS is structured like the WBS, with the top level as the identified categories. Subcategories may be included to help provide focus for additional areas of uncertainty.

This can be done after the risks have been identified or be used to help identify risks associated with different categories.

Risk Analysis

All identified risks will be prioritized through qualitative assessment and analysis. Based on the overall organization risk threshold, those that fall into the high or possibly medium risk categories will be further subject to a quantitative assessment.

Qualitative Assessment

*The process of **prioritizing** individual project risks for further analysis or action by assessing their probability of occurrence, impact, and other characteristics.*

The first step after identifying risks is to start subjectively evaluating the probability and impact of each risk.

The qualitative process relates to the subjective assessment and prioritization of all previously identified risks. This may only include identification of low-, medium-, or high-risk measures.

If further understanding is needed, or the organization considers the risk of falling near or outside the risk threshold, then a quantitative assessment may be required.

Probability and Impact Matrix

A grid for mapping the probability of occurrence of each risk and its impact on project objectives if the risk occurs.

There are often two versions of this risk matrix correlating to the likelihood and severity of a risk.

Initially, a simple color-coded matrix is used to determine the high, medium, and low categories of each risk based purely on subjective factors identified by the organization according to its risk appetite. Each identified risk should be equated to a cell representing individual risks' combined likelihood and severity.

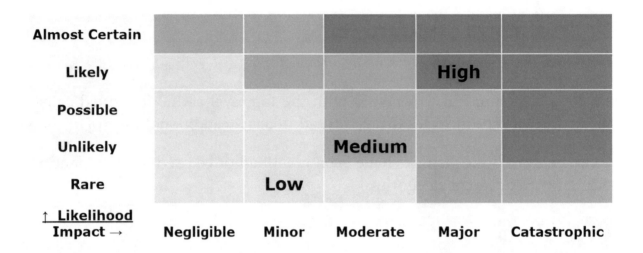

Later risk categories can include actual percentages and numerical impact amounts to support quantitative analysis, using more specific, quantitative probabilities and impact (including cost, schedule, or quality—or a combination of these). During quantitative risk analysis, these are applied to risks identified as high or medium (depending on the overall risk tolerance).

Additionally, numeric values can be assigned to the individual cells representing the combination of probability and impact. This is often used to aid in determining the risk exposure of individual and overall risks included in the risk register.

Quantitative Assessment

The process of numerically analyzing the combined effect of identified individual project risks and other sources of uncertainty on overall project objectives.

This process quantifies the overall project risk exposure and captures additional risk information to support the choice of appropriate risk responses.

This analysis is normally only performed on high or possibly medium risks and is often dependent on the quality requirements of the project. Because of the additional time required, and therefore the cost, it is usually best applied for large, complex, or strategically important projects or when required by a contract or key stakeholder(s).

Quantitative Risk Analysis Methods

Additional analysis may be beneficial for those risks falling into the high or possibly medium category because of the qualitative risk assessment activity results.

There are a few methods to help provide additional information regarding the probability of the risk affecting the outcome of the project. These can include:

– *Simulations*

An analytical technique to model the combined effect of uncertainties to evaluate their potential impact on objectives.

These models involve calculating several possible outcomes by applying varying sets of assumptions. The model is run many times using different variables. The result is a calculated probability distribution. These are often used in larger projects and incorporate models and estimates of risk. When used in risk analysis, they translate the risk uncertainty into potential impacts on project objectives.

– *Monte Carlo Simulation*

A risk management technique to estimate the impacts of various risks on the project cost. With this method, one can easily find out what will happen to the project schedule and cost if any risk occurs. It is used at various times during the project life cycle to get an idea of a range of probable outcomes during various scenarios.

The most used mathematical modeling technique for risk analysis is the Monte Carlo simulation. It requires the use of statistical analysis tools to render the model and has a wide range of applications in many fields, including finance and engineering, working with large quantities of numbers.

Rather than using the limited factors with either triangular or PERT distributions, Monte Carlo analysis can combine hundreds or thousands of data points into an overall model. It also works well for complex project management problems, with only a few schedule and/or cost inputs required to produce an integrated quantitative cost-schedule analysis of risk.

Exam Tip: You will most likely see the Monte Carlo simulation technique associated with quantitative risk analysis, but it can also be used for estimating schedule or budget numbers.

– *Sensitivity Analysis*

An analysis technique to determine individual project risks or other sources of uncertainty having the greatest potential impact on project outcomes, by correlating variations in project outcomes with variations in elements of a quantitative risk analysis model.

This method helps determine individual risks or areas of uncertainty having the greatest potential impact on the outcome of a project. This technique changes one element, while all other elements are held constant. It correlates the variations of the outcomes with the variations of elements in the quantitative risk analysis model. The result of this analysis makes it easier to understand how variation in one element will impact the overall project objectives. It is usually shown using a tornado diagram.

– *Tornado Diagram*

A horizontal bar chart comparing the relative importance of various opportunities and threats, with the highest one shown on the top.

	Opportunities			Risks			
Opportunity A	███	███	███				
Risk A				███	███	███	███
Opportunity B		███	███				
Risk B				███	███		
Opportunity C			███				
Risk C				███			

This diagram shows the results of sensitivity analysis. It is a special type of bar chart with the various elements and their variations displayed and then arranged to show the threat and/or opportunity with the highest importance on the top. The y-axis lists the various types of uncertainty or risks—with highest strength of correlation at the top, and the x-axis contains the spread of the uncertainty. It represents the opportunities and threats from high to low.

This tool and technique are often used as part of quantitative risk analysis to show the relative importance and impact of items within the project with a high degree of uncertainty compared to those relatively known and more stable.

– *Decision Tree Analysis*

A diagramming and calculation technique for evaluating the implications of a chain of multiple options in the presence of uncertainty.

Decision trees allow decision-makers to evaluate both the probability and impact for each branch of decisions under

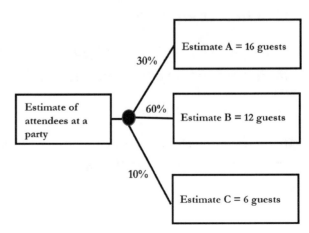

consideration, making it a useful tool for value/benefit analysis and risk analysis. It is used for more complex decision-making with multiple possible decisions and complex uncertainties. Branches of the decision tree represent different decisions or events, each with associated costs (impact) and uncertainty (probability). The endpoints of branches of the tree represent each path's outcome (positive or negative).

Solving the decision tree indicates the decision providing the greatest expected value when all the uncertain implications, costs, rewards, and subsequent decisions are quantified.

This technique is commonly used in both Six Sigma and Lean Six Sigma methods.

- *Influence Diagrams*

A graphical representation of situations showing causal influences, time ordering of events, and other relationships among variables and outcomes (also commonly used in quality management decisions).

These are a graphical way to show the various elements of uncertainty and how they influence or impact each other. They were introduced when the decision tree analysis became overwhelming for most practitioners.

- *Expected Monetary Value (EMV)*

A quantitative method of calculating the average outcome when the future is uncertain. The calculation of EMV is a component of decision tree analysis. Opportunities will have positive values, and threats will have negative values.

Expected Monetary Value, or EMV, is a statistical technique calculating the average outcome when the future includes scenarios that may or may not occur. It is also called analysis under uncertainty and often uses the decision tree analysis process. EMV assumes a risk-neutral position and will identify opportunities as positive amounts and threats as negative amounts.

The EMV is calculated by multiplying the value of each possible outcome by the probability of the outcome and then adding all the results together for each branch of the decision tree. The branch with the most optimal EMV is then recommended for selection.

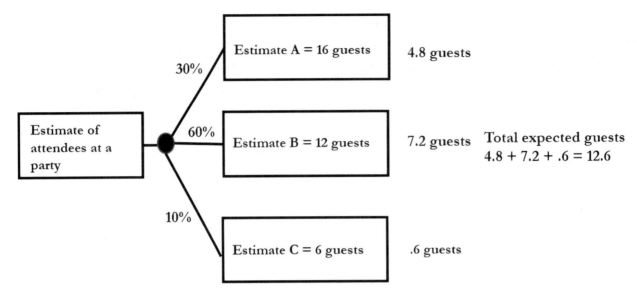

Exam Tip: Because the math used to create and analyze the decision tree can become very complicated, you should not have to perform any calculations to determine the correct answer. The answer to the question will probably be determined from its definition alone.

Risk Register

A repository where the outputs of risk management processes are recorded.

An essential planning document for project risk analysis and control, the risk register contains a list of the most important risks to the project's completion. For each risk, it identifies the likelihood of occurrence, the impact to the project, the priority, and the applicable response plans.

Content of the risk register is dependent on the risk appetite of the stakeholders and/ or organization and is continually monitored and updated throughout the project. Information included for each individual risk includes:

- Identified risks — categories and event description
- Probability, impact, risk score/exposure definition
- Trigger
- Planned response (primary and secondary)
- Contingency reserves
- Roles:
  - Risk owner — person responsible for monitoring and managing the risk and for selecting and implementing an appropriate risk response strategy
  - Risk action owner — person responsible for carrying out the approved risk actions when responding to a given risk

Additional information may be added to the risk register as project work proceeds, including:

- Current risk status
- WBS reference
- Timing of potential occurrence
- When no longer relevant
- Deadline for acting

Risk descriptions can be described by formatted risk statements including:

- EVENT may occur, causing IMPACT
- IF CAUSE exists, EVENT may occur, leading to EFFECT

Project Management Principle:

Optimize Risk Responses [41]

Continually evaluate exposure to risk, both opportunities and threats, to maximize positive impacts and minimize negative impacts to the project and its outcomes.

Plan Risk Response

An action to address a risk.

It is important to determine the action needed for the identified risks prior to their occurrence. This includes developing options, selecting strategies to use, and agreeing on actions to address overall risk exposure and response. If the impact of a risk is high, the process decision program chart (PDPC) (also known as a contingency planning tool) may be used to identify various options available for different situations.

The trigger condition identified for a risk signals that a risk event can or is about to happen. Responses should be identified for risks, so these are considered and analyzed before the event happens.

Risks and their responses need to be reassessed throughout the project. This reassessment is normally done at the beginning of a phase or release, as some risks may no longer be applicable if the time when they should have occurred has passed.

---

41 *The Standard for Project Management, Section 3.10 – Project Management Principles*

Risk Response Strategies

Several strategies are applied to both threats (negative risks) and opportunities (positive risks).

Strategies for Threats (from most serious to least)

- *Escalate*

For threats clearly exceeding the project manager's threshold for management, escalate or hand off the risk to the designated party. If the risk can't be handled, the project may be postponed, modified, or canceled.

- *Avoid*

If overall project risk may cause a significant negative impact to the project and is outside the agreed-upon risk thresholds for the project, adopt an avoid strategy to take focused action to reduce the negative effect of uncertainty on the project and move it back inside the threshold.

- *Transfer*

Suppose the overall level or that of an individual project risk is high, and the organization is unable to address it effectively. In that case, a third party may be involved to manage the risk on behalf of the organization. Where overall project risk is negative, a transfer strategy for all or a large portion of the project is required, often involving a substantial payment to offset the impact of the risk.

The transfer response can be used to cover an insurable risk where there is potential for loss, including direct property, indirect property, liability, and personnel related risks. Insurance or a bond may be purchased to reduce or offset the possible loss of the risk occurring.

- *Mitigate*

The level of overall or individual project risk is modified by reducing the chances of not achieving the project's objectives—e.g., replan the project, change the scope and boundaries, modify project priority, change resource allocations, adjust delivery times, etc. This includes actions to lower the probability of occurrence, the impact if it happens, or a combination of both.

- *Accept*

Where no proactive risk response strategy can address overall individual project risks, the organization may choose to continue with the project as currently defined, even if overall project risk is outside the agreed-upon thresholds.

Acceptance can be either active or passive. The most common active acceptance strategy is to establish an overall contingency reserve for the project, including amounts of time, money, or resources to be used if the project exceeds its thresholds. These contingencies may also be established for individual risks at the activity or work package level.

Passive acceptance involves not taking any proactive action apart from the periodic review of the level of overall project risk to ensure it does not change significantly. Basically, "It is what it is" and will be dealt with it, and when the risk occurs.

Strategies for Opportunities (from most positive to least)

- *Escalate*

If the team uncovers a great opportunity for the organization outside the scope of the project, identify and inform the relevant party who can act on it. This is likely one of the key stakeholders.

- *Exploit*

Where the level of overall project risk is significantly positive and outside the agreed-upon risk thresholds for the project, an exploit strategy is adopted. This involves taking focused action to capture and implement activities that apply to the positive effect of uncertainty on the project. This could include adding additional high-benefit elements of scope to the project to add value or benefits to stakeholders. Alternatively, the risk thresholds for the project may be modified with the agreement of key stakeholders to embrace the opportunity.

- *Share*

If the level of overall project risk is high but the organization is unable to address it effectively, a third party may be involved to share the risk. Where the overall project risk is positive, a sharing strategy is often required, and a cost-sharing type contract is put in place with another organization. The outside organization may have the necessary expertise to take advantage of the opportunity presented.

- *Enhance*

The level of overall project risk is changed through additional activities to optimize the chances of achieving the project's objectives—e.g., replan the project, change the scope and boundaries, modify project priority, change resource allocations, adjust delivery times, etc.

- *Accept*

Where no proactive risk response strategy is possible to address overall or an individual project risk, the organization may choose to continue with the project as currently defined, even if the risk is outside the agreed-upon thresholds. Acceptance can be either active or passive.

Exam Tip: The top and bottom strategies (Escalate and Accept) are the same, while other strategies are the opposite between a threat and an opportunity:

- *Avoid vs. Exploit*
- *Transfer vs. Share*
- *Mitigate vs. Enhance*

Strategies for Threats	Strategies for Opportunities
Escalate	Escalate
Avoid	Exploit
Transfer	Share
Mitigate	Enhance
Accept	Accept

Strategies for overall project risk (rather than individual risks) are the same for threats and opportunities, except for the escalate strategy.

Contingency Responses

For some of the risks which are accepted, but may require additional reserves for time or money, a contingency plan and responses are developed for use only if those specific events occur.

Risk Response Guidelines

One principle of project management is to optimize risk responses. This means continually evaluating the project's risk exposure, including opportunities and threats.

It is important to maximize the positive impacts and minimize any negative impacts to the project and outcomes.

Some guidelines include:

- Consider risks from the start of the project.
- Remember risks are always in the future.
- Risk is uncertainty—it may or may not occur.
- Risk can be known or unknown.

- Risk can cause a negative impact (threat) or a positive impact (opportunity).
- Understand the organization's and key stakeholders' risk appetite, risk tolerance, and risk threshold.
- Ensure the risk response is appropriate for the significance of the risk.
- Make the response cost-effective.
- Keep the response realistic within the context of the project.
- Receive agreement to the response by the relevant stakeholder.
- Identify a responsible person as owner of the risk and response.

Additional Risk Concepts

- *Secondary Risk*

A risk that arises as a direct result of implementing a risk response.

These secondary risks may be identified during risk planning or occur because of a risk response being implemented. In these situations, the primary and secondary risks, and their responses, are dependent upon each other.

- *Residual Risk*

The risk that remains after risk responses have been implemented.

These might be discovered and identified during risk planning, and then a contingency plan may be developed. If not identified, then the residual risk could linger in the organization.

- *Contingency Plan*

A risk response strategy developed in advance before risks occur; and is meant to be used if and when identified risks become reality.

Secondary plans are developed for specific risks that were accepted. They are only executed under predefined conditions and when there is sufficient warning to implement. This is also known as a "fallback plan."

Contingent response strategies are only identified if some predefined condition(s) exist and there is sufficient warning to implement the planned response.

A contingency or fallback plan should also be created and put in place if the primary risk response fails.

    – *Contingency Reserve*

Time or money allocated in the schedule or cost baseline for known risks with active response strategies.

Any necessary costs or time to cover the identified risks and their response strategies, including the fallback plan, should be added to the appropriate baselines before baselining the entire project.

Contingency reserves handle "known unknowns" where risks have been identified and quantified and a risk category determined.

Management reserves handle "unknown unknowns" where risks have not been identified by the project team or by management. The amount of reserve is usually at the organization level and not known to the project manager or the project team. Only when there is no other way to handle additional needed costs does the project manager request funds from the management reserve. This could also happen if a requirement is overlooked but needs to be included later, and additional time or money is needed.

Exam Tip: Contingency reserves allocated for known risks on activities, work packages, or the project overall are included in the project's cost baseline (BAC) when using a predictive approach.

Project Risk Management: Adaptive

Uncertainty is often the reason an adaptive approach was chosen. This approach provides for smaller increments of work, enabling feedback and the continual progressive elaboration of the scope to help reduce the risk of rework.

The product owner may continually review the impact of uncertainty on the product backlog. This often results in a "risk-adjusted" backlog, with items being moved up or down on the list depending on the impact of a risk.

In the case of a feature or function that is essentially a make-or-break item for the project, those related stories are often prioritized as high and handled early in the project or release. If those items are not delivered successfully, often the project will need to have the scope reduced, canceled, or postponed until the issue can be resolved.

Risk List (Disciplined Agile)[42]

Adaptive teams might use a risk list, which functions like a risk register but also may include risk information transferred and managed on an issue log.

---

42   *https://www.pmi.org/disciplined-Agile/Agile/risklist*

This is often a simple spreadsheet to capture a description of the risk, the probability and impact scores on a 1–10 scale (or percentages), and then the magnitude determined by multiplying the two risk factors.

Additional columns might include:

- Owner—the person who has taken responsibility for seeing the risk is addressed
- Status—current state of the risk, typically—identified, accepted, in progress, resolved, or issue (the risk has happened)

Additional information is more closely associated with an issue, including a potential risk or unknown that has happened and would be managed on an issue log.

- Date identified—when the risk was first identified
- Date resolved—when the risk was resolved
- Days active—a calculated field
  - For an unresolved risk, it is current date minus the date identified.
  - For a resolved risk, it is the date resolved minus the date identified.
- Resolution strategy—the strategy to address the risk

Regardless of whether a risk register or a risk list is used by an adaptive project, the information is displayed on the information radiator (including possibly a risk burndown chart), continually addressed during the backlog refinement process by the product owner and discussed during various planning meetings and retrospectives.

Project Risk Management: Hybrid

Hybrid approaches often are more focused on weighing the risk opportunity with the threat.

These projects will implement more adaptive approaches in areas with uncertainty, while other project aspects will be handled using traditional risk management techniques.

Key Concepts Covered

- Risk strategy
- Risk management plan
- Risk identification
- Probability and impact matrix

- Qualitative risk assessment
- Quantitative risk assessment
- Risk register
- Risk responses

ECO Coverage

- Assess and manage risks (2.3)
  - Determine risk management options (2.3.1)
  - Iteratively assess and prioritize risks (2.3.2)

- Plan and manage project compliance (3.1)
  - Determine potential threats to compliance (3.1.3)
  - Determine necessary approach and action to address compliance needs (risk, legal) (3.1.6)

Check Your Progress

1. Your project team and stakeholders completed the risk register when one of the stakeholders called you about a new risk that seems to have been missing and is not included in the risk register. This stakeholder is very concerned about this risk. What should be your first course of action?

   A. Update the risk management plan

   B. Update the risk register

   C. Use your contingency reserve

   D. Call for a meeting of the stakeholders to discuss the new risk

2. Which one of the following is not true about issues in a project?

   A. An issue is recorded in the issue log and requires a solution

   B. There should be only one person assigned to each issue as a point of contract for resolution

   C. Issues and risks are the same thing

   D. A risk is recorded in the risk register and becomes an issue when the risk has occurred

3. You and your family have made the arrangements for your daughter's wedding, which will be held outside at a resort near a beach. You have assigned one of your family members to monitor the weather and she has reported that the weather

forecast suggests a chance of light rain, seven days away from the wedding day. You have reserved umbrellas and a few tents just in case you need them. Which of the following risk response strategies are you using in this case?

A. Acceptance

B. Mitigation

C. Avoidance

D. Enhance

4. Residual risk is a risk that remains after a risk response has been implemented. Is this statement true or false?

A. True

B. False

5. What are the risk strategies for opportunities (Choose 3)

A. Avoid

B. Exploit

C. Share

D. Enhance

E. Mitigate

Answers

1. B
2. D
3. B
4. True
5. B, C, D

Plan Project Quality

Project Management Principle:

Build Quality into Processes and Deliverables[43]

Maintain a focus on quality that produces deliverables that meet project objectives and align to the needs, uses, and acceptance requirements set forth by relevant stakeholders.

Quality aspects of a project address the management of the project as well as its deliverables. They apply to all projects, regardless of the nature of the deliverables. They also apply to the processes used and are tied to the identified quality requirements for the project and product. These quality measures and techniques are specific to the type of deliverables produced by the project.

Quality dimensions may include:

- Performance—functioning as intended
- Conformity—fit for use and meeting specifications
- Reliability—producing consistent metrics
- Resilience—the ability to cope with unforeseen failures and recover quickly
- Satisfaction—eliciting positive feedback from end users
- Uniformity—showing parity with other deliverables produced in the same manner
- Efficiency—producing the most significant output with the least amount of inputs and effort
- Sustainability—producing a positive impact on economic, social, and environmental parameters

Quality

The degree to which a set of inherent characteristics fulfills requirements.

Quality represents what the stakeholders expect from the project to fulfill requirements. In today's customer-focused business environment, end-user happiness is often critical to defining quality. Stated and implied quality needs are used to identify project quality requirements.

Quality requirements should be feasible, modifiable, and measurable.

---

43   *The Standard for Project Management, Section 3.8 – Project Management Principles*

Quality is also a project component governed by internal (organizational) quality policy and external policies such as commercial standards and regulations. All of these must be satisfied. At the beginning of the project, quality policies and procedures should be planned to incorporate, manage, and control quality requirements into work cycles and backlog items throughout the project consistent with the organization's quality management system.

Quality is a key focus of continuous process improvement activities and is addressed during lessons learned activities or retrospectives. The benefits of planning the management of quality on the project include:

- Sharper focus on the project's value proposition
- Cost reductions
- Mitigate schedule overruns from rework

Effective Quality Management

The five levels of effective quality management from "best to worst" include:

- Best case — create a culture within the project to ensure awareness and commitment to quality in the processes performed as well as the products delivered.
- Incorporate quality into the planning and delivery of both the project activities and the product itself.
- Use quality assurance practices to review and continually improve the process itself.
- Detect and correct internal defects before they are released to the customer — including costs for prevention, inspection and internal failures.
- Let the customer find the escaped defects — obviously the most expensive method.

Cost of Quality (CoQ)

All costs incurred over the life of the product by investment in preventing nonconformance to requirements and appraisal of the product or service for conformance to requirements and failure to meet requirements.

The CoQ includes all costs incurred over the life of the product and is based on Philip Crosby's 1979 book *Quality is Free*. He believed that a company that established a quality program would experience savings that more than offset the cost of that program. Even though the focus was on manufacturing, the paradigm is useful in other industries and helps us think about all costs incurred over the life of the product. This includes identifying what methods and procedures can be implemented to systematically remove defects from the process—or achieve zero defects. Once these methods have been developed, they become standardized as part of the process.

The costs associated with the monetary value of quality for a project are separated into the categories of cost of conformance and cost of nonconformance.

Cost of Conformance

Money spent during the project to avoid failure, including:

- *Preventive Costs*

Costs to build a quality product include training, documentation of processes, data analysis, equipment, resources, infrastructure expenses, and the time to do things right. Additional methods include:

- Reliability engineering
- Shigeo Shingo's Poka-Yoke (mistake proofing) and Zero Quality Control (100% source inspection)
- Test engineering—failure modes and effects analysis (FMEA)
- Voice of the customer (VOC)—originated in Japan and focuses on capturing what the customer is asking for from the process, including the stated and implied needs

- *Appraisal Costs*

Costs to assess quality, including testing, destructive testing tasks, calibration, and inspections. This can also include Gage's R&R (repeatability and reproducibility) and calibration and test equipment.

Cost of Nonconformance

Cost incurred both during and after the project because of poor quality. Crosby stated that "The cost of quality is the expense of doing things wrong. It is the scrap, rework, service after service, warranty, inspection, test, and similar activities made necessary by nonconformance problems."[44]

- *Internal Failure Costs*

Costs to discover failures found during the project, including rework, scrap, excessive inspections, and "service after service."

- *External Failure Costs*

---

44   *Crosby PB. Quality is Free. New York: Mc Graw-Hill, 1980*

The cost to handle failures, or escaped defects, found by the customer. This includes warranty work and potential lost business, reputation, sales, and customers, which could lead to the demise of the business. Some additional costs include:

- High liability/insurance costs
- Excessive warranty costs
- Low team morale
- Decreased efficiency
- Negative press—increased competitive pressure

Quality Standards and Regulations

Project quality may be affected by applicable standards and regulations and needs to be continually recognized and managed throughout the project.

- *Standard*

A document established by an authority, custom, or general consent as a model.

Standards are typically voluntary guidelines or characteristics approved by a recognized body of experts such as the International Organization for Standardization (ISO). In some cases, the standards body will provide certification indicating conformance by suppliers to the requirements of the standards. Often, conformance to standards is a customer requirement.

- *Regulations*

Requirements imposed by a governmental body.

These requirements can establish product, process, or service characteristics, including applicable administrative provisions with government-mandated compliance.

- *De Facto Standards or Regulations*

Standards widely accepted or adopted through use, including best practices that describe a preferred approach but are not officially endorsed.

- *De Jure Standards or Regulations ("From the Bench")*

Result of a legal decision and therefore mandated by law or approved by a recognized body of experts.

Quality Techniques

Quality metrics identify project or product quality elements, including how to measure them, and are used during testing with various tools and processes to ensure compliance.

Tolerance level for quality is the quantified description of variation for a product quality requirement that will be acceptable to the customer. It can be applied to the acceptance of a product through the understanding of the acceptance criteria and DoD. Adaptive teams additionally use retrospectives and small batch cycles to help ensure compliance to any applicable quality standard.

Additional quality tools and techniques for the project are identified in the quality management plan, possibly including:

- Quality function deployment (QFD)
- Design for X (DfX)
- Design of experiments (DoE)
- Process decision program charts (PDPC)
- Tree diagrams—risk
- Statistical sampling
- Cause-and-effect diagrams
- Interrelationship digraphs
- Checklists
- Flowcharts
- Histograms
- Pareto charts
- Failure models and effects analysis (FMEA)

Quality Institutions

There are several international institutes devoted to quality with guidelines to help identify and manage quality to the level required for the project, including:

- The Chartered Quality Institute (CQI)
- ASTM International (formerly known as the American Society for Testing and Materials)
- American Society for Quality (ASQ), including the highly accepted and implemented global standard of quality—ISO 9000 series certifications
- Software Engineering Institute—Capability Maturity Model Integration (CMMI)

Quality Management: Predictive

Quality Management Plan

A component of the project management plan describing how applicable policies, procedures, and guidelines will be implemented to achieve the quality objectives.

Predictive projects create a quality management plan to develop the product or deliverable. This plan identifies how the quality aspects of the project will be conducted and is an extension of the organization's quality management plan (especially regarding testing and rollout/implementation activities).

It should be continually reviewed throughout the project. Often, organizations create the quality standards in the OPAs and label them as Quality Policies and Procedures, or something similar, for all projects to consider when developing their project management plan. The content of the plan includes:

- Quality standards (industry, product, or regulatory)
- Quality metrics, specifications, or measures
- Quality roles and responsibilities
- Deliverables and processes subject to quality reviews
- Quality management approaches (timing and content of quality audit)
- Quality control approach (measurement of quality, including testing approach)
- Applicable quality procedures (nonconformance and rework; corrective actions; continuous improvement)

The plan also addresses project quality processes, verifications, and requirements. These are often identified during elicitation activities. These quality processes undergo observation and checking throughout the project for conformance to the quality policy.

The formality, detail included, and style are determined by the project quality requirements, especially regarding products rather than service or process improvement results.

Exam Tip: A quality policy must be in place for the project. Even if this is often the responsibility of an organizational quality function, if a quality policy does not exist, the project needs to create one.

Quality Metrics

Quality metrics provide specific detailed measurements about a project or product element and how it should be measured to verify compliance. Metrics are reviewed continually to ensure the processes used and results delivered will meet the metric and be acceptable. If not, corrective action or rework may be necessary.

These metrics are individually specified, including the element to be measured, the specific, quantifiable measurement of an indicator, and the method of measuring at a particular point in time (including any equipment or procedures).

Quality metrics can be determined as part of the requirement specification if the requirement is stable, including both precision and accuracy.

- *Precision*

Focuses on the consistency of measurements and targets repeated measurements that yield the same value.

- *Accuracy*

Looks at how close the true value is to the measured value. Closer values indicate higher reliability and less uncertainty.

Additional quality terms which are often used synonymously even though there are differences include:

- *Quality*

The degree to which characteristics fulfill requirements. Can be considered subjective, based on the recipient's needs, perspectives, and requirements.

- *Grade*

A category assigned to products having the same functional use but different technical characteristics. The grade is measurable and therefore objective, even though a high grade does not ensure high quality.

Quality Management: Adaptive

The quality aspects of the product using an adaptive approach are quite different, especially when the product's metrics and quality levels have not been specified.

It is still important to have or develop a quality management plan. This plan identifies how the quality aspects of the project will be conducted and often refers to the alignment with the organization's quality management plan. If the organization does not have a quality policy, then the project needs to create one.

Adaptive teams focus on small, iterative cycles allowing for frequent feedback about the quality of the product being developed. This feedback often uncovers inconsistencies and quality issues earlier in the project life cycle when the overall costs of change are lower. In addition, it is used to improve the product and outcome by incrementally refining the backlog. This also includes continuous checking against various quality standards.

Self-organizing teams focus on their way of working and work processes consistently at regular intervals—daily stand-ups or sprint retrospectives, for example. These discussions allow the team to improve the quality of their process and procedures, as well as the product, on an ongoing basis.

Quality Metrics

The quality metrics will also evolve and change with evolving or changing requirements, often using prototypes and experimentation to determine the appropriate metric.

Quality Management: Hybrid

A quality management plan should still be developed, including the alignment with the organization's quality plan and required processes.

As in other planning areas, the hybrid approach will identify those portions of the project where quality is easily understood and defined and utilize a more predictive approach in those areas.

In areas where no specific quality standard is provided, research and development efforts, prototypes, and even usage of an exploratory life cycle help determine the acceptable level of quality.

Exam Tip: PMI stresses prevention over correction or inspection as the preferred approach.

Continuous improvement is a recurring quality theme.

Everyone is responsible for the quality of the project, product, or service.

Key Concepts Covered

- Quality management
- Cost of quality (CoQ)
- Standards and regulations
- Quality approaches
- Support compliance

ECO Coverage

- Plan and manage quality of products/deliverables (2.7)
  - Determine quality standard required for project deliverables (2.7.1)

- Plan and manage project compliance
  - Use methods to support compliance (3.1.4)
  - Measure the extent to which the project is in compliance (3.1.7)

Check Your Progress

1. Which quality activity should be considered first?

   A. Perform quantitative analysis

   B. Plan how quality management will be done on the project

   C. Determine the Definition of Ready

   D. Perform a quality audit

2. The cost of fixing defects of a product that is discovered by a customer is considered part of which cost of quality (CoQ) category?

   A. Internal failure cost

   B. Preventive cost

   C. Appraisal cost

   D. External failure cost

3. 3. A Kaizan team has identified wasted steps in developing your project's product. They have recommended a few actions for process improvement and have requested that some of the manufacturing processes be updated. Which of the following best describes what they performed?

   A. Continuous improvement activity

   B. Cost-benefit analysis

   C. Sprint retrospective

   D. Assessment of a change request

4. Cost of nonconformance is the cost incurred both during and after the project is finished because of poor quality. Crosby stated that "The cost of quality is the expense of doing things wrong which is the scrap, rework, service after service, warranty, inspection, test, and similar activities made necessary by nonconformance problems." Is this true or false?

A. True

B. False

5. 5. The quality tools and techniques for the project are identified in the quality management plan. Which of the following are considered quality tools or techniques? (Choose 3)

A. Design for X (DfX)

B. Design of experiments (DoE)

C. Checklists

D. Precedence Diagramming Method (PDM)

E. Quality gate

Answers

1. D

2. D

3. A

4. True

5. A, B, C

Integrate Project Plans

The development of the initial project management plan should be addressed as soon as the project charter is completed, but the plan will continually be reviewed throughout the project delivery to make any required mid-course corrections.

At this time in a project, it is important to coordinate and evaluate all applicable plans and activities used throughout the project. All the previous planning activities to support the delivery of the vision and expected value are now integrated into the project management plan. The combined scope, requirements, schedule, budget, resources, procurement, quality, risk, communications, and stakeholder plans must support the project's desired outcomes.

These plans should continually be reviewed as more information becomes known. For scope, schedule, and cost baselines, an effective strategy for change management or control is needed to continually compare what was planned and agreed upon to what is occurring as part of the project effort.

Focusing on an integrated view of all the plans can:

- Identify and correct gaps or discrepancies
- Align efforts and improve understanding of how the various activities depend on each other
- Help the assessment and coordination of project work throughout the life cycle

No matter the life cycle, some level of planning is needed to provide support for the project work. This activity is the responsibility of the project manager and cannot be delegated to other team members.

Predictive

For projects using a predictive approach, at the end of the planning stage, all the planning results from the various project management knowledge areas and performance domains are reviewed and combined. This includes subsidiary plans, baselines, and any information regarding the way the project will be managed.

Except for the baselines, these are "plans," and as a result will need to be monitored and possibly adjusted as the actual project results are reviewed and compared to initial estimates.

Adaptive

Plans are developed and reviewed more frequently with a smaller scope and/or time frame.

Adaptive processes and Agile ceremonies provide a structure to continuously review and integrate plans or aspects of a project.

Hybrid

For hybrid projects, this is modified to reflect the process of "planning integration" rather than necessarily creating specific deliverables or documented plans.

It is important to determine a way to work with and adapt the various planning elements where needed. Teams may opt for a de facto integrated working process and refine and adapt it while working on the project.

Project Management Plan Components

Subsidiary Plans

Subsidiary management plans include:

- Scope management plan
- Requirements management plan
- Schedule management plan
- Cost management plan
- Quality management plan
- Resource management plan
- Communications management plan
- Risk management plan
- Stakeholder engagement plan
- Procurement management plan

Baselines

Once the individual baselines are agreed upon (and often signed off on), they become the content used to measure all subsequent changes.

Baselines include:

- Scope baseline
- Schedule baseline
- Cost baseline

An additional performance measurement baseline (PMB) may also be included to measure and manage performance against the approved combined scope-schedule-cost plans. It includes the contingency reserve amounts but excludes the management reserve.

Additional Content

There may be other components included in this project management plan representing additional, overall management areas. These often include how changes will be handled and how different versions of project artifacts will be maintained, often based on OPAs.

Additional components may include:

- Artifacts
- Configuration management plan
- Change (control) management plan
- Compliance management plan
- Implementation/rollout plan
- Transition management plan
- Benefits realization plan
- Development approach
- Project life cycle and project governance
- Management reviews for content, extent, and timing
- Tailoring areas
- Prioritization techniques

The plan may identify and include the actual development approach and life cycle chosen for the project. Depending on how the project result is to be delivered, an additional implementation or rollout plan, transition plan, and benefits realization plan may be specified here, along with key management, quality, and compliance reviews.

The baselines, if changed, will need to go through the defined change control system. Even though these non-baselined components are not subject to change control, the sponsor and key stakeholders should review and approve them.

Artifacts

Any documents prepared in support of a project — for example, requirements, specifications, contracts with vendors, design documents, test plans, and publications delivered to the client along with the final product.

In addition to the key planning documents developed by the project manager, several other documents are created during the project. These are referred to as project artifacts and may include deliverables or required documents according to the organization's OPAs.

Project artifacts are like historical artifacts, showing us what work was done and how it was developed. They are elements of a historical repository useful for future projects.

Artifacts are developed and maintained by the project team during the life of the project and are often archived at the end of the project. Any documentation, plan, or item used to reconstruct the history of the project or product, especially where changes were made, should be maintained, and archived once the project is complete. Even though OPAs are provided by the PMO for use on projects, the project manager and/or team select and adapt the appropriate artifacts for use on their specific project, tailoring them to the project's unique needs.

Many of the artifacts listed below were previously identified as project documents prepared in support of a project, but not required as deliverables identified on agreements.

Examples include:

Activity attributes	Activity cost estimates	Activity resource requirements	Activity list
Assumption log	Basis of estimates	*Burndown chart	*Burnup chart
Change log	Cost forecasts	Duration estimates	Issue log
Lessons learned register	Lessons learned repository	Milestone list	Physical resource assignments
*Product backlog	*Product road map	Project calendars	Project communications
*Project road map	Project schedule	Project schedule network diagram	Project scope statement
Project team assignments	Quality control measurements	Quality metrics	Quality report
*Release plan	*Requirements backlog	Requirements documentation (BRD)	Requirements traceability matrix
Resource breakdown structure	Resource calendars	Risk register	Risk report
Schedule data	Schedule forecasts	*Sprint/Iteration plan	Stakeholder register
*Story Points	*Task board/ Kanban board	Team charter	Test and evaluation documents

The artifacts listed above are not all-inclusive and include documents used both by predictive and adaptive approaches. The adaptive artifacts are indicated by *. Not every process, input, tool, technique, or output is required on every project.

Artifacts produced using a predictive approach include:

- Project management plan
- Project charter
- Change requests and change logs
- Lessons learned
- Requirements
- Requirements traceability matrix
- Scope baseline (including the scope statement, WBS, and WBS dictionary)
- Schedule baseline
- Cost baseline

Artifacts produced using an adaptive approach include:

- Product road map
- Product vision statement
- Product, release, and iteration/sprint backlogs
- Release and iteration plans
- Task board/kanban board
- Burndown/burnup charts

- Experiments (sometimes referred to as spikes)

In addition to those artifacts from predictive and adaptive approaches, artifacts produced using a hybrid approach include:

- Agreements
- Acceptance criteria
- Assumptions
- Constraints
- Business case
- Benefits management plan
- Minutes of status meetings
- Presentations and slide decks
- Project communications

These lists can be considered "typical" and are not exclusive.

Project Management Information Systems (PMIS)

A PMIS is an information management system component consisting of the tools and techniques used to gather, integrate, and disseminate the outputs of project management processes.

The project management information system (PMIS) has been used as a tool for project managers to conduct work and share information. It is not a single tool but rather a combination of automated or software tools and techniques. Depending on the maturity of project management in the organization, these are available through different formats to help ensure consistency in the collection of project information. They also provide the information required for reporting, work processing, spreadsheet applications, and other software applications a project manager needs. The most common tools are Microsoft Project, MS Teams, or a similar project management applications.

The PMIS frequently includes tools to support the management of project artifacts. These are usually provided through a sharing platform to enable both the storage and maintenance of project artifacts. This is usually determined by and based on recommendations of the organization and the PMO to best support the team environment as well as the project approach being used.

Information Storage and Distribution

Because of the sheer number of artifacts created during a project, it is important to have a place for their storage and access by team members and others requiring the information. The decisions regarding the storage and distribution of information is a part of information management.

Some good practices for storage and distribution of artifacts include:

- Store artifacts in an easily accessible location for users.
- Utilize information radiators to make appropriate work visible and transparent.
- Use a storage and distribution system to match the complexity of the project.
- Use cloud-based document storage and retrieval systems for larger projects, especially where team members are virtual and/or geographically distributed.

Standardization of Artifacts

Many organizations and PMOs have created standard systems for working with project artifacts. These often are part of the OPAs available to project managers and include:

- A simple way to produce and control documents
- Standardized formats and templates

- A structured process for the review and approval of documents
- Built-in version control
- Document checkout and check-in capability to maintain the integrity of the document when undergoing changes
- Automatic alerts when documents are added or changed, often via email
- User-based document security
- Capability to support timely distribution of documents

Configuration Management Plan

A component of the project management plan describing how to identify and account for project artifacts under configuration control and how to record and report changes to them.

Artifacts are maintained according to the configuration management plan.

This describes how to identify and account for project artifacts under configuration control and record and report changes to them. This is often provided as part of the OPAs' procedures and processes. It relates to how changes impact configurable items. It also includes the activities necessary to validate that the configuration items have been identified, approved, tracked, and correctly implemented.

Change Management Plan

A component of the project management plan that establishes the change control board, documents the extent of its authority, and describes how the change control system will be implemented.

A change management plan is used with predictive approaches to provide direction for managing changes, including the process and assigned roles. Identification of change requests and the process to be followed should be specifically defined in the project management plan.

This is often specified as an OPA, which then would be included as part of the project management plan to show how it will be incorporated into the project.

A key component of this plan is determining the specific project authority levels to approve changes and determine what constitutes a change.

Areas to consider and determine include:

- Who can propose a change — with roles identified
- What exactly constitutes a change, compared to an adjustment or clarification

- The impact of the change on project objectives—including recommendation of an evaluation or impact assessment method

- The steps to evaluate a change request before approving or rejecting it—documenting the required steps per the change control system and quality policy

- Who has the authority to approve various types and levels of change—with designated approvers and levels of approval

- When a change request is approved, what project documents will record the next steps (actions)—including a change log or similar artifact to track the status of a change request

- How actions to confirm completion and quality of approved change requests will be monitored—including processes and artifacts to be used

Exam Tip: Change control is important because it impacts all aspects of the project, from scope, schedule, and budget to quality, resources, risks, and procurement. It includes understanding the processes, artifacts, and approval levels for requested changes.

Key Concepts Covered

- Project management plan components
- Subsidiary plans
- Baselines
- Artifacts
- Project management information system (PMIS)
- Configuration management plan
- Change management plan

ECO Coverage

- Integrate project planning activities (2.9)
  - Consolidate the project/phase plans (2.9.1)
  - Assess consolidated project plans for dependencies, gaps, and continued business value (2.9.2)
  - Analyze the data collected (2.9.3)
  - Collect and analyze data to make informed project decisions (2.9.4)
  - Determine critical information requirements (2.9.5)

- Manage project changes (2.10)
  - Determine strategy to handle change (2.10.2)

– Manage project artifacts (2.12)

• Determine the requirements (what, when, where, who) for managing project artifacts (2.12.1)

Check Your Progress

1. You established a change control board for your project, and you also want to follow the established change control process. Which of the following are the primary goals for performing the established change control process? (Choose 3)

   A. Prevent unnecessary changes in your project

   B. Set up a mechanism to delay or reject changes

   C. Analyze the possible impacts of the changes in your project

   D. Manage changes as they occur

2. When can a project manager make changes to the project scope baseline?

   A. When a change is identified as necessary

   B. When a key stakeholder identifies a missing requirement

   C. Based on the configuration management plan

   D. After a change request has been approved

3. The components of the integrated project management plan for a predictive approach reviewed by the sponsor and key stakeholders are: (Choose 3)

   A. Subsidiary management plans

   B. 3 baselines

   C. Configuration management plan

   D. Project charter

4. A PMIS is an information management system component consisting of the tools and techniques used to gather, integrate, and disseminate the outputs of project management processes. Is this true or false?

   A. True

   B. False

5. A project artifact is any document prepared in support of a project—for example, requirements, specifications, contracts with vendors, design documents, test plans, and communications delivered to the client along with the final product. Which of the following are considered agile artifacts? (Choose 3)

   A. Product road map

B. Release plan

C. Story points

D. Assumption log

E. Requirements traceability matrix

Answers

1. A, C, D
2. D
3. A, B, C
4. True
5. A, B, C

Team Leadership

Project Management Principle:

Demonstrate Leadership Behaviors45

Demonstrate and adapt leadership behaviors to support individual and team needs.

This chapter focuses on the leadership skills of a project manager and corresponds to the "People" domain of the ECO and the "Power Skills" leg of the PMI Talent Triangle.

In this chapter, you will:

- Understand the role of the project manager
- Learn leadership competencies and skills
- Understand leadership styles, whether in-person or virtual
- Understand characteristics and core functions of empowered teams
- Learn strategies and forms of collaboration in a project team environment
- Understand the value of training and coaching for a team
- Understand the importance of conflict management, the causes and levels of conflict, and their outcomes

Topics in This Chapter:

- Role of the Project Manager
- Leadership Competencies and Skills
- Collaborative Work Environment
- Team Member Empowerment
- Team Member Performance
- Stakeholder Collaboration
- Team Development
- Manage Conflict

---

45 *The Standard for Project Management, Section 3.6 – Project Management Principles*

Role of the Project Manager

The leadership role of the project manager, working with the project team, is important to achieve project objectives. Most of a project manager's time on a project is spent managing communications with management, team members, and stakeholders. The project manager is the "glue" holding the project together. They act like an orchestra conductor synchronizing all the musicians, as they synchronize the work of project team members and stakeholders. This role should be visible throughout the project, even though often a project manager may initially plan a project and then turn the execution over to another project manager. The role of the project manager is frequently adapted to the organization, just as the project activities are also adapted to individual projects.

Role On a Project

A project manager's role is to lead the project team to meet not only the project's objectives but also stakeholders' expectations, while balancing constraints with the resources previously provided.

This balance requires the project manager to communicate effectively with executives and leaders and consult on the best approach to advance the strategic objectives, while utilizing interpersonal/soft skills to achieve the expected results. Customer expectations can be managed and met through the project activities and results.

Changes can be realized through the results of project improvements to organizational performance, including continuous improvement efforts. The role of a project manager in this area becomes that of a change agent.

Role Within the Organization

The role of the project manager goes beyond just the project and extends into the overall organization where the project is being delivered.

It is important for a project manager to understand the organization and how it operates. This is a critical and necessary component of business acumen skills. This includes the business strategy, financial performance, marketing and competitors, operations, and products or services provided, as well as the organization's functions and management structure.

The project goals and objectives must be continually aligned with the organizational strategy to ensure project managers realize why their project has been selected and understand the organizational goals supported by the project result.

Since very few organizations have only one project at a time, there is a need for the project manager to interact with other project managers, especially since resources must often be shared by multiple projects, which requires cooperation with other project managers as well as resource managers.

Often deliverables for a project are either needed by other project efforts or must be received from the work of other projects. This coordination between various projects within the organization is key to ensuring project results meet their expected delivery time frames.

Because organizations rarely have unlimited resources and funding to commit to project efforts, project managers must always be aware of the organizational priorities supported by their projects.

Role Within the Industry

Even though project management can be applied to any industry, it is important to understand the industry where the project is being conducted to help communicate with stakeholders and managers effectively. This includes not only understanding industry-specific terminology but also current trends, new products, external forces, technology, and strategies that may impact the project.

Role Within and Across Disciplines

As a professional in the project management discipline, it is critical to continually share and increase personal project management knowledge. This includes mentoring others in the profession as well as promoting project management, which emphasizes one area required for recertification as a project management professional through training and continuing education. Additionally, contributing to project management knowledge and expertise through blogs and presentations is recognized as "giving back" to the profession.

In addition to participating in activities in the project management discipline, it is important to interact with professionals in other disciplines. This enables project managers to educate others on the value of incorporating project management approaches into an organization. These approaches help improve the timeliness, quality, innovation, and management of organizational resources.

This cross-discipline approach also increases project managers' knowledge in areas where they may not have as much experience, such as business analysis, risk management, contracting and procurements, financial management, knowledge management, scheduling, and quality.

Exam Tip: Project managers are expected to provide the team with challenges and opportunities, offer feedback and support, collaborate in problem-solving and decision-making activities, effectively and openly communicate between team members and stakeholders, manage disagreements and conflicts in a constructive manner, and establish an environment of collaboration, teamwork, and cooperation.

Leadership Competencies and Skills

"Effective leadership is not about making speeches or bring liked; leadership is defined by results not attributes."

-- Peter Drucker

The project manager is both a leader and manager of the team and should be aware of different aspects influencing the team, including the team environment, geographical locations of team members, communications among stakeholders, organizational change management, internal and external politics, cultural issues, and organizational uniqueness.

Project managers should spend the appropriate amount of time to acquire, manage, motivate, and empower the team members responsible for the collective work needed to achieve shared project goals. When project team members are included in the planning activities, their expertise can be utilized to improve and strengthen their commitment to the project.

The project manager is also responsible for proactively developing the skills and competencies of team members while retaining and improving team satisfaction and motivation. The project manager must ensure all team members are aware of and always subscribe and adhere to professional and ethical behavior.

Leadership ≠ Management

Even though leadership and management are often used interchangeably, they are very different.

Leadership refers to guiding the team by using discussion and an exchange of ideas, whereas management refers to directing actions using a prescribed set of behaviors. Project managers need to employ both leadership and management depending on the situation.

Management	Leadership
Direct using positional power	Guide, influence and collaborate using relational power
Maintain	Develop
Administrate	Innovate
Focus on systems and structure	Focus on relationships with people
Rely on control	Inspire trust
Focus on near-term goals	Focus on long-range vision
Ask how and when	Ask what and why
Focus on the bottom line	Focus on the horizon
Accept the status quo	Challenge the status quo
Do things right	Do the right thing
Focus on operational issues and problem solving	Focus on vision, alignment, motivation, and inspiration

These changes from a focus on management to leadership include:

- Moving from directing and using positional power to guiding, influencing, and collaborating using relational power.
- Rather than just maintain, we develop—rather than administrate, we innovate.
- Instead of focusing on systems and structure, we focus on relationships with people, including moving from relying on control to inspiring trust.
- Rather than focusing on near-term goals, we focus on the long-range vision.
- Instead of asking how and when, we ask what and why.
- Management focuses on the bottom line and accepting the status quo, while leadership focuses on the horizon and challenges the status quo.
- Rather than just doing things right, we ensure and do the right things.
- Management focuses on operational issues and problem-solving, while leadership focus is on vision, alignment, motivation, and inspiration.

Not all team members and other stakeholders are motivated and inspired the same way. The project manager must recognize and act upon the most suitable and reasonable approach to lead the project team. This may require taking charge or quietly working behind the scenes. A project manager must adapt their leadership style to the situation and the stakeholders. This demands awareness of individual and team goals, working relationships, and emotional intelligence.

Power Skills

The role of project professionals continues to evolve as they become more collaborative leaders, innovators, and change makers. These power skills also help maintain influence with stakeholders to deliver the project's expected outcomes critical for effecting change.

The interpersonal power skills required to lead teams and individuals include collaborative leadership, communication, an innovative mindset, an orientation to understand purpose, and empathy.

Leadership Skills

Teams are made up of individuals with different skill sets, backgrounds, experiences, and attitudes.

Cohesive, collaborative teams typically are productive and effective. Leadership is a trait required of everyone on the project team. The project lead will also need to implement and utilize the appropriate leadership style.

As a project professional, it is important to possess and apply leadership skills to enable a good work environment and provide guidance to the project team toward accomplishing the desired result. This requires a balance of ethical, interpersonal, and conceptual skills helping with the analysis of situations and ability to interact appropriately.

Project managers work and communicate with several people throughout the life cycle of a project, so strong people and leadership skills are critical. Depending on the project professional's personality and a project's environment, their leadership style can vary from a servant leadership style to a more direct approach.

These leadership skills and competencies include:

- Coaching
- Communication, clear and effective, both written and verbal
- Conflict management
- Critical thinking
- Decision-making
- Emotional Intelligence (EI or EQ)
- Ethical approach—including the PMI Code of Ethics and Professional Conduct
- Expert judgment
- Facilitation

- Leadership
- Meeting management
- Negotiation and influencing
- Networking
- Political and cultural awareness
- Team building
- Presentation and public speaking

Leadership Styles

Leadership styles are different from interpersonal power skills. These styles vary depending on the situation at the time, and changes may be required as the result of multiple factors.

It is important to know a few of these and learn the differences between them; but on the job, the most important aspect is to adapt and tailor the leadership style to the situation. Factors influencing this choice include the team members, how they relate to leadership and your leadership characteristics, and the project's organization and environment.

Another area to be considered is the team's and organization's experience with the type of project being conducted—a new kind of project or a new development approach

Leadership is closely tied to the maturity of the team, including experience levels, team working experience, and personality types and combinations. These are all factors in determining the appropriate style to employ.

Some of the most common styles are laissez-faire, where the team can make their own decisions, and transactional, where the leader focuses on transactions, delivery of goals, and feedback, using management by exception.

The avoiding style is a little different from the laissez-faire. Rather than the team not needing leadership, the leader refuses to act, become involved, or make decisions.

The organization's governance structure will also affect the leadership style of the project. This reflects the influence of organizational culture.

The location of team members, especially when virtual, will impact how the project manager can support and enable them to work at their best under potentially challenging conditions.

Additional leadership styles include:

- Analytical—technical expertise making technical decisions for the project
- Autocratic—decisions made unilaterally by the leader
- Bureaucratic—focus on following documented procedures exactly without deviation
- Charismatic—energizing style motivating and inspiring the team to a high level of performance
- Consensus/Collaborative—team operates autonomously; the style frequently used in adaptive projects
- Consultative—leader factors in opinions from the team but may need to make the final decision
- Direct—hierarchical, with project manager making all decisions
- Driver—issues orders and expects team to follow; sometimes viewed as micromanagement
- Influencing—emphasizes collaborative decision-making and focuses on teamwork and team building
- Interactional - combination of transaction, transformational, and charismatic styles
- Situational—style changes to fit context and maturity/experience of team
- Servant Leadership—leader models desired behaviors supporting the team
- Transformational—empower others through sharing ideals, encourages innovation and creativity

Aspects to consider tailoring the leadership style include:

- Experience with the type of project
- Maturity of the project team members
- Organizational governance structures
- Virtual or distributed project teams

Servant Leadership

The practice of leading through service to the team, by focusing on understanding and addressing the needs and development of team members to enable the highest possible team performance.

Servant leadership means leading by supporting the team and addressing their needs. In this style the leader serves and puts other people first, concentrating on relationships, community, collaboration, understanding the team's needs, and taking action to enable the team to perform and deliver. Leadership becomes secondary and only emerges after service has been provided.

Servant leadership principles include:

- *Listening*
- *Empathy*
- *Healing*
- *Self-awareness*
- *Persuasion*
- *Conceptualization*
- *Foresight*
- *Stewardship*
- *Commitment to growth*
- *Building community*

Rather than managing projects and teams and trying to keep the project on plan and the team in line, servant leaders help teams develop and grow as a group and as individuals. They facilitate the team's work by providing coaching and training, removing blocks impeding work progress from people or processes, and focusing on team accomplishments rather than team misfires.

Servant leadership behaviors include:

- Obstacle removal
- Diversion shield
- Encouragement and development opportunities

To become a servant leader an individual should:

- Lead by example
- Show team members why the work they do is important
- Encourage collaboration, communication, and engagement
- Help the team members grow and develop
- Take interest and support team members personally
- Request feedback

To help reflect and support this change in orientation, some organizations use the term project leader rather than project manager.

Every team member should also strive to be a servant leader and support other team members.

Interpersonal and Team Skills

Additionally, project managers need interpersonal and team skills to meet the expectations of a team leader. Many of these have been identified previously, but another critical skill today includes awareness of the political and cultural state within the organization, and thus its possible impact on the project.

Some key interpersonal skills include:

- Active listening
- Communication styles assessment
- Nominal group technique
- Emotional intelligence
- Influencing
- Motivation
- Political and cultural awareness
- Transparency
- Building trust
- Resolving disagreements or conflicts
- Being a change agent

Personality

Personality refers to the differences in individuals through patterns of thinking, feeling, and behavior. Project managers need some level of each of these characteristics to successfully manage the various situations, projects, and organizations they encounter.

Most of these styles are very familiar—including being authentic, courteous, creative, culturally sensitive, emotional, intellectual, and political.

Competencies

As the vital link between the project and the organization and its strategies, the project manager must possess some core competencies, including knowledge of project management concepts and the ability to apply that knowledge to projects.

There are also some personal competencies or behaviors required in this leadership role, including attitude, personality characteristics, and ethics, as well as the leadership required to achieve the project objectives while balancing the various project constraints.

Additional competencies of project managers include:

- Skills to effectively lead a project team, coordinate, collaborate, solve problems, and make decisions
- Ethical and appropriate personal behavior while performing project activities

Leadership Competencies

Some general guidelines to help develop leadership competencies include:

- Tailoring the leadership style to meet the needs of the project.
- Using emotional intelligence and interpersonal skills to lead with empathy, being mindful of individual and team objectives and working relationships.
- Examining differing motivations and working styles of individuals and groups, which can vary greatly based on their experiences, age, culture, job roles, and many more influences. This includes cultural and diversity elements.
- Maintaining transparency and a sense of openness within a psychologically safe environment to build trust and collaboration, so team members feel empowered and free to contribute, learn from others, and offer suggestions.
- Ensuring all required external resources are included to support the needs of the project.

Team Building

Team building is critical to ensure the team functions in a cohesive manner, working together in the same direction. This is a significant component of leading a successful team.

Team-building activities facilitate bonding between team members in addition to focusing on the team aspects of unity, trust, and empathy rather than on the individual. Working collaboratively toward a shared goal is a great way for team members to help each other reach a higher level of performance.

These activities can be:

- Formal or informal
- Over a brief or extended period
- Facilitated by the project manager or a professional facilitator

Tuckman Stages of Team Development

Project team formation is the subject of Dr. Bruce Tuckman's ladder model and is very helpful when managing project team dynamics. It is often used both at the initial startup of a project and continually throughout the project, especially when new team members are added.

The first four stages of the team development model were proposed and developed by Dr. Bruce Tuckman in 1965. In 1977, Tuckman teamed up with Mary Ann Jensen and added the fifth stage—adjourning.

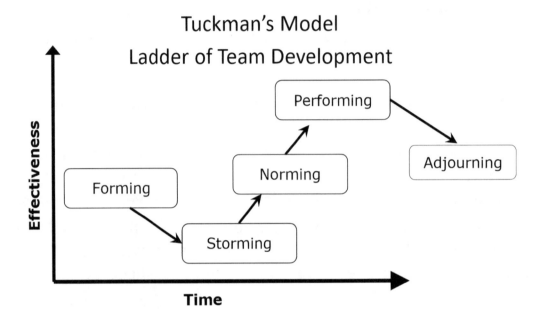

At the beginning of a project, the team is "forming." They meet and begin to know and trust each other.

As team members begin to assert themselves and compete for control of different situations, they enter the "storming" stage. This stage can be very detrimental to the success of the project if allowed to continue for any length of time. The development or refinement of the ground rules and the team charter help the team move into the "norming" stage. In this stage the team begins to work together, minimizing personal objectives or the need to individually be in control.

In adaptive teams, "storming" and "norming" can happen very quickly. Since it is assumed adaptive team members are assigned full-time throughout the project, these stages only happen when the initial team is formed. These stages are more often seen with predictive teams and can be very tricky, with team members coming and going throughout the project. The project manager's role is to help make sure these stages go smoothly and the team emerges as a cohesive unit.

After the team has determined their most effective way of working together and collaborating, they are able to move to the "performing" stage. Here the team is working at optimum productivity, often utilizing group decision-making techniques, communicating effectively, and solving problems and conflicts.

During a project, teams can get stuck in a particular stage or even revert to an earlier one. This is especially likely when a disruption occurs as the project is in progress, such as new team members joining or leaving, or perhaps a change or shift in roles. Project managers must help the team move through the "storming" stage as quickly as possible, regardless of the situation prompting the change.

The "adjourning" stage is reached at the end of the project, or when a team member moves on to the next project.

Team Tone and Culture

It is important to provide a positive environment where team members feel valued and are empowered to contribute to the overall success of the project.

This includes leading through continual positive and fluid communications and engagement with the team and stakeholders through encouragement of collaboration. This reinforces the understanding of the project's importance and vision, showing the team why the project matters, and in turn helping create relevancy and commitment to delivering the expected value.

There is also a need to help the team cultivate and establish a sense of urgency to be able to provide their best work in the shortest time.

The key is balance, consistency, motivation, and emphasizing a sense of shared understanding of the value of the project.

Types of Power and Authority

Often it is necessary to get things done, and various skills must be used. This includes using one's influence through various types of power, as perceived by others.

Power and its use can be complex, and its various forms are often needed at different times during a project.

- Formal, legitimate power is the result of the person's position in the organization, assigned by senior management and described in the project charter. It often carries with it an authoritative power.

- Reward and/or punitive power includes the power of the project manager to reward, or provide positive consequences, for team members who deliver good results—or the power to "punish," or enact negative consequences when work is not done appropriately.

- Representative power is bestowed because the team thinks an individual would be the best person to represent its needs and interests. This often happens if there is not a clearly designated project manager.

Additional types of power to be considered, either positively or negatively by others, include:

- Pressure-based power limits freedom of choice or movement by restricting choices to encourage a certain performance or compliance for a desired action.

- Guilt-based power often is used to make either team members or stakeholders feel guilty if they do not comply or conform to various areas within the project.

- Informational power is often seen as a negative power resulting in the control, gathering, or distributing of information, rather than providing transparency and sharing information with others.

- Situational power often results from having previously been in a specific or unique situation and applying those lessons learned to similar situations in the future.

Additional powers often used on a personal basis include:

- Ingratiating power to gain favor through flattery.

- Relational power from participating in networking, connections, and alliances—and often based on who knows who.

- Persuasive power utilizing influence and negotiation skills to help move toward a desired conclusion or action.

- Transformational power empowering through idealized elements and behaviors and considering the individual through encouragement of innovation and creativity.

- Personal or charismatic power based on individual charm or attraction, including having a warm personality that others like to be around. Charismatic leaders can inspire using high energy, enthusiasm, and self-confidence while also holding strong convictions.

- Interactional power combining the factors of transactional, transformational, and charismatic leadership styles.

The two last types of powers are earned powers:

- Referent power is based on the respect others hold for this individual, which is often based on credibility and experience. It also includes the person's charisma or example as a role model.

- Expert power is perceived because of special knowledge or expertise based on experience, training, education, and skills.

Exam Tip: According to PMI, referent, expert and reward are the best forms of power. Penalty power is the worst.

Key Concepts Covered

- Role of a project manager
- Leadership vs. management
- Leadership skills and competencies
- Interpersonal and team skills
- Servant leadership
- Team building
- Types of power

ECO Coverage

- Lead a team (1.2)

  - Value servant leadership (e.g., relate the tenets of servant leadership to the team) (1.2.3)

  - Determine an appropriate leadership style (e.g., directive, collaborative) (1.2.4)

  - Distinguish various options to lead various team members and stakeholders (1.2.7)

Check Your Progress

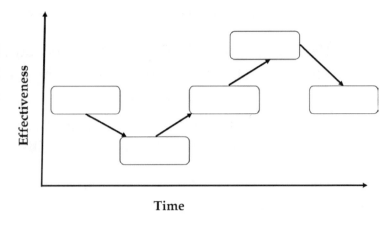

1. List the stages of Tuckman's Ladder of Team Development in the adjacent diagram from the beginning to the end.

   A. Storming

   B. Performing

   C. Storming

   D. Forming

   E. Adjourning

2. Which of the following are principles of servant leadership? (Choose 3)

   A. Buffer the team from interruptions

   B. Remove impediments

   C. Get lunch and coffee for the team

   D. Manage the team schedule

3. There are general guidelines to help project managers with the development of their leadership competencies. Which of the following are a part of these general guidelines? (Choose 4)

   A. Tailoring the leadership style to meet the needs of the project.

   B. Using emotional intelligence and interpersonal skills to lead with empathy, being mindful of individual and team objectives and working relationships.

   C. Examining differing motivations and working styles of individuals and groups, which can vary greatly based on their experiences, age, culture, job roles, and many more influences.

   D. Maintaining transparency and a sense of openness within a psychologically safe environment to build trust and collaboration, so team members feel empowered and free to contribute, learn from others, and offer suggestions.

   E. Good leaders always distance themselves from their team.

4. Referent power is perceived because of special knowledge or expertise based on experience, training, education, and skills and expert power is based on the respect others hold for this individual, which is often based on credibility and experience. It also includes the person's charisma or example as a role model. Is this statement true or false?

A. True

B. False

5. 5. Project managers need interpersonal and team skills to meet the expectations of a team leader. Which of the following are interpersonal and team skills? (Choose 3)

A. Active listening

B. Being assertive regarding the project schedule and costs

C. Emotional intelligence

D. Building trust

Answers

1. ⟶

2. A, B, C

3. A, B, C, D

4. False

5. A, C, D

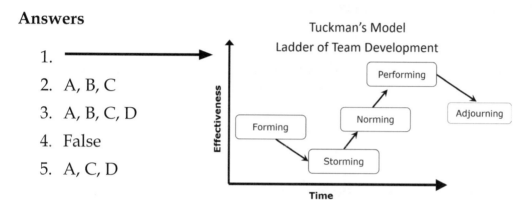

Tuckman's Model
Ladder of Team Development

Collaborative Work Environment

In addition to leading the people on the project, it is important to review best practices to ensure work can happen smoothly. This includes creating a physical and virtual working environment, including workspace management, project artifact and document creation, and configuration management.

Team Work Environment

Colocation – An organizational placement strategy where the project team members are physically located close to one another to improve communication, working relationships, and productivity.

The environment and location of a project team are extremely important elements to leading and managing projects. These could be physically shared spaces or virtual environments. The environment and location need to be considered when supporting team performance. If the team feels involved and engaged, their interactions will be more meaningful. This physical space for the project team members and stakeholders is often referred to as agile space or a war room, encouraging collaboration, communication, transparency and visibility through colocation.

Team members need to be given autonomy in their work and empowered to take initiative when needed. This includes respecting the content of the team charter or ground rules.

Collaboration and Transparency

Transparency is one of the three pillars of empirical process (transparency, inspection, and adaptability) promoting real-time, accurate progress on every aspect of the project.

Setting up the physical environment supports the whole team's engagement. Colocating all involved in a shared workspace fosters more informal and immediate collaboration and exchange of information. Ensure private spaces for those who need to work in solitude, including the use of "caves and commons."

Even the passive information absorbed from the surroundings—such as ad hoc discussions, side conversations, whiteboard drawings, and physical body language—has value. This is referred to as "osmotic communication."

Being immersed in the team physically and mentally improves the team's ability to work faster, more collaboratively, and with greater unity.

In adaptive projects, meaningful interaction is a core tenet. To encourage frequent, free-flowing interaction, the team structure and workspaces must be conducive to this need. It is important to have a team able to contribute everywhere and at any time.

These ideas apply to hybrid teams as well.

Virtual Teams

It is easy for team members to feel disconnected from other team members when working in a virtual environment.

Because the team is not colocated, project managers of virtual teams will spend a substantial amount of their time "knocking down virtual walls" to ensure that teams are able to effectively collaborate and operate as a team, not just a series of isolated individuals.

It is important to check in with each team member in a one-on-one setting as often as possible to understand the personal situations impacting the work of the individual.

Additionally, it is important to support the needs of virtual team members, including encouraging shared goals and a clear understanding of both the purpose of the project and their individual roles, responsibilities, and expectations of performance. This often includes positive network-building activities for members of the team, whether virtually located or colocated.

There are both pros and cons for virtual teams to support a project. Some best practices to consider during the performance of the project work include:

- Manage the inherent risk of virtual team members feeling isolated.
- Focus on shared commitments and team goals vs. individual accomplishments.
- Instill a sense of shared commitments in the team.
- Start with the team charter or ground rules and continually reassess and refine those to support current situations.
- Adopt and encourage behaviors to reinforce collaboration and transparency.
- Encourage teams to be accountable for deliverables, rather than individuals.
- Enable teams to self-organize where possible.
- Use appropriate tools such as shared calendars to plan meetings and coordinate feedback.
- Provide tools to improve visibility to goals and activity status.

Virtual Team Member Engagement

Managing continued engagement with virtual team members requires persistence and a focus on good team dynamics, especially transparency, accountability, and active attention to effective communications.

Teams communicate better in a face-to-face environment, and there is lots of evidence for the criticality of assessing body language and tone of voice to ensure team members have bought into the approaches they are using together to solve problems. Using and configuring videoconferencing tools for the team is essential to ensure the appropriate method provides the desired results.

Virtual Team Member Needs

To ensure teams can effectively collaborate and operate as a team, not just a series of isolated individuals, consideration and planning are required. This collaboration must be a priority. It is often the responsibility of the project manager to facilitate any actions to address these needs.

The basic needs include:

- Cohesion
- Shared goals

- Clear purpose
- Clarity on roles and expectations

These can be addressed in several ways, including:

- Investment in and active use of videoconferencing tools to enable team meetings allowing fuller integration of all aspects of the team and to ensure the team members are committed to their solution approaches.
- Visibility into work and work status, since even a small team will have trouble aligning its work activities unless effective tools are implemented to collaborate and promote visibility.
- Use of kanban-style boards to visualize the work to do, to track (and limit) work in progress, and to note when work activities are completed, and objectives have been met.

Key Concepts Covered

- Team work environment
- Collaboration and transparency
- Virtual teams

ECO Coverage

- Engage and support virtual teams (1.11)
  - Implement options for virtual team member engagement (1.11.3)

- Manage project artifacts (2.12)
  - Validate that the project information is kept up to date (i.e., version control) and accessible to all stakeholders (2.12.2)

Check Your Progress

1. For virtual teams to support a project, some of the best practices to consider during the performance of the project work are included below. Which of the following are considered best practice of virtual teams? (Choose 3)

   A. Establish effective, and sustainable technology to support team members working remotely

   B. Manage the inherent risk of virtual team members feeling isolated

   C. Encourage teams to be accountable for deliverables, rather than individuals

   D. Concentrate on individual team members to accomplish their goals since they work from home with little interruptions

2. For a project manager leading an agile project team in a virtual environment, what should be the first step the agile project manager should take?

    A. Determine what software tools should be used to help the team collaborate

    B. Learn the team members needs

    C. Determine where to set up a virtual co-location environment

    D. Work with the hiring manager to recruit the most experienced team members

3. In adaptive projects, meaningful interaction among team members is important. To encourage frequent, free-flowing interaction, the team structure and workspaces must serve this need. It is important to have a team able to contribute everywhere and at any time. Is this statement true or false?

    A. True

    B. False

4. Colocating all involved in a shared workspace fosters more informal and immediate collaboration and exchange of information. The project manager or scrum master should try to create private spaces for those who need to work in solitude, known as 'caves' from where the team works in a conference room known as "commons." Is this true or false?

    A. True

    B. False

5. Virtual team member basic needs include:

    A. Cohesion as a team

    B. Shared goals

    C. Clarity on their role in the project

    D. Scheduled break times for each team member to be scheduled on their respective calendars

Answers

1. A, B, C
2. B
3. True
4. True
5. D

Team Member Empowerment

The idea of empowerment is a critical part of the Agile mindset and has made its way into hybrid projects. Predictive team environments can also benefit from empowering team members to assist the project manager in making decisions based on their previous experience and expert judgment.

In all contexts, strive to create an environment where individual team members are empowered to contribute ideas.

Empowerment, Unity, Autonomy

Empowerment, team unity, and autonomy are characteristics of high-performing teams that should be cultivated in any project team. Other factors include:

- Open communication
- Shared understanding
- Shared ownership
- Trust
- Collaboration
- Adaptability
- Resilience
- Empowerment
- Recognition

People contribute their best when they feel proud of their work and are empowered by being given shared responsibility. When challenges arise during the project, empowered teams can act with a greater sense of responsibility.

It is important to encourage the team to foster team collaboration and decision-making. The team does not depend on heavy-handed discipline. The team must recognize the power and influence they possess. As an empowered cohesive unit, they depend on each other to make decisions and solve problems to deliver targeted value quickly.

In projects, the team is the most important component. Without a unified team, the project falls apart and project management becomes insufficient. Teams should be shaped with a healthy culture of working autonomy. This shows trust in the individual, inspires collaboration and innovation, and in turn boosts the productivity of the entire team.

Use a light management touch and one appropriate to the situation. Any interference with the team is disruptive and can reduce the members' motivation to work.

In the shift from leading a team to empowering team members, it is important to recognize the knowledge and domain expertise of team members. The project manager becomes more of a servant leader, utilizing emotional intelligence approaches and enabling effective communication among team members.

Psychological Safety

Psychological safety is showing and employing oneself without fear of negative consequences of status, career, or self-worth — we should be comfortable being ourselves in our work setting.46

Psychological safety is a condition that is required for high-performing project teams. It means team members should be comfortable being themselves in their work setting, while remembering they are part of a team.

It is important to empower the team by creating and maintaining a healthy work setting that embraces diversity and is built on trust and mutual respect for all team members.

This adaptive team concept is also useful in predictive team settings.

Diversity, Equity, and Inclusion (DEI)

Teams are composed of individuals, and many global organizations have initiatives related to diversity and inclusion strategies. Individuals must be respected even as the team is empowered to work together as a cohesive unit.

Based on what is appropriate for the team, it is important to create an environment that acknowledges diversity in a positive way and builds a team climate of mutual trust.

Diversity is important to a team's success because it enables greater innovation. The more diverse our team, the better our ideas will be, the better our work will be, and the more we'll learn from each other.

DEI development objectives for the team might include:

- Improving team knowledge and skills to reduce cost and time and improve quality
- Improving trust to raise team morale, reduce conflict, and improve teamwork
- Creating a collaborative culture to improve individual and team performance and facilitate cross-training and mentoring

---

46 *https://www.pmi.org/disciplined-Agile/mindset/promises/safety*

- Empowering the team to participate in decision-making and own the solutions they create

Situational Leadership

Developed by Paul Hersey and Ken Blanchard in the 1960s, situational leadership describes how project managers change their leadership style based on the project's current situation. This includes applying more influence when managing inexperienced team members and using a more directive approach, telling team members exactly what to do. As the skills and capabilities of team members increase, a more delegated approach, with very little guidance, is needed. The various stages between these two extremes include:

- *Directing/Telling*—Defines the roles and tasks of the "followers" and supervises closely, with decisions made and expressed by the "leader."
- *Coaching/Selling*—Roles and tasks still defined, but ideas and suggestions from the "followers" are encouraged—including more two-way communications.
- *Supporting/Participating*—Day-to-day decisions, including task assignments and processes, are given to the "followers," but the leader plays the role of facilitator while remaining in control.
- *Delegating*—Even though the "leader" is still involved in decisions and problem-solving, the "followers" are in control.

OSCAR Model

The OSCAR coaching and mentoring model was developed by Karen Whittleworth and Andrew Gilbert. It helps individuals adapt their coaching and leadership styles for individuals with a personal development plan. The five contributing factors include:

Outcome—An outcome identifies the long-term goals of an individual and the desired results

Situation—Evaluation of the current knowledge level and how that level impacts performance and peer relationships

Choices/consequences—Identification of potential means for attaining the desired outcome and the consequences of each choice

Actions—Commitment to specific improvements by focusing on immediate and attainable targets within a specified time frame

Review—Regular meetings to offer support and help ensure that individuals remain motivated and on-track

Team Charter and Ground Rules

The team charter and ground rules can and should be reviewed and updated as needed on a periodic basis.

When the project is in progress, the team should always have the ground rules close at hand and visibly displayed. This helps identify when any of the rules are not being followed—and maybe a modification is needed. If the project experiences change, the team charter or ground rules might need updating.

The team may go through the "forming" stage again whenever team members change, which is one of the reasons for preferring a full-time and long-standing team.

If a ground rule has been violated, the team needs to initiate the appropriate response using servant leadership to help coach individual team members back into alignment.

Key Concepts Covered

- Team work environment
- Team member empowerment
- Diversity, equity, and inclusion (DEI)

ECO Coverage

- Lead a team (1.2)
  - Support diversity and inclusion (e.g., behavior types, thought process) (1.2.2)
  - Inspire, motivate, and influence team members/stakeholders (e.g., team contract, social contract, reward system) (1.2.5)

Check Your Progress

1. The new project manager just finished his first meeting with his team members, He noticed that often during the meeting, team members would talk on top of each other, interrupt other team members as they were speaking and poking fun at one team member where the project manager realize from their body language, he was offended. What should the project manager have done before this meeting?

   A. Conduct a ground rules meeting to set the stage for the behavior for all team meetings

   B. Create a project charter to identify the ground rules

   C. The project manager should have called out each problem during the meeting to correct their behavior

    D. This team behavior is normal during all team meetings so the project manager must learn to deal with it

2. Situational leadership describes how project managers change their leadership style based on the project's current situation. This includes applying more influence when managing experienced team members and using a more directive approach, telling team members exactly what to do. For less experienced team members a more delegating approach, with very little guidance, is needed. Is this statement true or false?

    A. True

    B. False

3. An Agile team had been working together for just two weeks when a team member violated a ground rule. How should this violation be handled?

    A. The team needs to initiate the appropriate response using servant leadership to help coach individual team members back into alignment

    B. The scrum master is responsible for coaching the team member back into alignment

    C. The H.R. department is responsible for coaching the team member back into alignment

    D. The Agile team should ignore the violation and hope the team member will figure out what he did wrong.

4. Psychological safety is a condition that is required for high-performing project teams. It means team members should be comfortable being themselves in their work setting, while remembering they are part of a team. Is this statement true or false?

    A. True

    B. False

5. DEI development objectives for the team might include: (Choose 3)

    A. Creating a collaborative culture to improve individual and team performance and facilitate cross-training and mentoring

    B. Empowering the team to participate in decision-making and own the solutions they create

    C. Setting direction for all team meetings

    D. Improving team knowledge and skills to reduce cost and time and improve quality

Answers

1. A, B, C
2. False
3. A
4. True
5. A, B, D

Team Member Performance

Supported team members perform better and are motivated to do their best work. Project managers need strategies to maintain support for the individual as well as for the whole team. These are focused mainly on emotional intelligence and communications.

Team Motivation

As project work is being performed, it is important as a project manager to stay focused on keeping the team motivated.

It is also important to continually assess the team to see what they need to perform at their best. Strong leadership power skills are essential.

Motivational Theories/Approaches

Motivational theory is standard reading for business practitioners, and most should be familiar with these names, their contributions to motivational theory, and why their work from the mid-20th century is still relevant to project professionals today.

Project managers and team members can benefit as part of their personal professional development through several topics in motivational theory.[47]

Maslow's Hierarchy of Needs

Psychology professor Abraham Maslow founded the humanistic psychology discipline. In 1943, his paper "A Theory of Human Motivation"[48] presented what we refer to as Maslow's Hierarchy of Needs. He also included this in his book *Motivation and Personality*.[49]

---

47 Further reading: https://www.pmi.org/learning/library/motivation-increase-project-team-performance-7234

48 Maslow, A. H. (1943). A Theory of Human Motivation, Psychological Review 50, 370-96.

49 Maslow, A. H. (1943). Motivation and personality. New York: Harper.

Maslow grouped human needs into five categories humans fulfill progressively, from bottom to top. This means the underlying needs must be fulfilled before the ones above are attempted.

The levels of the hierarchy, starting from most basic, include:

- *Physiological needs*—the basic elements the human body needs to survive. These are food, water, and sleep
- *Safety needs*—the items a person needs to feel safe from physical or economic harm
- *Social needs*—the desire to give and receive affection and to be part of a group
- *Esteem needs*—the recognition received from others as well as through self-esteem
- *Self-Actualization needs*—an individual's desires for self-fulfillment and developing to their full potential

Motivating a team requires facilitating or encouraging accordingly, so people are empowered to strive to reach the fifth level of self-actualization.

Herzberg's Motivation-Hygiene Theory

Frederick Herzberg performed studies to determine which factors in an employee's work environment caused satisfaction or dissatisfaction and published these in his 1959 book *The Motivation to Work*.[50] He identified two dimensions to job satisfaction: "hygiene factors" and "motivators."

Herzberg's Motivation-Hygiene theory states that success in the workplace is based upon those two elements:

- *Hygiene factors*—relate to working environment, salary, a stable job, good relationships with management and coworkers
  - Hygiene topics include company policies, supervision, salary, interpersonal relationships, and working conditions—issues related to the employee's working environment.
  - Hygiene issues cannot motivate employees but can minimize dissatisfaction if handled properly. They can only "dissatisfy" if they are absent or mishandled.

- *Motivation factors*—relate to feelings of engagement, recognition, and career advancement
  - Once the hygiene areas are addressed, the motivators will promote job satisfaction and encourage production.

---

50   *Herzberg, F., Mausner, B. & Snyderman, B.B. (1959). The Motivation to Work. New York: John Wiley.*

- Motivators create satisfaction by fulfilling an individual's needs for meaning and personal growth. They include issues such as achievement, recognition, work, responsibility, and advancement.

McGregor's Theory X and Theory Y[51]

Douglas McGregor's Theory X and Theory Y apply to the management of labor in the field of social psychology. He developed this while working at the MIT Sloan School of Management in the 1950s.

His book *The Human Side of Enterprise* refers to two styles of management—authoritarian (Theory X) and participative (Theory Y). These describe two different attitudes regarding workforce motivation and provide ways to categorize individuals in the workforce.

- *Theory X*—assumes that people dislike work, have little ambition, and are unwilling to take responsibility
  - Theory X presumes team members are only interested in their own goals, are unmotivated, dislike work, and must be forced to be productive.
  - These team members will require an authoritative management style, constant supervision, and an enticing incentive program to achieve the results required for the project.
  - Work in organizations managed like this can be repetitive, and people are often motivated with a "carrot-and-stick" approach.

- *Theory Y*—assumes that people are more self-motivated and ambitious with self-control
  - Theory Y is essentially the opposite from Theory X: people want to work and enjoy it, and management does not need to hover and constantly supervise.
  - These team members need very little external motivation, will seek responsibility, and can be trusted to work on their own to achieve the project's goals.

Sometimes, Theory X is called the "old-school" approach to management, and it is often used with a predictive approach. Theory Y is a more modern approach that supports an adaptive mindset.

This theory most often applies to the composition of teams working in a more Agile or adaptive environment, where the team is expected to be self-organizing and self-starting, without the need for a "command and control" leader more representative of Theory X.

---

51 *McGregor, D. (1960). The Human Side of Enterprise. New York: McGraw-Hill Book Co.,*

A Theory X project manager often wants to micromanage the team members, whereas the Theory Y project manager holds back and lets the team members determine the way to proceed. But this doesn't always have to be negative, especially when the team needs more direction, as identified as a part of Situational Leadership.

The problem arises when there is a conflict between these styles, such as a Theory X manager who manages a Theory Y person, or conversely, when a Theory Y manager is responsible for directing Theory X individuals.

McClelland's Achievement Motivation Theory[52]

David McClelland's Achievement Motivation theory, described in his 1961 book, *The Achieving Society*, states that an individual's needs are shaped by life experiences, largely depending on culture. The theory suggests that everyone has three needs, and one becomes dominant in our personalities at various times. The dominant need can change based on life experiences. Most people possess and exhibit a combination of all three characteristics, and the mix affects their behavior and managing style.

One of these needs is dominant at any given time, but project managers must be able to discern when a change has occurred. This information and understanding can help influence goal setting, feedback, and the use of motivation and reward systems. It is important, where appropriate, to understand team members' strengths and utilize this knowledge when establishing team roles.

A balance of these three motivators within the project team helps with establishing a high-performance team. The motivators are:

- *Achievement*
  - Has a strong need to set and accomplish challenging goals
  - Takes calculated risks to accomplish their goals
  - Likes to receive regular feedback on their progress and achievements
  - Often likes to work alone, taking personal responsibility
  - Make the best leaders but may demand too much of their team, believing that everyone is also highly achievement-focused and results-driven
- *Affiliation*
  - Wants to belong to a group
  - Enjoys friendship and wants to be liked
  - Will often go along with whatever the rest of the group wants to do

---

52 *McClelland, D. The Achieving Society (1961). D. Van Nostrand*

- Favors collaboration, and cooperation over competition
- Doesn't like high risk or uncertainty
- May undermine a manager's objectivity because of their need to be liked, affecting decision-making capabilities

- *Power*
    - Wants to be in charge, including control and influence over others
    - Likes to win arguments
    - Enjoys competition and winning
    - Enjoys status and recognition
    - Produces a determined work ethic and commitment to the organization
    - Often attracts individuals to a leadership role, but they may not possess the required flexibility and interpersonal skills

Vroom's Expectancy Theory[53]

Victor Vroom, in his 1994 book *Work and Motivation*, stated that for a person to be motivated, performance and motivation must be linked. This includes recognition of effort from motivation, performance, and outcomes. Three variables were identified:

- *Expectancy*—belief that increased effort will lead to a specific outcome; affected by:
    - Having the right resources available (materials, time)
    - Having the right skills to do the job
    - Having the necessary support to complete the work (management support, appropriate and necessary information)

- *Instrumentality*—belief that a valued outcome will be received if you perform well
- *Valence*—importance, or value, the individual places on the expected outcome

Motivation: Right Way

- Consider ways to inspire and motivate the team by providing opportunities, not emphasizing obligations.
- Encourage moments or opportunities to self-assess and reflect on areas for professional growth.
- Provide appropriate training opportunities by asking the team what they need.

---

53 *Work and Motivation, Victor Vroom, Jossey-Bass 1994*

– Make sure virtual teams continue to feel connected through constant and regular contact.

Motivation: Wrong Way

– Heavy-handed, one-size-fits-all approaches to improvement or support for team members.

– Constantly scheduling meetings to have meetings, causing interruptions to planned activities.

– Requiring additional non-project work and causing distractions. Meeting other obligations may be necessary, and team members will have other commitments, but try to keep the team focused as much as possible.

Objectives

Teams are typically more productive when they have clear objectives to meet. Project managers can support the team by setting objectives collaboratively with them. Ensure that these objectives are clearly and effectively communicated throughout the project to enable a more productive and driven team.

Project managers and the team can determine joint objectives that are challenging yet attainable.

Objective setting can be conducted at the start of a project or phase but is commonly done throughout the project life cycle. In an iteration planning session, the team sets the targets and commitments for the upcoming period.

Today's leadership of projects often includes management by objectives including.

– Using clear objectives to guide productivity and encourage aspiration
– Setting objectives collaboratively with team members
– Creating challenging, yet attainable, objectives
  • At the beginning of the project or a phase
  • Throughout the life cycle as part of an iteration planning session

Performance Assessment

In structured teams with a project manager, performance assessments can be carried out for team members for skills, aptitude, attitude, work style, and other characteristics.

A formal assessment can include the activities and in-house templates provided by the organization, but the information included will be standard. This is often done by the project manager and provided as a courtesy to the team member's manager, often referred to as the resource manager. This evaluation of work on the project becomes part of the more formal, overall individual performance assessment.

Use performance assessments to review and evaluate work on the project, including:

- Comparison of performance to goals
- Reclarification and performance in assigned roles and responsibilities
- Ability to deliver and receive positive as well as negative feedback
- Discovery and support of unknown or unresolved issues
- Creation and monitoring of individual training plans
- Establishment of future goals
- Successful delivery on technical requirements

Assessments: Predictive

For predictive approaches, assessments are often done to help identify potential team members, then when individuals are assigned and become part of the team, and again after the team is established. The assessments are monitored throughout the project. These assessments can utilize either formal or informal methods, often recommended by the organization.

Discover Opportunities for Improvement

Adaptive teams are self-organizing and operate in psychologically safe environments, meaning there is an accepted level of trust among team members to continuously assess each other as well as regulate their own performance.

Personalities Assessment[54]

Everyone can be considered an introvert, extrovert, pragmatist, innovator, or process-follower, among other categories.

Personality assessments can be useful to achieve better understanding of team members. Typically used in a human resource (HR) or recruitment function, they attempt to measure human psychology and are helpful when evaluating a team or team environment.

Some teams use personality tests and indicators to create more meaningful interactions. These often provide insight into individual personalities to help shape motivation

---

54   *Psychological team roles research: https://hbr.org/2017/01/great-teams-are-about-personalities-not-just-skills*

options, as well as improvement of interactions and communications with other team members and stakeholders.

They can also help the project manager build trust and empower team members by aligning their strengths with knowledge-sharing or coaching roles.

Commonly used tools include:

- Big Five Personality Model (OCEAN)
- Myers–Briggs Type Indicator
- DISC
- And many others

When using these tools, make sure that their use is clearly explained, and permission is received. The personal information captured must not be shared with others without the individual's permission.

Use the results as predictors, not as absolutes, as they are heavily based on how the individual responds to the questions. Don't make fixed assumptions or judgments based on the results. They can be used as an icebreaker or a team-building activity to help team members get to know each other better.

Personality affects an individual's project management role within the team, their interactions with the rest of the team, and whether their values, or core beliefs, align with those of other team members.

In addition to personality tests, psychological metrics, or psychometrics, can be useful in analyzing personality indicators. This allows the project manager to make adjustments within the team to support team members' and key project stakeholders' emotional and other needs.

Psychological team roles are useful for understanding how people think, and therefore, what types of roles or tasks they may be best suited for, or conversely, not readily suited for. They include:

- Results-oriented — e.g., product testing
- Relationship-focused — e.g., communication leader, meeting facilitator
- Innovative and disruptive thinkers — e.g., Agile software developer/team member
- Process and rule-followers — e.g., transcriber in meetings, prototype builder
- Pragmatic — e.g., archive project documents

Emotional Intelligence

An important interpersonal skill of all project managers is emotional intelligence (EI). EI helps with the understanding of personal emotions and those of others to help minimize conflict. The notion of EI evolved in the 1990s and is now recognized as a key set of personal and interpersonal skills.

The personal side includes self-awareness, self-regulation, and motivation, whereas the interpersonal side comprises social skills and empathy.

- Self-awareness measures how well individual emotions are recognized in a variety of situations.
- Self-regulation defines how well those emotions can be controlled.
- Motivation describes various intrinsic reasons for achievement.
- Empathy is how well the emotions of others can be read and understood.
- Social skills address how well relationships and rapport with others are built.

Emotional Intelligence Components[55]

Each emotional intelligence skill is made up of, or influenced by, several components.

Self-Awareness

- How do you affect the team?
- How does the team affect you?

Self-Management

- Think before you act
- Build trust

Social Awareness

- Be empathetic
- Employ active listening

Social Skill

- Establish rapport
- Build effective teams
- Manage attitude

---

55   *Goleman, D. (1995). Emotional Intelligence: Why It Can Matter More Than IQ*

– *Self-Awareness Elements*

Self-awareness enables an individual to read and interpret the emotions and feelings of others, as well as recognizing how emotions and behaviors positively or negatively affect others.

This is crucial for effective management and team performance. From self-awareness, people can begin self-regulating and become more socially aware.

This leads to better relationship management capability, which is essential for healthy project team cultures.

– *Empathy*

Empathy is a critical emotional intelligence skill profoundly affecting the ability to relate to and establish a rapport with others. It expands vision and decision-making beyond the immediate circumstance and individual priorities.

Having empathy helps us to help ourselves (inward) and to help our team (outward). It helps individuals:

- Understand others
- Be of service to others based on their particular needs and emotions
- Readily observe emotional cues and listen carefully
- Display tact and appreciate or share others' points of view
- Happily, provide proper help
- Understand a customer's point of view and serve as a faithful guide
- Look for strategies to increase consumers' contentment and loyalty
- Recognize consumers' needs and match them to products or services

Establishing an empathetic culture helps teams:

- Make developing others a priority
- Recognize and reward the talents and achievements of others
- Provide helpful criticism and determine people's development needs
- Coach and mentor, when appropriate, and provide tasks to stretch and nurture a person's abilities

- *Social Skills*

Social skills draw on other emotional intelligence skill sets to build strong relationships with people and effect change in the organization.

High-performing team members are adept at:

- Communicating
- Building bonds
- Collaborating and cooperating
- Catalyzing change
- Managing conflict
- Influencing
- Leadership
- *Motivation Elements*

To lead people toward having the desired social skill set, project managers need to motivate them.

Motivation is the EI skill associated with an individual's internal abilities. It's about raising ambition to attain peak performance. As a project manager, it is important to understand how to nurture and grow these factors personally as well as for the project team.

- *Achievement/Drive*
  - Setting tough goals and taking chances
  - Driving hard to get results and satisfy or exceed aspirations and ideals
  - Discovering how to upgrade capabilities
  - Striving to minimize uncertainty and discover ways to improve

- *Commitment*
  - Relying on the team's core principles to make decisions
  - Realizing a benefit in a comprehensive quest (holistic participation)
  - Gladly sacrificing to fulfill a substantial company goal
  - Enthusiastically searching for opportunities to help achieve the team's mission

- *Initiative*
  - Working toward goals beyond what's essential or anticipated
  - Inspiring others through extraordinary, resourceful feats
  - Being prepared to grab opportunities

- *Optimism*
  - Hoping to succeed instead of fearing failure
  - Seeing reversals as caused by controllable factors instead of a personal defect
  - Steadily working toward goals regardless of barriers and glitches

Key Concepts Covered

- Motivation theories
- Performance indicators
- Team member performance assessment
- Emotional intelligence

ECO Coverage

- Support team performance (1.3)
  - Appraise team members' performance against key performance indicators (KPIs) (1.3.1)
  - Verify performance improvements (1.3.4)

- Promote team performance through the application of emotional intelligence (1.14)
  - Assess behavior through the use of personality indicators (1.14.1)
  - Analyze personality indicators and adjust to the emotional needs of key project stakeholders (1.14.2)

Check Your Progress

1. Emotional intelligence is made up of, or influenced by, several components. What are the components of emotional intelligence? (Choose 4)

   A. Self-Management

   B. Social skills

   C. Self-Awareness

   D. Social Awareness

   E. Esteem Awareness

   F. Self-Actualization Awareness

2. Which of the following are the right way to motivate a team? (Choose 4)

   A. Consider ways to inspire and motivate the team by providing opportunities, not emphasizing obligations

   B. Encourage moments or opportunities to self-assess and reflect on areas for professional growth

   C. Provide appropriate training opportunities by asking the team what they need

   D. Make sure virtual teams continue to feel connected through constant and regular contact

   E. Use a one-size-fits-all approach to improvement or support for team members

3. Maslow's Hierarchy of Needs, identifies accomplishments, respect, attention, and application of skills are categorized as: (Choose 3)

   A. Physiological need

   B. Self-actualization needs

   C. Esteem needs

   D. Social needs

4. As a team member, working conditions, salary, status, and job security matter a lot to you on the other hand, you feel that you will be more motivated and will contribute more if you are rewarded for your contribution to the project given the opportunity to grow professionally. Which motivational theory are you referring to?

   A. McGregor's theory X and theory Y

   B. Maslow's Hierarchy of Needs

   C. Herzberg's Motivation-Hygiene theory

   D. McClelland's Achievement Motivation Theory

5. Empathy is a critical emotional intelligence skill profoundly affecting the ability to relate to and establish a rapport with others. It expands vision and decision-making beyond the immediate circumstance and individual priorities. Which of the following are characteristics of empathy? (Choose 3)

   A. Understand others

   B. Concentrate on getting team members to meet their task completion dates.

   C. Readily observe emotional cues and listen carefully

   D. Check on virtual team members through constant and regular contact to make sure they are working their regular hours

   E. Display tact and appreciate or share others' points of view

Answers

1. A, B, C, D
2. A, B, C, D
3. A, B, C
4. C
5. A, C, E

Stakeholder Collaboration

Project Management Principle:

Effectively Engage with Stakeholders[56]

Engage stakeholders proactively and to the degree needed to contribute to project success and customer satisfaction.

Effective project leadership means establishing meaningful and collaborative relationships with all stakeholders through appropriate and effective engagement.

Stakeholder Engagement

Keeping track of stakeholder activity and engagement in a project is needed on every project team, regardless of the approach. Depending on the project composition and the ways of working, multiple methods might be appropriate.

The power/interest or power/influence grid was used to capture the "position" of a stakeholder relative to the project when the initial stakeholders were identified and analyzed. Since there are many situations during the project where this might change, it is important to frequently review these grids, as the preferred engagement method may need to be modified. Placement on the grids often dictates the appropriate management strategies and engagement approaches.

Additional analysis and expert judgment are often needed to correctly update this information. It is important to keep track of changes and the reasons for them if there is a need to understand when and why a change was made.

---

56 *The Standard for Project Management, Section 3.3 – Project Management Principles*

Stakeholder Engagement Assessment Matrix (SEAM)

A matrix comparing current and desired stakeholder engagement levels.

It is important to use expert judgment, emotional intelligence, and interpersonal skills to assess stakeholders and their level of engagement at various times during the project. This not only requires continual review of the expected engagement level but also updating based on the current work and the current stakeholder engagement level.

The SEAM matrix identifies the current and desired engagement levels for each key stakeholder. This is reviewed and modified continuously throughout the project, as interests and concerns may change for different areas of the project.

The key labels used for this matrix include:

- Unaware—stakeholders who don't realize they are stakeholders or are unaware of the focus of the current project effort
- Resistant—against the project or the current focus
- Neutral—knowledgeable but have no strong opinion on the project
- Supportive—in favor of the project and/or current focus and are helpful promoters.
- Leading, aka "Champions"—advocates for the project or current focus

It is important to understand their current level of engagement and then work with them individually to help achieve the desired level of engagement. This is especially challenging for those who are resistant, as it requires understanding their resistance and what will be necessary to move them to at least a neutral position.

Communication

"Communication is the real work of leadership."[57]

Communications are both personal and strategic. There is a need to manage volumes of informal and formal conversations, emails, documents, and so on. Establishing healthy, collaborative working relationships within the team and with stakeholders is important. The key to both is effective communication.

Project managers spend a great deal of time communicating with stakeholders, so it is essential to ensure the right information is getting to the right stakeholder so timely decisions can be made, issues addressed, and expectations met.

---

57 *Nitin Nohria, Dean of the Harvard Business School, 2010-2020*

Effective project teams rely on healthy, active communication to enable collaborative learning. Collaboration with stakeholders looks different in each project, but there are some general guidelines to creating a project culture tied together with fluid communication.

Communications Management

Managing project communications includes planning how communications will be managed and identifying actual communications distributed by the project manager to the appropriate stakeholders. This identification continues throughout the project, not just initially, when the communication management plan was developed.

A communications matrix is a shorter version used in all types of team environments that helps organize information related to communications. The matrix is usually described and managed using a spreadsheet, whiteboard, or other media tailored to the team's needs.

It represents the communication requirements assessed for the various stakeholders, as well as any reporting requirements identified in other subsidiary project plans. Some reports are required to have multiple formats and content around the same subject, due to individual stakeholders' needs and authority to know the specifics included.

The type of information for individual communications, or reports, captured in the matrix for a predictive project approach includes:

- Information to be communicated, including language, format, content, and level of detail
- Reason for communication
- Time frame and frequency
- Receipt of acknowledgment, or response, if required
- Sender of the communication
- Authorizing person, in the case of confidential information
- Receivers — including their needs, requirements, and expectations
- Methods or technologies used for communications — e.g., email, press release, social media

Optimize Communication

Communication is clearly the key for successful teams and projects.

Successful teams become successful by working together to execute work, solve problems, and produce solutions. In a virtual team, the need for effective communication is even greater due to the lack of opportunity for osmotic learning from just being around other team members.

Effective Communication

Effective communications include:

- Integrating and implementing retrospectives appropriately with the project work to continually focus on where improvements can be made, both on the product and the way of working
- Communicating regularly and positively to internal and external stakeholders and team members based on the communication management plan and communication matrix
- Reviewing team communications as identified in the team charter, ground rules, and team communications plan and continually determining whether changes or adjustments are needed
- Utilizing both technology and tools to support the work and communication sharing within the team
- Regularly encouraging feedback on the usage of the tools and where tailoring or adjustment is needed to increase their effectiveness and efficiency

Active listening and providing feedback are two critical communication techniques every project team member should practice as part of effective listening.

Nonverbal Communication

Nonverbal communication includes conveying information without using words, adding additional layers of meaning to what is being spoken. This may include as much as four times the number of nonverbal communications over verbal communications. Often, nonverbal communication reveals who an individual is and how they relate to others.

The various types of nonverbal communication types, effects and expressions which can vary between cultures include:

- Facial expressions (happiness, sadness, anger, fear, etc.)
- Gestures (waving, pointing, giving a "thumbs up" sign, etc.)
- Paralinguistics (tone of voice, loudness, inflection, and pitch))
- Body language (indicating feelings and attitudes, often subtle and less definitive)

- Proxemics or personal space (influenced by social norms, cultural expectations, situational factors, and level of familiarity)
- Eye gaze (looking, staring, and blinking)
- Haptics (touch)
- Appearance (culture, first impressions)
- Artifacts (objects and images including avatars)

Active Listening

A communication technique involving acknowledgment of what is heard and clarifying the message to confirm that what was heard matches the message the sender intended. (From glossary: an interpersonal skill that requires listening closely and participating actively while communicating.)

Using active listening, the listener must focus on the person. Listen to not only the words but the nonverbal communication and feeling included in the message to the end, rather than trying to formulate a response prematurely. Be sincerely interested in what the person is talking about. The receiver should confirm receipt and understanding of the message, often by restating or paraphrasing the message or using body language such as nodding, etc.

Feedback

Feedback is a crucial part of communication. It should be done regularly and, in both directions, — giving and receiving.

The most important aspect of feedback is to provide confirmation that the message sent was understood. This can be done through ensuring that feedback is:

- Clear, specific, and offered in a timely way
- Objective and critical
- Positive or effective — if received and understood objectively

If feedback is not received, it becomes an implicit acceptance of the message by the receiver. This is especially true when team members don't feel comfortable openly discussing issues directly with others, especially during retrospectives with team members. Nonparticipation by key stakeholders at times during the project can lead to misunderstanding or the need to spend more time explaining situations previously discussed.

In the case of key stakeholders who are not participating as expected, the reason will need to be uncovered and may require escalation to help resolve the situation or provide a replacement.

Feedback is a key part of adaptive projects regarding product development. It also is important to ask for feedback from the team, showing a willingness to listen to them, which encourages continued feedback. Regardless of the type of feedback, it should be given in a timely manner, especially if it requires some action to be taken. It also should be requested frequently as well as when needed.

Communication regarding technical and "soft" performance aspects should be done at the appropriate level of detail. This includes determining the most appropriate communication method to transfer information among project stakeholders—e.g., public or private, individual or group, written or verbal.

Active listening and providing feedback are two critical communication techniques every project team member should practice as part of effective listening.

Reports and Formal Communication

Projects using a predictive approach utilize formal reporting at appropriate milestones to maintain continuous communication with stakeholders. Reports also become the information to support approval of milestones or governance checkpoints. These are often used to obtain sign-off or approval of work.

Because of the overlap between communications being distributed and stakeholders receiving them, the stakeholder register and engagement plan, and the communications management plan incorporate the required reports, including any formal communications.

Visible Information

"Information radiator" is the generic term for visual displays placed in a visible location so everyone can quickly see the latest information. In Agile practices, this is also known as a "Big Visible Chart."

Having open communications and transparency are some of the pillars of Agile. They support effective collaboration, but it may take time to develop trust and become comfortable displaying project information openly.

In adaptive teams, the term "psychological safety" is key. It is the ability to speak openly and freely about the work, in the interest of the work. This can seem difficult at first but remember that the team should establish clear ground rules of respect. Ensure that the team members stay respectful but are open to speaking up and offering helpful opinions.

Project information can be openly shared using electronic or physical methods or a combination of both. One additional important benefit of this sharing is that it promotes accountability by increasing the responsibility of individual team members to contribute to the overall project effort.

Another benefit is that by providing progress and project information, additional conversations and collaboration among team members and stakeholders may lead to innovation. This might not happen if that sharing, and discussion do not take place.

Collaboration

It is important to foster an environment of effective collaboration between the entire team, including stakeholders as well as the core team. It is a key to building trust between all parties.

Open dialogue and meaningful communication optimize the understanding of the project's aims, as well as the expectations of the results and what needs to be done to realize those expectations.

Everyone's involvement and engagement in the project may fluctuate or remain constant depending on the focus of the project at that time. That level of engagement needs to be evaluated and re-evaluated throughout the project.

Keeping discussions open and transparent ensures appropriate stakeholders are knowledgeable and expectations are set. Engagement also builds appreciation for others' needs and constraints.

Communication skills, interpersonal skills, feedback, and meeting management, among other management skills, can be leveraged to maximize the feedback loop and engagement between stakeholders.

This can be enhanced by using effective collaboration tools, including shared whiteboards, wikis, and shared file structures.

Collaboration Activities

Stakeholders and team members collaborate every day on a project. Some stakeholders may be engaged less frequently. The frequency of engagement is based on mutual needs and expectations. The stakeholder engagement assessment matrix is especially helpful in evaluating individual stakeholders' current and desired engagement levels at different times during the project.

Nearly constant engagement among the core project team members is common. This regular collaboration can be encouraged by daily stand-up meetings and collocating teams near each other for more face-to-face communications, where possible.

More infrequent collaboration can be supported by scheduled sessions such as milestone reviews, backlog refinement sessions, and project update meetings. These facilitate the sharing of knowledge, as well as providing opportunities for pairing or coaching.

Determining and optimizing collaboration activities is an ongoing team effort required by the project manager in predictive settings.

Effective Meetings

Whether meeting with stakeholders in person or online, always try to make the most of meeting times. Everyone's time is valuable, and it is important to ensure that the right participants are included in the meeting, and the topics discussed are of interest and concern to them.

Strategies related to communication and collaboration skills include:

- Be organized and clear about the purpose of the meeting and the desired objective.
- Timebox the meeting: start and end the meeting on time, including creating timings for discussion content.
- Practice active listening and feedback techniques during the meeting.
- Facilitate collaboration, remaining open to and encouraging ideation or problem resolution during meetings.

Task Accountability

Promote accountability by empowering people to take responsibility for work. Effective project managers generally encourage team members to self-organize. This determination includes the following:

What work must be done to meet a requirement?

How to develop, perform, and deliver the results.

Who should perform individual tasks?

Regardless of the method used, it is important to keep work and progress visible to support transparency and demonstration of work completed. This includes visibility of who is performing various tasks and when, which helps ensure effective collaboration and use of team resources. This may be tracked and managed as part of a large project schedule or more simply on team task boards, including task or kanban boards that facilitate collaboration and promote visibility across the team.

Tasks are assigned in predictive settings, so those team members become accountable for completing specific work. The WBS dictionary and work package descriptions help provide additional information regarding the work to be done. The assignment to the various work packages or tasks can be summarized and shown by either a RAM or RACI chart.

In hybrid and adaptive teams, kanban or task boards are typically used to visually depict progress on user stories or requirements. The team determines the detail and information shown. All team members must have easy access to the board, not only so they can see the overall progress of teamwork but also to update their individual progress. This can be located as part of the information radiator on a wall or board in a colocated area or supported by an automated tool. Regardless of the method used, it is key to keep information up-to-date, based on the frequency determined by the team.

Key Concepts Covered

- Stakeholder engagement (SEAM)
- Effective communication
- Stakeholder collaboration
- Task accountability

ECO Coverage

- Lead a team (1.2)
  - Analyze team members' and stakeholders' influence (1.2.6)

- Support team performance (1.3)
  - Determine appropriate feedback approach (1.3.3)

- Collaborate with stakeholders (1.9)
  - Optimize alignment between stakeholder needs, expectations, and project objectives (1.9.2)
  - Build trust and influence to accomplish project objectives (1.9.3)

- Manage communications (2.2)
  - Communicate project information and updates effectively (2.2.3)
  - Confirm communication is understood and feedback is received (2.2.4)

- Engage stakeholders (2.4)
  - Engage stakeholders by category (2.4.3)

- Evaluate and deliver project benefits and value (3.2)
  - Apprise stakeholders of value gained progress (3.2.5)

Check Your Progress

1. You are the project manager managing a software development project to implement a restaurant food and beverage menu application on an iPad. Currently, you are executing the project plan and conducting a project status meeting with the stakeholders. This activity is closely related to which of the following?

   A. Approval of the project deliverables

   B. Verify quality requirements

   C. Provide transparency of project activities

   D. Update project risks

2. During your first requirements meeting with stakeholders, you notice that Alex, who is an important stakeholder, is unaware and has no clue about what is happening in the project. Since he can contribute to your project success, you decide to bring him from an unaware state to a supportive state. Which of the following will help you to achieve your goal with this stakeholder?

   A. Send additional project status reports

   B. Since he is unaware of the project objectives, you should ignore him

   C. Since he has been assigned to the project but is unaware of the project, assign him insignificant tasks

   D. Involve him in some project activities

3. Stakeholders play a major role in the success of a project. To ensure that stakeholder expectations are managed properly throughout the project, the project manager needs to do which of the following? (Choose 3)

   A. Resolve conflicts among stakeholders

   B. Build trust with stakeholders

C. Listen to concerns of stakeholders

D. Create ground rules for the stakeholders to follow

4. Information radiator is the generic term for visual displays placed in a noticeable location so everyone can quickly see the latest project information. In Agile practices, this is also known as a "Big Visible Chart." How is a project handled when all the stakeholders and team members are virtual?

A. Create a big visible chart on a monitor in a high traffic area so when the stakeholders and team members visit the office, they can see it

B. The I. T. staff should create a landing page where the virtual information radiator can be viewed when the stakeholder and team members log into their project application

C. Since everyone is working from home, the virtual information radiator can be ignored since everyone will pay little attention to it since it is difficult to view it using current technology

D. Most stakeholders, team members and management ignore the information radiator when it was in the office environment, so there is no need to create a virtual information radiator

5. You have been assigned as the project manager for a new and highly complex project. There are twelve key stakeholders identified for the project, and you are working on a communication plan for the stakeholders. You do this by determining what information is needed, when, to whom, what method, what format, and how frequently. When is it important that you develop your communication plan?

A. Concurrently with identifying stakeholders and then continuously updating it throughout the project

B. You only need to create a communication plan at the beginning of the project

C. Upon completion of the stakeholder project plan

D. At the start of the executing phase

Answers

1. C
2. D
3. A, B, C
4. B
5. A

Team Development

Throughout the project there are always areas in which additional knowledge can fill in gaps for team members and stakeholders. This can be addressed formally through training, coaching, or ad hoc discussions. It is all part of the larger aspect of knowledge sharing.

Growth Mindset

The belief that a person's capacities and talents can be improved over time.

It is important to utilize past experiences and processes to help understand situations, but they should not dictate the way things must be done. It is also important to continuously look to improve and innovate. Considering the status quo can open new ideas and perspectives.

Challenging the way things were done, or are currently being done, helps ensure all involved consider that the best approach is being used given the circumstances, and the best product will result.

The best approach is often discovered through discussion and introspection, examining your own mental and emotional state. It also breaks complacency and blind acceptance. Using an elicitation approach helps stakeholders not overlook anything or assume too much.

Training, Coaching, and Mentoring

Training, coaching, and mentoring are three activities related to knowledge sharing. Project management practitioners will engage in all three at some point in their careers.

- *Training*
  - Training provides specialized skill building for individuals and the team. It can be formal or informal, on almost any topic from "soft" to technical skills. It may address any topic but usually provides upskilling based on identifying gaps in knowledge.

- *Coaching*
  - Coaching can be provided individually or to a group, including the entire project team. This helps put knowledge into practice over an extended period of collaboration with other individuals.

- *Mentoring*
  - Mentoring is a long-term relationship between individuals and aims to transfer skill sets and knowledge from more experienced to less experienced individuals. It usually addresses activities that reach beyond the project with external individuals or organizations.

Team Knowledge

Knowledge is an asset to both the team and the organization and should be managed appropriately.

Knowledge can be divided into two main types: explicit and tacit.

Understanding and management of both types of knowledge is needed to take advantage of the knowledge, skills, and experiences that project team members have gained throughout the project.

- *Explicit Knowledge*

Knowledge that can be codified using symbols such as words, numbers, and pictures. This type of knowledge can be easily documented and shared with others.

Although collecting and gathering explicit knowledge is relatively easy to do, there is the risk of capturing only the facts and not the context surrounding them. Both are important to know. This often becomes the difference between "collecting" and "eliciting" requirements for the project.

- *Tacit Knowledge*

Personal knowledge, such as beliefs, experience, and insights, can be difficult to articulate and share.

Tacit knowledge includes personal knowledge, which is often hard to articulate and share and requires elicitation techniques to extract. To manage tacit knowledge, it is necessary to create and maintain trust among those involved in the project, so they are willing to share their experiences with everyone else. By obtaining those personalized experiences of the project, the team can more fully understand and leverage this knowledge. This is often obtained using elicitation techniques.

Knowledge-Sharing Culture

The project leader is consistently learning and teaching others in daily interactions and collaborations. These activities occur as part of projects as well as being external to projects, including as part of an individual's professional development path.

Team members can both learn from and teach others and should always avail themselves of training, coaching, and mentoring opportunities. This also includes stakeholders and customers as part of the project work and continuous improvement efforts.

In adaptive projects, there are dedicated roles for these activities. Agile coaches or scrum masters help teams to develop their Agile practice and foster greater effectiveness and cohesion.

An Agile coach is often a process role on an adaptive project team. By coaching teams across the enterprise on applying Agile practices and choosing their best way of working, the coach helps organizations achieve true agility

Training is also important as part of product delivery and support for the transition from the project team to the customer or end user. A separate stakeholder training is done at the end of the project as part of the transition plan—to prepare those stakeholders (normally not involved in the project effort) to utilize the results of the project. These training requirements are identified as transition requirements during the initial planning efforts.

Knowledge-Sharing Value

Time and resources are limited, so scheduling and participating in training, coaching, and mentoring activities at the most appropriate time is often challenging. These various ways of increasing knowledge should be viewed as an asset.

When considering training for current team members, it often helps to determine potential cost savings by a cost-benefit analysis to compare the cost of the training to the cost of adding outsourced labor resources to the project.

Improving skills and knowledge for team members, stakeholders, and project leaders better equips the team to increase the project effort's quality, output, and value.

Training and coaching also contribute to better relationships and trust with stakeholders and team members.

Gap Analysis

Gap analysis is a key activity, especially when reviewing the capability and skills of newly assigned project team members. This helps determine current competencies and their comparison to those desired. There are several ways to help individual team members and key stakeholders acquire the additional knowledge desired for the project. The SEAM matrix can also be used to help determine the needs of key stakeholders.

A skills list can provide details of all the current skills the team possesses, including skills irrelevant to the current project, while some are highly relevant to achieving the project goals.

It is important to identify the specific needs of the various team members, including the topics and depth of knowledge required. Not only should technical skills be reviewed, but also interpersonal skills needed to establish and maintain relationships with other people. The schedule for any identified training often is dependent on the timing of the needs of the project and the availability of training opportunities. This will also determine the best way to provide the training.

Some training may be provided by key stakeholders to team members at the beginning of the project to better familiarize the team with the customer's business, culture, desired outcomes, and project vision and context.

Because of the conflicts with potential training offerings, individual or group coaching may present a better training opportunity. This is preferred when an experienced team member can work directly with other team members in specific areas.

Mentorships should be encouraged, but it is often an individual decision to establish a long-term mentorship relationship with another individual, especially for increased knowledge in personal development or leadership beyond the project context.

Training Team Members

Training is a well-known and versatile way of imparting knowledge and skills to individuals, small groups, or whole teams. It is well suited for covering management, technical, or administrative topics. It also can be easily tailored to meet the specific needs of the team members and the organization.

Training can be provided via several methods, including:

- Instructor-led, classroom—physically present or colocated
- Virtual classroom, instructor-led
- Self-paced e-learning—scalable including rich media video, simulated lab exercises, etc.
- Document review
- Interactive simulations—including hands-on labs or test simulators to provide support when studying for an exam
- On-the-job training and coaching

Planning Training

There may be a differentiation between the training of team members and stakeholders.

Training in the process and knowledge to perform the project work is done during the project and provided both to the team members and the appropriate stakeholders involved in the work.

A separate stakeholder training is done at the end of the project as part of the transition plan—to prepare those stakeholders and end users (not normally involved in the project effort) to utilize the project results.

During resource management planning, required training and coaching may have been identified. As specific individuals are added to the project, the gap analysis of their knowledge and skills may need to be reviewed. Training and coaching offerings can be arranged based on the project team's combined needs.

The training requirements identified may include support for technical skills, interpersonal or "soft" skills, or be included as part of team-building activities.

Timing is important. Training to help a team member understand how to perform an activity should occur just prior to utilizing that skill. Training for customers to utilize the product or service should occur shortly before implementation as part of the transition planning activities.

In addition to specific skills for project activities, it may be valuable for team members to extend their training and formalize their learning through attainment of certification in specific areas. This additional level of understanding benefits both the individual and the organization.

Individuals benefit not only from being mentored but also from becoming mentors and sharing their professional knowledge and experience with others.

Training Outcomes

After training sessions, it is important to acknowledge completion with certificates, including letters or badges from the awarding organization.

Post-training performance assessments can be used to evaluate improvements resulting from the training. These can be performed with formal exams or by observations of knowledge or skill improvements. Training outcomes are often discussed and shared as part of team retrospectives.

Since training cannot completely fill the required knowledge gap, it is often augmented through coaching. Training usually helps with the understanding of why and how but converting that into knowledge requires applying what was learned to actual work activities. This may include pairing team members to help provide this additional understanding.

If the desired outcomes of the training are not achieved, record this in the lessons learned and try to find out why as part of a retrospective session.

Coaching Team Members

Coaching team members with others is a key aspect of Agile projects. Group coaching is often the result of working together to complete a task, rather than assigning the responsibility to a single individual. Everyone involved is learning and increasing their knowledge because of the activity.

Coaching can be formally established or offered more informally with teammates assisting each other.

- *Informal Coaching*

  Informal coaching of project management knowledge can be done with team members in multiple ways.

  - Delegate tasks, observe, and then provide feedback.
  - Observe work done by team members and provide feedback if applicable.
  - Encourage others to take the lead on activities.
  - Collaborate on project planning and management activities.
  - Practice taking on new roles.

- *Formal Coaching*

  Formal coaching opportunities can include:

  - Facilitating meetings and sessions
  - Transferring skills by pairing individuals
  - Modeling and observing behaviors

Adaptive methods often include a specific role to help hybrid or adaptive teams learn processes and methods. This includes understanding the transition and differences in tools and techniques and incorporating an Agile mindset.

This concept was derived from the extreme programming (XP) method, where the lead resource was identified as a coach to help focus the team on the activities. This is critical because the timebox in XP is usually only one week to deliver and implement results.

The two roles that are often utilized for coaching on adaptive projects include:

Agile coach — process role on a project team that helps organizations achieve true agility by coaching teams across the enterprise on applying Agile practices and choosing their best way of working.

Scrum master — coach of the development team and process owner in the scrum framework. Removes obstacles, facilitates productive events, and protects the team from disruptions.

Team and Individual Coaching

Coaching stakeholders and team members on any topic can be done individually or in groups.

In adaptive teams, coaching is more common than training or mentoring. Team members are coached on individual skill areas, with the aim of getting the work done and professional improvement.

Coaching is done on two levels and at different times within an iteration or release.

- *Team Coaching*

  Happens more at the iteration boundaries (planning, reviews, and retrospectives) with the entire team.

- *Individual Coaching*

  Happens while the iteration is in progress and is often one-on-one, confidential, and private.

Tacit Learning

Coaching often results in the sharing of tacit knowledge that is difficult to articulate and goes beyond knowledge acquired in traditional methods (explicit knowledge), including training, research, and discovery. Individuals aspiring to move into a higher leadership position can gain an understanding of the role by observing servant leadership activities.

Job shadowing and coaching often follow formal training sessions to ensure the transfer of knowledge and skills from the team to the organization during the transition of the solution.

An Agile coach is not necessarily needed to learn and apply adaptive methods. Self-organizing teams coach and mentor each other every day in their work. Project managers and other experienced team members can help coach individuals to work with and contribute to other project roles.

Mentorships[58]

Mentorships are long-term partnerships that provide tremendous value for professional growth. They may include job shadowing to reinforce explicit knowledge with additional tacit knowledge. This is also very valuable to project managers as they enhance their management skills.

As part of a training and coaching strategy within a project, mentorships complement training and coaching efforts. They are often used to train project managers and those individuals aspiring to move into leadership roles in the future.

Advocate mentorships to the team, so they can continue with fruitful relationships after the project is closed.

Key Concepts Covered

- Knowledge-sharing culture
- Tacit learning
- Training team members
- Coaching team members
- Mentoring stakeholders

ECO Coverage

- Support team performance (1.3)
  - Support and recognize team member growth and development (1.3.2)

- Ensure team members/stakeholders are adequately trained (1.5)
  - Determine required competencies and elements of training (1.5.1)
  - Determine training options based on training needs (1.5.2)
  - Allocate resources for training (1.5.3)
  - Measure training outcomes (1.5.4)

- Build a team (1.6)
  - Appraise stakeholder skills (1.6.1)

- Mentor relevant stakeholders (1.13)
  - Allocate the time for coaching/mentoring (stakeholders) (1.13.1)
  - Recognize and act on coaching/mentoring opportunities (1.13.2)

Check Your Progress

1. What are three activities related to sharing team members' knowledge? (Choose 3)

   A. Training

   B. Coaching

   C. Mentoring

   D. On the job experience

2. You are trying to identify the training coaching, and mentoring needed to improve the team's performance and effectiveness by making formal or informal assessments of the project team's effectiveness. Which of the following is the project manager performing?

   A. Team performance assessment

   B. Project performance appraisal

   C. Observations

   D. Team building activities

3. An organization recently moved to adaptive project management and the team is not sure how to estimate the amount of work they can get done in a sprint. What should the project manager do to help the team?

   A. Conduct training sessions about sprint team velocity

   B. Conduct research regarding team velocity on the Internet

   C. Ask the sponsor to conduct a team training on sprint methods

   D. Acquire new team members that are knowledgeable of sprint methods

4. Explicit knowledge is personal knowledge, such as beliefs, experience, and insights, that can be difficult to articulate and share while tacit knowledge is knowledge that can be codified using symbols such as words, numbers, and pictures. This type of knowledge can be easily documented and shared with others. Is this statement true or false?

    A. True

    B. False

5. What is the role of an agile coach in an adaptive project? (Choose 3)

    A. Coach team members on the agile approach to estimation, planning, and story mapping

    B. Remove obstacles for team members

    C. Interact with stakeholders to increase business value

    D. Create a project plan, and assign tasks to team members, and track their progress

6. Dan has been assigned to an agile project as the scrum master/project manager. His new team does not have any agile experience. What would you recommend as Dan's first engagement with his team?

    A. Train the team members in the fundamental of the agile mindset and principles

    B. Train the team members in the scrum method

    C. Train the team members in the eXtreme programming methods

    D. Train the team members in the Kanban approach

    E. There is no need to train the team members in the agile methods, they will learn on the job as they go

Answers

1. A, B, C

2. A

3. A

4. False

5. A, B, C

6. A

Manage Conflict

An extremely important part of the project manager role is maintaining a peaceful, productive work environment, including recognizing and handling potential team member or stakeholder disagreements and conflict.

Conflict as Part of Team Culture[59]

Team members need to exchange ideas and points of view about work. Disruptions to the status quo can lead to conflict and the discovery of new opportunities or improvements.

A psychologically safe team environment, where exchanges and disagreements are encouraged and welcomed, is essential. This is a basic and widely recognized Agile concept, but it can be used in any project context.

There are numerous approaches to handling disagreements before they escalate to the level of a conflict. It is important to recognize the benefits of encouraging disagreements among team members to arrive at the best solutions.

Effective conflict management can lead to improved understanding, performance, and productivity.

Conversely, ineffective or nonexistent conflict management can lead to destructive behavior, animosity, poor performance, and reduced productivity. All of these can threaten successful completion of the project's deliverables.

Causes of Conflict

Conflict arises in most groups and working situations. Project managers should be aware of certain characteristics of conflict that will help them effectively handle conflicts when they arise.

Conflict is natural and forces the need to explore alternatives. It is a team aspect; openness about the situation or opinions can resolve conflicts.

While resolving conflicts, the focus should be on the issues, not individuals. Also, attend to the present situation while not dwelling on the past.

Causes of conflict include:

- Schedule milestones
- Resource unavailability and impact on schedule

---

59   https://www.pmi.org/disciplined-Agile/mindset/promises/safety

- Budget constraints
- Project priorities
- Technical opinions
- Competition
- Differences in objectives, values, and perceptions
- Disagreements about role requirements, work activities, and individual approaches
- Communication breakdowns
- Administrative overhead

All of these are a normal part of most human interactions. Use expert judgment and root cause analysis tools to drill down to determine the core issue, or root of the conflict.

Conflict Management Roles

Managing conflict is the responsibility of all stakeholders.

The project manager heavily influences the direction and handling of conflict. It is important to utilize interpersonal and team skills to ensure positive results when handling conflict. These interpersonal skills not only apply to conflict resolution but also drive to the strengths of the project team members, including:

- Leadership—sharing the vision and inspiring the team to achieve high performance
- Influencing—utilizing interactive listening skills, seeing all sides of a disagreement, and not taking sides on disagreements or issues, especially in a matrix organization structure
- Decision-making—having strong negotiation skills to influence the organization to achieve a successful result

As a servant leader, the removal of obstacles or impediments for the team often reduces potential sources of conflict. The team charter or ground rules should document how conflict and disagreements are handled.

In adaptive projects, the team lead may assist in facilitating conflict resolution sessions and empowering the team to resolve conflicts as they see fit.

Conflict Management Techniques

Several techniques can be used to manage conflict. These can include interpersonal skills and emotional intelligence to address personal aspects of the conflict.

When the conflict revolves around an actual problem or situation, utilizing root cause analysis techniques helps to move from the situation or symptom to discovering the actual root cause.

Traditional projects often utilize cause-and-effect diagrams (also known as fishbone or Ishikawa diagrams).

Agile approaches have adopted a Lean questioning technique called the 5 Whys method, developed by Sakichi Toyoda, a Japanese inventor and industrialist. Using this approach when you identify a cause you repeatably ask, "Why did that happen?" Asking why at least five times will either get you to the root cause of the problem or identify a point where you need further information to understand the cause. You may start or alternate asking "how" along with "why."

Handling Conflict[60]

Team members need to work in a safe environment where they are empowered and able to exchange ideas and points of view about work. It is important to understand when a disagreement moves beyond just being a disagreement and becomes a conflict.

The team would have previously collaborated to create ground rules, including how to address conflict. These rules need to be continually reviewed and updated as necessary. This especially applies to decisions regarding the need for escalation, rather than coming to an agreement within the team.

Adaptive teams often consider conflict management strategies when determining and tailoring their way of working (WoW). This includes being supported through a culture of trust among team members.

Regardless of the project approach or the type of disagreement or conflict, it is important to always focus on the issues, not individuals.

---

60   *https://www.pmi.org/disciplined-agile/mindset/promises/safety*

Conflict Management Approaches

The approach to managing conflict will depend on:

- The intensity and importance of the conflict
- The time given to resolve the conflict
- The positions of the conflicting parties
- The motivation to resolve conflicts on a short-term or long-term basis

An additional approach—arbitration and mediation (ADR)—is used for contract disputes and involves escalating to an outside panel rather than pursuing legal resolution.

Conflict Resolution Methods

There are five basic approaches for handling conflicts in project situations. Each is effective in different circumstances. Leadership skills and expert judgment are needed to assess the situation and choose the appropriate conflict resolution method.

Based on Thomas-Kilmann Conflict Modes

- *Smooth*
  - Emphasize areas of agreement rather than areas of difference.
  - Concede your position to the needs of others to maintain harmony and relationships.
  - Retreat from an actual or potential conflict situation.
  - Postpone the issue to be better prepared or to be resolved by others.

- *Compromise/Reconcile*
  - Search for solutions that bring some degree of satisfaction to all parties.
  - Temporarily or partially resolve the conflict through compromise.

- *Force/Direct*
  - Pursue individual viewpoints at the expense of others.
  - Offer only win-lose solutions, usually enforced through a power position to resolve an emergency.

- *Collaborate/Problem Solve*

- Incorporate multiple viewpoints and insight from differing perspectives.
- Enable cooperative attitudes and open dialogue to reach consensus and commitment.

Exam Tip: PMI considers the best approach to be collaborate, with the worst approach being force. Compromise, smoothing, and withdrawing can lead to lose-lose situations.

Leas' Level of Conflict[61]

This model by Speed B. Leas is widely used to manage project teams. It describes how conflict emerges and evolves from a task orientation with possible resolutions to intractable situations often nearly impossible to resolve.

This model can help clarify the context of a disagreement, when it is possible to intervene, and how. Additionally, it is important to know when to escalate matters that are beyond resolution.

Note that the levels are not self-contained, and behaviors may overlap and change.

- Level 1 — Problem to solve: Differences are identified, shared, and discussed among members. This level is a problem- or task-oriented conflict, not a person- or relationship-oriented conflict.
- Level 2 — Disagreement: Personalities and issues mix; therefore, problems cannot be identified. People begin to distrust one another and make problems personal at this stage.
- Level 3 — Contest: Win-lose dynamic emerges, followed by taking sides, distorted communication, and personal attacks. Conflict objectives shift from focus on self-protection to winning the argument. People feel threatened or invigorated and ready to fight.
- Level 4 — Fight/Flight: Conflict participants may shift from winning to trying to hurt or get rid of their opponents. Intervention is required.
- Level 5 — Intractable situation/War: People are now incapable of clearly understanding issues. Efforts to destroy others' reputations, positions, or well-being are common. This eventually ruins the relationship.

---

61 *Leas, Speed B. Leadership and Conflict. Nashville: Abingdon Press, 1983*

Conflict Stages and Outcomes[62]

It is important to understand the levels of a conflict and the outcomes that will result.

Interpersonal skills and conflict management strategies are possible for conflicts in levels 1 through 4.

- *Level 1 – Problem to solve*: Often task-oriented where differences are identified and discussed.
  - Outcome: Collaborate to solve the problem by moving parties toward an acceptable agreement.

- *Level 2 – Disagreement:* Issue is obscured as it becomes personalized, with distrust starting to set in.
  - Outcome: Attempt a collaborative solution or negotiate an acceptable agreement.

- *Level 3 – Contest:* Win-lose environment emerges, with communications becoming distorted and aggressive.
  - Outcome: Third-party decision-making, compromise, or mediation may be required for a resolution.

- *Level 4 – Fight/Flight:* Efforts move from winning the argument to inflicting harm on opposing party.
  - Outcome: Minimal chance of compromise and a high probability of someone quitting, requiring intervention.

- *Level 5 – Intractable situation/War:* Understanding of each side by the other is impossible.
  - Outcome: Highly destructive environment where further escalation is needed.

The outcomes can be positive in levels 1 to 3. At higher levels, parties may become embittered.

Managing Conflict

Following the guidance provided by the Leas model, use of interpersonal skills is possible for Levels 1–4.

---

62   Alban Institute. *"Levels of Conflict."* https://www.vnim.org/Resources/Leas'%20Five%20Levels%20of%20Conflict.pdf

As a servant leader, a project manager can assist in removing impediments or sources of conflict to support the team's performance. It is important to always remain mindful of the interactions of those involved in the disagreements.

The utilization of interpersonal and team skills plays a major role in ensuring the results of a disagreement or conflict are positive rather than negative.

Some interpersonal skills that can be used to manage conflict include

- Emotional Intelligence—utilizing empathy to understand the situation and help defuse it.
- Influencing—persuading all parties to reconsider or modify their tone, approach, or mindset.
- Leadership—moving beyond influencing and steering the discussion more positively.
- Decision-Making—if the parties can't reach a decision, offering a solution to move the situation forward.
- Active Listening—continue listening for language, especially as it becomes personalized or accusing with a bitter or caustic tone. Defensive or aggressive physical postures may also accompany it.

Key Concepts Covered

- Causes of conflict
- Conflict management
- Conflict resolution

ECO Coverage

- Manage conflict (1.1)
  - Interpret the source and stage of the conflict (1.1.1)
  - Analyze the context for the conflict (1.1.2)
  - Evaluate/recommend/reconcile the appropriate conflict resolution solution (1.1.3)

- Build shared understanding (1.10)
  - Break down situations to identify the root cause of a misunderstanding (1.10.1)
  - Investigate potential misunderstandings (1.10.4)

- Define team ground rules (1.12)
  - Discuss and rectify ground rule violations (1.12.3)

Check Your Progress

1. What are common causes of conflict in projects? (Choose 3)

   A. Schedule milestones

   B. Budget constraints

   C. Mentoring

   D. Communications breakdown

2. During a one-on-one meeting with one of your team members, both of you agree on a training program to address the concerns of conflicts with other team members. You also make sure that he understands the need to submit his task status report every Wednesday of each week. Which action are you currently engaged in with the team member?

   A. Observation

   B. Project performance appraisals

   C. Conflict management

   D. Team performance assessment

3. There are five basic approaches for handling conflicts in project situations. Each is effective in different circumstances. Leadership skills and expert judgment are needed to assess the situation and choose the appropriate conflict resolution method. What is the best practice to resolve conflicts?

   A. Smooth/Accommodate

   B. Withdraw/Avoid

   C. Compromise/Reconcile

   D. Force/Direct

   E. Collaborate/Problem solve

4. Agile approaches have adopted a Lean questioning technique called the 5 Whys method. Using this approach when you identify a cause you repeatably ask, "Why did that happen?" Asking "why" at least five times will either get you to the root cause of the problem or identify a point where you need further information to understand the cause. Is this statement true or false?

   A. True

   B. False

5. The approach to managing conflict in a project will depend on which of the following?

    A. The intensity and importance of the conflict

    B. The time given to resolve the conflict

    C. The positions of the conflicting parties

    D. Deciding on which of the conflicting parties should be removed from the project

Answers

1. A, B, D
2. C
3. E
4. True
5. A, B, C

Project Performance

This chapter addresses the tools, techniques, and additional leadership skills to help get the best performance from the project team by staying on track to achieve successful project outcomes.

In this chapter, you will:

- Explain the various methods for performance measurement.
- Understand the value of a continuous improvement mindset.
- Compare these methods, with a focus on communication and accountability.
- Identify the methods for implementing a project and the issues and impediments that arise during a project.
- Describe the methods for implementing changes during a project.

Topics in This Chapter:

- Project Work
- Continuous Improvement Mindset
- Business Value Delivery
- Project Measurement
- Project Challenges
- Managing Changes

Project Work

Performance Domain:

Project Work[63]

The Project Work Performance Domain addresses activities and functions associated with establishing project processes, managing physical resources, and fostering a teaming environment.

---

63 *PMBOK Guide, Seventh Edition, Section 2.5 – Project Performance Domains*

The following items defined in the glossary relevant to the Project Work Performance Domain:

- *Bid Documents — All documents used to solicit information, quotations, or proposals from prospective sellers*

- *Bidder Conference — Meetings with prospective sellers prior to the presentation of a bid or proposal to ensure all prospective vendors have a clear and common understanding of the procurement. Also known as contractor conferences, vendor conferences, or pre-bid conferences*

- *Explicit Knowledge — Knowledge that can be codified using symbols such as words, numbers, and pictures*

- *Tacit Knowledge — Personal knowledge that can be difficult to articulate and share such as beliefs, experience, and insights*

After the project management plan has been developed, the project manager and project team can focus on ensuring that the project activities are running smoothly including:

- Managing the flow of existing project work, new work, and changes to work
- Keeping the project team focused
- Establishing efficient project systems and processes
- Communicating with stakeholders
- Managing material, equipment, supplies, and logistics
- Working with contracting professionals and vendors to plan and manage procurements and contracts
- Monitoring changes that can affect the project
- Enabling project learning and knowledge transfer

The project manager's role in a predictive project includes more involvement in overseeing and monitoring project work throughout the project life cycle.

This starts with developing a project management plan to help identify the activities and information to be developed and maintained as part of the project work. This plan must continually be reviewed and updated as necessary as the work is done.

Overall, the role of the project manager in a predictive approach is to steer the team toward successful project outcomes. This role often includes areas that can be delegated to other experienced team members.

This can include involvement and oversight in many areas, including:

- Measure and monitor progress, taking appropriate action where necessary.
- Ensure alignment of due dates for project deliverables and project phase completion requirements.
- Manage phase transitions when necessary.
- Manage project performance and changes to project activities.
- Create and use appropriate knowledge provided to and distributed from the project.
- Collect, analyze, and communicate project information to relevant stakeholders.
- Participate in integrated decisions about critical changes that impact the project.
- Ensure completion of all project work and formally close each phase, contract, and project.
- Ensure alignment with the benefits realization plan.

In a hybrid project, the project manager oversees the integration of project plan components but delegates control of detailed product planning and delivery to the product owner, including requirements prioritization.

The project manager focuses on building a cross-functional team and collaborative decision-making environment and ensuring the team can respond appropriately to changes. The actual team configuration, management, and process roles are unique in the adaptive portion of a hybrid project—but they always remain team-centered.

The process role of the scrum master or coach helps the team understand the Agile mindset and use the appropriately tailored scrum processes. This role may change based on the context of the project.

To develop the product, the team, with the domain expert, plan how best to conduct the work, while the product owner focuses on value creation.

Team performance assessments help identify each team member's potential to help improve the interaction between team members, solve issues, and deal with conflicts.

Continuous Improvement Mindset

Supporting the team and the work requires a servant leader who is continually looking to improve the process, product, and individuals. These are all part of the continuous improvement mindset.

Improvements can be supported by additional training, processes, or technology that may have been overlooked initially. These project needs should be reviewed continually.

Adopting a "fail fast" mindset allows the team to focus first on those areas that are essential or "must work." In that way, additional time isn't wasted on developing requirements that cannot be implemented if the "must work" item is unsuccessful. Decomposing items into smaller pieces makes it easier to discover and "fix" those areas.

Continuous Improvement

An ongoing effort to improve products, services, or processes.

This is often supported by employing organizational knowledge from previous project efforts and continuously capturing lessons learned (like retrospectives) throughout the project.

Continuous improvement is one of the fundamental principles of Agile and is applied to processes, products, and individuals. It can be applied to small, incremental, or considerable "breakthrough" improvements.

This is often a business strategy identified at the organizational level for all projects to adopt and utilize. The organization's project management office (PMO) provides implementation support through OPAs or a continuous improvement framework such as Agile, Lean, or Six Sigma.

Continuous Improvement (CI) Assessment

Supporting the team's performance extends beyond the measurement tools, feedback, and methods. It is essential to review the results of continuous improvement processes continually. Team members should know various quality and continuous improvement methods and utilize appropriate concepts to tailor the project work.

Additionally, the risk register may indicate the awareness of potential quality threats and the current CI measures that may have been identified. Reviewing the risk register and ensuring that it is updated continually is important. The present method is to benchmark existing against established models and standards.

International Standard Organization (ISO)

ISO is an independent, nongovernmental international organization established in 1946 that develops consensus-based, market-relevant international standards in many areas. In 1987, ISO published its first quality management standard, ISO 9000, to help organizations improve the quality of their products and services and consistently meet their customers' expectations. This now includes ISO 9001 certification by many organizations, helping ensure that customers get consistent, good-quality products and services.

Capability Maturity Model Integration (CMMI)[64]

CMMI replaced the original capability maturity model from the Software Engineering Institute at Carnegie Mellon University in 2006. It is a process-level appraisal designed to help organizations improve their software design, development, and deployment. Philip Crosby described the original model in his book *Quality is Free*.

The levels in the CMMI model include:

Level 1 — Initial: processes unpredictable, poorly controlled, and reactive

Level 2 — Managed: processes characterized by project and often reactive

Level 3 — Defined: processes characterized for the organization and proactive; processes tailored from the organization's standards

Level 4 — Quantitatively managed: processes measured and controlled

Level 5 — Optimizing: focus on continuous process improvement

The Software Engineering Institute (SEI) uses this to audit organizations desiring to be assessed at Level 2 or above in the CMMI model. The level of assessment is often applied to software products, used as an evaluation method, and is usually required for government contracts.

Continuous Improvement Approaches

To continuously focus on reflection and improvement, it is beneficial to understand some of the prominent quality theories that focus on continuous improvement. Even though these approaches originated in manufacturing, they are now widely applied to other processes. The approaches include:

- Plan-Do-Check-Act (PDCA) — continuous process improvement to meet customer needs (W. Edwards Deming)
- Juran Trilogy — break quality management into planning, control, and improvement (Joseph M. Juran)
- Total Quality Management (TQM) — an organizational approach centered on quality, based on the participation of all employees to achieve long-term success through customer satisfaction

---

64 *http://www.sei.cmu.edu/cmmi, Software Engineering Institute, Carnegie Mellon*

- Kaizen Technique—small changes or improvements from workers and continually improving
- Six Sigma—respond to customer needs through improving processes by removing defects (William Smith Jr.)
- Lean Six Sigma—improves performance by eliminating waste and defects (Michael George and Robert Lawrence Jr.)

Valuable personal understanding and knowledge on various aspects of continuous improvement can be obtained through training or certifications, including Lean Six Sigma, PMI-ACP, DASM, DASSM, and Scrum Master.

Widely utilized approaches and quality theories for incorporating continuous improvement to support project performance include:

- *Plan-Do-Check-Act (PDCA)*

In the USA in the 1920s, Walter Shewhart took inspiration from the scientific method of inductive and deductive thinking, used in hypothesis testing, and converted it to a simple notion:

When we do something, we Plan it, Do it, Check it, and Act on its results—resulting in the PDCA cycle.

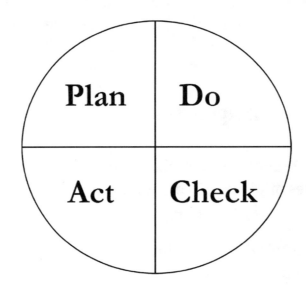

By using the PDCA cycle as an empirical process, repeatedly, incremental improvements can be realized that benefit both the business and the customer.

In the context of manufacturing and the Bell Telephone Company, workers could understand how this process helped build telephones. Shewhart felt management needed to understand variation in a process and who was responsible for addressing the variation.

He defined two types of variation:

- Special cause — occurs when a process exceeds its control limits; can be addressed by the process owner or operator
- Common cause — natural variation or randomness in the process, measured by standard deviation and a measure of precision; must be addressed by management

W. Edwards Deming championed the Plan-Do-Check-Act (PDCA) method. Deming later changed the third step, "check," to "study" (PDSA), because he felt that "check" emphasized inspection over analysis.

This continuous improvement methodology systematically tests possible solutions, assesses the results, and implements those that work. The cycle is then repeated to further improve a process or product in this methodology:

- Plan — Define objectives and processes to deliver desired results.
- Do — Execute the plan and collect data to determine the effectiveness of the processes.
- Study — Evaluate the data and compare the results to expected outcomes.
- Act — Identify issues with the process, determine their root causes, and modify the process to improve them. Planning for the next cycle can then proceed.

Exam Tip: PDSA is also known as the Deming Cycle, or PDCA (Plan-Do-Check-Act), depending on the region. It also served as the basis for the Process Groups identified in the PMBOK Guide through the sixth edition and the Process Groups: A Practice Guide.

- *Juran*

The Juran Trilogy, also known as the quality trilogy, was presented by Joseph M. Juran in 1986 and has become the basis for most quality management best practices today. It is a universal way of thinking about quality pertaining to all functions, products, and services at all levels.

Quality consists of three universal processes:

- *Quality Planning* (quality by design, or design for Six Sigma) — with designs that correspond to customers' needs and process features used by organizations as part of their development processes, including corrective actions and elimination of waste.
- *Quality Control* (process control and compliance, or regulatory control) — moving from inspections (detection control) to prevention (proactive control). This includes compliance with international standards or regulatory authorities such as ISO 9000.

- *Quality Improvement* (Lean Six Sigma)—every organization performs daily activities to make incremental improvements. It looks back, using lessons learned or retrospectives to discover areas preventing the current performance from meeting customer needs and identifying areas to increase the rate of improvement with a few vital breakthroughs.

- *Total Quality Management (TQM)*

TQM was introduced in the early 1900s by Walter A. Shewhart and is defined by ISO 8402:1994 as *"a management approach for an organization, centered on quality, based on the participation of all its members and aiming at long-term success through customer satisfaction, and benefits to all members of the organization and society."*

It is an ongoing process of detecting and reducing or eliminating errors to provide unparalleled customer satisfaction by continuously measuring the quality of products and services.

All members of an organization participate in improving processes, products, services, and the culture in which they work to provide continuous delivery of quality results. The primary elements and principles of TQM include:

- Customer first
- Employee ownership
- Based on the process
- System integration
- Communication
- Data-driven
- Constant improvement

- *Kaizen*

An important idea emerged from Japanese business in the 1980s. It refers to "change for the better," a culture and mindset of continuous improvement and self-motivation. These small incremental changes create an impact over time.

Its key features include:

- Management commitment to, and follow-through on continuous improvement, so the rest of the organization will develop a kaizen, or continuous improvement mindset.
- Focus on activities that reduce cost and cycle times, which drive higher customer satisfaction and improve overall quality.

- Improvements are based on many small changes and do not necessarily require capital expenditure.

- Ideas come from workers—not expensive research, consultants, or equipment.

- All employees are expected to improve their performance continually.

- Everyone is encouraged to take ownership of their work and improve motivation.

- Managers perform a Gemba (meaning real place) walk to learn or review exactly how a specific process works and gain insights from workers about possible implementations.

The kaizen process includes:

- What is the root cause of the problem—Gemba walk and root cause analysis.

- How can we address the root cause of the problem—5 Whys analysis.

- Are changes being carried out consistently, by everyone, and in all areas—centralization of kaizen management.

- What impact do our continuous improvement efforts create—A3 or 8D report to identify, analyze and resolve, or prevent complex issues or problems.

- How else can we keep improving—an unending process.

- *Six Sigma*

A collaborative team method that provides an enhanced ability to target customer needs and measure performance during project execution and monitoring.

American engineer Bill Smith, Jr. introduced this while working at Motorola in 1986.

Six Sigma originates from statistical quality control, referencing the fraction of a normal curve within six standard deviations of the mean. It is used to represent a defect rate of 3.4 or less out of 1 million opportunities.

Six Sigma includes a set of techniques and tools for process improvement, seeking to improve quality by:

- Identifying and removing the causes of defects
- Minimizing variability in manufacturing and business processes
- Using empirical and statistical quality management methods
- Following a defined methodology with specific value targets
- Utilizing quality tools, including brainstorming, FMEA, and design of experiments (DOE)

Six Sigma uses a five-step process (DMAIC), a variant of the PDCA, to implement improvements to existing processes.

- **D**efine the system, requirements, and goals.
- **M**easure critical aspects of the current process and collect relevant data (as-is process).
- **A**nalyze the data to verify cause and effect, seeking out the root cause of the defect.
- **I**mprove and optimize the current process to implement a new, future state process, including process capability (to-be process).
- **C**ontrol the future state process by implementing statistical tools to measure the result of the change and ensure that any deviations from the target are corrected before resulting in defects.

- *Lean*

Lean principles are a set of management practices that produces value for customers through a focus on reducing delays and eliminating waste. It is based on two pillars: respect for people, and continuous improvement.

Principles used to improve efficiency and quality include:

- *Define value*
- *Map value stream*
- *Create flow*
- *Establish pull*
- *Pursue perfection*

Additional principles have been added to apply more specifically to adaptive approaches including:

- *Eliminate waste*
- *Empower the team*
- *Deliver fast*
- *Optimize the whole*
- *Build quality in*
- *Defer decisions*
- *Amplify learnings (like retrospectives)*

- *Lean Six Sigma*

Today most organizations refer to Lean Six Sigma, combining the key concepts and processes of Six Sigma and Lean. This emerged in the 1990s as US manufacturers attempted to compete with Japan's better-made products.

This approach was initially applied to manufacturing and focused on eliminating waste within the manufacturing process. It then expanded its focus to reducing or eliminating various kinds of waste. This helps organizations deliver customer value through efficient operations and quality standards.

Lean Six Sigma modified the DMAIC process to develop a DMADV approach, which addresses the design process:

- **D**efine the process and design goals.
- **M**easure and identify critical characteristics, including risk and production capabilities.
- **A**nalyze the data to find the best design.
- **D**esign and test the product, service, or process.
- **V**erify that the design result meets requirements (verification) and performs satisfactorily for the intended use (validation).
- **O**ptimize—added to prioritize the need for the organization to optimize the design after implementation.

Kaizen and multiple Agile frameworks, including kanban, have incorporated Lean Six Sigma tools, processes, and principles into their adaptive approaches, especially the value-stream mapping technique to help discover and eliminate waste in processes.

- *Just-in-Time*—another Lean concept often applied to planning and monitoring portions of the project schedule to identify when resources are needed, rather than building up unnecessary inventory. However, trade-offs must be made to ensure that critical resources are available, especially when long lead times are required to acquire those resources.

Ongoing Improvements

"Balance attention to quality with action to achieve customer satisfaction" is the goal.

Continuous improvement is vital to continually striving to provide the highest quality and value of the result delivered by the project. The project management plan may include an additional process improvement plan to address how these activities will be incorporated into the project.

Continuous Improvement Techniques

Two continuous improvement techniques which have become best practices on projects include:

- *Lessons Learned Register* – collecting and implementing small improvements continuously

Lessons learned should be captured constantly and at scheduled times throughout the project, and that learning should be applied to determine and implement appropriate actions to improve the project's performance and environment.

- *Retrospectives* – looking back at completed work and planning improvements for the next phase

Supporting the team's performance extends beyond the measurement tools, feedback forums, and methods. Retrospectives can be done frequently, and the work performed reviewed quickly, like a milestone, deliverable, or iteration. It can also be done in a more structured manner, usually at the end of a phase or release.

Regardless of when they are held or the breadth of the review included, they focus on performance and potential improvements. In adaptive projects, retrospectives are the most important practice for gathering lessons from the team on improving and recognizing success. Retrospectives can occur at the end of a milestone or phase, as well as at the end of every project.

Conducting a retrospective encourages the team to review what went well and what could have been done better. This assessment includes the work on the product and the processes, team dynamics, and other areas that influence the team's effectiveness.

Guidelines that can be used when conducting retrospectives:

- Prepare for topics to be discussed.
- Identify two columns for discussion: "What went well" and "What needs improvement."
- Encourage participants to add items to these lists, including the reason for the needed improvement.
- Decide on and indicate common items that need improvement.
- Narrow the list of improvements to those items that can bring value in the next iteration.
- Get consensus on an improvement plan.
- Identify the tasks that will be affected or improved by the items selected.

- Implement the changes.
- Review the change area's result at the next retrospective to see if it made a difference.

Both lessons learned and retrospectives must be taken seriously by the team. This is when challenges are identified, and potential actions can be taken immediately to improve quality. These support an effective continuous improvement mindset.

Regardless of the method employed to identify and make improvements, any change should be measured to determine whether the desired effects have been achieved. If successful, incorporate it into the "way of working" for future activities and efforts.

Improvement Methods—Predictive

Some additional methods can be used to implement improvements for items that have been identified.

- *Experiments*

Experiments can be used to test and gather feedback to identify improvements and potential solutions. This usually provides verification of the effectiveness of items being tested. It is essential to apply controls to experiments and testing efforts and only change one aspect at a time to isolate the results. Experiments include team feedback and A/B testing to identify improvements.

- *A/B testing*

A marketing approach used to determine user preferences by showing different sets of users similar services — an Alpha and a Beta version — with one independent variable.

Customers and others do A/B testing as a type of experiment by comparing different versions of the product. The one most often selected is considered for further development.

- *Feedback*

Team feedback can come from many sources and in many ways. The project result is improved throughout development by utilizing small increments with continual review and approval. This prevents developing a larger item only to find that changes must be made, resulting in additional work and cost.

Improvement Methods—Adaptive

Adaptive teams already use retrospective ceremonies and the steps for making them effective.

There are additional quality improvement theories that should be reviewed to determine whether they might be helpful to the team and project.

Disciplined Agile has adopted a version of the kaizen loop strategy for reviewing and implementing small improvement areas. This combination of kaizen and experimentation is called guided continuous improvement (GCI)[65].

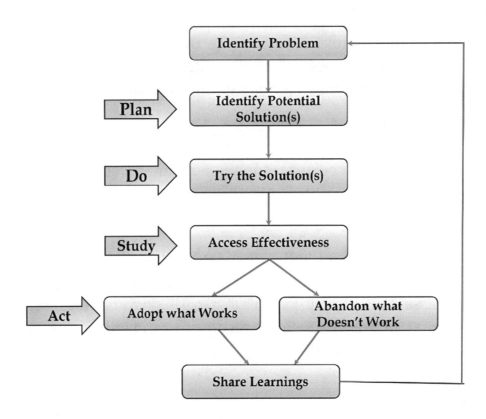

During a kaizen loop, small changes are chosen and tested for potential improvement. If they work, they are adopted, and if not, they are abandoned, and another approach is tried.

GCI extends the kaizen loop strategy by using previously abandoned guidance to help increase the probability that the chosen technique will work, decreasing the effort required to achieve process improvement.

Continuous Improvement to Processes and Standards

The information from lessons learned or retrospectives at the individual project level can apply to the organization's continuous improvement and project management processes.

---

65   *https://www.pmi.org/disciplined-Agile/gci/guided-continuous-improvement*

Providing these lessons for evaluation at the organizational level to the PMO or CoE, either during the project, or as part of the project closure.

Key Concepts Covered

- Continuous improvement approaches
- Implementation of ongoing improvements
- Improvement techniques

Check Your Progress

1. What are the different types of continuous improvement for an adaptive project? (Choose 3)

    A. Plan-Do-Study-Act

    B. Kaizen techniques

    C. Lean Six Sigma

    D. Lesson learned repository

2. Match the DMAIC terms on the left with their definitions on the right.

Define	Define the system, requirements, and goals.
Measure	Control the future state process by implementing statistical tools to measure the result of the change and ensure that any deviations from the target are corrected before resulting in defects.
Analyze	Improve and optimize the current process to implement a new, future state process, including process capability.
Improve	Analyze the data to verify cause and effect, seeking out the root cause of the defect.
Control	Measure critical aspects of the current process and collect relevant data (as-is process).

3. Quality consists of three universal activities. What are the three quality activities? (Choose 3)

    A. Smooth quality

    B. Plan quality

    C. Improve quality

    D. Control quality

    E. Assure quality

4. Adopting a "fail fast" mindset allows the team to focus first on those areas that are essential or "must work." In that way, additional time isn't wasted on developing requirements that cannot be implemented if the "must work" item is unsuccessful. Decomposing items into smaller pieces makes it easier to discover and "fix" those areas. Is this statement true or false?

   A. True

   B. False

5. What is the objective of using the Kaizen method in project management?

   A. Large improvements for large benefits

   B. Smal improvements for small benefits carried out on a continuous basis

   C. Large improvements for small benefits

   D. Small improvements for large benefits over a short time

Answers

1. A, B, C

2. Define the system, requirements, and goals.

   Measure critical aspects of the current process and collect relevant data (as-is process).

   Analyze the data to verify cause and effect, seeking out the root cause of the defect.

   Improve and optimize the current process to implement a new, future state process, including process capability.

   Control the future state process by implementing statistical tools to measure the result of the change and ensure that any deviations from the target are corrected before resulting in defects.

3. B, D, E

4. True

5. B

Business Value Delivery

Examining the business value of the work is interconnected with how the project is being conducted (ways of working) and the expected urgency required to deliver business value (business acumen).

To meet the expectations for today's projects, this may be one of the most critical aspects of the project manager's job. It is always important to consider how the project can deliver value for the business.

Project managers have a toolkit of processes, methods, and leadership skills to expedite and fine-tune value delivery. How well the approach is tailored, and these tools, techniques, and skills are used can determine the project's success in the delivery and stewardship of value.

Realign with Value Delivery

Throughout the project, the team must stay focused on delivering value. This requires continual prioritization of team cohesion, coherence, collaboration, and consensus.

Performance Measurement

Performance Domain:

Measurement[66]

The Measurement Performance Domain addresses activities and functions associated with project performance and taking appropriate actions to maintain acceptable performance.

The following items defined in the glossary relevant to the Measurement Performance Domain:

- *Metric — A description of a project or product attribute and how to measure it*
- *Baseline — The approved version of a work product used as a basis for comparison to actual results*
- *Dashboard — A set of charts and graphs showing progress or performance against important measures of the project*

Metrics, baselines, and thresholds, including test/evaluation procedures, were established during planning. As the project team performs the work of the project, it

---

66 *PMBOK Guide, Seventh Edition, Section 2.7 – Project Performance Domains*

is important to continually measure the variances of actual performance against those planned measures and evaluate project progress.

Many areas can be measured during the project. They can be used to:

- Evaluate performance compared to plan
- Track utilization of resources, work completed, budget expenditures, etc.
- Accountability
- Provide information to stakeholders
- Assess whether project deliverables are on-track to deliver planned benefits
- Ensure project deliverables meet customer acceptance criteria

Tailor what needs to be measured and *"only measure what matters."* This phrase is commonly attributed to John Doerr, also known for championing the usage of OKRs (Objectives and Key Results) to set goals.

Most methods of tracking performance show the actual work being done by the team, compared with a baseline or an expectation. This comparison utilizes the variance analysis technique to determine the difference and the potential impact on the project of that difference. Even though it is done differently, it can be used in any project life cycle.

Although the evaluation of project progress may be done differently and different measures used, most projects still need to measure progress in some manner for the following areas:

- Scope—the percentage of work completed and change requests
- Schedule—actual duration of work compared to projected start and end dates
- Budget—actual costs compared to budgeted costs, assessment of procurement usage
- Resources—team and procured resource allocations/availability, team and vendor performance appraisal, contract management
- Quality—technical performance, quality audits, escaped defects
- Risk—risk register reassessment

Performance Reporting

While adaptive teams do not create typical formal reports, most projects find a need for a hybrid reporting method to generate this more standard data output, especially to meet organizational reporting requirements.

Even if teams are empowered to use Agile methods and processes, some contexts may require formal reporting. For example:

- A highly regulated industry
- A cultural context that uses formal reports
- A stakeholder or stakeholder group that requires a detailed or formal approach

The various types of performance reports may include:

- *Status reports*—where the project effort currently stands, including milestones reached, risk and issue status, requested changes, and expected deliverables by the next reporting period
- *Progress reports*—what has been accomplished to date
- *Forecast reports*—predictions of future performance of schedule, budget, scope, risks, quality, or other factors of concern
- *Milestone and network diagrams*—including updated milestone charts, dependencies, and sequences
- *Quality reports*—charts and reports based on the quality metrics collected that meet requirements
- *Earned value management (EVM) reports*—graphs and values based on EVM equations using performance measurement baseline requirements
- *Variance analysis reports*—graphs and their analysis comparing actual results to planned and expected results
- *Trend reports*—measurement of performance over time to determine whether performance is improving, deteriorating, or staying constant
- *Dashboards*—physical or electronic progress summaries, usually with visuals or graphics representing the more extensive data set
- *Work performance reports*—physical or electronic representation of work performance information compiled in project documents to support decisions, actions, or awareness

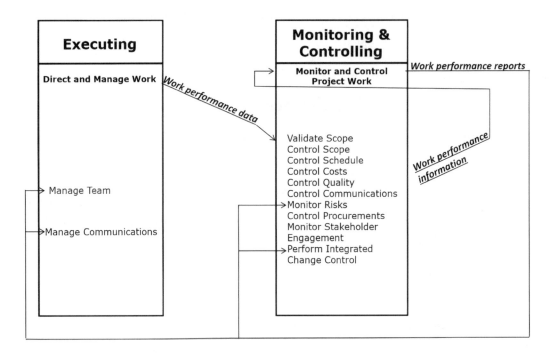

Scope Performance Measurement

Evaluation of scope progress varies according to the life cycle or development approach used.

Predictive

The approved scope baseline, including the scope statement, WBS, and WBS dictionary, is used to measure the scope. The work by the team is then measured against the completion of requirements specified in the scope baseline as identified on the requirements traceability matrix (RTM).

As the project's work continues, it is essential to ensure that the scope baseline is adhered to. This includes a clear understanding of any requested changes to the scope, where they come from, their impact on the project, and whether they have been accepted or rejected.

The key to controlling scope and not allowing undocumented, unapproved changes to "creep" into the project is continuously enforcing the change control procedures identified in the project management plan. These include:

- Requested scope changes must be documented with a change request form and entered on the change control log.

- Requested scope changes must undergo an appropriate impact assessment.

- Requested scope changes must be reviewed by the appropriate customer, performing organization, and identified approver (including possibly the change control board (CCB)), based on previously identified approval levels.
- Change requests must be accepted, rejected, or deferred, and the change control log notes the decision.

Adaptive

The scope evolves from the initial product road map to user story items in a release backlog, selected by the product owner and prioritized into the iteration backlog. The product owner continually reprioritizes the items on the release backlog to determine the work the team will address during an iteration. Confirmation is continuously done to check user stories against the definition of done (DoD) and customer feedback to determine the completion of product requirements.

Hybrid

Uses a combination of these approaches, depending on the portion of the scope being planned and delivered using a predictive approach versus an adaptive one.

Scope Validation/Acceptance

The scope is validated when the customer formally accepts the deliverable(s). The term comes from the predictive process, but the meaning is the same in adaptive life cycles. The actual timing of the validation of deliverables often differs depending on the approach used.

The success criteria, determined by the customer (needs and wants) and the team (product requirements), must be in place. The team establishes a definition of done, reviews wherein the team and customer inspect the product, and the final acceptance criteria.

Exam Tip: Do not confuse validation with verification. Verification is performed to ensure deliverables are correct and meet quality requirements as part of testing activities. (The "e" in verification is similar to the "e" in test.) Validation is formal acceptance of deliverables. (The "a" in validation is similar to the "a" in acceptance.)

- *Predictive*

The acceptance criteria for requirements are listed along with each requirement, possibly for the phase or project.

Requirements can be accepted at the end of a phase or major milestone. Still, they should be reviewed and may be conditionally accepted throughout the project rather than waiting until the final user acceptance testing (UAT).

In addition to validating the scope, organizational requirements must often be met to complete a phase or satisfy any production readiness requirements.

- *Adaptive*

Each user story has acceptance criteria, often included on the back side of the user story "card." This acceptance criteria is measured against the team's DoD and the result of the review with the product owner and stakeholders.

The story could be "accepted" at that time, or when a group of related stories has together met the criteria, and then again possibly at the end of the release, just prior to releasing it to the customer.

This final approval may also need to meet organizational requirements for production readiness.

In a continuous flow approach, individual backlog items, or requests, are prioritized as they are received ("to do") and then work is performed ("in progress") by various individuals or in stages towards completion ("done".)

Schedule Performance Measurement

There are various ways to track performance across projects according to the delivery schedule determined during planning, including:

- *Gantt charts* — a visual display of schedule performance over time
- *Earned value* — a measure of work performed expressed in terms of the budget authorized for that work
- *Quality metrics* — a description of a project or product element and how to measure it
- *Variance analysis* — a technique for determining the cause and degree of difference between the baseline and the actual performance

One method that measures the performance of the schedule and budget is earned value management (EVM), which evaluates the progress of the combined project identified during planning as part of the performance measurement baseline measures.

Predictive

Schedule tracking is usually done against the schedule baseline and shown through either a milestone or Gantt chart. The Tracking Gantt chart displays the activity's actual progress toward completion compared to the planned duration and dates for a work package or activity.

If it is necessary to act on the schedule as a result of measuring performance, three methods are typically used:

- Adjust the schedule model due to the demand and supply of resources.
- Consider the use of smoothing leveling techniques.
- Utilize schedule compression techniques, including fast-tracking.

Even though most predictive project efforts can determine the schedule for the entire project, it may be beneficial to use more of a rolling method and progressive elaboration, leaving most of the schedule detail activities until closer to the phase being delivered.

Adaptive

The schedule for work using an adaptive approach is done differently, not only compared to a predictive approach but also depending on whether timeboxed or continuous flow methods are used.

A few ways to monitor the project's progress are based on an agreed-upon schedule.

- *Timebox Approach*

The time frame when progress is measured could be a sprint or iteration using a timeboxed approach or the delivery of completed individual requests using a continuous flow approach.

Even though the schedule or time frames are set when using timeboxed approaches, the scope delivery and acceptance of the work within those time frames determine the progress.

When work has been done but not accepted at the end of an iteration or sprint as part of a sprint review or demo, it is important to discuss during the retrospective why the work was not accepted. This might be due to not understanding the user story (not meeting the DoR) or accepting more work than can be completed (velocity is too high).

In some Agile methods all backlog items (either in a product or release backlog) are defined and measured against the targeted completion of those items. This assumes that all items in the backlog will be completed. Those items removed by the product owner from the backlog are then determined to be "out of scope."

Note: In most adaptive projects which need the continual flexibility to respond to changes, the final decision as to the content of the backlog is fluid, with final decision on implementation of items is made as part of the backlog refinement. Even though user stories have been added to either the product or release backlog, because of priorities, they may not be addressed until later, if at all.

- *Continuous Flow Approach*

Measurement of progress is shown by the stage in which an item is currently shown, including potentially in a queue awaiting the next available resource.

The time required to complete a request may be based on an SLA.

Hybrid

Uses a combination of these approaches, depending on the portion of the schedule or time frames being planned and delivered using a predictive approach versus the portion that is using an adaptive approach. Because an individual request, or increment of work is time-dependent, a schedule variance results when work is not completed as scheduled. With this information, the project manager can identify appropriate corrective actions.

Schedule Management Techniques

Performance can be shown visually or in reports as identified in the communications management plan.

Reporting and displaying team progress and accomplishments, including committed versus completed work, is extremely important to motivate the team, as are communicating and providing transparency to others about the team's work. This could include:

- *Information Radiators*
  - Various visual representations are displayed in a highly visible location, either in a virtual or physical wall display.
  - Provides the latest up-to-date information at a glance, supporting transparency.
  - Can include velocity, issues, ground rules, and testing results or other schedule-related charts and graphs.

- *Matrices*

- A requirements traceability matrix is a thorough way to track and visualize progress against the completion of requirements.

- Task or kanban boards are used in most adaptive methods and vary by detail, including burndown, burnup, and velocity charts displaying progress using a timeboxed approach.

- Throughput, cycle time, and lead time are calculated and often used in a continuous flow approach.

Other generic visualization methods can include to-do lists, procedure checklists, or simple versions of the requirements traceability matrix.

Predictive

Project progress can be tracked and reported to upper management and stakeholders based on the schedule performance.

The project schedule can be presented in different formats, depending on the audience as well as the approach and circumstances, including:

- *Road map*
- *Milestone chart or list*
- *Gantt chart*
- *Project schedule network diagram*

Adaptive

Providing visualizations is a powerful way of showing work contributions. These various visual representations are displayed in a highly visible location, either in a virtual or physical wall display.

Timeboxed Approach

In timeboxed approaches, a task board can range from a straightforward chart to one with more columns to track the progress of individual tasks. Primary columns include: To Do, In Progress, and Done. Individual teams can add columns for various stages of a user story or task development, if applicable.

- *Burndown Chart (Iteration)*

Adaptive teams use a burndown chart to show the progress toward the work committed to for the iteration. Each user story or task has a value (usually represented as story points) which is tracked to completion in an iteration, based on the definition of done (DoD).

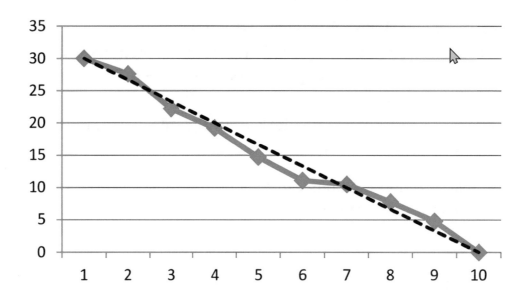

The vertical axis shows the number of story points determined by the team during the iteration planning meeting. The horizontal axis represents the iteration periods when the completed story points are tracked and recorded.

A diagonal line is drawn between the total number of story points (velocity) agreed upon for the current iteration during the iteration planning meeting and zero on the vertical axis.

The team agrees on the criteria for when credit can be taken for completing story points, which are then displayed as "burned down."

As work progresses, the number of story points completed in each iteration is noted and connected to visibly track progress. This helps determine whether the current team velocity is on track, the remaining work needed, and the expected completion status.

‒ *Burnup Chart (Release)*

This chart displays the number of story points completed or accepted based on the DoD for each iteration. Those numbers are accumulated during the release to show the overall value of the release. This value can be used when an agile earned value measurement (AEVM) is done.

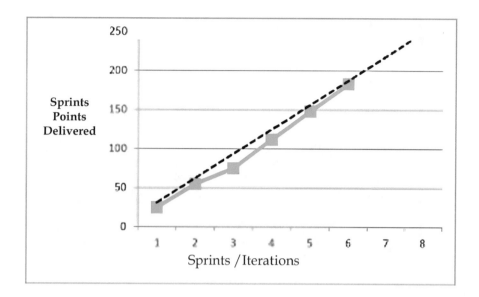

When a Feature-Driven approach is used, a baseline, or total number of story points for the release can be determined after estimating the total value of the release backlog.

Most adaptive approaches incorporate the Lean principle, "decide as late as possible," and agree upon the stories to include in each iteration during the iteration planning meeting. Therefore, the number of story points or value included in the release is not estimated at the start of a release. Many stories may end up not being prioritized high enough to be included in the release.

- *Task Board*

Task boards are a fantastic way of enabling shared understanding and evaluating progress. By making data visible, everyone has knowledge regarding work in progress. This creates an atmosphere of transparency and information sharing.

Different task boards vary based on the adaptive approach, with the main difference being the detail and number of columns shown on the boards. The columns and detail tracking need to be tailored for the project, and the stages or iterations are displayed on the board.

Regardless of the method used, the board organizes the tasks from the user stories or requirements into "cards." These cards allow visualization of the work being done.

- *Velocity*

Just as we estimate the duration of activities using a predictive approach, estimating how much work a team can complete during a timeboxed iteration is useful. This measure is referred to as the velocity of the team. The team's velocity may vary at the beginning of a project but should be consistent as additional iterations are completed.

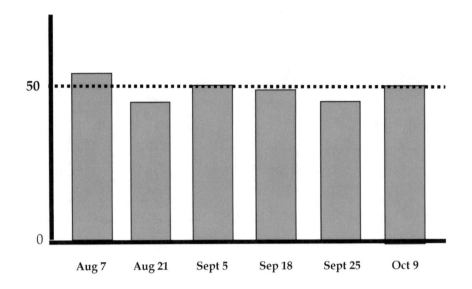

Velocity is calculated by estimating the number of story points that can be completed during an iteration. It will be modified as additional iterations refine the number of story points completed and accepted. The goal is to achieve a constant velocity from one iteration to the next.

Velocity is a useful metric for a project, but it is also unique. One team's velocity cannot be compared with another's. Teams differ in ability and skill, their work and schedules are different, etc.

Continuous Flow Approach

The kanban board is used for continuous flow methods and tracks the progress of individual requests or requirements from arrival until completion.

To Do	Stage 1 WIP 4	Que	Stage 2 WIP 3	Que	Stage 3 WIP 4	Que	Stage 4 WIP 5	Done
User Story 1								✓
User Story 2							✓	
User Story 3							✓	
User Story 4				✓				
User Story 5						✓		
User Story 6		✓						
User Story 7					✓			
User Story 8	✓							
User Story 9			✓					
User Story 10					✓			

It uses columns, queues, and work in progress (WIP) limits to visualize work using a pull system with each story's progress as it moves toward completion. This allows the analysis of blockages with items in columns or queues for an extended period.

- *Cumulative Flow Diagram*

In continuous flow approaches, lead time, cycle time, and throughput show progress for individual items, requests, or requirements that can be measured.

The cumulative flow diagram (CFD) is an analytical tool fundamental to kanban or other continuous flow methods. It allows teams to visualize both effort and progress. It also shows where impediments have impacted the delivery of results.

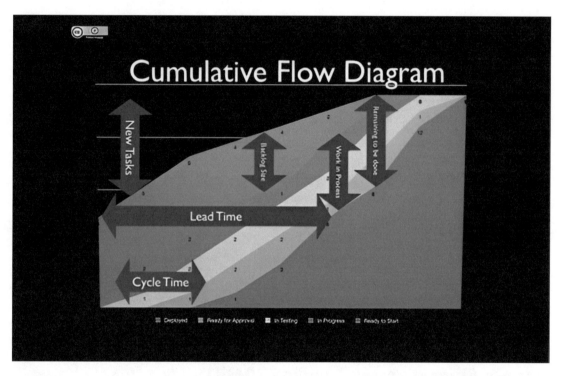

This chart often displays the following:

- *Lead time*—the time required for an item to go through the entire process, from arrival to delivery
- *Cycle time*—the actual time worked on an item, from start to delivery
- *Throughput*—number of items entering or exiting the system at any time
- *WIP*—a measure of work in progress but not completed at any point

Analysis of this diagram includes:

- Lines should be smooth and rise gently, as the graph tracks the number of work items entering and exiting the queue. Ideally, this rate should be constant.

– A bump or sudden ascent/descent indicates a surge or lag in some additional requests.

Budget Performance Measurement

Budget challenges on projects are typical, and their impact and resolution require close monitoring.

Even though the project manager needs to continually track the costs and expenditures of project activities, that function may be centralized and included in a functional department's or organization's budget. Regardless of who has the final responsibility, communications need to identify any problems or challenges.

Budget changes can occur for a variety of reasons, including:

– New or changed project requirements

– Risks or changes to risk probability or impact

– Changes to activity cost estimates resulting from economic factors like inflation, procurement contract modifications, resource costs, etc.

Remember, "time is money," and therefore schedule and cost performance are tied closely and usually analyzed together. When cost and schedule variance analysis is conducted at the appropriate time intervals and levels, it can effectively control further cost and schedule problems.

Since the budget is tied to the schedule and scope requirements and is part of the overall project baseline, any changes must be handled through the project change management system.

Performance Measurement Baseline (PMB)

The performance measurement baseline (PMB) is a component of the project plan that relates to a project's scope, schedule, budget, or control accounts. It helps the project manager evaluate the progress being made concerning the combination of the scope, schedule, and budget.

The indicators for this baseline are defined individually in the scope, schedule, and cost management plans. These identify how the delivered work and consumed resources will be tracked and documented, especially when using earned value management. Of special importance is the determination of "earning rules" or metrics to quantify the accomplishment of work, especially for earned value (EV) or actual cost (AC). Earned value is determined and credited at the end of the reporting period.

Factors to measure performance include:

- *Discrete* — *describes the activities that are likely to be planned/measured for all outputs, including:*

  - *Fixed formula* — a percentage of the budget is given to a work package when work starts and the remaining percentage when the work is completed (50/50, 20/80, 0/100)

  - *Percentage complete* — earned value computed by multiplying the work package BAC by the percent complete (only if completion percentage can realistically be determined)

  - *Weighted milestones* — divides longer duration work packages into smaller measurable sections with specific value earned for each interim deliverable and then accumulated as milestones are completed

  - *Physical measurements* — any measurable unit explicitly connected with the completion of the work

- *Apportioned* — *describes the work that shares a direct/supporting relationship toward discrete work, including:*

  - Non-discrete activities (quality assurance, testing, inspection, project management activities)

  - Calculated as a percentage of discrete work

- *Level of Effort* — *planned value for activities not producing definitive products or deliverables during a measurement period. These activities do not have a schedule variance but can have a cost variance measured by actual cost (AC), including:*

  - Helpdesk activities

  - Database performance and tuning

  - Troubleshooting

Earned Value Management (EVM)

Earned value management (EVM) is a technique used by project managers and project teams to measure project progress by comparing actual schedule and cost performance against planned performance as laid out in the schedule and cost baselines.

EVM can be used in any life cycle or development approach, but it has historically been applied to and possibly mandated for predictive approaches. The original method has been modified slightly for usage by projects using an adaptive method.

EVM combines the analysis of scope completion or "value earned" compared to what was planned to be completed at a point in time and the actual cost needed to earn that value.

Assessing the value of work requires first determining what work has been performed and usually approved, and therefore, what it has contributed to the project. These performance reviews are typically included in project status review meetings.

During planning, project work is broken down into work packages and activities. Each work package is assigned a budget and a schedule. This is where performance information is captured based on performance measurement baseline metrics in the various subsidiary management plans.

Even though progress is captured continuously throughout the project, EVM is typically performed and communicated at a designated reporting time, usually at the end of a month.

Earned Value Management Variables

EVM utilizes three independent metrics to assess and monitor project cost and schedule performance progress against the completion of work. These three variables are used to determine whether the work is being accomplished as planned and to forecast project cost at completion. The variables are:

Planned Value (PV)—the authorized budget assigned to scheduled work.

This amount is specified in the project's schedule baseline. PV indicates the value of work scheduled during a particular time.

Earned Value (EV)—the measure of work performed expressed in terms of the budget authorized for that work.

EV is a measurement of the value of the work completed at a point in time. The metrics determining this value are usually specified in the performance measurement baseline. Since this really refers to scope, it is important to understand how value can be "earned," e.g., percent complete, 50/50 credit at the beginning and end, or some other agreed-upon measure.

Earned value can be determined by multiplying the percentage of work completed by the budgeted cost for the activity as laid out in the cost baseline (EV = % completed x BAC).

Actual Cost (AC)—the actual cost incurred for the work performed on an activity during a specific period. AC refers to the total costs incurred while performing work, either during a scheduled activity or the completion of a WBS component, depending on the specified earned value metric.

It is important to know these three factors and what they represent, as well as understand the progress of the project by comparing them at any time.

This method often subdivides the reporting based on planning packages (especially when some work is being done internally and other work is performed under a contract, and performance monitoring is critical).

In the best case, the earned value should be greater than the planned value and the actual cost at any time. This indicates that more value has been "earned" than planned or scheduled (i.e., ahead of schedule). It also should determine whether the value "earned" was greater than the actual cost to achieve value (i.e., under budget).

EVM Measures for Schedule Control

The two commonly used EVM measures for schedule control are:

Schedule Variance (SV) — a measure of schedule performance expressed as the difference between the earned and planned values. $(SV = EV - PV)$

- Positive SV indicates the project is ahead of schedule.
- Zero SV indicates the project is on schedule.
- Negative SV indicates the project is behind schedule.

The Schedule Performance Index (SPI) — a measure of schedule efficiency as the ratio of earned value to planned value. $(SPI = EV / PV)$

This is a much more valuable metric since it can be compared to the tolerance in the schedule management plan, so any necessary adjustments can be made to get the schedule back on track.

- SPI greater than 1.0 indicates the project is ahead of schedule.
- SPI = 1.0 indicates the project is on schedule.
- SPI less than 1.0 indicates the project is behind schedule.

EVM Measures for Cost Control

The most used EVM measures for cost control are:

Cost Variance (CV) — the accumulated budget spent at a given time, expressed as the difference between earned value and actual cost. $(CV = EV - AC)$

- Positive CV indicates the project is under budget.
- Zero CV indicates the project is on budget.
- Negative CV indicates the project is over budget.

The Cost Performance Index (CPI) — a measure of budget efficiency, expressed as the ratio of earned value to actual cost. (CPI = EV / AC)

This is a much more valuable metric since it can be compared to the tolerance included in the cost management plan, so any necessary adjustments can be made to get the budget back on track.

- CPI greater than 1.0 indicates the project is under budget.
- CPI = 1.0 indicates the project is on budget.
- CPI less than 1.0 indicates the project is over budget.

	Planned Value (PV)	Earned Value (EV)	Actual Cost (AC)
	Schedule		**Cost**
Variance	Schedule Variance (SV) SV=EV-PV		Cost Variance (CV) CV=EV-AC
	Minus		*Minus*
Performance Index	*Divided By*		*Divided By*
	Schedule Performance Index (SPI) SPI=EV/PV		Cost Performance Index (CPI) CPI=EV/AC

EVM Forecasting

Budget at Completion (BAC) — the initial baselined budget established for the work. As new baselines are established, they are referred to as the Estimate at Completion (EAC).

Two helpful EVM factors are estimate to complete (ETC) and estimate at completion (EAC).

These help determine whether additional analysis and possibly more funds are required. This includes looking at efficiencies and deciding how they work.

Exam Tip: ETC is usually used first, before EAC to determine when an increase should be requested.

- *Estimate to Complete (ETC)*

Based on current work and expenditures, this is used to determine whether additional money will be required to complete the project.

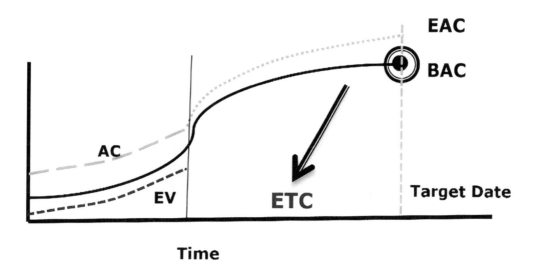

The estimate to complete (ETC) is calculated to help determine if additional funds are necessary. *(ETC = BAC - AC).*

- *Estimate at Completion (EAC)*

The current projected final cost of the project is referred to as the EAC. This often indicates that the original budget amount (BAC) has been modified or re-baselined.

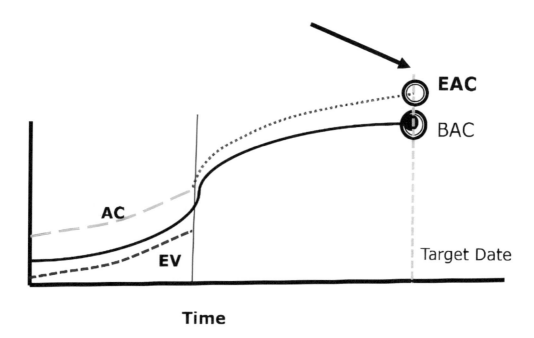

It is based on the current spending efficiency (the CPI) and can be calculated with several formulas. The simple way to calculate the estimate at completion (EAC) is to divide the BAC by the current CPI. Given the current progress, this will give us the minimum amount needed to complete the project. *(EAC = BAC / CPI)*

- *Variance at Completion (VAC)*

Variance at completion compares the project's actual cost with the budgeted amount. It is the difference between the original budget at completion (BAC) and any updated baselines to the original budget (EAC).

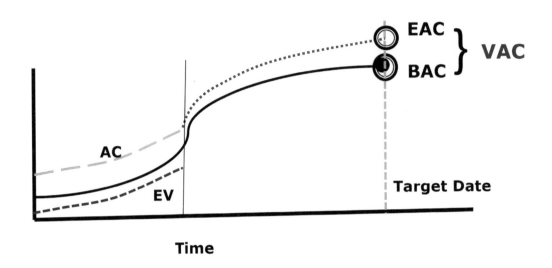

Exam Tip: In preparing for the current exam, only two formulas are essential to remember.

- *CPI = EV/AC provides the current spending rate.*
- *EAC = BAC/CPI provides the minimum amount needed to meet the completion of the work based on the current spending rate.*

By remembering the formula for CPI and realizing it includes the cost factor (AC), it is easy to then determine the SPI = EV/PV by substituting the schedule factor (PV).

Agile EVM

EVM has been adapted for use in adaptive and hybrid projects because it has been proven effective as a set of forward-looking metrics for monitoring and controlling complex and risky projects.

Because most adaptive projects are not concerned with time constraints, most performance measures are related to the time or schedule. This enables the comparison of items in the release plan against the actual work done and helps teams to identify areas where they are experiencing problems and ensure they can complete the prioritized requirements/user stories within the specified release time frame.

As with predictive projects, a performance measurement baseline (PMB) needs to be established. It is also essential to understand:

- How many iterations are planned for the release
- How many story points were identified for the release (provided the method used identifies these at the release level)
- The release budget based on the resources and time (not necessarily based on the number of story points)

The following data, collected at the end of each iteration, have been modified slightly from how the EVM factors are determined for a predictive approach.

- Planned value: the budgetary value for planned work in an iteration
- Earned value: the budgetary value for completed work in an iteration
- Actual cost: actual cost incurred to complete an iteration deliverable

Funding Limit Reconciliation

Funding limits are imposed by the project sponsor or the organization to help protect against overspending.

Most budgets are created with the assumption that there will be a steady flow of money to pay for the various expenditures, rather than large amounts of money available from the start of the project.

It is vital to align work and expenditures on the schedule to level out the rate of expenditure while being aware of the timing of funding. The distribution or acquisition of resources based on the required expenditure may be affected, which can result in rescheduling project work and eliminating or postponing work packages in a change request to the approved scope baseline.

When the project nears the target end date and the budget has been exhausted, the project will need to get additional funding or end with only the work completed.

Resource Performance Measurement

The project manager must continually monitor, manage, and inform stakeholders of any issues regarding relevant resources.

Any impact on the schedule or cost baselines must be handled and approved by the project's change control system process.

This process of monitoring resources, both work and physical, must be performed continually throughout the project.

– *Work Resource Management*

Leading human resources, including team members and external contractors, requires leadership power skills and applying tailored tools to performance measurement.

As team members change, the team often experiences regression from the current stage in the Tuckman ladder to a previous stage, hopefully only temporarily. The project manager must be aware of the change and help the team re-norm as seamlessly as possible.

New team members should be welcomed and considered a potential source of new and additional knowledge. It is vital to ensure they understand and accept the project goals and vision.

While introducing new members to the team, take time to determine how they can add value to the team through discussions and collaboration with the entire team.

Any changes in the project team's composition may cause disruptions and potential conflict. This requires the project manager to help support these situations in a constructive and positive way.

Continual monitoring of project suppliers and vendors during the contract period is needed to ensure the contracted work is progressing and determine whether any changes might impact the budget, timeline, quality, or risk.

– *Physical Resource Management*

Controlling resources concerns the physical resources required for the project, including equipment, materials, facilities, and infrastructure. Management of physical resources is often more of a controlling process. When resources are scarce, many organization may include methods including lean management, just-in-time (JIT) manufacturing, Kaizen, total productive maintenance (TPM), and the theory of constraints (TOC).

It is critical to continually ensure that those physical resources identified as being required are available as planned. This includes their availability at the right time, in the right place, and in the right amount. It is also important to release these resources when they are no longer needed, to avoid recurring additional expenses.

In addition to monitoring availability, this process also monitors the usage or consumption of materials, supplies, and equipment. This enables the project manager to determine whether additional resources may be needed to complete the work. This is often referred to as resource allocation.

To manage physical resources, it is necessary to understand what has been used and what is still needed at any given time. This includes reviewing the usage and whether it aligns with what was planned. It also includes the expenditures for the various resources and the reporting utilization identified in the project management plan.

Monitoring the usage of resources is directly tied to the cost of these resources and whether additional resources will be required besides those initially identified. This is critical if there is a potential delay in acquiring additional items. It also addresses releasing or removing excess supplies when no longer required.

Contract Performance Measurement

Measuring performance on contracts includes managing the various sellers, and ensuring the seller's performance aligns with delivery requirements in the contract. This includes documentation and review of the work performed based on contract requirements and may require corrective actions to be initiated. This may be managed at the project level by the project manager, or at the organizational level by a procurement administrator.

Various aspects regarding measuring contract performance include:

- *Communications*

The subsidiary communications management plan and contract terms and conditions will help identify communications and activities pertaining to working with resources obtained through contracts.

The organization, contract, or agreement may require formal progress reports—typically documented in the SOW or agreement. If formal reports are not required, it is important to continually check with suppliers to ensure work is proceeding as expected, on time, and within cost parameters. Additional contract checks may include compliance with the procurement process.

- *Contract Change*

The way changes in contracts are usually handled is specified in the contract itself. This may be in addition to the organization and project change processes. Regardless of the approach used, the contract should continually be reviewed regarding how changes must be handled.

  – *Completion of Contract*

When work is complete, a formal acceptance of the deliverables from the supplier will need to be arranged.

Suppliers and vendors are given instructions on how to submit invoices for payment—usually in the SOW. However, project managers need to notify the appropriate financial entity when work has been completed, which includes authorizing payment of the final invoice.

Activities to measure the performance on any contract include:

- Continually update and maintain documentation of all contract and procurement activities, often in a record management system or similar functionality as part of the information management system and PMIS.
- Ensure payments to the vendor are made according to the terms and conditions in the contract.
- Perform necessary or required performance reviews, including performance successes and failures, progress against the SOW, and the seller's ability to perform the contracted work (or not).
- Utilize inspections and audits to identify weaknesses in the seller's processes or deliverables.
- Report on the seller's performance, in accordance with the terms and conditions of the contract.
- Resolve any disputes or claims, especially regarding compensation for changes.

  – *Predictive*

Changes to baselines and contract issues impacting the approved baselines must be assessed for impact and approved or rejected by the appropriate change control system.

  – *Adaptive*

Because change is expected using an adaptive approach, the deliverables are not specified in typical Agile contracts. Changes to the work are determined and prioritized by the product owner.

Quality Performance Measurement

The objective of quality activities is the same whether dealing with an up-front, well-defined set of requirements or a group of conditions progressively elaborated and incrementally delivered.

Quality is closely linked to acceptance criteria for the project's deliverables and is also relevant to the project approaches and activities used to produce the deliverables.

While project teams evaluate the quality of a deliverable through inspection and testing, project activities and processes are assessed through reviews and audits, often by a quality assurance function or the guidelines provided. These include executing quality activities defined in the quality management plan, ensuring appropriate standards and processes are implemented in the project, and auditing quality requirements and measurements used in quality control testing activities.

In all approaches, the team should incorporate quality activities within their work and always focus on detecting and preventing errors and defects.

Quality Measurement

Quality is linked to both the product and the processes the project uses and is specified in the acceptance criteria described in the statement of work (SOW) and the requirements and design documents.

Regardless of the terminology and approach, the quality metric of each requirement or user story must be met to obtain approval for the work completed.

A variety of methods are used to measure quality, including:

- Service level agreements (SLAs)
- Key performance indicators (KPIs)
- Measures stipulated in contracts

- *Predictive*

As the project team produces deliverables, the project manager will incorporate a quality process to:

- Review the deliverable and verify it meets both functional and nonfunctional requirements.
- Identify and suggest potential improvements.
- Validate whether the deliverable aligns with compliance requirements.
- Provide feedback on any variances identified.

Additionally, the project manager is often responsible for monitoring the quality assurance (QA) reports and recommendations and coordinating with the project team to address identified defects or noncompliance issues.

- *Adaptive*

Quality management is usually part of the process—everyone is responsible. The team, customer, and product owner define quality goals and metrics.

They use feedback from iterations, identified and discussed during retrospectives, to monitor quality continuously.

Adaptive approaches can use the quality tools usually associated with predictive approaches, but some additional quality evaluation and management activities are also used. (Because of the increase in hybrid approaches, these concepts are now often seen in predictive approaches as well.)

- Definition of done (DoD)—determined by the team to help identify the requirements for something to be "done"
- Acceptance criteria—tied to each user story or requirement to identify what must exist before the requirement is accepted, especially by the product owner or stakeholder

Adaptive projects associate the acceptance criteria with individual stories, whereas predictive projects identify these criteria for each deliverable in the scope statement within the scope baseline.

Verify Outcomes

Verified results must deliver outcomes to meet the requirements specified for a deliverable or user story.

The products and outputs are measured against the project's quality standards regardless of the approach used. Corrections must be made when those quality standards are neither met nor within the acceptable ranges.

Regardless of the approach, it is important to continually reflect on the work done and the quality achieved and identify and implement corrections and controls when quality standards are outside of acceptable ranges.

- *Predictive*

The project team verifies the deliverable based on the quality standards and requirements, usually through testing by team members, or demonstration and review to the product owner. This verification includes checking to see if the quality metrics are being met, possibly within an identified tolerance or acceptable variation for the metric.

Once the deliverables have been verified, they are presented to and accepted (or validated) by the customer—resulting in accepted deliverables.

– *Adaptive*

In adaptive approaches, the story is not accepted if the user story within an iteration does not meet the product owner's expectations. It is then put back on the backlog for further analysis, understanding, and prioritization compared to other backlog items.

Acceptance of deliverables or stories can be done upon individual completion or at the end of the phase, project, or release.

Quality Tools

Several quality tools are used to help control project quality within the quality management discipline. They are often used to support other project activities as well.

Regardless of the processes or tools used to monitor quality aspects of a project, it is important to visualize the work, which requires incorporating the Agile principle of transparency.

Tools to evaluate quality include:

- *Data-Gathering Tools*
    - Checklists/check sheets
    - Statistical sampling
    - Questionnaires and survey

- *Data Analysis Tools*
    - Performance reviews
    - Root cause analysis
    - Design for X (DfX) (to optimize a specific aspect of design)
    - Failure mode and effects analysis (FMEA) (process analysis tool to identify all possible failures)
    - Design of experiments (DOE) (usually identified during planning)

- *Data Representation/Visualization*
    - Cause-and-effect diagram
    - Scatter diagrams
    - Control charts
    - Flowchart
    - Histograms
    - Pareto chart

- *Checklist/Check Sheet*

Checklists are a simple way to ensure the product's quality and process for accuracy and completeness. This includes checking that all steps in a process are followed or that a result meets all requirements or specifications. Many organizations have standard templates that can be tailored to meet the specific needs of the project or product being reviewed. These can be used for a quality audit or to continually verify the work being performed.

A check sheet is used to collect data in real time as a process is being performed, often at the location where the work is being performed. This usually is a simple tally sheet with marks or checks to quantify observed results. It can also be the collection of multiple readings, especially in manufacturing, which is then analyzed for conformance to standards and tolerances.

- *Statistical Sampling*

Rather than test every individual result, random sampling is often used to determine whether the expected quality of the result has been met. The number of samples taken, and the sampling frequency depend on the applicable quality metrics.

The individual element sampling results from the tests are recorded and then combined to see trends in the results. These are often charted using a control chart to help indicate whether the results are increasing, decreasing, or fluctuating as expected around the mean or specified element metric.

The trends help indicate when appropriate action must be taken to bring the results back into conformance.

Example: In one project there were only a few critical product elements (one being the percentage of sugar in the product). A single product was pulled off the assembly line on an hourly basis and that element was checked to ensure conformance within specified tolerances. If the results started trending close to the tolerance limits further examination was required, including possibly other factors causing the change (e.g., temperature, humidity, etc.). If the metric reached the control limit it required, the line being stopped until a correction could be made .

- *Cause-and-Effect Diagram (Root cause analysis)*

Cause-and-effect diagrams break down the causes of a problem statement, helping to identify the primary or root cause of a problem. These are also called fishbone or Ishikawa diagrams.

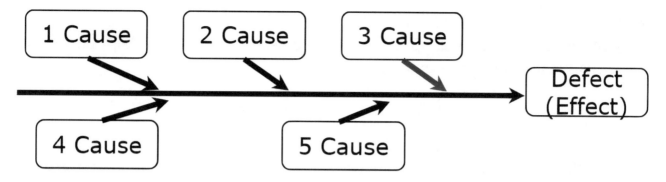

Kaoru Ishikawa, a Japanese quality guru, developed the Ishikawa diagram. It is a tool used to analyze root causes in a graphic format.

The diagram breaks down the problem into parts, with the main effect at the head end of the chart. The spines on the remaining portion of the graph indicate high causes (the main branches or spines), with contributing causes on the smaller spines. Further breakdown can be done at each branch to understand the problem better.

This analysis can be done by continually drilling down into the causes using the Agile approach of "5 Whys." This method continually asks "why" to the previous reason until a potential root cause of the problem is found. Asking "why" at least five times will either get you to the root cause of the problem or identify a point where you need further information to understand the reason.

– *Scatter Diagram*

Scatter diagrams use a traditional graph for trending and regression analysis to represent the relationship between any process, environment, or activity element on one axis and a quality defect (usually) on the other.

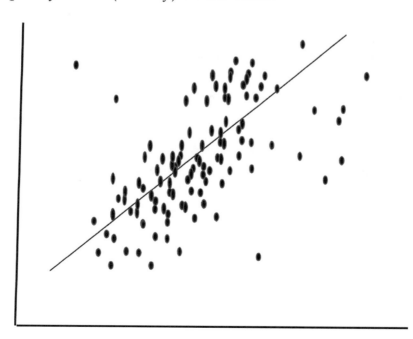

For the scatter diagram to be practical or valuable, the compared elements must be causally related in some way. If unrelated data sets are compared, false-positive or false-negative measurements may occur.

They are often used in trending and regression analysis, comparing the two variables and resulting changes.

- Positive correlation—An increase in X corresponds to an increase in Y, trending in a positive direction.
- Negative correlation—An increase in X corresponds to a decrease in Y, trending in a negative direction.
- Neutral correlation—An increase in X leads to neither an increase nor a decrease in Y, showing no correlation of any impact between the measurements.

Exam Tip: The detail regarding a scatter diagram is most likely not needed for the exam. It is important to understand that this diagram is used to compare two related variables.

- *Control Chart*

A control chart is a tool used to determine a process's predictability, behavior, and stability over time. It can also be referred to as a variability control chart when used to analyze and communicate the variability of a process or project activity over time.

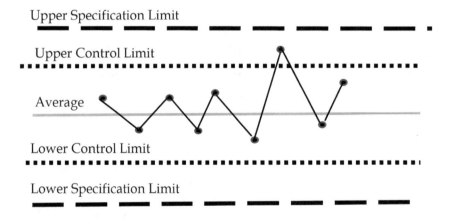

These charts are ideal for repetitive processes with predictable results and can be plotted against those control limits. They also provide visibility to where corrective actions can prevent further problems.

A control chart graphically displays project results against established control limits, including maximum and minimum acceptable values.

The centerline is the mean or average expected or planned result.

The process sets the control limits and shows the area of three standard deviations on either side of the centerline, reflecting the expected variation in the data. This equates to 99.96% of the results falling within the control limits.

The customer sets the specification limit to meet specified requirements for a product or service. This area is usually greater than the area defined by the control limits.

Since this is a statistical process chart, the data is supposed to fall randomly within the control limits, but there is no way of predicting where the data points will land at any given time. This is especially true when it is used to analyze the results of statistical sampling.

There is a rule of seven that helps expose when corrective action may be needed. A set of seven data points consecutively increasing or decreasing may reflect a trend (either positive or negative), or seven consecutive points below or above the mean. Usually, the points will vary above and below the mean but within the control limits. (Obviously in manufacturing where there are many points being recorded, the "seven" is a relative measurement, and maybe referring to the top or bottom measurements.)

– *Flowchart*

The flowchart has been used since the 1920s to analyze processes and decision points. It analyzes and verifies processes, rules, and potential waste. It also helps document, study, plan, improve, and communicate often complex processes with clear, easy-to-understand diagrams. It has been used for many years to show the steps (shown by rectangles) and decision points (shown by diamonds) in a process.

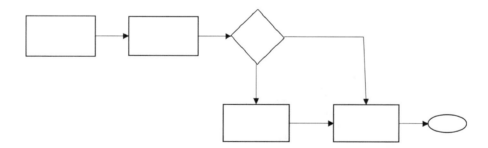

These diagrams are often expanded by using a swim lane diagram, placing the various processes and decision points within a "lane" representing the function performing the action. This enhances the analysis to show where efficiencies can be achieved by reducing the number of "lanes" involved.

These are often referred to as process maps, process diagrams, process flows, or process flow diagrams. A common versions of the flowchart is the SIPOC model showing the flow of suppliers, inputs, process, outputs, and customers.

– *Histogram*

A histogram is a vertical bar chart that captures or categorizes group-specific data elements over time. Data is captured, associated with a category, and then displayed graphically, showing any category's density or number of occurrences. Typical project usage includes resource overallocation and defect categories.

When the vertical bars of this graph are sorted, with the category/bar with the greatest numbers appearing first, it becomes a Pareto chart.

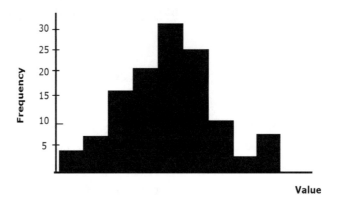

– *Pareto Chart*

A histogram used to rank causes of problems in a hierarchical format based on the Pareto principle (also known as the 80/20 rule), which contends that a relatively large number of problems or defects, typically 80%, are commonly due to a relatively small number of causes, typically 20%.

The areas for improvement can be identified using a Pareto chart or the 80/20 rule.

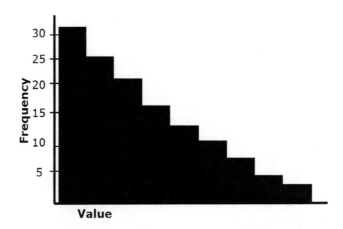

The Pareto chart was named for the Italian economist Vilfredo Pareto in the late 19th century. He discovered that 80% of the wealth in Italy was held by 20% of the population. He applied this as a principle, proposing that roughly 80% of the outcomes result from 20% of the conditions for many events. The Pareto chart is a key tool in kaizen to help indicate the conditions yielding the most significant outcomes.

The Pareto chart aims to highlight the most important among a set of categories through prioritization. It helps find and prioritize the defects to determine where the most significant overall improvement can be made. The most common sources are displayed in the order of frequency, highest to lowest.

This chart does not help define a problem's root cause but only visually indicates where problems may need further analysis.

Exam Tip: The Pareto chart is often used as a prioritization tool to help identify critical issues in descending order of frequency, identifying those problems that should be addressed first.

Quality Audit

A structured, independent process to determine whether project activities comply with organizational and project policies, processes, and procedures.

Quality audits can be used to formalize the quality management components, including continuous review and improvements in predictive or adaptive approaches.

Quality audits, whether conducted regularly, on a schedule, or in an ad hoc fashion, improve the quality performance of a project. The audit result is usually communicated in the form of a quality report.

Audits can be scheduled or conducted at random intervals and often are specified in the quality management subsidiary plan. Topics that can and should be audited include adherence to the following:

- Quality management policy
- Collection and use of information (especially confidential or sensitive information)
- Analytical techniques, methods, and the results achieved when these methods are used
- Cost of quality (both conformance and nonconformance aspects)
- Quality process design and usage

Risk Performance Monitoring

Risk monitoring and analysis are closely tied to project and product quality management.

As the project proceeds, it is important to continually monitor risks and their triggers. When the time arrives and if the risk occurs, the actual implementation of the planned risk response is set in motion.

Risk requires constant reevaluation. This may include identifying possible new risks, risks that have changed based on additional information, and risks whose "time has passed." It also includes assessing the effectiveness of the chosen risk response.

In addition to determining whether the project assumptions used to identify risks are still valid, the threat itself may have changed, or the time when it could have occurred may have passed. Therefore, the risk register will require modifications.

Risk management policies and procedures need to be reviewed to ensure the project is adhering to those previously defined and determine whether the subsidiary risk management plan requires any changes.

Contingency Reserves

A method used to evaluate the amount of risk on a project and the amount of schedule and budget reserve to determine whether the reserve is sufficient for the remaining risk.

The way in which contingencies should be applied to the project should be identified in the subsidiary risk management plan, often with best practices through policies and procedures in the OPAs.

– *Predictive*

Predictive approaches are more methodical toward risk, including identification and specification of the risk approach for the project in the subsidiary risk management plan.

Reserve analysis is a method used to evaluate the project's risk and determine whether additional money or time needs to be set aside in a reserve account to be allocated for identified accepted risks. This is often referred to as the contingencies (whether time or money), which can be identified for individual activities or work packages and added to the project budget.

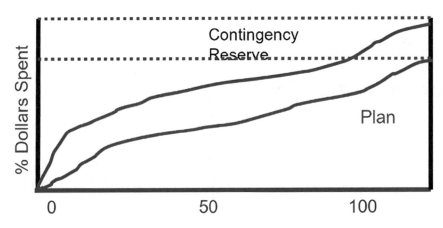

The reserve analysis is often done to determine how much, if any, reserve remains, especially after a problem has occurred and contingency has been required to cover the resolution.

Exam Tip: Contingency reserve amounts can be applied to individual activities or work packages where risks have been identified, or a percentage applied to the project overall.

Example: I had a project where a 38% contingency was added by the PMO to the cost of the project based on the evaluation of various aspects of the project where uncertainty was perceived to possibly occur. I had already estimated and included contingencies on individual activities, not realizing that the final review of my submitted budget would be reassessed for potential risks or uncertainties. This resulted in additional costs being added and increasing the final cost to exceed the project budget, and the customer's expectations.

- *Adaptive*

Risk management is incorporated throughout the project with iterative and incremental practices.

Adaptive projects don't usually identify contingencies and reserves but handle these situations by prioritizing and estimating the effort required on individual stories.

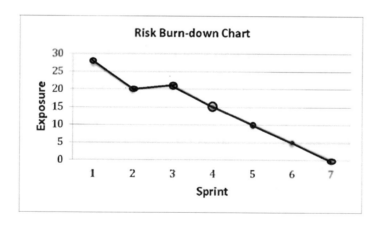

A risk burndown chart can identify the top anticipated risks for a release, and as the threat is either handled or no longer presents a risk to the project, it is "burned down."

Risk Register Updates

Even though risks are initially identified at the beginning of a project, release, or iteration, they should be continually addressed.

Risks raised during the daily stand-up meetings, iteration reviews, other meetings, or everyday conversations are added to the risk register.

Both newly identified and existing risks in the risk register must be updated to include the current knowledge and situation.

Adaptive teams may use a simplified risk register, sometimes called a risk list or log.

Risk Audits

If a risk has occurred, both the initial response chosen and the actual response required should be reviewed. Often this is done through a risk audit. Also, the contingency reserve should be reviewed, especially if contingency was required to handle the risk.

Risk audits are a specific type of project audit performed to examine and document the effectiveness of the implemented risk responses. They also review the complete risk management process, its effectiveness, and how closely the activities follow the initial risk management plan. A risk audit is often performed by individuals external to the project who specialize in these activities.

The risk audit format should be defined before it is conducted, and if it is a common activity, it might be included in the subsidiary risk management plan. At a minimum, the policies and procedures regarding this risk audit should be part of the OPAs available to the project.

Compliance Monitoring

Compliance, and potential noncompliance, are the highest priority in any aspect of risk management. Noncompliance is the inability, or threat, of satisfying the compliance requirements.

When considering compliance in terms of the quality of deliverables, a designated stakeholder or group of stakeholders should be identified as being accountable for each compliance requirement in the project and authorized to sign off on and approve these requirements.

Many of these final approvals may only be possible shortly before project completion because they depend on integrated testing, verification, and validation throughout the project.

Regardless of when the final approvals are received, the continual review provides an early warning of potential threats to compliance and determines an appropriate course of action to remediate the issue before it impacts the project timeline, causes cost overruns, or creates significant project risks.

Key Concepts Covered

- Measure and report on performance
- Scope performance
- Schedule performance
- Budget performance
- Performance measurement baseline (PMB)
- Earned value management (EVM)
- Resource performance
- Contract performance
- Quality performance
- Quality tools
- Risk performance
- Compliance monitoring

ECO Coverage

- Execute project with the urgency required to deliver business value (2.1)
  - Examine the business value throughout the project (2.1.2)

- Plan and manage budget and resources (2.5)
  - Monitor budget variations and work with the governance process to adjust as necessary (2.5.3)

- Plan and manage the schedule (2.6)
  - Measure ongoing progress based on methodology (2.6.4)
  - Modify schedule, as needed, based on methodology (2.6.5)
  - Coordinate with other projects and other operations (2.6.6)

- Plan and manage the quality of products/deliverables (2.7)
  - Recommend options for improvement based on quality gaps (2.7.2)
  - Continually survey project deliverable quality (2.7.3)

- Plan and manage scope (2.8)
  - Monitor and validate scope (2.8.3)

Check Your Progress

1. For an agile project, the project manager would like to use a tool that allows the team to keep track of the flow of work while limiting the work in progress. What tool best meets these requirements?

   A. Gantt chart

   B. Kanban chart

   C. White board in a conference room

   D. Burn up chart

2. You are reviewing the earned value on your project with your team members and the CPI equals 1.15 and SPI equals 1.00. What should you do with the results of your analysis?

   A. Distribute the good results to project stakeholders as per your communication management plan

   B. You do not need to do anything since you are over budget

   C. Find out why you haven't spent as much money as planned

   D. Since the SPI and CPI are good, you don't need to report this analysis to the stakeholders

3. A project manager and the team members discovered a complex problem that can have a negative impact on the project. The project manager analyzed the problem using a fishbone diagram, identified a solution, and immediately implemented the solution. However, the same problem resurfaced. What did the project manager most likely forget to do?

   A. Validate the solution with the key stakeholders

   B. Confirm that the solution solved the problem

   C. The project manager should have used a Pareto chart instead

   D. The project manager should have used a control chart to discover a solution

4. The project manager reported to the sponsor that SPI is 0.85 and the CPI is 0.80 and the sponsor is very upset and would like the project manager to correct this action as soon as possible. What should the project manager do next?

   A. Meet with the team to determine how to fix the project schedule

   B. Meet with the team to determine how to fix the project cost

   C. Meet with the team to determine how to bring the project back on schedule and find out why they are overspending the budget

   D. Inform the sponsor the project is on schedule and on budget and no corrective actions needed

5. Please review the control chart and determine the status of this process.

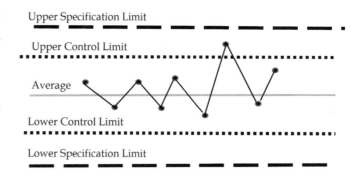

   A. This process was out of control but appears now to be back in control so it should be closely monitored going forward.

   B. The process has indicated that the product is near the upper specification limit and should be discarded

   C. This process is in control

   D. This process is out of control

Answers

1. B
2. C
3. B
4. C
5. A

Project Challenges

Risks are not always negative, but if they become project issues, they must be acted on and resolved.

Impediments, Obstacles, and Blockers

Problem-solving combines two different areas for project managers. These are addressing and removing obstacles as the team is performing the work and managing project issues.

The ECO refers to impediments, obstacles, and blockers as a task. The term "obstacle" is a general term in common project terminology, especially in Agile methods.

Exam Tip: An outcome of the review of materials has resulted in a recommendation to move away from distinguishing among the terms "obstacle," "blocker," and "impediment." However, the exam is aligned to the ECO and NOT the PMBOK Guide, and therefore exam questions may continue to be written using the ECO terminologies. We will continue to loosely differentiate between these distinctions.

— *Impediments*

Situations, conditions, and actions that are slowing down or hindering progress.

An obstacle is preventing the team from achieving its objectives. Also known as a blocker.67

— *Obstacles*

Barriers are movable, avoidable, or can be overcome with effort or strategy.

— *Blockers*

Events or conditions causing stoppages in the work or any further advancement.

Since the project team generates most of the business value, a critical role for the servant leader is to maximize delivery by removing impediments to their progress. Be responsible and proactive about problem-solving within the project team as a servant leader regardless of the process role, such as scrum master, team lead, or team member.

This includes solving problems and removing obstacles hampering the project team's work. By solving or easing these impediments, the project team can deliver value to the business faster.

All change comes with obstacles. Sometimes the blockages are outdated processes, sometimes they are based on the organizational structure, and sometimes they are people resistant to change. Regardless, all obstacles must be addressed, often requiring change management concepts.

Adaptive project teams identify obstacles during the daily stand-up, with the understanding that the scrum master will take these and help remove them, so the team can continue working.

Although problem-solving is not unique to any development approach or team, different terminology is often used. It can significantly impact the success of the project.

Any hindrance affecting the project team's work, or any team member reduces productivity and impacts the project's ability to meet its objectives.

Any actions a project manager can take to address and remove the conditions or causes restricting the team's productivity helps the team and the project produce value. The speed of action, as well as efficiency, are essential.

---

67 *Definitions in the PMBOK 7th ed. Glossary*

Risks and Issues[68]

There is a big difference between risks and issues.

A risk is generally defined as an event possibly impacting a project, whereas an issue is a risk that happened and has or will impact the project.

- *Risk – an uncertain event or condition that, if it occurs, has a positive or negative effect one or more project objectives*
  - Focus on a potential future event
  - Can be positive or negative
  - Documented in the risk register
  - Response is called a "risk response"
- *Issue – a current condition, or situation, that may have an impact on the project objectives.*
  - Focus on the present — it has occurred
  - Will always be negative
  - Documented in the issue log
  - Response is called a "workaround"

Exam Tip: Make sure you can differentiate between a risk and an issue.

Issues: Predictive

Issues can arise in many processes and project work, most often during monitoring and controlling — or in an adaptive project, at any moment.

Areas prone to issues include:

- Scope change control
- Schedule control
- Cost control
- Project variance analysis
- Quality
- Risk
- Procurement
- Communications

---

68   *https://www.pmi.org/learning/library/characterizing-unknown-unknowns-6077*

Issue Log

An issue log is used to record and monitor information on active issues. Issues are assigned to a responsible party for follow-up and resolution.

Predictive teams use an "issue log" to help identify and track issues having occurred and needing resolution. Guidelines for handling issues include:

- As issues are discovered, promptly add them to the issue log.
- Assign an owner to each issue who is the point of contact and responsible for tracking the progress of the workaround and reporting back status.
- Provide realistic due dates and make every reasonable attempt to meet them.
- Address open issues at every status meeting and retrospective.
- Limit open issues to a manageable number, often using a prioritization factor based on importance or impact.
- Don't hesitate to escalate an issue to the project sponsor or appropriate stakeholder if it exceeds the project manager's threshold and begins to significantly affect the project.

Impediments: Adaptive

Adaptive teams using scrum methods will approach problems in a slightly different way.

- *First step* — discovering and identifying a problem. This usually is by the team raising it as an obstacle during the daily stand-up meeting.
- *Next step* — determining how to solve it.

The scrum master is responsible for removing the impediment and finding consensus wherever needed. This often involves dealing with conflicting areas within the organization. Additionally, it may involve gathering and providing additional information from stakeholders or the organization to the team.

Scrum takes a "bigger picture" approach of solving from the organizational goals and strategy point of view, aligning any rift using commonly held goals. They say, "Strive for global optimization and not for local optimization, which is suboptimal for the whole."[69]

---

69   *https://resources.scrumalliance.org/Article/help-scrum-team-discover-solve-impediments*

Swarming

When needed, only one requirement may be chosen for the team members to address during an iteration, with all team members working together collectively to resolve a specific problem. This allows the team to deliver future work more quickly but requires trust between team members as they work on portions of the requirement which will then be combined at the end of the iteration.

Spike

A spike is a term from XP that refers to timeboxing work within an iteration to help answer a question or gather additional information. It is usually a very short period of time requested to further analyze a risk or architectural issue.

Address Impediments

General adaptive and hybrid approaches take a broader view of problem-solving or addressing impediments.

There are four main actions to take:

- *Track Impediments*

Use some systematic way of recording and managing them, like the issue or impediment log.

Impediment logs can take a variety of forms. They can be as simple as sticky notes denoting impediments, potential causes, responsibilities, and status posted on a whiteboard or wall near the project team's colocation or as complex as sophisticated software capturing greater detail and communication features.

- *Reprioritize Product Backlog*

While reviewing the work to be done, constantly look for potential problems and determine if those areas require further understanding or offer too much risk and may require postponement.

- *Use Daily Stand-Up Meetings*

Daily stand-up meetings are a great way to identify obstacles promptly. These can later be addressed during follow-on brainstorming, brainwriting, or decision-making sessions to solve the problem.

Obstacles can also be addressed during retrospectives to review whether the initial solution solved the problem.

- *Be a Servant Leader*

As a servant leader, a project manager aims to create an unobstructed path for the project team so they may contribute and deliver.

Project managers want to optimize the workplace to avoid obstacles and other impediments. This extends from the physical team space to shield the team from non-value activities.

Reprioritization

Impediments and obstacles may block work or planned efforts from moving forward. As a result, the product backlog, scheduled activities, and other work items must be assessed regarding these problems.

The evaluation of impediments against the pending or planned work forces the team and business stakeholders to assess the backlogged work regarding value and priority.

Backlog assessment and refinement can also explore alternatives to overcome or avoid the risk, or in some instances, to remove the work item or blockage altogether.

The prioritization is based not only on value, but may be based on risk, implementation difficulties or other factors. These often include:

- Grouping of backlog items according to predefined categories (MoSCoW)
- Ranking from most important to least
- Timeboxing/budgeting based on allocation of a fixed resource, using time or money
- Negotiation to establish a consensus regarding the prioritization.

Key Concepts Covered

- Impediments, obstacles, and blockers
- Issues and risk

ECO Coverage

- Address and remove impediments, obstacles, and blockers for the team (1.7)
  - Determine critical impediments, obstacles, and blockers for the team (1.7.1)
  - Prioritize critical impediments, obstacles, and blockers for the team (1.7.2)
  - Use the network to implement solutions to remove impediments, obstacles, and blockers for the team (1.7.3)

- Reassess continually to ensure impediments, obstacles, and blockers for the team are being addressed (1.7.4)

- Manage project issues (2.15)

  - Recognize when a risk becomes an issue (2.15.1)

  - Attack the issue with the optimal actions to achieve project success (2.15.2)

  - Collaborate with relevant stakeholders on the approach to resolve the issues (2.15.3)

Check Your Progress

1. There is a big difference between risks and issues. What are the characteristics of a risk? (Choose 3)

   A. Focus on a potential future event

   B. Can be positive or negative

   C. Documented in the risk register

   D. Focus on the present—it has occurred

2. An issue log is used to record and monitor information on active issues. How should the project manager handle the issue log? (Choose 4)

   A. Assign an owner to each issue who is the point of contact and responsible for tracking the progress of the workaround and reporting back status

   B. Provide realistic due dates and make every reasonable attempt to meet them

   C. Address open issues at every status meeting and retrospective

   D. Limit open issues to a manageable number, often using a prioritization factor based on importance or impact

   E. Ignore minor issues as they usually work themselves out

3. What is the primary responsibility of the scrum master after the daily standup meeting has concluded?

   A. Report the status of what each team member said about what they completed, what they are now working on, and any impediments slowing or blocking their progress

   B. The scrum master should start to work on eliminating the impediments the team members stated in the daily standup meeting

   C. The scrum master should ask each team member who reported an impediment when they can start to remove it

D. The scrum master does not need to do anything after the daily standup meeting since the team members are proactive in their responsibilities

4. The scrum master is responsible for removing the impediment and finding consensus wherever needed. This often involves dealing with conflicting areas within the organization. Additionally, it may involve gathering and providing additional information from stakeholders or the organization to the team.

A. True

B. False

5. Match the items on the left to their definitions on the right.

Impediments	Events or conditions causing stoppages in the work or any further advancement
Obstacles	Situations, conditions, and actions that are slowing down or hindering progress. Prevents the team from achieving its objectives
Blockers	Barriers that are movable, avoidable, or can be overcome with effort or strategy

Answers

1. A, B, C
2. A, B, C, D
3. B
4. True
5.

Impediments	Situations, conditions, and actions that are slowing down or hindering progress. Prevents the team from achieving its objectives
Obstacles	Barriers that are movable, avoidable, or can be overcome with effort or strategy
Blockers	Events or conditions causing stoppages in the work or any further advancement

Project Changes

Change is inevitable, but it is rarely insurmountable. There are strategies, tools, and techniques for managing project changes. The project's attitude toward change reflected by its life cycle and development approach.

A change in a project can come from anywhere internal to the project or from the organization. It can often impact the project and require changing one of the baselines.

Embrace Change

Many project management principles address the reality of dynamic and potential change, and therefore a hybrid approach is more frequently adopted. These principles include:

- Be a diligent, respectful, and caring steward.
- Recognize, evaluate, and respond to system interactions.
- Navigate complexity.
- Create a collaborative project team environment.
- Demonstrate leadership behaviors.
- Optimize risk responses.
- Effectively engage with stakeholders.
- Tailor based on context.
- Embrace adaptability and resiliency.
- Focus on value.
- Build quality into processes and deliverables.
- Enable change to achieve the envisioned future state.

Monitor External Business Environments

If changes are taking place in the business environment, they will likely influence what is happening in the project.

This includes things like the cost or availability of goods and resources and timing in the context of national or cultural holidays and events, or even natural disasters.

Project teams must operate appropriately, aware of what's happening outside the project to handle potential impacts.

Commonly used frameworks can help continuous exploration of what is happening outside of the project. These include:

- PESTLE — political, economic, social, technical, legal, environmental
- TECOP — technical, environmental, commercial, operational, political
- VUCA — volatility, uncertainty, complexity, ambiguity

Manage Project Change

Predictive approaches are used when the majority of the requirements can be specified up front and changes are controlled through a change request process. Adaptive approaches are used to quickly react to changes based on changing requirements through evaluation and feedback within short cycles.

Causes of Change

Change that impacts projects can have several causes. As teams move from a more predictive to a more adaptive approach, the impact on the project due to changes is significantly reduced.

It is important to be aware and alert to any of these areas possibly causing a shift in the project:

- *Inaccurate initial estimates* — These can come from lack of experience, lack of information, inaccurate data, excessive optimism, technological difficulties, or unreliable resources. Getting the estimates to be as realistic and accurate as possible makes the control process more manageable.

- *Specification changes* — Project work can open new ways of development and design not considered during the initial project work and scope or iteration planning. As new options for a product or service become apparent, customers, sponsors, or the project manager may broaden the project's scope or backlog to include new requirements.

- *New regulations* — As project work progresses, new governmental or industry-specific regulations may be enacted. This can be especially true for lengthy projects. Project change becomes necessary if the new regulations are related to the ongoing project. Accommodating new regulations or legislation can also mean revisiting the planning process to determine the effect these regulations will have on resource needs, schedule durations, and quality specifications.

- *Missed requirements* — The requirements are often understood by reviewing the documentation and interviewing the end users and policymakers. However, there are times when a complete and comprehensive understanding may not be possible. The stakeholder or product owner feels they have fully expressed the need, while the team members are not aware, or didn't understand that additional information is still needed or the definition of ready (DoR) has not been met.

Although a project scope statement and WBS are prepared in predictive projects or user stories identified in adaptive projects, confusion might arise when reviewing written or visual documents.

Prototyping may be beneficial to demonstrate and more fully understand functional and technical requirements.

Configuration Management

A component of the project management plan describing how to identify and account for project artifacts under configuration control and how to record and report changes to them.

The way configuration management is done for the project is through the configuration management system.

Configuration Management System

A collection of procedures used to track project artifacts and monitor and control changes to these artifacts.

This includes identifying items to be labeled and tracked by configuration procedures, referred to as configurable items. It relates to how changes impact configurable items and details how changes to these items will be handled, especially when resulting from an approved change request. This is often provided as part of the OPAs procedures and processes.

This describes how to identify and account for project artifacts under configuration control and record changes to them. It also includes the activities necessary to validate that the configurable items have been identified, approved, tracked, and correctly implemented.

A periodic review of standards and practices is necessary to determine whether changes to the configuration management system procedures are required and whether these are being followed appropriately. This should include reviews of configurable artifacts as part of continuous improvement efforts.

Exam Tip: Plans identify how activities and concepts are to be applied to the project.

Systems (including configuration and change control) are the actual processes to follow.

Version Control

A way of recording, tracking and managing changes to an artifact.

Version control is a subset of configuration management relating to the way artifacts, including documents and digital or electronic records, are changed. The way version control is applied is defined as part of the configuration management system.

Changes to specified artifacts should show updates, providing a digital "paper trail" of the document's history, including:

- Possibly a new version number, depending on the organizational or project rules for how version numbers are determined and applied to changes
- A date/time stamp as to when the change was made
- Name of the user who made the change
- Rationale for why the change was made

Version control should be applied to all important artifacts identified by the organization and the project, including subsidiary project management plans, baselines, and deliverables, upon approval via the change control system.

Artifact Maintenance

Project artifacts must be maintained appropriately. This can be facilitated by keeping artifact storage easily accessible and utilizing versions to identify the most recent revision. This includes checking that the artifact/file management systems provide effective and efficient access to artifacts, versions are maintained, and artifacts are being maintained in a consistent way. This may be identified as part of the information management system or PMIS for the project.

Some organizations, as well as projects, have data protection or security mandates which may apply to the project. If so, the configuration management system for artifacts must align with these requirements.

Determine the artifacts needing to be archived at the end of the project to ensure they are captured during the project and can be located when the project is completed. They will become a key component of the knowledge asset for the organization.

Change Control Systems

An effective change control system includes the forms, tracking methods, processes, and approval levels required for authorizing or rejecting requested changes.

A project performs differently than initially planned. Internal and external factors, new requirements, issues, and stakeholder influences, among other factors, influence projects. Some aspects of a project may fail or fall short of expectations, requiring the project team to regroup and rethink alternative solutions. Regardless of the type of project, the project team needs to address the situation and move forward. The view that projects should hold to plans and commitments made during the early stages even after new or unforeseen factors emerge is not beneficial to stakeholders, including customers and end users, as this limits the potential for generating value. Without proper change control processes scope creep may occur.

Manage Change: Predictive

Predictive life cycles and development approaches control change to a project methodically, following an approved change management system.

Predictive processes are developed to handle change with a structured method, including:

- Use of configuration management for version control of artifacts
- A change request process to review and assess the impact of all requested changes, including identifying alternatives
- A change control board (CCB) or other authorized body to review and approve or reject changes
- Communication regarding the status and ultimate decision on the change request
- Managing changes to deliverables, project documents, and the project management plan through management of artifacts
- Use of the established change control process and establishment of a change control system

Change Control Process

An effective change control system includes the forms, tracking methods, processes, and approval levels required for authorizing or rejecting requested changes.

Basic change control process steps include:

- Receive and log the change request or change control form
- Assess the possible impact on individual requirements or project objectives.
- Review the impact statement by the appropriate level of approval, identified as part of the overall change management plan.
- Determine the final disposition of the request, update the change log, and communicate the decision with the appropriate individuals.
- Incorporate the change, if approved, into the current project plans and activities.
- Update any applicable artifacts.
- Test the changes to ensure they have been properly executed.

Every change ends in one of three ways—either it is rejected, or postponed or deferred, or approved and the affected project areas are modified to accommodate the change.

Change Requests

The various types of change requests include:

- *Scope changes*—Additional functionality or other changes to the project scope.
- *Corrective action*—Adjust the project work to correct the identified situation.
- *Preventive action*—Ensure future performance of the project work by proactively preventing or avoiding anticipated future problems. It is often closely related to the identification of additional risks.
- *Defect repair*—Modify a nonconformance within the project.
- *Integrated change*—Change to baselined scope (often impacting other areas, including schedule, cost, quality, risks, resources, etc.).
- *Updates*—Updates to any formally controlled document or plan but does not include updates to the baselines.

Change Control Board (CCB)

A change control board (CCB) handles change requests based on approval levels of changes identified in the change management plan, included as a part of the project management plan. The CCB board is often composed of management level individuals from various business areas and may also be part of the project board or steering committee.

Not all change requests must be approved by the CCB. The approval level is defined as part of the project management plan in the change management plan.

Manage Change: Adaptive

Adaptive life cycles and development approaches incorporate and expect change in everyday work and continually modify their processes to handle it.

Adaptive life cycles and approaches also have controls for change. It is a myth that adaptive teams are a free-for-all where "anything goes." There are some experimental and developmental features, but these are still contained within a development approach by checks or guardrails.

The key aspects within the development and feedback cycles are:

- The product owner role—the key decision-maker for changes on the team, focusing on the intended value to the business of a change.
- Full participation by allowing everyone on the team to refine the backlog.
- Encouragement of feedback by stakeholders and potential customers, through participation in demos to ensure the changes work as intended and requirements are understood.
- Project team considers requested changes and identifies potential solutions. This allows for adaptation while the feedback is immediately relevant and should improve the quality of the change while reducing overall cost and product owner risk.
- Iterations or sprints are closed cycles. No changes are allowed during a sprint. The product owner handles change through the backlog refinement activities.

Manage Change: Hybrid

Any of these methods can be applied as appropriate to various aspects of the project. This especially applies to the predictive portions of the project, where deliverables or processes are agreed upon and then changes to those areas require approval.

The adaptive portions continually reprioritize requirements/user stories and support continual changes, especially for realignment to objectives or competitive advantages.

Manage Change: Contracts

Contract changes are treated separately, as they are legal documents and likely to be a shared responsibility with the organization—including procurement, finance, and a functional department.

It is important to work with the vendor when contract changes are required.

Additionally, other areas in the organization (procurement, finance, functional departments) should be notified, and changes or recommendations for changes should be offered within the project manager's or team's domain or threshold.

Escalation may be required of the sponsor, as well as legal representation when legal problems cause project issues.

Contract Change Control System

The contract change control system collects, tracks, adjudicates, and communicates changes to a contract. It often will be handled similarly to other changes and is either a component of the project's established change control system or a separate contract management system at the organizational level.

It is dedicated explicitly to controlling contract changes and specifies the process for such changes. This information is often included in the contract terms and conditions and should be clearly understood. It consists of the documentation, dispute resolution processes, and approval levels to authorize changes to contract specifications. It should also clearly identify who has the authority to approve and make changes to the contract.

Types of Contract Changes

Because of the legal aspects of a contract, any changes may require the involvement of other organizational functions, such as procurement, finance, and a functional department. Understanding the responsibility level of the project manager or team and the thresholds for handling contract changes is important.

If problems are encountered during the contract execution, assistance from the legal department may be needed to handle modifications to the contract.

There are several different types of contract changes, often described explicitly in the terms and conditions of each contract:

- *Administrative changes* are non-substantive and are usually about how the contract is administered. They are generally very limited, such as a change to an address, etc.

- *Contract modification* is a substantive change to the contract requirements, such as a new or different deadline or change in product requirements. This often requires extensive time and energy for all parties, including legal involvement, to agree to the modification.

- *Supplemental agreements* are addendums to the contract negotiated separately. This most often can be a work order or MOU with specifics for deliverables that augments a previously agreed-upon master agreement.

- *Constructive changes* are made or caused by the buyer through action or inaction and may have legal ramifications.

- *Termination* of contract happens when the vendor defaults or for the customer's convenience. Terminations are handled differently depending on who is terminating the agreement and the reason for termination. These should be specifically defined for each contract.

Legal Concepts When Managing Disputes

When a change leads to a dispute, it is critical to seek legal advice to ensure the terms of the contract are observed. Using negotiation skills to reach a final, equitable settlement of all issues, claims, and disputes is always the best approach.

Some essential legal concepts, as they relate to contracts, include:

- *Warranty*—This is the promise, explicit or implied, that goods or services will meet a predetermined standard. The standard may cover reliability, fitness for use, and safety.
- *Waiver*—A legally binding provision in which one party in a contract agrees to forfeit a claim without the other party becoming liable, even inadvertently.
- *Breach of Contract*—Failure to meet some or all contract obligations. It may result in damages paid to the injured party, litigation, or other ramifications.
- *Cease and Desist Letter*—A letter sent to an individual or a business to stop (cease) allegedly illegal activities and not undertake them again (desist). Often used as a warning of impending legal action if it is ignored.

Claims Administration

Claims administration is a procedure used to settle contract disputes. It includes processing, adjudicating (deciding), and communicating any claims made against the contract. These claims can also be known as disputes or appeals.

These can result from contested changes, including potential constructive changes.

The disagreement could result from the two parties needing help to agree on the compensation to cover a change or being unable to agree to a change that has occurred. These often involve negotiated settlements where a final, equitable, mutually agreed disposition is negotiated for all outstanding issues, claims, and disputes.

If these cannot be resolved promptly, they are often referred to and handled through alternative dispute resolution (ADR), often defined as part of the contract terms.

- *Alternative Dispute Resolution (ADR)*

A process with a neutral third party—a mediator or arbitrator—helping parties embroiled in a dispute agree. Methods such as mediation and arbitration are used to avoid costly and time-consuming litigation.

Settlement of any contract disagreements through negotiation and collaboration between both parties is preferred over ADR or the last resort of litigation.

Update Project Management Plan

Based on the scope of the approved change, updates to various items in the project management plan may need to be reviewed and possibly modified.

- *Predictive*

An approved request could impact baselines and other artifacts, including:

- Scope, including work packages and individual requirements
- Quality metrics and acceptance criteria
- Timelines in the project schedule
- Team member assignments
- *Adaptive*

The product owner or team might adjust the delivery of stories by reprioritizing to allow changes to be incorporated into the backlog.

Key Concepts Covered

- External changes
- Change control process
- Change control board (CCB)
- Contract changes

ECO Coverage

- Manage project changes (2.10)
  - Anticipate and embrace the need for change (e.g., follow change management practices) (2.10.1)
  - Execute change management strategy according to the methodology (2.10.3)
  - Determine a change response to move the project forward (2.10.4)

- Manage project artifacts (2.12)
  - Validate the project information is kept up-to-date (i.e., version control) and accessible to all stakeholders (2.12.2)
  - Continually assess the effectiveness of the management of the project artifacts (2.12.3)

- Evaluate and address external business environment changes for impact on scope (3.3)

- Survey changes to external business environment (e.g., regulations, technology, geopolitical, market) (3.3.1)

- Assess and prioritize impact on project scope/backlog based on changes in the external business environment (3.3.2)

- Recommend options for scope/backlog changes (e.g., schedule, cost changes) (3.3.3)

- Continually review the external business environment for impacts on project scope/backlog (3.3.4)

Check Your Progress

1. Because of the need to identify requirements, plan the project up front and then maintain changes with a change control system, it is important to be aware and alert to any of these areas possibly causing a shift in the project. Which of the following are reasons for project changes? (Choose 3)

    A. Inaccurate initial estimates were too low

    B. Specification changes because of misunderstanding of requirements from stakeholders

    C. New regulations that will impact the projects solution

    D. Because the project was staffed with inexperienced individuals, the requirements will need to be reduced

2. The Configuration Management System and the Change Control System are essential to project management. What sets the two apart from one another?

    A. Configuration Management System and the Change Control System are part of the Enterprise Environmental Factors

    B. The Change Control System is a component of PMIS, but the Configuration Management System is not a component of PMIS

    C. The Configuration Management System is a component of the PMIS, whereas the Change Control System is not a component of PMIS

    D. The Change Control System is used to manage the changes to the project baselines, while the Configuration Management System controls the configuration to versions of artifacts

3. A project stakeholder submitted a change request that will increase the scope of the project and asks you when you can add the changes to the scope baseline. How should you respond to this request?

    A. You can go ahead and make the desired adjustment to the scope baseline

B. Since the project charter has been approved and signed by the project sponsor, you can commence the work to add the additional changes to the project scope

C. Change requests are processed based on the change control management plan and must be approved before any change can be put into effect

D. You can tell the stakeholder that the project scope baseline has been frozen, and changes are not permitted to meet the project schedule target date

4. A change control board (CCB) handles change requests based on determined approval levels of changes identified in the change management plan, included as a part of the project management plan. Is this true or false?

A. True

B. False

5. You are the project manager in charge of a new multi-year project, and you are currently in the development of the project requirements. You want to make sure that your project stakeholders will receive the correct version of the various artifact that the project is creating. Which of the following plans will be used to specify how versioning of the artifacts will be tracked?

A. Quality management plan

B. Scope management plan

C. Change management plan

D. Configuration management plan

Answers

1. A, B, C
2. D
3. C
4. True
5. D

Project/Phase Closure

Regardless of whether the project is completed successfully or canceled prematurely, several activities are performed to close out the work for a project phase, a completed project, or a project that was canceled or postponed.

In this chapter, you will:

- Learn the reasons and activities related to the closure of a phase or a project
- Understand the benefits gained from a project or phase and how they are managed, sustained, etc.
- Understand the reasons for knowledge transfers and how they relate to the closure of a phase or project

Topics in This Chapter:

Project/Phase Closure

Benefits Realization

Knowledge Transfer

Project/Phase Closure

Whether it's the closure of an entire project or an individual phase, specific administrative closure activities are required by the organization, including:

- Validating the work was completed per the specified requirements
- Receiving formal acceptance of the phase or project deliverables
- Finalizing all required performance reporting
- Closing outstanding procurement contracts, if applicable
- Documenting and archiving lessons learned
- Documenting reasons for early termination, if applicable
- Transitioning/delivering project results
- Releasing organizational resources
- Updating archived OPAs, including project files, closure documents, and historical information

Closure: Predictive

A predictive project uses a closeout process often based on the organization's process assets (OPAs), using the traceability matrix to ensure all requirements have been completed and approved.

Closing activities at the end of a phase or the project include:

- Finalizing all project, phase, or contract activities
- Gathering retrospectives/lessons learned information
- Documenting any reasons for early termination of the project, if necessary
- Reviewing any outstanding work packages, change requests, issues, and potential risks
- Releasing project resources, including personnel, equipment, and funding
- Archiving all required information

These closing activities should be part of the project requirements and included in the WBS under the project management function.

- *Project Fulfillment*

A set of conditions is required to be met before deliverables are accepted.

Project fulfillment includes acceptance of the deliverables according to the acceptance criteria identified in the OPAs, to show they meet the quality and compliance requirements within the organization.

The acceptance of deliverables may include partial approval as part of individual reviews, with final acceptance covering the integration of individual requirements. This partial acceptance may also have a milestone sign-off or approval.

The requirements traceability matrix is often crucial to ensure all requirements for specified deliverables have been completed and approved.

- *Transition*

Some organizations and teams create a transition or rollout plan. This is especially important when a substantial change is being made to the organization because of the project. This is not a named subsidiary plan of the project management plan but supports any transition requirements and is usually the responsibility of a business analyst or domain SME, and often identified as additional content in the project management plan.

Closure: Adaptive

Adaptive approaches review complete work at the end of an iteration and obtain final acceptance before the release of the result to the customer. The team then continues to the next release.

Adaptive projects complete closing activities at the end of a release, including:

- Gathering retrospectives
- Documenting any reasons for early termination, if necessary
- Releasing project resources
- Archiving all required information

- *Project Fulfillment*

Definition of done (DoD) is the team's checklist of all the criteria to be met to prepare a deliverable for customer use.

At the end of an iteration, the team and stakeholders assess the product/service being demonstrated against the DoD. The final acceptance is prepared before the release of the product.

- *Transition*

The output from every iteration is handed over to the product owner and then integrated into the functionality delivered to customers as part of the release.

For a project using a continuous flow (kanban) approach, each user story or request is being worked on individually and approved. It may be that a number of stories need to be completed before they can be put into production. This approach usually has either a completion milestone and/or a budget for the resources needed for the work. Each requested user story can be measured by the cycle time and lead time to complete the request.

Example: The writing of this book used a continuous flow approach with individual tasks identified and tracked from identification, and development to completion. There were milestones identified to be met for certain tasks as well as any overall budget for the project.

It is often used to support an application after it has been put into production, by a DevOps organization, who address any escaped defects or requirements that were not included.

Example: After results of a contracted software development application was turned over to the requesting organization, additional testing had to be done to ensure that it could integrate with other applications (which were outside the scope of the contracted application). Each of the components of the application were identified as individual user stories and integration testing of those were performed using a continuous flow approach. Once all the integrations were approved, then the new application could be put into production.

Closure: Hybrid

Planned work is completed and meets the organizational definition of done (DoD), and project or phase information is gathered, consolidated, and archived.

- *Project Fulfillment*

The acceptance of deliverables may include partial approval as part of the individual demonstrations or review, with final acceptance covering the integration of individual requirements.

In adaptive and hybrid projects, teams may use the DoD to express the required state of completion against the individual results of an iteration or at the final release to the customer.

- *Transition*

Rather than waiting until the end of the project when all requirements have been met, hybrid projects often create a tailored solution delivering value to the organization iteratively, by a release, or in an incremental way.

Regardless of how it is done, what it is called, or who is responsible, it is essential to identify the work needed to meet the transition requirements as part of the project activities and schedule them appropriately.

Premature or Forced Closure

Whether a phase or project comes to a successful end with completion or an abrupt one, closing activities must be completed.

Some reasons for forced or premature closure of projects or phases include:

- Changes in requirements or needs
- Project no longer needed or feasible
- Blockers or significant risks encountered
- Cost exceeds the planned benefits
- Changes in technology

Transition Result

For effective handover, handoff, or transition of work in a project or phase, additional activities are usually required to transition the result to the customer or end user. These often include knowledge transfer through training and documentation and any necessary data conversion or procedure updates.

Even though transition activities are not specifically identified in the project management plan, these requirements for transition are identified along with other types of requirements. This is a key business analysis, project management, and program management activity.

Transition Readiness

Effective transition of knowledge and deliverables of project outcomes increases the likelihood that the result will be successfully implemented. Successful adoption impacts the realization of the expected benefits.

Before the project result can be transitioned to the end-users of the customer organization, additional parties including any organizations needed to support the result must also be ready.

Customer readiness or completion of the transition requirements must be evaluated before beginning the final transition or closing, especially when an existing product or service is being upgraded and conversion from the current to the new product is required.

Disciplined Agile includes a risk-based milestone, production ready, to ensure everything needed to move the result into production or to the customer has been completed.

Deploying the project's result without the customer readiness being met may reduce the expected value and possible rejection of the project outcome.

Predictive projects may have a time when the scope is "frozen," with only activities required to prepare for phase approval or pre-production activities defined by the organization. While adaptive projects often include a special Iteration H or "hardening" to ensure all defects have been corrected. No additional functionality is added during these times.

This final readiness check is often defined as part of the OPAs as a final phase gate and may be reviewed and approved through a Go/No-Go decision or final production approval meeting.

Transition Activities

Transition requirements identified during planning include the activities to be conducted before the release of the product to the customer including:

- Any required training on the new or updated product or service, or new technology employed. This may be delivered prior to implementation but also should be made available for later review, especially for individuals newly hired
- Development of user documentation regarding the new or updated product, service or technology, including updated policies and procedures
- Data conversion from old systems to the new system, if required
- Establishment of post-implementation support, either internally or by an outside support organization

Example: On one project many of the end-users were not available for or did not attend the training on the new system prior to implementation. As a result, when the product was "live" they were unaware of how to use the system. Supervisors and project team members had to provide "on the job" training for a number of days after the go-live date.

This transition plan often includes a sustainment plan to identify the requirements needed track the realization of the planned benefits.

In addition to activities during the project, it is important to gather feedback from the customers regarding their experience with the project or the product they have received. In addition to the typical evaluation types of questions asked, an additional net promoter score (NPS) is captured. This measures the customer's willingness to recommend a provider's products or services to other potential customers. Many organizations place more weight on the NPS than other evaluation metrics.

Contract Closure

Most projects work with contracted labor and suppliers, and those contracts must be completed before the project can be closed. This is not necessarily done at the end of the project but rather as soon as the work has been completed.

This includes ensuring the work under the contract has been completed. All invoices must be received, and payments completed before Accounts Payable can close out the contracts or accounts.

Additional steps for closing contracts may be specified in the contract, including:

- Verify completion of contract deliverables.

- Complete final contract performance reporting.
- Conduct any required procurement audits and vendor performance evaluations.
- Resolve any outstanding claims.
- Complete contract acceptance criteria.

Exam Tip: Closure of all contracts must be completed before the project can be closed.

Contract Artifacts

Contract documentation is archived, often based on OPAs or organizational requirements. This includes collecting, indexing, and filing several items to ensure easy access in the future if there is a need to refer to them.

Contract artifacts often include:

- Contract schedule, both planned and actual
- Scope requirements and deliverables
- Quality metrics and results
- Cost performance, both planned and actual
- Contract change documentation, including approval signatures
- Payment records and financial documents, including approved invoices
- Inspection documents
- Additional documents, manuals (including "as-built" or "as-developed"), and technical documents as needed for support

This closure of any contract should be done whenever the work is completed, not just at the end of the project.

Key Concepts Covered

- Administrative closure
- Premature or forced closure
- Transition of result
- Contract closure

ECO Coverage

- Negotiate project agreements (1.8)
  - Verify objective(s) of the project agreement is met (1.8.3)

    – Plan and manage project/phase closure or transitions (2.17)

       • Validate readiness for transition (e.g., operations team or next phase) (2.17.2)

       • Conclude activities to close out the project or phase (e.g., final lessons learned, retrospectives, procurement, financial, resources) (2.17.3)

Check Your Progress:

1. Gina is a senior project manager working on a new flight simulator for a new space vehicle for the Space Force. She just completed the work on the project and reported that the project is 100% complete. What is the best indicator that the project is completed?

    A. Completion of deliverables listed in the project charter

    B. Completion of the deliverables in the project scope statement

    C. Acceptance of project deliverables by the sponsor or key stakeholders

    D. Completion of project work packages in the project schedule

2. Because the product owner believes that the project you are managing no longer has any economic value, the project sponsor decides to cancel it. What should you do next?

    A. Reassign team members to other projects

    B. Refuse to stop the project and continue the work since it was already approved

    C. Check with your PMO team on how to use the rest of the unused budget

    D. Start to close the project, release the team members, and update the lessons learned

3. All the project work has been completed. Which of the following is part of closing a project or phase? (Choose 3)

    A. Release team resources, including team members

    B. Finalize open claims and unpaid vender invoices

    C. Validate project scope with the sponsor

    D. Complete the lessons learned and update the lessons learned repository

4. Many projects engage with contracted labor and suppliers to provide external resources. Those contracts must be completed before the project can be closed. This is not necessarily done at the end of the project but rather as soon as the work has been completed. Is this statement true or false?

    A. True

    B. False

5. Match the artifacts to their respective process group to ensure benefits are managed after they are delivered, through the development of the sustainment plan.

Lesson learned register	
	Process Group
Accepted deliverables	Initiating
	Planning
Project charter	Executing
Final product, service or result	Monitoring and Control
	Closing
Quality metrics	

Answers

1. C
2. D
3. A, B, D
4. True
5.

Project charter	Initiating
Quality metrics	Planning
Lesson learned	Executing
Accepted deliverables	Monitoring and control
Final product, service or result	Closing

Benefits Realization

Value is delivered when the customer organization can use or realize a project's requested benefits.

Benefits Management Plan

An artifact developed before the project, used along with the business case, and reviewed periodically by a business representative to verify benefit delivery.

The benefits management plan is a business document developed by the organization to define potential benefits for the project. It is a key input to portfolio management and project initiation processes.

This is often used to authorize the project by examining the requested benefits and determining whether the project effort can realize tangible and intangible business value.

It specifies the expected time frame for when both short- and long-term benefits will be realized.

- *Predictive* — Benefits are delivered at the end of the project.
- *Adaptive* — Benefits and value are delivered incrementally throughout the project.
- *Hybrid* — Benefits and value are delivered incrementally throughout the project.

Benefits Realization

While adaptive life cycles are designed to deliver incremental value as soon as possible, it may take years after a predictive project closes for benefits to be realized and value delivered. It all depends on the work's nature, the project type, and the desired outcomes.

The preferred method is for projects to deliver benefits early through identifying incremental outcomes, as utilized most often by an adaptive approach.

Other projects are only able to deliver the benefits when they are finished.

Benefits Owner

The benefits owner is one of the key resources that assists in transitioning the project outcome and the resulting benefits to the receiving organization. This includes various activities identified during planning based on the benefits management plan.

These activities begin as soon as the project work is implemented and transitioned to the receiving organization. This work includes the project manager and project team lead(s) (often a business analyst) on various activities, including:

- Ensuring the benefits are managed as they are delivered, through the development of the sustainment plan
- Assisting in the transition of the benefits to the receiving organization
- Ensuring the benefit measures and metrics identified in the sustainment plan are established and followed
- Providing reports to organizational management on the value and realization of delivered benefits

The benefits owner may be a business analyst, or operations manager in the receiving organization.

Predictive—Benefits owner is identified, along with the activities performed by this role, during the transitioning of the project work.

Adaptive or Hybrid—Product owner is responsible for ensuring the project work will provide benefits for the organization through continual reprioritization of requirements/stories.

Benefits Transition and Sustainment

In any project, the project team hands over the product or service, providing benefits and value to the customer or receiving organization. This transition is determined by reviewing the benefits management plan, including when benefits are expected to be delivered and how the benefits will be measured to ensure sustainment and realization.

As benefits are transitioned from the project team to the customer or organization, different aspects are based on the life cycle used.

Benefits Transition: Predictive

- Any ongoing activities beyond the project related to the delivered product or service are carried out by the receiving organization or a support organization to ensure the continued generation of benefits delivered by the project.
- The customer or business analyst implements monitoring of the metrics at suitable times.
- The customer or business analyst compares the actual performance to the planned, including identified key performance indicators (KPIs) and metrics specified in an optional benefits sustainment plan.
- The customer or business analyst ensures continued generation and reporting of delivered benefits, including capturing additional requirements.
- The customer or business analyst identifies risks, as well as the processes and tools necessary to mitigate them, including monitoring of risks affecting the delivered benefits.
- The customer or business analyst updates support information, often including frequently asked questions (FAQs).
- The business analysis reviews benefits measurements and works with the support organization or customer to identify requirements for desired improvements for a future project.

Benefits Transition: Adaptive

- The product owner works with the project team to determine suitable metrics.
- The product owner collaborates with the project team to use these metrics to determine whether performance is satisfactory.
- The team identifies remaining and outstanding risks preventing the realization of benefits.
- The product owner and business analyst works with the customer to identify work required for desired improvements in a future iteration or release.
- Business improvements are identified, placed on the backlog, and then reprioritized for subsequent or future iterations or releases.

Benefits Transition: Hybrid

Hybrid scenarios will mix the approaches, tailoring them to ensure efficient and effective delivery of benefits and planning for continued benefits creation.

The business analyst, product owner, or customer implements monitoring of the metrics based on previous decisions regarding timing and reporting content.

DevOps

DevOps is a combination of processes and tools created for organizations to facilitate the delivery of services and applications much faster than conventional software development processes.

It combines development and operations to provide continuous value to customers from development to deployment, focusing on automation and agility to accelerate the application deployment process.

It also utilizes a feedback loop from the customer after delivery of the result, enabling changes, corrections, or enhancements identified after release to be made quickly, rather than delaying and incorporating those changes in the next release or project. This is supported by automated and continuous testing of the development process, which enables new features and versions to be delivered through release management at any stage of development.

Benefits Realization Verification

In predictive projects, the benefits owner in the receiving organization, or a business analyst facilitates frequent reporting on the benefits obtained, both tangible and intangible.

In hybrid and adaptive projects, product owners or business analysts facilitate frequent reporting on realized benefits, both tangible and intangible.

The required content of these reports and their frequency are often determined by the type of benefit and its potential impact on the organization.

- Tangible benefits—progress made toward realization of the identified benefits
- Intangible benefits—qualitative or subjective determination of realization of benefits
- Benefits at risk of not being realized as planned
- Negative impact on strategic objectives if not met
- Potential cancellation of ongoing project team support

Key Concepts Covered

- Benefits realization
- Benefits owner
- Benefits transition
- DevOps

ECO Coverage

- Evaluate and deliver project benefits and value (3.2)
  - Document agreement on ownership for ongoing benefit realization (3.2.2)
  - Verify measurement system is in place to track benefits (3.2.3)

Check Your Progress

1. The benefits owner is one of the key resources that assists in transitioning the project outcome and the resulting benefits to the receiving organization. This includes various requirements and activities identified during planning based on the benefits management plan. Benefits may be realized soon after the project is completed. What are the roles of the benefit owner? (Choose 3)

    A. Ensuring the benefits are managed as they are delivered, through the development of the sustainment plan

    B. Assisting in the transition of the benefits to the receiving organization

    C. Ensuring the benefit measures and metrics identified in the sustainment plan are established and followed

    D. The role of the benefits owner is played by the project manager after the project is completed.

2. When are the short- and long-term benefits identified in the benefit management plan expected for predictive, adaptive and hybrid projects? (Choose 3)

   A. Predictive—Benefits are expected to start at the end of the project

   B. Predictive—Benefits are expected throughout the project

   C. Adaptive—Benefits and value are expected incrementally throughout the project

   D. Adaptive—Benefits and value are expected to start at the end of the project

   E. Hybrid—Benefits and value are expected incrementally throughout the project and/or at the end

3. One month after a project was implemented into the organization, one of the key stakeholders asks the project manager, "Why aren't we seeing the expected business value?" How should the project manager respond to this question?

   A. Refer to the project management plan

   B. Refer to the project communications plan

   C. Refer to the stakeholder engagement plan

   D. Refer to the benefits management plan

4. DevOps combines development and operations to provide continuous value to customers from development to deployment, focusing on automation and agility to accelerate the application deployment process. Is this statement true or false?

   A. True

   B. False

5. The benefits management plan often is used to authorize the project by examining the requested benefits and determining whether the project effort can realize the tangible but not the intangible business value as it cannot be quantified with realistic calculated figures. Is this statement true or false?

   A. True

   B. False

Answers

   1. A, B, C
   2. A, C, E
   3. D
   4. True
   5. False

Knowledge Transfer

Knowledge transfer occurs between team members and stakeholders during the project and at the end of the project or release. It also becomes an asset to the organization and future projects as part of historical information.

This includes archiving project artifacts per the OPAs and consolidating the individual lessons learned captured throughout the project into the organization's lessons learned repository.

Knowledge Management Discipline

Knowledge management is a discipline including a mixture of the experience, values and beliefs, contextual information, intuition, and insights people use to make sense of new experiences and knowledge.

Two main types of knowledge are captured throughout the project.

- *Explicit knowledge* — available by codifying words, numbers, and pictures. This is often done through data-gathering activities and categorized for ease of use in the future.
- *Tacit knowledge* — gained through work experiences in people's professional careers. It is often subjective, and difficult to share or express because it is based on personal beliefs and values. It is challenging to document this knowledge meaningfully to enable sharing with others.

Knowledge Management: Three Levels

Knowledge management can be thought of as a three-level system: individual, project, and organizational.

- *Individual Level*

Each team member needs to know how to perform their work by each assigned task's scope, schedule, and cost while maintaining an acceptable level of quality. If a person does not possess the required knowledge for a particular task, they must acquire it by one of the following methods:

- Research the topic to learn what they do not know.
- Collaborate with other team members to fill in the knowledge gap. This is often provided through coaching, on-the-job training, or job shadowing.
- Review the project's or organization's knowledge repository.

- *Project Level*

The focus is on achieving the goals of the current project. The project manager will solicit knowledge from project managers or project leaders involved with other projects. Their experience can then be applied to the current project. The project management office (PMO) is also an excellent source of knowledge, as it exists to define and maintain standards for project management within an organization.

- *Organizational Level*

This level is about managing programs or portfolios. The program manager or portfolio manager can seek information from peers who manage other programs or portfolios and adapt this knowledge to their needs.

Knowledge Management during Closing

Lessons learned register – A project document used to record knowledge gained during a project. The knowledge attained can be used in the current project and included in the lessons learned repository for future project use.

Lessons learned repository – A central store of historical lessons and learned information from various projects across the organization.

Knowledge is gained throughout the project and then combined at the end of a phase, the project, or a release, to provide historical information for future projects. It is essential to allocate time at the end of the phase, project, or release to reflect on the work, processes used, product challenges, and improvements made.

Activities traditionally done as part of project closure include:

- Final retrospectives to discuss the overall lessons learned from the project
- Archiving all project information to be part of the organization's historical knowledge base
- Incorporation of the lessons learned register into the knowledge management/ lessons learned repository
- Transition of any necessary knowledge from the project team to the organization, such as user documentation, updated policies and procedures, and training content

Structured Retrospective

It is essential to allocate time at the end of the phase, project, or release to reflect on the work, processes, and product improvements. This is usually a more formal and lengthier review than the retrospectives held continuously throughout the project.

This retrospective may utilize a more structured approach, reviewing previous retrospective results and the lessons learned register to consider qualitative (feelings) and quantitative (measurements) information. The data can be used for a more in-depth analysis of root causes, to design alternatives, and to develop action plans for the next phase, project, or release.

It is often led by an external facilitator, enabling all team members, including the project manager and key stakeholders, to participate.

In predictive teams, a final all-hands meeting is often held at the end of a phase or project. This is an opportunity to debrief and find ways to improve performance and participation for the next phase or project. This can also include technology issues, people issues, vendor relationships, and organizational culture.

Adaptive teams usually have a final meeting for the same purpose just before the product's release, looking back on all the improvements and challenges.

This should be a time to congratulate the team, recognize and celebrate a job well done.

Consolidate Lessons Learned

The information gained from lessons learned provide valuable knowledge assets for an organization. It is important to be thorough and diligent in reviewing and finalizing these documents.

Consolidating previous lessons learned and conducting retrospectives are valuable activities to help organizations improve their project management practices. The final consolidated lessons learned are archived and shared with the organization and future project teams through incorporation into the lessons learned repository.

The information on the project's lessons learned registers often includes:

- Strategic—Impact on some aspect of the organization's strategic objectives.
- Tactical—Guidance and recommendations for current projects underway as well as future projects.
- Scope changes—Significant impact based on scope changes and the source and handling of those changes.
- Schedule impacts—Relevant scheduling problems or issues and how these were dealt with, especially regarding resource constraints.
- Risks and issues—Issues within or between the team and customers including documentation of the nature and source of the issue and its impact on the project.

Note whether issues had been previously identified as risks. Indicate whether the appropriate reserves were determined and whether they had to be used.

- Conflict impacts—Nature and source of conflict, its impact on the project, and how it was handled.
- Stakeholder relationships—Significant stakeholder relationships, including preferences, specialties, or anything unique to their interaction.
- Customer and vendor relationships— Experience with the customer or vendor for consideration for future sales or collaboration—changing from a product-orientation to a customer-orientation.
- Artifacts—Any project artifacts making up part of the OPAs or templates, which will help future projects achieve more with the same resources and deliver work sooner.
- Recommendations—Recommendations to share with others, for creating appropriate implementation plans, and implementing those plans.

Final Report

A summary of the project's information on performance, scope, schedule, quality, cost, and risks.

The final report summarizes the result of the project or phase. The OPAs traditionally provide the actual requirements for this report and may include several reports or presentations to various audiences.

In addition to information regarding scope, quality, and cost objectives, the report will often include an account of the requirements validation, recommendations on artifacts as part of the OPAs or templates, and development and implementation of updates to current plans and execution strategy.

Information often included in the final report:

- Summary of the project's achievements.
- Project description—Activity that was undertaken, including deliverables or milestones.
- Strategic alignment—Objectives and benefits met and challenges.
- Approach used—Predictive, adaptive, or hybrid, and if hybrid, the project portions utilizing each approach.
- Scope—Objectives, evaluation criteria, and evidence of completion.
- Schedule—Verification of on time milestone delivery, including any variances, the reasons for them, and their effects, especially regarding resource constraints.

- Cost—Acceptable planned cost range, actual costs, and reasons for any variances.

- Change management—Source of changes, impact, and how handled.

- Quality objectives—Evaluation criteria for project and product quality, verification of objectives met, handling of variances.

- Risks or issues encountered—Critical risks and issues, whether they were previously identified, whether reserves were required, and how they were addressed.

- Validation information—Required approvals for the final product, service, or result including user satisfaction survey results and acceptance signatures if required.

- Stakeholder —Engagement, involvement, and relationships.

- Vendor relationships—Both positive and negative experiences.

- Benefits realization—How the final product, service, or result achieved the business needs and expected benefits. If partial, provide details of variance and realization fulfillment schedule.

There are a number of techniques that can aid in the analysis of data in the final report including:

- Document analysis—identification of information to be included in the final lessons learned register for historical information and improvement of OPAs

- Regression analysis—analysis of interrelationships between different project variables contributing to project outcomes that can be used to improve future project performance

- Trend analysis—evaluation of data points over time to validate the organization's models and implement adjustments for future projects

- Variance analysis—comparison of actual to planned performance to help with metrics based on differences between initial planning and actual end results

Key Concepts Covered

- Knowledge management
- Lessons learned consolidation
- Lessons learned repository
- Final report

ECO Coverage

- Ensure knowledge transfer for project continuity (2.16)
  - Confirm approach for knowledge transfers (2.16.3)

Check Your Progress:

1. Knowledge management identifies two types of knowledge used on a project, tacit and explicit knowledge. Which of the following statements is correct?

   A. Explicit knowledge is the type of knowledge that comes from experience

   B. Tacit knowledge is the knowledge that is internal to an organization

   C. Tacit knowledge can be conveyed through printed pictures, and diagrams

   D. Tacit knowledge is difficult to express and comes from experience

2. Knowledge management can be thought of as a three-level system: individual level, project level, and organizational level. Which of the following statements is correct. (Choose 3)

   A. Each team member needs to know how to perform their work by each assigned task's scope, schedule, and cost while maintaining an acceptable level of quality

   B. The project manager will solicit knowledge from project managers or project leaders involved with other projects

   C. The program manager or portfolio manager can seek information from peers who manage other programs or portfolios and adapt this knowledge to their needs

   D. Each team member needs to know how to perform their work by each assigned task regarding project scope, schedule, and cost and the project manager is responsible for all other knowledge for the project

   E. For hybrid projects, the program manager is responsible for all knowledge regarding the project

3. The project manager and all team members document lessons learned during and at the end of the project. Which of the following statements are correct regarding lesson learned? (Choose 2)

   A. The lessons learned register is a central store of historical lessons and learned information from various projects across the organization

   B. The lessons learned repository is a project document used to record knowledge gained during a project. The knowledge attained can be used in the current project

    C. The lessons learned register is a project document used to record knowledge gained during a project

    D. The lessons learned repository is a central store of historical lessons and learned information from various projects across the organization

4. The final report summarizes the result of the project or phase. The OPAs traditionally provide the actual requirements for this report and may include several reports or presentations to various audiences. Is this statement true or false?

    A. True

    B. False

5. The information contained in the project final report is identical to the lessons learned register and are consolidated and transferred to the lessons learned repository. Is this statement true or false?

    A. True

    B. False

Answers

    1. D

    2. A, B, C

    3. C, D

    4. True

    5. False

A small favor to ask

Now that you are finished studying the content of this book:

- What did you think of what you read?
- Were there any tips or information you found insightful?
- What do you think was missing from this book?

Please feel free to leave a review at <u>PMP® Certification Opportunities – Facilitated Methods</u> https://facilitatedmethods.com/pmp-landing-page/

It would also mean the world to us if you left an honest review on Amazon. Whether you found the information helpful or not, your candid review would help other customers make an informed purchase.

Also based on your review, we will continually improve this book and future editions.

Good luck with your project management journey.

Greta and Steve Blash

Appendix A: Project Management Framework

The framework identified on the following pages shows the five (5) process groups, the ten (10) knowledge areas, and the forty-nine (49) processes identified in *Process Groups: A Practice Guide*.

These processes may be done once, continually, or as needed during the project work. There is no expectation that processes will be conducted sequentially as shown in this framework—either by Process Group, or by Knowledge Areas —but related based on the output of a process and the inclusion of outputs as inputs into other processes.

It is important to understand the purpose of processes and the key outputs created, and then determine when and to what level of detail they should be performed.

Process Groups

Logical grouping of project management inputs, tools and techniques, and outputs. Project management process groups include initiating, planning, executing, monitoring and controlling, and closing processes.[70]

 - Basic nature of projects: Start, Work, End
 - Names are nouns ending in "-ing"

Process Group	Purpose
Initiating	Authorizes start of new project or phase
Planning	Establishes baselines and plans project activities
Executing	Performs the work planned
Monitoring & Controlling	Tracks, reviews, and regulates process and performance and administers change control
Closing	Completes or closes project or phase

---

70 *These definitions are taken from the Glossary of the (PMBOK Guide) 6th ed.*

These are NOT phases of a development life cycle.

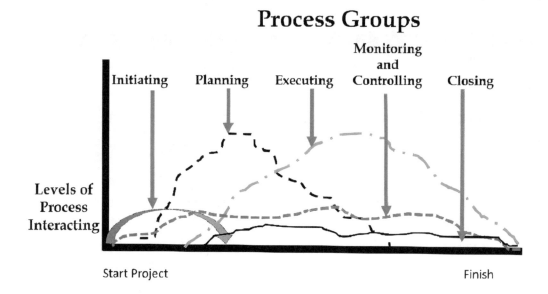

Process Groups

- All processes overlap.
- Initiating starts at the beginning and usually is complete at the end of planning.
- Planning starts almost immediately and continues almost to the end.
- Re-planning must be done when change requests are approved.
- Executing starts shortly after project initiation and winds down as deliverables are completed.
- Monitoring and Controlling continues throughout the project, with more emphasis during the middle portion of the project.
- Closing starts as soon as the first contract is completed, or the first deliverable is accepted and continues until the project is done.

Project Management Knowledge Areas

An identified area of project management defined by its knowledge requirements and described in terms of its component processes, practices, inputs, outputs, tools, and techniques.[71]

- Integration
- Scope
- Schedule
- Cost
- Quality

---

71 *These definitions are taken from the Glossary of the (PMBOK Guide) 6th ed.*

- Resource
- Communications
- Risk
- Procurement
- Stakeholder

PMBOK® V6	Project Management Process Groups	
Knowledge Areas	Initiating	Planning
Project Integration Management	Develop Project Charter	Develop Project Management Plan
Project Scope Management		Plan Scope Management Collect Requirements Define Scope Create WBS
Project Schedule Management		Plan Schedule Management Define Activities Sequence Activities Estimate Activity Durations Develop Schedule
Project Cost Management		Plan Cost Management Estimate Costs Determine Budget
Project Quality Management		Plan Quality Management
Project Resource Management		Plan Resource Management Estimate Activity Resources
Project Communications Management		Plan Communications Management
Project Risk Management		Plan Risk Management Identify Risks Perform Qualitative Risk Analysis Perform Quantitative Risk Analysis Plan Risk Responses
Project Procurement Management		Plan Procurement Management
Project Stakeholder Management	Identify Stakeholders	Plan Stakeholder Engagement

PMBOK® V6	Project Management Process Groups		
Knowledge Areas	Executing	Monitoring and Controlling	Closing
Project Integration Management	Direct and Manage Project Work Manage Project Knowledge	Monitor and Control Project Work Perform Integrated Change Control	Close Project or Phase
Project Scope Management		Validate Scope Control Scope	
Project Schedule Management		Control Schedule	
Project Cost Management		Control Costs	
Project Quality Management	Manage Quality	Control Quality	
Project Resource Management	Acquire Resources Develop Team Manage Team	Control Resources	
Project Communications Management	Manage Communications	Monitor Communications	
Project Risk Management	Implement Risk Responses	Monitor Risks	
Project Procurement Management	Conduct Procurements	Control Procurements	
Project Stakeholder Management	Manage Stakeholder Engagement	Monitor Stakeholder Engagement	

Project Management Institute, A Guide to the Project Management Body of Knowledge (PMBOK Guide) – Sixth Edition, Project Management Institute, Inc., 2017 Page 25.

Project Integration Management

Processes and activities needed to identify, define, unify, and coordinate the various processes and project management activities within the project management process groups.

Process	Key Deliverables
Develop Project Charter	Project Charter Assumption Log
Develop Project Management Plan	Project Management Plan
Direct and Manage Project Work	Deliverables Work Performance Data
Manage Project Knowledge	Lessons Learned Repository
Monitor and Control Project Work	Work Performance Reports
Perform Integrated Change Control	Approved Change Requests Change Log
Close Project or Phase	Final Product, Service, or Result Final Report

Project Scope Management

Ensure the project includes all the work required, and only the work required, to complete the project successfully.

Process	Key Deliverables
Plan Scope Management	Scope Management Plan Requirements Management Plan
Collect Requirements	Requirements Documentation Requirements Traceability Matrix
Define Scope	Project Scope Statement
Create WBS	Work Breakdown Statement Scope Baseline
Validate Scope	Accepted Deliverables
Control Scope	Work Performance Information

Project Schedule Management

Manage the timely completion of the project.

Process	Key Deliverables
Plan Schedule Management	Schedule Management Plan
Identify Activities	List of Activities, Activity Attributes
Sequence Activities	Project Schedule Network Diagram
Estimate Activity Duration	Activity Duration Estimates, Basis of Estimates
Develop Project Schedule	Project Schedule Schedule Baseline
Control Schedule	Work Performance Information Schedule Forecasts

Project Cost Management

Planning, estimating, budgeting, financing, funding, managing, and controlling costs so the project can be completed within the approved budget.

Process	Key Deliverables
Plan Cost Management	Cost Management Plan
Estimate Cost	Cost Estimates, Basis of Estimates
Determine Budget	Cost Baseline
Control Costs	Cost Forecasts

Project Quality Management

Incorporates the organization's quality policy regarding planning, managing, and controlling project and product quality requirements to meet stakeholders' expectations.

Process	Key Deliverables
Plan Quality Management	Quality Management Plan Quality Metrics
Manage Quality	Test and Evaluation Documents
Control Quality	Quality Control Measurements Verified Deliverables

Project Resource Management

Identify and acquire the resources needed for the successful completion of the project.

Process	Key Deliverables
Plan Resource Management	Resource Management Plan Team Charter
Estimate Activity Resources	Resource Requirements Resource Breakdown Structure
Acquire Resources	Physical Resource Assignments Project Team Assignments Resource Calendars
Develop Team	Team Performance Assessments
Manage Team	
Control Resources	Work Performance Information

Project Communications Management

Timely and appropriate planning, collection, creation, distribution, storage, retrieval, management, control, monitoring, and ultimate disposition of project information.

Process	Key Deliverables
Plan Communications Management	Communications Management Plan
Manage Communications	Project Communications
Monitor Communications	Work Performance Information

Project Risk Management

Risk management planning, identification, analysis, response planning, response implementation, and risk control on a project.

Process	Key Deliverables
Plan Risk Management	Risk Management Plan
Identify Risks	Risk Register Risk Report
Perform Qualitative Risk Assessment	Probability Impact Matrix
Perform Quantitative Risk Assessment	
Plan Risk Responses	Risk Responses
Implement Risk Responses	
Monitor Risks	

Project Procurement Management

Purchase or acquire products, services, or results needed from outside the project team.

Process	Key Deliverable
Plan Procurement Management	Procurement Management Plan Procurement Strategy Bid Documents Source Selection Criteria Statement of Work (SOW)
Conduct Procurements	Selected Sellers Agreements
Control Procurements	Closed Procurements Work Performance Information

Project Stakeholder Management

Identify people, groups, and organizations who could impact or be impacted by the project.

Analyze stakeholder expectations and their impact on the project.

Develop appropriate management strategies for effectively engaging stakeholders in project decisions and execution.

Process	Key Deliverables
Identify Stakeholders	Stakeholder Register
Develop Stakeholder Engagement Plan	Stakeholder Engagement Assessment Matrix
Manage Stakeholder Engagement	
Monitor Stakeholder Engagement	

Project Management Processes

A systematic series of activities directed toward causing a result, with one or more inputs being acted upon to create one or more outputs.

The selection of processes and the extent a specific project applies them should be based on the needs of the project along with any organizational policies, procedures, or governance requirements.

Processes can be used once or at predefined points in the project, performed periodically as needed, or performed continuously throughout the project.

Appendix B: How to Answer Exam Questions

I f you prepare by studying the material in a course and this guide and practicing PMI-supplied test questions in test banks and simulators, you will pass the exam.

The PMP exam consists of 180 questions, five of which are unscored practice questions. That leaves 175 questions that count toward your score. You have 230 minutes (3 hours and 50 minutes) to finish the exam. So, there is plenty of time to answer all the questions on the exam.

There are two optional 10-minute breaks scheduled: the first break after 60 questions and the second break after another 60 questions, followed by the remaining 60 questions before finishing the exam. Answer every question in each section before requesting the break. Be sure to click the button to indicate to the proctor when taking a break and when returning.

Exam Domains

The Exam Content Outline (ECO) lists three domains and the percentage of questions based upon each.

Power Skills—People (42% of the questions)

This domain includes various topics related to interpersonal skills, "soft" skills, or power skills from the PMI Talent Triangle including building and leading teams, interacting with stakeholders, supporting teams, managing conflict, and more.

Ways of Working—Process (50% of the questions)

This domain from the PMI Talent Triangle covers the traditional "technical" project management activities such as planning and managing scope, schedule, resources, budget, communication, risk, quality, stakeholders, and procurement.

Business Acumen—Business Environment (8% of the questions)

This domain focuses on topics such as organizational strategy, project compliance and regulations, benefits, organizational change, and external influence, the knowledge of which is needed to deliver successful projects.

Heuristics—Rule of Thumb

These helpful hints are heuristics—or rules of thumb—that work most of the time but not all of the time, but many students have found them very useful.

Organizations have a certain philosophy or a way of working, which you need to consider when answering questions, rather than the way you have worked. Some assumptions about organizations included in exam questions:

- Organizations use multiple project management techniques in their way of working on projects.

- No two projects, approaches (predictive, adaptive, or hybrid), or teams use the same techniques. They can vary quite a bit depending on the organization.

- There is a repository of knowledge available to every project manager, so always consider this previous experience of the organization when answering questions.

- Forget how you have managed projects in the past, especially the terminology and procedures you used in your organization.

- You need to understand how PMI thinks about projects. Their underlying philosophy is that you are managing an organization that has a well-established PMO with governance and project management processes and templates in place, referred to as organizational process assets or OPAs.

- There is also an assumption that historical information from previous project efforts will be available to you when you start a project. When you finish the project, you will in turn add your project documentation to that historical database.

- Remember that the various publications and guidelines from PMI and other sources can help you determine the activities that best fit your project. The exam is NOT based on the *PMBOK Guide* (either Sixth or Seventh Edition). There is no single rigid methodology by any means.

- To pass the exam, you will need to answer the questions based on PMI's project management philosophy and mindset. This may not be in total agreement with the way you currently manage projects, but for the exam you must put on your "PMI hat."

- What often throws people off is incorrectly thinking that the *PMBOK* is a regulation to be followed. It was developed by project managers all over the world and contains a body of knowledge for project management, so it sometimes works on some types of projects. The *PMBOK Guide* provides excellent guidance for project managers applying good project management practices within predictive, adaptive/Agile, or hybrid environments.

Types of Questions

The questions are based upon project management situations that require you to select the best or most correct answer.

There are several types of questions:

- Multiple-choice (select one answer)
- Multiple response (choose two, three or four answers. All correct answers must be selected, or else it is scored as wrong.)
- A few true/false questions
- One or two fill-in-the-blank questions
- One or two matching items (where you drag items on the right of the screen to items on the left of the screen)
- And a few hot spot questions (where you move an item to an area on the screen or simply click the correct position on a chart or diagram)

Math questions have been changed to interpret the answer rather than needing to memorize formulas to determine the correct answer. Often you can select the correct answer without having to calculate a specific number.

For earned value questions, compare the figures in the question to determine whether a project is:

- Behind schedule and over budget
- Ahead of schedule and over budget
- Behind schedule and under budget
- Ahead of schedule and under budget

Level of Difficulty Questions

Some people think that all the questions on the exam are difficult or tricky. That's not true.

Easy Questions: About 30% of the questions are straightforward and easy to answer. (You will probably get 85%–90% of these questions correct.)

Moderate Questions: About 40% of the questions are of moderate difficulty. (You will probably get 65%–70% of the answers correct.)

- For moderate level of difficulty questions, you will usually see that you can strike through two of the answers, giving you a 40%–50% chance, depending upon the number of answers.

- Read the question again and compare the differences to determine which is the best answer for the question.

- Look for keywords to answer the question. Remember that many of the questions look like they contain two correct answers, but you are looking for the most correct answer based upon the keywords of the question or the project management situation the question is describing.

Difficult Questions: About 30% of the questions are difficult to answer. (You will probably get 55%–60% of these answers correct.)

When answering questions, try to determine whether the situation refers to before or at the start of a project, the planning of the project, performing the activities or work of the project, controlling the scope, schedule, cost, etc., or completing a phase or closing a project.

Next, consider the subject matter the question is referencing. This will lead to the activity that the question is referring to and perhaps what should be considered next. If the situation question is referring to scope, then the answer(s) should be related to project scope. You will probably see answers related to schedule, cost, risks, etc. that you can eliminate.

The questions will usually ask *what you will do next or first.*

Avoid Extreme Words

When you see words in an answer such as all, always, never, only, or none,

this hints that it is not the correct answer.

Example Question:

The *PMBOK Guide is the standard for:*

    A. Managing all projects all the time across all industries.

    B. Managing all projects all the time across some types of industries.

    C. Managing most projects most of the time across many types of industries.

    D. Managing some projects some of the time across some types of industries.

Answer:

You see the word "all" several times in the first two answers, so they are wrong.

Now compare the words "most" and "some" in the last two answers.

"C: most projects, most of the time, across many types of industries "

would be harder to accomplish than

"D: some projects, some of the time across some types of industries."

The last answer (D) is correct.

Avoid the Word "All"

Let's look at another example of avoiding the word ALL in an answer.

Question:

Which of the following is the best approach for estimating effort?

  A. The project manager estimates **all** the work.
  B. A team lead estimates **all** the work.
  C. The work is estimated by the people who will be asked to do the work.
  D. The estimates are inflated to avoid second-guessing from the customer.

Answer:

The project manager or a team lead estimating all the work is not considered a best practice, even though many project managers in the past had to estimate a project by themselves.

In Answer D, "inflated" is an extreme word. *We don't exaggerate the numbers!*

Inflating the estimates would be considered an unethical practice.

More Suitable Words

Here is a list of more suitable words that indicate a correct answer. When you see words like best, may, least, ensure, update, investigate, or advise, they may lead you to a correct answer, but keep in mind that these hints work most of the time but not always. You still need to read the question thoroughly.

Look for the Keyword "Ensure" in the Answer

When you see the word "ensure," that answer is correct more often than not. When you read the other answers, you may see that they don't address answering the question at all, so the word "ensure" is a very helpful hint to getting the correct answer.

This works when only one of the answers contains the word "ensure." For questions that include the word "ensure" several times in the answers, you need to consider other options.

You will probably see five to seven such questions on the exam.

What Should You Do—First, Next, Best Course of Action Questions

Many questions focus on what the project manager should do first or next or following best practice.

The answer refers to the need to gather or seek out information and analyze the situation before deciding to act. It might require referring to an artifact, such as a project management plan, quality management plan, or change management plan, to determine how the project was originally planned and how it should now be updated to reflect changes, especially based on actual results.

Best Leadership Styles

Several questions will address the best leadership styles for project managers. This includes identifying and engaging all team members and stakeholders throughout the project from beginning to end.

Project managers need to take ownership of any problems or issues and not pass them off to someone else. PMI believes project managers should be proactive and preventive; therefore, doing nothing will not be a correct answer.

Some questions will illustrate servant leadership by putting the team first to address whatever they need to overcome obstacles. Additionally, the project manager exhibits emotional intelligence by recognizing how to behave in difficult situations and collaborate with team members in a constructive and empathetic way.

Best Practices

Project managers should not only be involved in the creation of the project scope, schedule, budget, quality, and risks but also be aware of scope creep, schedule slippage, uncontrolled costs, and unidentified risks.

They should continually review the project assumptions, constraints, and risks and be aware of any changes to them.

They should prioritize the quality, governance, compliance, and safety requirements and never skip steps or artifacts to finish sooner.

They should be proactive rather than reacting to situations, especially risks, and practice transparency, collaboration, and good communication with all team members and stakeholders.

Project Management Terminology

There is a difference in the naming and terminology of the various project management concepts based on the difference between predictive and adaptive approaches. Understanding these differences will help you answer the questions correctly.

There will be questions about artifacts that refer to documents, deliverables, or other work products produced during a project. The names of these may differ depending on the approach (predictive, adaptive, or hybrid) being used. The major artifacts are referred to as deliverables, and you need to understand their purpose, what they include, and how they are used during the project. These include the project charter, project management plan, scope statement, scope baseline, risk register, issue log, etc.

You should also be familiar with the predictive and adaptive techniques that can be used for data gathering, data analysis, and data representation. This includes understanding the differences between the various techniques.

Soft versus Harsh Approach

Most organizations such as PMI recommend the use of a softer approach to people and project activities and not the hard approach when encountering problems. If an answer sounds harsh, then it probably isn't correct.

Examples:

When you see wording such as a **waste of time** to estimate, team member **is not allowed** to be assigned to another project, **reprimand** the team member, or **ignore** the issue in the answers, then they are not the correct answer to the question.

Questions Based upon Definitions

Some of the questions are derived from the definition of an artifact, a person's role in the project, or a tool or technique.

Let's look at this question:

Question with explanations:

Which statement best describes project stakeholders?

> A. Anyone making money from the project (*May be part of strategic or project objectives but not for stakeholders*)
>
> B. A customer paying for the project's output (*Partially true but not the definition*)
>
> C. The organization delivering the project's products (*Partially true but not the definition*)
>
> D. Anyone affected by the project, its outputs, and its operation (*Derived from the definition you see below from PMI, and it sounds like a PMI question*)

Doubt Answers with Unfamiliar Terms

If a term in the answer is unfamiliar to you or doesn't match terminology presented while studying, then it probably is not a valid answer. Some exam takers may think they missed it during preparation, but the exam creators add these false terms to confuse you or throw you off, so ignore them.

Negative Questions

You will see a few questions that include a negative word, such as not, except, or excluding.

Question:

Agile feedback methods include all the following except?

> A. Sprint retrospective
>
> B. Reflective improvement

C. **Team performance reviews**

D. Timebox closeout

Agile feedback methods are sprint retrospective, reflective improvement, and timebox closeout, which mean the same thing but are from various Agile methods.

Team performance reviews are a predictive method activity.

Note: You may have a few negative type questions like this, but most of the questions are positive, where you will have to select two, three, or four answers to a question.

Know Agile Terminology

If you are not familiar with Agile or only know one Agile method such as scrum, then study Agile methods and terminology in a course because there are a lot of Agile questions on the exam.

Question:

Bringing the entire project team, customer, or product owner on-site to work together is an example of:

A. Team integration *(Pulling everyone together – sounds good but not the correct term)*

B. Active participation *(Getting everyone to participate – also sounds good but not the correct term)*

C. **Colocation** *(Correct Agile term)*

D. Osmotic communication *(Overhearing conversations – the team is already colocated and is hearing conversations)*

Similar Wording

When there are similar words in the answers, read the answers carefully to compare them.

Here is an ethics question:

PMI considers the four supporting values of the Code of Ethics that are most important to be:

A. **Responsibility,** loyalty, **fairness,** and **respect**

B. **Responsibility, respect, fairness, and honesty**

    C. Loyalty, profitability, **fairness,** and **honesty**

    D. Diversity, **responsibility, fairness,** and **honesty**

Compare the words. You see responsibility in A, B, and D, so being responsible sounds like an ethics value.

Loyalty appears in A and C, but loyalty is not an ethical value, so eliminate A and C.

Fairness appears in all four answers, so you know fairness is correct.

Respect shows up in A and B, but we eliminated A.

Profitability is only in answer C and is not an ethical value, plus we eliminated C.

So that leaves diversity in D compared to respect in B.

Responsibility, fairness, and honesty are the same in D and B.

Respect is treating others with dignity; it promotes diversity in the project team.

So, the correct answer is B.

Of course, you should have memorized these four core values of the Code of Ethics.

Other ethical questions are based upon not taking something of value or going out to an expensive restaurant in order for a vendor to gain preference over other vendors. These are not ethical things to do.

Similar Questions

Using the content of one question to answer another question could help you with a previous question you are not sure of. The testing software allows you to go back to a previous question within the active portion of the exam (the set of 60 questions before a break or just before the end of the exam). Once a break has been taken, you cannot go back to those previous questions again.

The way something is worded in one question may help you determine the answer in another question. This happens with questions regarding earned value, network diagrams, PDM method, critical path, and forward and backward pass questions. These are all related concepts, and there is a high likelihood that several questions will provide you with the correct answer to another question. This seems to happen two to four times during the exam for some test takers.

Agile Tools and Techniques

Agile is an iterative approach to project management that helps teams deliver value to their customers faster instead of only at the end of a project. An Agile team delivers work in small increments. Requirements, plans, and results are evaluated continuously, so teams have a natural mechanism for responding to change quickly.

Know the correct names and purpose of Agile tools and techniques.

Know all the basic Agile principles.

Adaptive/Agile Keywords

Certain adaptive/Agile terms are based on definitions. There will probably be one question about the Manifesto for Agile Software Development, which has four values.

Through this work we have come to value:

Individuals and interaction over process and tools

Working software over comprehensive documentation

Customer collaboration over contract negotiation

Responding to change over following a plan

You will also need to know the 12 Agile principles.

Agile Framework Source

Remember and understand the different Agile tools and techniques by their respective Agile frameworks referred to in the question.

Question:

Which of the following is not an Agile extreme programming (XP) role?

(This question is expecting you know the difference between XP and scrum.)

     A. Product owner *(scrum role)*

     B. Coach *(XP — similar to scrum master)*

     C. Tracker *(unique to XP to track progress, which is a project manager role in a predictive approach, but they use the term "review project" or "team performance")*

     D. Tester *(XP official test role)*

Skip the Question

Remember, about 30% of the questions are difficult or lengthy and it can be a struggle to answer them, so go ahead and skip them for now. Go back to answer the questions before the break or at the end of the exam. The software will prompt the test taker if a question is unanswered.

Trust Your Intuition

For those questions where you don't know the answer and are guessing, trust your intuition and don't change your answer.

This is especially true when you get close to the end of the testing time. Do your best to eliminate at least one answer. Also look at the longest answer, as it is often the correct one.

Final Recommendation

Practice many legitimate tests several times. Legitimate tests are based upon the most recent test requirements of the ECO and are often provided by PMI. When searching on the Internet, be aware that many old practice tests are available at a very cheap price, but they won't help in passing the exam because they do not reflect the content of the current exam.

When you answer a practice test question incorrectly, try to understand why you got it wrong. Many times, it will be because you didn't read the question correctly or didn't understand it.

Always try to eliminate two answers, so you have a 50/50 chance of a correct answer.

Read the last sentence of the question first, and then look at the answers to determine whether you can answer it correctly. Some questions have more information than needed to answer them.

Remember to study and prepare for the exam and retake the practice tests many times until your test scores are in the 80% range. These hints and the practice questions will help you to not only pass the exam but also score above target.

If you want practice questions provided to Authorized Training Partners (ATP) from PMI that are very similar to those on the current PMP exam, please check the Facilitated Methods website: www.facilitatedmethods.com. Available test banks include PMP Lesson Questions 2023 (20 questions at a time) and Simulated PMP Exam Questions (60 questions at a time).

Good luck and let us know when you pass the exam.

Glossary of Terms

5 Whys Method

> An effective tool for root cause analysis in which the question "Why?" is asked of a problem in succession until the root cause is found. Developed by Sakichi Toyoda, a Japanese inventor and industrialist, the 5 Whys method is an integral part of the Lean philosophy.

80/20 Rule

> A general guideline with many applications; in terms of controlling processes, it contends that a relatively large number of problems or defects, typically 80%, are commonly due to a relatively small number of causes, typically 20%. See also "*Pareto Chart*".

A/B Testing

> A marketing approach is used to determine user preferences by showing different sets of users' similar services—an 'Alpha' and a 'Beta' version—with one independent variable.

Accept

> A strategy for managing negative risks or opportunities that involves acknowledging risk and not taking any action until the risk occurs.

Acceptance Criteria

> A set of conditions that is required to be met before deliverables are accepted.

Accepted Deliverables

> Deliverables that meet the acceptance criteria and have been formally signed off and approved by the customer or sponsor as part of the scope validation process.

Active Listening

> A communication technique that involves acknowledging the speaker's message and the recipient clarifying the message to confirm that what was heard matches the message that the sender intended.

Activity

> A distinct portion of work, scheduled with a beginning and an end, must be performed to complete work on the project. Also known as a scheduled activity. See also "*Task*".

Activity Attributes

> Multiple attributes associated with each activity can be included within the activity list.

Activity Cost Estimates

Each task is assigned a budget, and the aggregate of these estimates results in the project budget. Activity cost estimates include labor, materials, equipment, and fixed cost items like contractors, services, facilities, financing costs, etc. This information can be presented in a detailed or summarized form.

Activity Dependency

A logical relationship that exists between two project activities. The relationship indicates whether the start of an activity is contingent upon an event or input from outside the activity.

Activity Duration Estimates

The quantitative assessments of the likely number of time periods that are required to complete an activity.

Activity List

A documented tabulation of schedule activities that shows the activity description, activity identifier, and a sufficiently detailed scope-of-work description so project team members understand what work is to be performed.

Activity on Arrow or Activity on Node

A graphical diagram on which schedule activities are represented by nodes (rectangle boxes) and their dependencies are depicted by arrows.

Activity Resource Requirements

The resources (physical, human, and organizational) required to complete the activities in the activity list; often expressed as a probability or range.

Actual Cost (AC)

Earned Value Management term for the realized cost incurred for the work performed on an activity during a specific time.

Adaptive

A type of project life cycle or methodology that values responding to change over following a set plan. Adaptive methodologies seek solutions that deliver maximum value to the customer.

Administrative Closure

Involves verifying and documenting project results to formalize project or phase completion.

Affinity Diagram

A technique that allows large numbers of ideas to be classified into groups for review and analysis.

Affinity Estimating

Technique designed to rapidly estimate large stories (epics or features) in the backlog. For example: T-Shirt sizing, coffee cup sizes, or Fibonacci sequence.

Agile

A term used to describe a mindset of values and principles as set forth in the Agile Manifesto.

Agile Coach

A process role on a project team that helps organizations achieve true agility by coaching teams across the enterprise on how to apply agile practices and choose their best way of working. See also *"scrum master."*

Agile Estimating

An approach that assists with planning a project appropriately from the beginning to ensure the team can focus on the quality of each deliverable.

Agile Life Cycle

An approach that is both iterative and incremental to refine work items and deliver frequently.

Agile Manifesto

In 2001, a group of 17 software developers met in Snowbird, Utah to discuss lightweight software development. Based on their experience, they came up with the four core values of agile software development as stated by the Agile Manifesto are: individuals and interactions over processes and tools; working software over comprehensive documentation; customer collaboration over contract negotiation; and responding to change over following a plan.

Agile Modeling

A representation of the workflow of a process or system that the team can review before it is implemented in code.

Agile Practitioner

A person embracing the agile mindset who collaborates with like-minded colleagues in cross- functional teams. Also referred to as an *agilist*.

Agile Principles

A set of 12 guidelines that support the Agile Manifesto and which practitioners and teams should internalize and act upon.

1. Customer satisfaction by early and continuous delivery of valuable software
2. Welcome changing requirements, even in late development
3. Deliver working software frequently (weeks rather than months)
4. Close, daily cooperation between business and technical people
5. Projects are built around motivated individuals, who should be trusted
6. Face-to-face conversation is the best form of communication (colocation)
7. Working software is the primary measure of progress
8. Sustainable development, able to maintain a constant pace
9. Continuous attention to technical excellence and good design
10. Simplicity is essential
11. Best architectures, requirements, and designs emerge from self-organizing teams
12. Regularly, the team reflects on how to become more effective, and adjusts accordingly

Agile Release Planning

A process in which a team determines the number of iterations or Sprints that are needed to complete each release, the features that each iteration will contain, and the target dates of each release.

Agile Space

Team space that encourages colocation, collaboration, communication, transparency, and visibility.

Agreements

Any documents or communication that defines the initial intentions of a project. Examples include contracts, memorandums of understanding (MOUs), service-level agreements (SLAs), letters of agreement, letters of intent, verbal agreements, email, or other written agreements.

Allowable Costs

Costs that are allowed under the terms of the contract. Typically, allowable costs become relevant under certain types of cost-reimbursable contracts in which the buyer reimburses the seller's allowable costs.

Analogous Estimating

A technique for estimating the duration or cost of an activity on a project using historical data from a similar activity or project. Also known as *"Top-Down Estimating"*.

Analytical Techniques

A logical approach that looks at the relationship between outcomes and the factors that can influence them.

Approved Change Requests

Change requests that have been reviewed and approved by the change control board (CCB) and are ready to be scheduled for implementation.

Artifact

Any project management processes, inputs, tools, techniques, outputs, EEFs, and OPAs that the project management team uses on their specific project. They are subject to configuration management and are maintained and archived by the team.

Assumption

Anything considered to be true while planning. Assumptions should be documented and validated and are often closely linked to constraints.

Assumption and Constraint Analysis

A process that explores the validity of the project assumptions within the constraints and identifies risks from any incompleteness or inaccuracy of these project assumptions.

Assumption Log

A list of all uncertainties that are treated as true for the purpose of planning.

Attribute Sampling Data

Data that is counted such as the number of product defects or customer complaints.

Audit

An examination of a project's goals and achievements, including adequacy, accuracy, efficiency, effectiveness, and the project's compliance with applicable methodologies and regulations. It tends to be a formal, one-sided process that can be extremely demoralizing to team members.

Autocratic

A group decision-making method in which one member of the group makes the decision. In most cases, this person will consider the larger group's ideas and decisions and will then make a decision based on that input.

Avoid

A strategy for managing negative risks or threats that involves changing the project management plan to remove the risk entirely by extending the schedule, changing the strategy, increasing the funding, or reducing the scope.

Backlog

The prioritized list of all the work, presented in story form, for a project team. See also *"Iteration Backlog"*.

Backlog Refinement

The progressive elaboration of project requirements and/or the ongoing activity in which the team collaboratively reviews, updates, and writes requirements to satisfy the need of the customer request.

Backward Pass

Technique for calculating the late start and late finish dates of the scheduled activities. This is part of the critical path method and is paired with forward pass to determine activity and schedule float along with the critical path.

Bar Chart

A graphic display of schedule-related information. In the typical bar chart, schedule activities or WBS components are listed down the left side of the chart, dates are shown across the top, and activity durations are shown as date-placed horizontal bars. See also *"Gantt Chart"*.

Baseline

Original objectives plus approved change requests for scope, schedule, cost, and resources required to finish the project. Baselines represent the approved plan, and they are useful for measuring how actual results deviate from the plan.

Benchmarking

The comparison of actual or planned products, processes, and practices to those of comparable organizations to identify best practices, generate ideas for improvement, and provide a basis for measuring performance.

Benefit Cost Ratio (BCR)

The ratio of the expected benefits and the anticipated costs.

Benefits Management Plan

The documented explanation defines the processes for creating, maximizing, and sustaining the benefits provided by a project or program. It also describes how and when the benefits of a project will be derived and measured. Both the business case and the benefits management plan are developed with the benefits owner prior to the project being initiated. Additionally, both documents are referenced after the project has been completed. Therefore, they are considered business documents rather than project documents or components of the project management plan.

Bidder Conferences

The meetings with prospective sellers prior to the preparation of a bid or proposal to ensure all prospective vendors have a clear and common understanding of the procurement. Also called vendor conferences, pre-bid conferences, or contractor conferences.

Bottom-Up Estimating

A method of estimating project duration or cost by aggregating the estimates of the lower-level components of the WBS.

Brainstorming

A simple technique used to generate a list of ideas. It should be led by a facilitator with a group consisting of stakeholders, team members, and subject matter experts. After quickly generating a list of alternatives, the group then performs analysis of the alternatives and generally chooses a particular option for action.

Breach of Contract

The failure to meet some or all the obligations of a contract.

Budget

A time-phased plan for when funds will be disbursed on a project. It helps the organization anticipate when money will be coming in and/or going out, for the duration of the project. Budget accuracy is dependent upon a well-defined project scope and schedule. The total project budget is the cost baseline plus management reserves. See also *"Cost Baseline"*.

Budget at Completion (BAC)

The sum of all budgets established to provide financial support for the work to be performed.

Buffer

A planning term related to contingency. See also *"Reserve"*.

Burn Chart

A tool that is used to track the progress of the project by plotting the number of days of sprint against the number of hours of work remaining. It is used to communicate progress during and at the end of an iteration/sprint/ increment, showing the number of stores that have been completed and the ones that remain. The concept is as the project progresses over time, the backlog of work will "burn down"/lessen.

Burn Rate

The rate at which the project consumes financial resources, representing negative cash flow. Burn rates are often used by agile projects to budget costs for planned iterations/ sprints/increments.

Burndown Chart

A graphical representation of the work remaining versus the time left in a timebox.

Burnup Chart

A graphical representation of the work completed toward the release of a product.

Business Case

A documented economic feasibility study used to establish the validity of the benefits of a selected component lacking sufficient definition and that is used as a basis for the authorization of further project management activities.

Business Document

An artifact developed prior to the project, used as part of the business case, and which is reviewed periodically by a project professional to verify benefit delivery.

Business Requirement

A representation of goals, objectives, and outcomes that describe why a change has been initiated and how success will be assessed.

Business Requirement Documents (BRD)

Listing all requirements for a specific project.

Business Risk

The inherent risk in any business endeavor carries the potential for either profit or loss. Types of business risks are competitive, legislative, monetary, and operational.

Business Value

The net quantifiable benefit derived from a business endeavor. The benefit may be tangible, intangible, or both.

Cadence

A rhythm of execution. Also see *"time box."*

Capability Maturity Model Information (CMMI)

The CMMI provides a framework for the integration of process improvement for multiple process areas. Associated with quality management.

Cause and Effect Diagram

This diagram shows the relationship between causes and effects. Primarily used in root cause analysis (risk and quality) to uncover the causes of risks, problems, or issues. See also *"Fishbone Diagram"* and *"Ishikawa Diagram"*.

Cease and Desist Letter

A legal document sent to an individual or a business with the direct intention of stopping specific activities and preventing their occurrence or recurrence.

Centers of Excellence (CoEs)

Groups to support dissemination of skills and knowledge within the organization.

Certified Associate in Project Management (CAPM)

PMI® Certification that offers recognition to practitioners who are interested in or are just starting a career in project management, as well as project team members who wish to demonstrate their project management knowledge. This certification denotes that the individual possesses the knowledge in the principles and terminology of *A Guide to the Project Management Body of Knowledge (PMBOK® Guide)*, which outlines generally recognized good practices in project management.

Change Control

Purposeful management of changes to the project (scope, schedule, cost, or quality). In change control, a change request goes through a formal process before a decision (approve/deny) is made.

Change Control Board (CCB)

A formally chartered group responsible for reviewing, evaluating, approving, delaying, or rejecting changes to the project and for recording and communicating such decisions.

Change Control Form

A document used to request a project change. They can also be recommendations for taking corrective or preventive actions. See also *"Change Request"*.

Change Control System

A set of procedures that describes how modifications to the project deliverables and documentation are managed and controlled.

Change Log

A living list of all project change requests (CR). This log is used to track and provide accurate status of each CR (requester, owner, details, impact analysis, decision, etc.)

Change Management

A comprehensive, cyclic, and structured approach for transitioning individuals, groups, and organizations from a current state to a future state in which they realize desired benefits. It is different from project change control, which is a process whereby modifications to documents, deliverables, or baselines associated with the project are identified and documented, and then are approved or rejected.

Change Management Plan

A component of the project management plan that establishes the Change Control Board, documents the extent of its authority, and describes how the change control system will be implemented.

Change Request (CR)

Request for change sent to upper management or the Change Control Board (CCB) for its evaluation and approval. See also *"Change Control Form"*.

Charter

A shortened name for the project charter. A formal document that starts the project. Typically used by the project sponsor and the project manager, this document provides the reason for the project (based on business case) and may include high-level requirements, assumptions, constraints, milestone(s), and preliminary budget. See also *"Project Charter"*.

Checklist

A set of procedural instructions used to ensure that a product or component quality is achieved.

Checklist Analysis

A technique for systematically reviewing materials using a list for accuracy and completeness.

Claim

An issue with the contract brought by one party against another. Claims must be resolved before the contract can be properly closed out.

Close Project or Phase Process

The project management process of finalizing all activities for the project, phase, or contract.

Close-Out Meetings

Sessions held at the end of a project or phase during which teams discuss work and capture lessons learned.

Closing Process Group

One of the five Project Management Process Groups. It consists of those processes performed to formally complete or close the project, phase, or contract.

Coach

An agile servant leader role that exists to help the team and identify and remove any impediments (obstacles).

Coaching

The act of giving guidance and direction to another person to facilitate personal and/or professional growth and development.

Code of Accounts

A numbering system used to uniquely identify each component of the WBS.

Code of Ethics and Professional Conduct

A PMI® published body of knowledge that describes the ethical, professional behavior and expectations of an individual working as a project management professional (PMP®).

Collaboration

The act of working together and sharing information to create deliverables, work products or results.

Collect Requirements Process

The project management process in which requirements documentation is developed. Precedes the Define Scope project management process.

Colocation

An organizational placement strategy in which the project team members are physically located close to one another to improve communication, working relationships, and productivity.

Cause

A reason contributing to a quality problem that is usually considered acceptable. Common causes are considered unpreventable or if they are preventable, the cost of prevention would not justify the benefit. Opposite of "*Special Cause*".

Communication

Act of accurately encoding, sending, receiving, decoding, and verifying messages. Communication between sender and receiver may be oral or written, formal or informal.

Communication Channels

The number of possible communication paths on a project. The formula for calculating communication channels is: $[n(n-1)]/2$; n=number of people on the project.

Communication Method

A systematic procedure, technique, or process used to transfer information among project stakeholders.

Communication Models

A description, analogy, or schematic is used to represent how the communication process will be performed for the project.

Communication Requirements Analysis

An analytical technique to determine the information needs of the project stakeholders through interviews, workshops, or study of lessons learned from previous projects, etc.

Communication Styles Assessment

A technique to identify the preferred communication method, format, and content for stakeholders for planned communication activities.

Communication Technology

Specific tools, automated systems, computer programs, etc., used to transfer information among project stakeholders.

Communications Management Plan

A component of the project, program, or portfolio management plan that describes how, when, and by whom information about the project will be administered and disseminated.

Community of Practice (CoP)

As described by E. Wenger in his book, *Cultivating Communities of Practice*, the CoP uses the same basic idea as used by Shell in their offshore drilling platforms to establish local forums of "experts" with the specific mandate to create an arena in which project managers would feel comfortable sharing their findings and learnings from their projects.

Completion Contract

A type of contract that is completed when the vendor delivers the product to the buyer and the buyer accepts the product.

Complexity

A characteristic of a program, project, or its environment, which is difficult to manage due to human behavior, system behavior, or ambiguity.

Compliance

The state of meeting — or being in accord with — organizational, legal, certification or other relevant regulations.

Compromise

An option in conflict management in which both parties give up something to reach an agreement.

Conduct Procurement Process

The project management process of obtaining seller responses, selecting a seller, and awarding a contract.

Cone of Uncertainty

Agile term describing the difficulty of estimating early due to unknowns and how that should improve over time.

Configuration Item

Any component or project element that needs to be managed to ensure the successful delivery of the project, services, or result.

Configuration Management

A tool used to manage changes to a product or service being produced as well as changes to any of the project documents—for example, schedule updates.

Configuration Management Plan

A component of the project management plan that describes how to identify and account for project artifacts under configuration control and how to record and report changes to them.

Configuration Management System

A collection of procedures used to track project artifacts and monitor and control changes to these artifacts.

Conflict

Difference of opinion or agenda on a project amongst team members, stakeholders, or customers.

Conflict Management

The application of one or more strategies for dealing with disagreements that may be detrimental to team performance.

Conflict Resolution

The process of working to reach an agreement after a conflict situation arises.

Consensus

Group decision technique in which the group agrees to support an outcome even if the individuals do not agree with the decision.

Constraint

An external factor that limits the ability to plan. Constraints and assumptions are closely linked.

Context Diagram

A visual depiction of the product scope showing a business system (process, equipment, computer system, etc.), and how people and other systems (actors) interact with it.

Contingency Plan

A risk response strategy developed in advance before risks occur; it is meant to be used if and when identified risks become reality.

Contingency Reserve

Time or money allocated in the schedule or cost baseline for known risks with active response strategies.

Contingency Theory

A theory credited to Fred. E. Fielder which states that the set of skills and attributes that helped a project manager in one environment may work against them in another environment.

Continuous Improvement (CI)

The ongoing effort to improve products, services, or processes.

Continuous Integration

The practice of regularly merging all software code into a shared environment, several times a day, to check code quality and functionality.

Continuous Process Improvement

The systematic, ongoing effort to improve products, services, or processes in an organization.

Contract

A mutually binding agreement that obligates the seller to provide the specified project or service or result and obligates the buyer to pay for it.

Contract Change Control System

The system used to collect, track, adjudicate, and communicate changes to a contract.

Control Account

A management control point at which scope, budget, actual cost, and schedule are integrated and compared to earned value for performance measurement.

Control Charts

A graphic display of process data over time and against established control limits, which has a centerline that assists in detecting a trend of plotted values toward the control limits. These charts are often associated with control limits, specification limits, means, and standard deviation. Control charts are used to analyze and communicate the variability of a process or project activity over time. See also *"Variability Control Charts"*.

Control Costs Process

Project management process to monitor and control project costs to ensure they align with the cost baseline/budget.

Control Procurements Process

The project management process of managing procurement relationships, monitoring contract performance, making changes and corrections as appropriate, and closing out contracts.

Control Quality Process

Part of the Monitoring and Controlling Process Group, this project management process focuses on the quality of deliverables.

Control Resources Process

Part of the Monitoring and Controlling Process Group, this project management process ensures that the flow and usage of physical resources line up with the plan.

Control Schedule Process

Part of the Monitoring and Controlling Process Group, this project management process compares the planned work to the actual work.

Control Scope Process

Part of the Monitoring and Controlling Process Group, this project management process ensures that changes to scope are properly controlled.

Controlling PMO

A type of PMO that provides support and requires compliance through various means. Compliance may involve adopting project management frameworks or methodologies; using specific templates, forms, and tools; or conformance to governance.

Corrective Action

Steps (action) to bring future results in line with the plan; this can change the plan or the way the plan is being executed.

Cost Aggregation

Summing the lower-level cost estimates associated with the various work packages for a given level within the project's WBS or for a given cost control account.

Cost Baseline

The approved version of the time-phased project budget, excluding any management reserves, can be changed only through formal change control procedures and is used as a basis for comparison to actual results. See also "*Budget*".

Cost-Benefit Analysis

A financial analysis method used to determine the benefits provided by a project against its costs.

Cost Forecast

Cost estimates adjusted based on performance—i.e., Estimate at complete, budget at completion, estimate to complete, etc.

Cost Management Plan

A component of a project or program management plan that describes how costs will be planned, structured, and controlled.

Cost of Conformance

The money spent during a project to avoid failures. This includes prevention costs that build a quality product and appraisal costs that assess the quality.

Cost of Non-Conformance

The money spent after a project is complete because of failures. This includes internal and external failure costs.

Cost of Quality (CoQ)

All costs incurred over the life of the product by investment in preventing nonconformance to requirements, appraisal of the product or service for conformance to requirements, and failure to meet requirements.

Cost Performance Index (CPI)

A measure of the cost efficiency of budgeted resources expressed as the ratio of earned value to actual cost.

Cost Plus Award Fee (CPAF) contract

A category of contract that involves payments to the seller for all legitimate actual costs incurred for completed work, plus an award fee representing seller profit.

Cost Plus Fixed Fee (CPFF) contract

A type of cost-reimbursable contract in which the buyer reimburses the seller for the seller's allowable costs (allowable costs are defined by the contract) plus a fixed amount of profit (fee).

Cost Plus Incentive Fee (CPIF) contract

A type of cost-reimbursable contract in which the buyer reimburses the seller for the seller's allowable costs (allowable costs are defined by the contract), and the seller earns its profit if it meets defined performance criteria.

Cost Variance (CV)

The amount of budget deficit or surplus at a given point in time, expressed as the difference between the earned value and the actual cost.

Cost-Benefit Analysis

A cost-benefit analysis allows project managers to compare if the benefits of an action outweigh the costs or, conversely, if the costs outweigh the benefits. This can be an important criterion in decision making.

Cost-Reimbursable Contract

A type of contract involving payment to the seller for the seller's actual costs, plus a fee typically representing the seller's profit.

Crashing

Applying additional resources to one or more tasks/activities to complete the work more quickly. Crashing usually increases costs more than risks. In comparison, fast-tracking increases risks. See also "*Fast Tracking*".

Create WBS Process

A project management planning process that involves creating the work-break-down (WBS) structure, along with the WBS dictionary. This process produces the schedule baseline, which consists of the WBS, WBS dictionary and the scope statement. The scope statement is produced from the Define Scope project management process.

Critical Path

The sequence of activities that represents the longest path through a project determines the shortest possible duration.

Critical Path Activity

Any activity on the critical path in a project schedule.

Critical Path Method (CPM)

A technique of schedule analysis in which the schedule activities are evaluated to determine the float or slack for each activity and the overall schedule. To calculate critical path, use the forward and backward pass along with float analysis to identify all network paths, including critical.

Cross-Functional Team

Teams that have all the capabilities to deliver the work they've been assigned. Team members can specialize in certain skills, but the team can deliver what they've been called on to build. See also "self-organizing teams."

Crystal Family of Methodologies.

A collection of lightweight agile software development methods focused on adaptability to a particular circumstance.

Cultural Awareness

Understanding the cultural differences of the individuals, groups, and organizations in the project stakeholder community to adapt communication strategies to avoid or reduce miscommunication and misunderstandings.

Customer

The individual or organization that will accept the deliverable(s) or product. Customers can be internal organizational groups or external to an organization.

Cycle Time

Refers to the period from the time a team starts a task until the time it is completed. See also *"lead time."*

Daily Standup

A short, 15-minute meeting in which the complete team gets together for a quick status update while standing in a circle. Also referred to as a *"daily scrum"* or *"standup"*.

Data

Refers to gathered empirical information, especially facts and numbers.

Data Analysis

The act of scrutinizing facts and numbers for typical purposes of decision-making, verification, validation, or assessment.

Data Gathering

Techniques used to solicit and document ideas—i.e., brainstorming, interviews, focus groups, questionnaires, surveys, and so on.

Data Representation

A way of depicting data visually to aid in its communication/comprehension to various audiences.

De Facto Regulations

Regulations that are widely accepted and adopted through use.

De Jure Regulations

Regulations that are mandated by law or have been approved by a recognized body of experts.

Debriefing

An informal, collaborative means of discussing the positives and the negatives of a project, what worked, and what will be done differently next time. This discussion includes technology issues, people issues, vendor relationships, and organizational culture.

Decision Making

The process of selecting a course of action from among multiple options.

Decision Tree Analysis

A diagramming and calculation technique for evaluating the implications of a chain of multiple options in the presence of uncertainty.

Decomposition

A technique used for dividing and subdividing the project scope and project deliverables into smaller, more manageable parts.

DEEP

An acronym used in agile projects that describes desirable attributes of a product backlog. Stands for: **D**etailed, **E**stimable, **E**mergent and **P**rioritize.

Define Activities Process

Part of the Planning Process Group, this project management process defines the activities (tasks) necessary to complete work packages/stories.

Define Scope Process

Part of the Planning Process Group, this project management process produces a scope statement that depicts a detailed and complete understanding of the project's vision.

Definition of Done (DoD)

A team's checklist of all the criteria required to be met so that a deliverable can be considered ready for customer use.

Definition of Ready (DoR)

A team's checklist for a user-centric requirement that has all the information the team needs to be able to begin working on it.

Deliverable

Any unique and verifiable product, result, or capability used to perform a service that is required to be produced to complete a process, phase, or projects.

Delphi Technique

A form of gathering expert opinions in which members of a group are asked or polled anonymously.

Demo

A review at the end of each iteration with the product owner and other customer stakeholders to review the progress of the product, get early feedback, and review an acceptance from the product owner of the stories delivered in the iteration. See also *"Sprint Review"*.

Dependency

A relationship between one or more tasks/activities. A dependency may be mandatory or discretionary, internal or external. See also *"start-to-start"*; *"start-to-finish"*; *"finish- to-start"*; and *"finish-to-finish"*.

Design for X (DfX)

A set of technical guidelines that may be applied during the design of a product for the optimization of a specific aspect of the design. DfX can control or even improve the product's final characteristics.

Design of Experiments (DoE)

A data analysis technique to determine the optimal condition; typically used with multiple variables.

Determine Budget Process

Part of the Planning Process Group, this project management process produces the cost baseline/project budget.

DevOps

A collection of practices for creating a smooth flow of delivery by improving collaboration between development and operations staff.

Develop Project Charter

Part of the Initiating Process Group, this project management process produces the project charter, which officially starts the project.

Develop Project Management Plan Process

A project management planning process which is a guide on how the project will be managed. It is composed of 19 components.

Develop Schedule Process

Part of the Planning Process Group, this project management process arranges activities to create the schedule baseline.

Develop Team Process

Part of the Executing Process Group, this project management process enhances and empowers the team to improve teamwork and individual skills.

Diagramming Techniques

Various means of depicting a system or virtual concept such as a business or process flow that indicate entities, relationships, and interactions.

Dictatorship

A group decision technique in which one person makes the decision for the entire group.

Direct and Manage Project Work Process

A Monitoring and Controlling project management process that reviews the entire project and analyzes what is planned vs. actual (with schedule forecast and cost forecast as an input) to determine the overall project status.

Direct Cost

Costs that are reported against the project, which may include salaries for resources, materials, and other expenses. It does not include shared expenses or overhead expenses.

Directions of Influence

A classification model that groups stakeholders based on how they influence the project and/or the project team: upwards (senior management); downwards (team or specialists); outwards (external); sidewards (project manager's peers).

Directive PMO

A type of PMO that takes control of projects by directly managing the projects.

Disaggregation

Breaking down epics or large stories into smaller stories. This is similar to decomposition on predictive projects.

Discretionary Dependency

A relationship that is established based on knowledge of best practices within a particular application area or an aspect of the project in which a specific sequence is desired.

Document Analysis

A technique used to gain project requirements from current document valuation.

Duration

Amount of time needed to complete an activity/task or work package.

Early Finish

Used in a networking diagram, this represents the earliest date that the activity can finish.

Early Start

Used in a networking diagram, this represents the earliest date that the activity can start.

Earned Value (EV)

A measure of work performed expressed in terms of the budget authorized for that work.

Earned Value Management (EVM)

A methodology that combines scope, schedule, and resource measurements to assess project performance and progress.

EEF

Any or all environmental factors, either internal or external to the project, can influence the project's success. Enterprise Environmental Factors (EEFs) include culture, weather conditions, government regulations, political situation, market conditions, and so on.

Effect-Based Risk Classification

A way of analyzing the major risks inherent to a project that could have an impact on its success. These major risks include time, cost, quality, and scope.

Effort

The number of labor units required to complete a scheduled activity or WBS component, often expressed in hours, days, or weeks.

Elapsed Time

The actual calendar time required for an activity from start to finish.

Emotional Intelligence (EI)

The ability to identify, assess, and manage the personal emotions of oneself and other people, as well as the collective emotions of groups of people. EQ (emotional quotient) is also a commonly used abbreviation.

Empathy

Part of emotional intelligence (EQ or EI). The ability to understand others' viewpoints and be a team player. It enables us to connect with others and understand what moves them.

Empowerment

An essential attribute of agile teams to enable localized decision-making capabilities. The quality of granting or being granted, nurturing, or motivating a team member or team to exercise one's own knowledge, skill, and ability — or that of a team.

Engagement Roadmap

Another name for "stakeholder engagement roadmap" - a guideline based on stakeholder analysis that sets forth processes for engaging with stakeholders at current and all future states of the project.

Enhance

A strategy for managing positive risks or opportunities that involves increasing the probability that the opportunity will happen, or the impact it will have by identifying and maximizing enablers of these opportunities.

Epic

A block of work with one common objective, such as a feature, customer request or business requirement. A helpful way to organize work and create a hierarchy, epic helps teams break their work down, while continuing to work towards a bigger goal.

Escalate

The act of seeking helpful intervention in response to a threat that is outside the scope of the project or beyond the project manager's authority.

Estimate

A number, figure, or representation that denotes cost or time.

Estimate Activity Durations Process

A project management planning process that determines the estimate time needed to complete a work package and/or activity.

Estimate Activity Resources Process

Part of the Planning Process Group, this project management process estimates the materials and human resources needed to perform the project activities.

Estimate at Completion (EAC)

The expected total cost of completing all the work is expressed as the sum of the actual cost to date and the estimate to complete.

Estimate Costs Process

Part of the Planning Process Group, this project management process determines the financial estimate for each work package and/or activity.

Estimate to Complete (ETC)

The expected cost of finishing all the remaining project work.

Executing Process Group

One of the five Project Management Process Groups. It consists of those project management processes performed to complete the work defined in the project management plan to satisfy the project requirements.

Exit Gate

Logical point at the end of a project phase at which an independent party and/or relevant stakeholders reviews that phase's deliverables to determine whether or not they were completed successfully, and the subsequent project phase should be initiated. Used in predictive or traditional projects. See also "*Kill Point*".

Expectancy Theory

Motivational theory which proposes that the team makes choices based on the expected outcome.

Expected Monetary Value (EMV)

A quantitative method of calculating the average outcome when the future is uncertain. The calculation of EMV is a component of decision tree analysis. Opportunities will have positive values and threats will have negative values.

Expert Judgment

Judgment provided based upon expertise in an application area, knowledge area, discipline, industry, etc., as appropriate for the activity being performed. Such expertise may be provided by any group or person with specialized education, knowledge, skill, experience, or training.

Explicit Knowledge

Knowledge that can be codified using symbols such as words, numbers, and pictures. This type of knowledge can be easily documented and shared with others.

Exploit

A strategy for managing positive risks or opportunities that involves attempting to make sure that the opportunity happens.

External Dependency

Types of activity dependencies that exist between project activities and non-project activities and can be out of the project's control.

Extreme Programming (XP)

Agile methodology in which iterations last for one week and programmers work in pairs.

Facilitated Workshops

Organized working sessions held by project managers to determine a project's requirements and to get all stakeholders together to agree on the project's outcomes.

Facilitation

A skill used to lead or guide an assembled group toward a successful conclusion such as making a decision or finding a solution.

Fast Tracking

A schedule compression technique in which activities or phases normally done in sequence are performed in parallel for at least a portion of their duration. See also "**Crashing**".

Feature

A group of stories that delivers value to the customer.

Fibonacci Sequence

A mathematical sequence in which the value of each number is derived from the sum of the two preceding numbers. Used in agile estimating or relative estimating techniques, such as planning poker. 0,1,1,2,3,5,8,13,21, Simplified sequence: 0,1,2,35,8,13,20,40,100.

Final Report

A summary of the project's information on performance, scope, schedule, quality, cost, and risks.

Finish-to-Finish (FF)

A logical relationship in which a successor activity cannot finish until a predecessor activity has finished.

Finish-to-Start (FS)

A logical relationship in which a successor activity cannot start until a predecessor activity has finished.

Firm Fixed Price Contract (FFP)

A type of fixed price contract in which the buyer pays the seller a set amount (as defined by the contract), regardless of the seller's costs.

Fishbone Diagram

See "*Cause and Effect Diagram*".

Fixed Price Contract

An agreement that sets the fee that will be paid for a defined scope of work regardless of the cost or effort to deliver it.

Fixed Price Incentive Fee (FPIF) contract

A type of contract in which the buyer pays the seller a set amount (as defined by the contract), and the seller can earn an additional amount if the seller meets defined performance criteria.

Fixed Price with Economic Price Adjustment (FPEPA) contract

A fixed-price contract, but with a special provision allowing for pre-defined final adjustments to the contract price due to changed conditions, such as inflation changes, or cost increases (or decreases) for specific commodities.

Float

Also called slack. See "*Total Float*" and "*Free Float*".

Focus Groups

An elicitation technique that brings together pre-qualified stakeholders and subject matter experts to learn about their expectations and attitudes about a proposed product, service, or result.

Forward Pass

Technique for calculating the early start and early finish dates of the scheduled activities. This is part of the critical path method and is paired with backward pass to determine activity and schedule float along with the critical path. See also "*Backward Pass*".

Free Float

The amount of time that a scheduled activity can be delayed without impacting the early start date of any subsequent scheduled activity.

Functional Manager

Supervisory organizational role in a specialized area or department.

Functional Organization

An organizational structure in which staff is grouped by areas of specialization and the project manager has limited authority to assign work and apply resources.

Functionality

In an agile context, an action that the system performs and adds value to the customer/ user.

Funding Limit Reconciliation

The process of comparing the planned expenditure of project funds against any limits on the commitment of funds for the project to identify any variances between the funding limits and the planned expenditures.

Gantt Chart

A bar chart of schedule information on which activities are listed on the vertical axis, dates are shown on the horizontal axis, and the activity durations are shown as horizontal bars placed according to start and finish dates.

Generalizing Specialist

Refers to a project team member who has a particular area of deep expertise but also has experience in many other areas that may not be directly related to their core area. These team member types are valued on agile projects because of their ability to be interchangeable.

Gold Plating

Adding more scope than the customer requested and/or that the team planned for.

Group Decision Techniques

Team working techniques to move a group towards consensus or decision. Examples are unanimity, majority, plurality, and dictatorship.

Growth Mindset

A growth mindset, as conceived by Stanford psychologist Carol Dweck and colleagues, is the belief that a person's capacities and talents can be improved over time.

Ground Rules

Expectations regarding acceptable behavior by project team members.

Hardening Iteration/Iteration H

Specialized increment/iteration/sprint dedicated to stabilizing the code base so that it is robust enough for release. No new functionality is added. Primarily used for refactoring and/or technical debt.

Herzberg's Motivation-Hygiene Theory

In 1959, behavioral scientist Frederick Herzberg proposed that 'hygiene' or environmental factors can cause workers to feel satisfied or unsatisfied with their job and this factor affects their performance. The theory also proposes that a worker's independent drive associated with motivation also affects performance and that workers respond to feelings of connection with their work. Therefore, leaders should encourage workers to accept more authority as well as promote feedback. Also known as Two Factor Theory, Herzberg's Motivation Theory, and The Dual Structure Theory.

Histogram

A bar or column chart that graphically represents numerical data—for example, the number of defects per deliverable, a ranking of the cause of defects, the number of times each process is noncompliant, or other representations of project or product defects.

Historical Information

Archived information from previous projects that can be used for a multitude of reasons, including estimating cost, schedule, resources, and lessons learned.

Ideal Time

An estimation technique that refers to the time it would take to complete a given task assuming neither interruptions nor unplanned problems arise

Identify Risks

Performed throughout the project, this is the project management process of identifying individual project risks as well as sources of overall project risk and documenting their characteristics. The key benefit of this process is the documentation of existing individual project risks and the sources of overall project risk. It also brings together information so the project team can respond appropriately to identified risks.

Identify Stakeholders

Performed periodically, throughout the project as needed, this is the project management process of identifying project stakeholders regularly and analyzing and documenting relevant information regarding their interests, involvement, interdependencies, influence, and potential impact on project success. The key benefit is enabling the project team to identify the appropriate focus for engagement of each stakeholder or group of stakeholders.

Impediment

An obstacle that prevents the team from achieving its objectives.

Implement Risk Response Process

A part of the Executing Process Group, this is the project management process of implementing agreed-upon risk response plans. The key benefit is to ensures that agreed-upon risk responses are executed as planned to address overall project risk exposure, minimize individual project threats, and maximize individual project opportunities. This project management process is performed throughout the project.

Increment

A functional, tested, and accepted deliverable that is a subset of the overall project outcome.

Incremental Delivery

Agile concept that the functionality should be delivered in small pieces or stages rather than as a complete solution.

Incremental Life Cycle

An adaptive project life cycle in which the deliverable is produced through a series of iterations that successively add functionality within a predetermined time frame. The deliverable contains the necessary and sufficient capability to be considered complete only after the final iteration.

Estimates

Estimates generated by experts outside the project for the purposes of comparing them with those made by the team.

Indirect Costs

A cost is usually tracked as part of a contract, that is not expended directly for the project's benefit.

Influence Diagram

Used in quality management decisions. A graphical representation of situations showing causal influences, time ordering of events, and other relationships among variables and outcomes.

Influence/Impact Grid

Used in stakeholder management. A classification model that groups stakeholders on the basis of their involvement in and impact on the project.

Influencing

The act of presenting a good case to explain why an idea, decision, or problem should be handled a certain way, without resistance from other individuals.

Information

Data that has been analyzed, organized, and processed to make it more meaningful.

Information Management

A system to allow the team to collaborate, share, and capture project work.

Information Management System

A way to collect, manage, and distribute project information.

Information Radiator

The generic term for visual displays placed in a visible location so everyone can quickly see the latest information. Also known as "Big Visible Chart" in agile.

Initiating Progress Group

One of the five Project Management Process Groups. It includes the project management process(es) performed to define a new project or a new phase of an existing project by obtaining authorization to start the project or phase.

Input

Something needed or used by a process to create the process output.

Inspection

Reviewing the functionality or suitability of a product, service, or result against the plan (requirements/story).

Insurable Risk

A risk that has only the potential for loss and no potential for profit or gain. An insurable risk is one for which insurance may be purchased to reduce or offset the possible loss. Types of insurable risks are direct property, indirect property, liability, and personnel related.

Interactions

In an agile context, this generally refers to face-to-face conversations between members, customers and stakeholders.

Interactive Communication

An exchange of information between two or more individuals ensures common understanding for everyone participating in that exchange.

Internal Dependency

A type of activity dependency that exists between project activities and is usually under the project's control.

Internal Rate of Return (IRR)

The interest rate that makes the net present value of all cash flow equal to zero. This rate is a function of the cost of capital for project implementation.

Interpersonal Skills

Skills used to establish and maintain relationships with other people or stakeholders.

Interview

A formal or informal approach to elicit information from stakeholders by talking with them directly.

INVEST

Acronym describing the desirable attributes of a good story. Stands for: **I**ndependent, **N**egotiable, **V**aluable, **E**stimable, **S**mall and **T**estable.

Invitation for Bid (IFB)

A type of procurement document most commonly used when deliverables are commodities for which there are clear specifications and when quantities are very large. The invitation is usually advertised, and any seller may submit a bid. Negotiation is typically not anticipated. These are sometimes used interchangeably with RFPs.

Generally, this term is equivalent to RFP. However, in some application areas, it may have a narrower or more specific meaning.

Ishikawa Diagram

See *"Cause and Effect Diagram"*.

Issue

A current condition or situation that may have an impact on the project objectives.

Issue Log

An issue is a current condition or situation that may have an impact on the project objectives. An issue log is used to record and monitor information on active issues. Issues are assigned to a responsible party for follow up and resolution.

Iteration

A timeboxed cycle of development on a product or deliverable in which all the work needed to deliver value is performed.

Iteration Backlog

The work that is committed to be performed during a given iteration and is expected to burn down the duration. The work does not carry over to the next iteration.

Iterative Life Cycle

A project life cycle in which the project scope is generally determined early in the project life cycle, but time and cost estimates are routinely modified as the project team's understanding of the product/service increases. Iterations progressively develop the product/service through a series of repeated cycles, while increments successively add to the functionality of the product/service.

Job Shadowing

Techniques used to gain knowledge of a specific job role, task, or function to understand and determine project requirements. See *"Observations"*.

Joint Application Design (JAD)

Specialized workshops that include both SMEs and the development team together to discuss and improve on the software development process.

Kaizen

A management concept adapted by the project management community which refers to project activities that continuously improve all project processes. It usually involves all stakeholders. The concept originated in Japan and generally involves "change for the better" or "continuous improvement".

Kanban

Japanese management philosophy that means "signal". This philosophy focuses on promoting visibility of the work in progress (WIP) and limiting the amount of WIP that the team allows.

Kanban Board

A visualization tool that enables improvements to the flow of work by making bottlenecks and work quantities visible. It is a popular framework used to implement agile and DevOps software development. Also referred to as a signboard.

Kano Model

A mechanism, derived from the customer marketing industry, to understand and classify all potential customer requirements or features into four categories

Key Performance Indicator (KPI)

A set metric used to evaluate a project, an organizational unit, or a project team's performance against the project vision and objectives. KPI can be time bound.

Kill Point

The stage gate or phase review point. At this point, the progress of the project is evaluated, and a decision is made whether to continue or cancel the project. A set of criteria may be developed to assist with the decision to be made. See also *"Exit Gate"*.

Knowledge Area

An identified area of project management defined by its knowledge requirements and described in terms of its component processes, practices, inputs, outputs, tools, and techniques. The knowledge areas intersect with the five respective Project Management Process Groups. Although the Knowledge Areas are interrelated, ten are defined separately in the Project Management Body of Knowledge (PMBOK®).

Knowledge Management

A business area dedicated to connecting individuals to shared knowledge and general collaboration on project work. The modality used for connection can be face-to-face and/or virtual.

Lag

Refers to the amount of time whereby a successor activity will be delayed with respect to a preceding activity on the critical path.

Late Finish

The latest date an activity can finish, without delaying the finish of the project.

Late Start

The latest that a project activity can start without having to reschedule the calculated early finish of the project.

Lead

The amount of time whereby a successor activity can be advanced with respect to predecessor activity.

Leadership

The ability to guide others to achieve results. Leadership abilities are gained through experience, building relationships, and taking initiatives.

Leading

The act of establishing direction, aligning the team to a vision, and inspiring/motivating them to achieve a project's objectives.

Lead Time

Refers to the period from the time the team places a task on the board until delivery. Because the order of the items in the Ready column can be changed, this can be unpredictable. See also "**cycle time**."

Lean

An agile method used primarily in manufacturing that focuses on achieving outcomes with little or no waste.

Lean Six Sigma

A collaborative team method that provides an enhanced ability to target customer needs and measure performance during project execution and monitoring. It was introduced by American engineer Bill Smith while working at Motorola in 1986.

Legitimate Power

The authority granted to an individual due to his/her position within a group or an organization.

Lessons Learned

The knowledge gained during a project which shows how project events were addressed or should be addressed in the future for the purpose of improving performance.

Lessons Learned Register

A project document used to record knowledge gained during a project. The knowledge attained can be used in the current project and entered into the lessons learned repository for subsequent use.

Lessons Learned Repository

A central store of historical lessons learned information from various projects across jurisdictions.

Life Cycle Costing (LCC)

Life cycle costing is an approach that assesses the total cost of an asset over its life cycle including initial capital costs, maintenance costs, etc. LCC is an important economic analysis used in the selection of alternatives that impact both pending and future costs. The concept is also known as lifetime cost and is commonly referred to as "cradle to grave" or "womb to tomb" costs.

Logical Relationship

Those relations between the elements of discourse or thought that constitute its rationality, in the sense either of reasonableness or intelligibility.

Majority

A group decision-making method in which a course of action is agreed upon by a pre-defined quorum.

Make-or-Buy Analysis

The process of gathering and organizing data about product/service requirements and analyzing data against available alternatives including the purchase or internal manufacture of the project.

Make-or-Buy Decisions

Decisions made regarding the external purchase versus internal manufacture of a product.

Manage Communications

The project management process of creating, collecting, distributing, storing, retrieving, and the ultimate disposition of project information in accordance with the communications management plan defined within the project.

Manage Project Knowledge

The project management process of using existing knowledge and creating new knowledge to achieve project objectives and contribute to organizational learning. The process must include tools that allow converting data into information, and information into knowledge.

Manage Project Quality

The project management process of continually measuring the quality of all activities and taking corrective action until the desired quality is achieved. Quality management lowers the risk of product/service failure or unsatisfied clients.

Manage Project Team

The project management process of tracking team member performance, providing feedback, resolving issues, and managing team changes to optimize project performance. The key benefit of this process is that it influences team behavior, manages conflict, resolves issues, and appraises team member performance.

Manage Stakeholder Engagement Process

The project management process of communicating and working with stakeholders to meet their needs/expectations, address issues as they occur, and foster appropriate stakeholder engagement in project activities throughout the project life cycle.

Management Reserve

An amount of the project budget held outside of the performance measurement baseline (PMB) for management control purposes, that is reserved for unforeseen work that is within the scope of the project. Usually 5 – 10% of the project budget. This should not be confused with contingency reserve. See also "*Contingency Reserve*".

Managing

The exercise of executive control or authority.

Mandatory Dependency

A relationship that is contractually required or inherent in the nature of the work.

Market Research

The process of evaluating the feasibility of a new product or service, through research conducted directly with potential consumers.

Maslow's Hierarchy of Needs

A theory of psychology explaining human motivation based on the pursuit of different levels of needs. The theory states that humans are motivated to fulfill their needs in a hierarchical order. This order begins with the most basic needs before moving on to more advanced needs. The goal, according to this theory, is to reach the fifth level of the hierarchy: self-actualization.

Matrix Organization

An organizational structure in which the project manager shares responsibility with the functional managers for assigning priorities and for directing the work of individuals assigned to the project.

McClelland's Three Needs Theory

A human motivation theory which states that every person has one of three main driving motivators: the needs for achievement, affiliation, or power. Those with a strong need for affiliation don't like to stand out or take risk, and they value relationships above anything else.

Milestone

A specific point within a project life cycle used as a measure in the progress toward the ultimate goal. A milestone marks a specific point along a project timeline. The point may signal anchors such as a project start and end date, a need for external review, or input and budget check. It is represented as a task of zero duration and is displayed as an important achievement in a project.

Milestone Charts

A graphical representation of milestones. A type of project schedule bar chart that only includes milestone or major deliverables and their corresponding points in time.

Milestone List

Refers to an input or an output of various processes. A document that contains the milestones of a project.

Mind Mapping

A graphical technique used to consolidate ideas created through individual brainstorming sessions into a single map - image/display is used to reflect commonality and differences in understanding and to generate new ideas.

Minimum Business Increment (MBI)

The smallest amount of value that can be added to a product or service that benefits the business.

Minimum Viable Product (MVP)

The smallest collection of features that can be included in a product for customers to consider functional. In Lean methodologies, it can be referred to as "bare bones" or "no frills" functionality.

Mitigate

A strategy for managing negative risks or threats and that involves taking action to reduce the probability of occurrence or the impact of a risk.

Modeling

An approach used in schedule management and risk management. This can assist in the identification of problems or areas of risk with the project before they actually occur. See also *"What-If Scenario"* and *"Monte Carlo Analysis"*.

Monitor and Control Project Work

Performed throughout the project, the project management process of tracking, reviewing, and reporting the overall progress to meet the performance objectives defined in the project management plan. The key benefits of this process are that it allows stakeholders to understand the current state of the project, to recognize the actions taken to address any performance issues, and to have visibility into the future project status with cost and schedule forecasts.

Monitor and Controlling Process Group

One of five Project Management Process Groups. Monitoring and controlling project management processes measure work results against the plan and adjust where variance exists.

Monitor Communications Process

This project management process determines if the planned communications artifacts and activities have had the desired effect of increasing or maintaining stakeholders' support for the project's deliverables and expected outcomes.

Monitor Risks

The project management process of monitoring the implementation of agreed-upon risk response plans, tracking identified risks, identifying and analyzing new risks, and evaluating risk process effectiveness throughout the project. The key benefit of this process is that it enables project decisions to be based on current information about overall project risk exposure and individual project risks.

Monitor Stakeholder Engagement Process

Performed throughout a project, this is the project management process of monitoring project stakeholder relationships and tailoring strategies for engaging stakeholders through modification of engagement strategies and plans. The key benefit of this process is that it maintains or increases the efficiency and effectiveness of stakeholder engagement activities as the project evolves and its environment changes.

Monitoring and Controlling Process Group

One of the five Project Management Process Groups. It consists of those project management processes required to track, review, and regulate the progress and performance of the project; identify any areas in which changes to the plan are required; and initiate the corresponding changes.

Monte Carlo Analysis

Refers to a simulation technique in project management by which the project manager computes and calculates the total project cost and the project schedule using various scenarios. A set of input values are selected taking into consideration the probability distributions, potential costs, and potential durations. It allows a project manager to calculate the probable total cost of a project as well as to find a range or a potential date of completion for the project.

Monte Carlo Simulation (risk analysis)

A risk management technique, which project managers use to estimate the impacts of various risks on the project cost and project timeline. Using this method, one can easily find out what will happen to the project schedule and cost in case any risk occurs. It is used at various times during the project life cycle to get the idea on a range of probable outcomes during various scenarios.

Moscow Analysis

A prioritization technique used in management, business analysis, project management, and software development to reach a common understanding with stakeholders on the importance they place on the delivery of each requirement; it is also known as MoSCoW prioritization or MoSCoW analysis.

Motivation

The inner drive or external encouragement that keeps people involved and wanting to complete work of high quality in a timely fashion

Multi-Criteria Decision Analysis

A technique that utilizes a decision matrix to provide a systematic, analytical approach for establishing criteria, such as risk levels, uncertainty, and valuation, to evaluate and rank many ideas.

Negative Float

The amount of time that must be saved to bring the project to completion on time.

Negotiated Settlements

> The product or output of negotiation, representing a final, equitable, mutually agreed disposition of all outstanding issues, claims, and disputes.

Negotiation

> An approach used by more than one individual or group to come to an agreement or resolution that is mutually agreed by all parties.

Net Present Value (NPV)

> The difference between the present value of cash inflows and the present value of cash outflows over a period of time. NPV is used in capital budgeting and investment planning to analyze the financial viability of a projected investment or project.

Net Promoter Score (NPS)

> Measures a customer's willingness to recommend a provider's products or services to another on a scale of -100 to 100.

Network Diagram

> A graph that shows the activities, duration, and interdependencies of tasks within a project.

Node

> Represents the start or end of an activity in a sequence.

Nominal Group Technique

> A technique that enhances brainstorming with a voting process used to rank the most useful ideas for further brainstorming or for prioritization.

Nonfunctional Requirements (NFRs)

> A term from agile software development. NFRs define system attributes such as security, reliability, performance, maintainability, scalability and usability. They serve as constraints or restrictions on the design of the system across backlogs.

Non-Verbal Communication

> The use of body language and other means besides the spoken word—posture, gestures, dress and appearance, facial expressions, and the like—to communicate.

Observations

> Techniques used to gain knowledge of a specific job role, task, or function to understand and determine project requirements. See "*Job Shadowing*".

Opportunity

> A risk that, if developed, could create a positive effect on one or more project objectives.

Opportunity Cost

A concept applied to quantify the missed opportunity when deciding to use a resource (e.g., investment dollars) for one purpose versus another. Alternately opportunity cost is the loss of potential future return from the second-best unselected project. In other words, it is the opportunity (potential return) that will not be realized when one project is selected over another.

Organizational Chart

A diagram that shows the structure of an organization and the relationships and relative ranks of its parts and positions/jobs. It is typically a diagram that visually conveys a company's internal structure by detailing the roles, responsibilities, and relationships between individuals within an entity.

Organizational Culture

The underlying beliefs, assumptions, values, and behaviors that contribute to and define the unique social and psychological environment of an organization.

Organizational Process Assets (OPA)

Refers to all the implicit input or assets on processes used by an organization in operating a business. This may include business plans, processes, policies, protocols, and knowledge.

Organizational Silo

Occurs when employees or an entire department are isolated or refuse to share information or interact with others in the same company. Thus, the flow of critical information will be contained within that department. See also "**Silo**".

Organizational Theory

The study of how people, teams, and organizations behave. It is part of the search for common themes for the purpose of maximizing efficiency and productivity, problem solving, and meeting the stakeholder requirements of a project.

Osmotic Communication

Communication which occurs informally or indirectly and through means such as overhearing, as a result of people sitting in the same room/environment.

Output

A product, result, or service generated by a process. May be an input to a successor process.

Outsourcing

Moving beyond the organization to secure services and expertise from an outside source on a contract or short-term basis.

Overlapping Relationships

A type of phase-to-phase relationship characterized by phases that start prior to the ending of the previous phase. Therefore, activities in different phases run concurrently with one another.

Paralingual Communications

The effect of pitch, tone, and inflections in the sender's voice on the message being sent. For example, facial expressions, hand gestures, and body language contribute to the message.

Parametric Estimating

An estimating technique in which an algorithm is used to calculate cost or duration based on historical data and project parameters. This technique is scalable and linear.

Pareto Chart

A histogram that is used to rank causes of problems in a hierarchical format. See also "*80/20 Rule*".

Path

The sequence of project network activities.

Payback Period

The interval required to amass (via profit or value) the initial investment made for a project.

PDCA/PDSA

Plan Do Check/Study Act – also known as the "Deming Wheel". A process or method used to solve problems and implement solutions.

Penalty Power

The ability to gain support because project personnel perceive the project manager as capable of directly or indirectly dispensing penalties that they wish to avoid. Penalty power usually derives from the same sources as reward power, with one being a necessary condition for the other.

Perform Integrated Change Control

The project management process of reviewing all change requests, approving changes, and managing changes to deliverables, project documents, and the project management plan. These decisions are communicated to stakeholders.

Perform Qualitative Risk Analysis

A project management process used to identify individual risks by looking at how likely they are to happen (probability of occurrence) and how bad they would be for the project if they did happen (impact).

Perform Quantitative Risk Analysis

The project management process of numerically analyzing the effect of identified risks on overall project objectives.

Persona

An imaginary person or identity created by the team to model interactions with the system to gather requirements.

Phase

Refers to a collection of activities within a project. Each project phase is goal oriented and ends at a milestone.

Phase Gate

A point review at the end of a phase in which a decision is made to continue to the next phase, to continue with modification, or to end a project or program.

Plan Communications Management

Performed periodically, as needed, throughout the project, this is the project management process of developing an appropriate approach and plan for project communications activities based on the information needs of each stakeholder or group, available organizational assets, and the needs of the project. The key benefit of this process is a documented approach to engage stakeholders effectively and efficiently by presenting relevant information in a timely manner.

Plan Cost Management

Performed once or at predefined points in the project, this is the project management process of defining how the project costs will be estimated, budgeted, managed, monitored, and controlled. The key benefit of this process is that it provides guidance and direction on how the project costs will be managed throughout the project.

Plan Procurement Management Process

Performed once or at predefined points in the project, this is the project management process of documenting project procurement decisions, specifying the approach and identifying potential sellers. The key benefit of this process is that it determines whether to acquire goods and services from outside the project and, if so, what to acquire as well as how and when to acquire it. Goods and services may be procured from other parts of the performing organization or from external sources.

Plan Quality Management

Performed once or at predefined points in the project, the project management process of identifying quality requirements and/or standards for the project and its deliverables and documenting how the project will demonstrate compliance with quality requirements and/or standards. The key benefit of this process is that it provides guidance and direction on how quality will be managed and verified throughout the project.

Plan Resource Management

Performed once or at predefined points in the project, this is the project management process of defining how to estimate, acquire, manage, and use team and physical resources. The key benefit of this process is that it establishes the approach and level of management effort needed for managing project resources based on the type and complexity of the project.

Plan Risk Management

Performed once or at predefined points in the project, this is the project management process of defining how to conduct risk management activities for a project. The key benefit of this process is that it ensures that the degree, type, and visibility of risk management are proportionate to both risks and the importance of the project to the organization and other stakeholders.

Plan Schedule Management

Performed once or at predefined points in the project, this is the project management process of establishing the policies, procedures, and documentation for planning, developing, managing, executing, and controlling the project schedule. The key benefit of this process is that it provides guidance and direction on how the project schedule will be managed throughout the project.

Plan Scope Management

Performed once or at predefined points in the project, this is the project management process of creating a scope management plan that documents how the project and product scope will be defined, validated, and controlled. The key benefit of this process is that it provides guidance and direction on how scope will be managed throughout the project.

Plan Stakeholder Engagement Process

Performed periodically throughout the project as needed, this is the project management process of developing approaches to involve project stakeholders based on their needs, expectations, interests, and potential impact on the project. The key benefit is that it provides an actionable plan to interact effectively with stakeholders.

Planned Value (PV)

The approved value of the work to be completed for a specific period.

Planning package

A WBS component below the control account with known work content but without detailed schedule activities.

Planning Poker

Agile exercise to help the team estimate work.

Planning Process Group

One of the five Project Management Process Groups. It consists of those project management processes required to establish the scope of the project, refine the objectives, and define the course of action required to attain the objectives that the project was undertaken to achieve.

Plurality

Decisions made by the largest block in a group, even if a majority is not achieved.

PMBOK®

PMBOK® stands for *Project Management Body of Knowledge*, and it is the entire collection of project management processes, best practices, terminologies, and guidelines that are accepted as standard within the project management industry.

PMBOK® Guide

A Guide to the Project Management Body of Knowledge (PMBOK® Guide) is the Project Management Institute's flagship publication representing standards in the business area of project management. It is currently in its Seventh Edition.

Political Awareness

The ability to recognize the power structure internal to the organization, and the ability to navigate relationships.

Portfolio

Projects, programs, subsidiary portfolios, and operations managed as a group to achieve strategic objectives.

Portfolio Management

The centralized management of one or more portfolios to achieve strategic objectives.

Power/Influence Grid

A classification model that groups stakeholders on the basis of their levels of authority and involvement in the project.

Power/Interest Grid

A classification model that groups stakeholders on the basis of their levels of authority and interest in the project.

Precedence Diagramming Method (PDM)

A technique used to create the network diagram. It constructs a schedule model in which activities are represented by nodes and are graphically linked by one or more logical relationships to show the sequence in which the activities are to be performed.

Precedence Relationship

A logical dependency used in the precedence diagramming methods.

Predictive Life Cycle

Project management approach in which activities are completed in a distinct or linear fashion and a new phase begins only when the previous phase is completed. Value is delivered at the completion of the project in the form of deliverables. Also known as *"Waterfall"*.

Present Value (PV)

The current value of a future sum of money or stream of cash flows given a specific rate of return.

Preventative Action

Action taken to proactively prevent or avoid anticipated future problems. This is closely tied to risk management.

Prevention

A concept in quality management that indicates that quality cannot be inspected into a product but should be planned for from the start to avoid problems.

Probability and Impact Matrix

A grid for mapping the probability of occurrence of each risk and its impact on project objectives if that risk occurs.

Probability Distribution

The scattering of values assigned to likelihood in a sample population. It can be visually depicted in the form of a probability density function (PDF).

Process

A systematic series of activities directed towards causing a result such that one or more inputs will be acted upon to create one or more outputs.

Process Improvement Plan

A component of the project management plan, this document describes the processes used in the production of the project's deliverables, how they will be monitored, and under what conditions they may be changed.

Procurement

The acquisition of goods and services from an external organization, vendor, or supplier to enable the deliverables of the project.

Procurement Audit

The review of procurement contracts and contracting processes for completeness, accuracy, and effectiveness.

Procurement Documents

Documents used in bid and proposal activities, which include the buyer's invitation for bid, expression of interest (EOI); invitation for negotiations; request for information (RFI); request for quotation (RFQ); request for proposal (RFP); and seller's responses.

Procurement Management Plan

A component of the project or program management plan that describes how a project team will acquire goods and services from outside the executing organization.

Procurement Statement of Work (SOW)

Describes the procurement item in sufficient detail to allow prospective sellers to determine their capability of executing the tasks necessary to deliver the deliverables, products, services, or outputs.

Product

An artifact that is produced is quantifiable and can be either an end item in itself or a component item. See also "*Deliverable*".

Product Analysis

For projects that deliver a product, this is a tool to define scope. It generally means asking questions about a product and forming answers to describe the use, characteristics, and other relevant aspects of what is going to be manufactured.

Product Backlog

A Scrum term. A prioritized list of customer requirements that will improve a product/ service. This list represents the single source for work.

Product Box Exercise

> A technique used to explain a desired solution or outcome. Stakeholders try to describe aspects of a solution in the same way a marketer might describe product features and benefits on a box.

Product Owner

> An individual or an organization who is responsible for gathering inputs about a product from the customer and translating the requirements into the product vision for the team and stakeholders.

Product Life Cycle

> A series of phases that represent the evolution of a product, from concept through delivery, growth, maturity, and retirement.

Product Management

> The integration of people, data, processes, and business systems to create, maintain, and evolve a product or service throughout its life cycle.

Product Roadmap

> A high-level visual summary of the product or products of the project that includes goals, milestones, and potential deliverables.

Product Scope

> The functions and features that characterize a product or a service.

Program

> Related projects, subsidiary programs, and program activities that are managed in a coordinated manner to obtain benefits not available from individual management of them. A project may or may not be part of a program, but a program will always have projects.

Program Management

> The application of knowledge, skills, and principles to a program to achieve program objectives and obtain benefits and control not available by management of program components individually.

Program Management

> The process of managing programs mapped to business objectives that improve organizational performance. Program managers oversee and coordinate the various projects and other strategic initiatives throughout an organization.

Progressive Elaboration

The iterative process of increasing the level of detail in a project management plan as greater amounts of information and more accurate estimates become available.

Project

A temporary endeavor undertaken to create a unique product, service, or result.

Project Artifact

Any document related to the management of a project.

Project Calendar

The project calendar specifies the working and non-working days and times for activities.

Project Charter

A document issued by the project initiator or sponsor that formally authorizes the existence of a project and provides the project manager with the authority to apply organizational resources to project activities.

Project Coordinator

A project coordinator handles administrative tasks for the project manager and team members to manage a project effectively and efficiently. Tasks may include procuring project resources such as equipment and supplies, managing deadlines, workflow, and scheduling project meetings and other appointments on behalf of the project team.

Project Documents

Any documents that are prepared in support of a project – for example, requirements, specifications, contracts with vendors, design documents, test plans, and publications that will be delivered to the client along with the final product.

- Activity attributes
- Activity list
- Assumption log
- Basis of estimates
- Change log
- Cost estimates
- Cost forecasts
- Duration estimates
- Issue log
- Lessons learned register
- Milestone list
- Physical resource assignments
- Project calendars
- Project communications

- Project schedule
- Project schedule network diagram
- Project scope statement
- Project team assignments
- Quality control measurements
- Quality metrics
- Quality report
- Requirements documentation
- Requirements traceability matrix
- Resource breakdown structure
- Resource calendars
- Resource requirements
- Risk register
- Risk report
- Schedule data
- Schedule forecasts
- Stakeholder register
- Team charter
- Test and evaluation documents

Project Expeditor

Role or position on a project team that works as an assistant and coordinates communications on behalf of the team. Individuals performing in this role cannot make or enforce decisions but can communicate with the contractors or suppliers of project resources to ensure the timely delivery of materials.

Project Funding

The means by which the money required to undertake a project, program or portfolio is secured and then made available as required.

Project Funding Requirements

Budgetary requirements that specify when funds will be needed to be provided for the project.

Project Governance

The framework, functions, and processes that guide project management activities to create a unique product, service, or result to meet organizational, strategic, and operational goals.

Project Life Cycle

The series of phases that a project passes through from its start to its completion.

Project Management

The application of knowledge, skills, tools, and techniques to project activities to fulfill the project plan.

Project Management Information System (PMIS)

An information system consisting of the tools and techniques used to gather, integrate, and disseminate the outputs of project management processes. See also *"Project Management Software"*.

Project Management Institute (PMI®)

A professional membership association for project managers.

Project Management Office (PMO)

A management structure that standardizes the project-related governance processes and facilitates the sharing of resources, methodologies, tools, and techniques. PMOs are more common in larger organizations because of the number of projects that can be in process at the same time.

Project Management Plan

The document describes how the project will be executed, monitored and controlled, and closed.

Project Management Process Groups

Refers specifically to five logic-oriented groupings of project management processes. These include:
- Initiation
- Planning
- Executing
- Monitoring and Controlling
- Closing

Project Management Software

An automated application that helps plan, organize, and manage project resources and develop resource estimates for activities. See also *"Project Management Information System (PMIS)"*.

Project Manager

The person assigned by the performing organization to lead the team that is responsible for achieving the project goals and objectives.

Project Meetings

In-person or virtual communication events held with stakeholders that intend to generate group decisions, such as discussing issues, creating proposals, and approving or rejecting offers which can contribute to quicker project deliverables, planned goals, and expected results. Project meetings are an effective method of distributing information and communicating with the team and stakeholders.

Project Methodology

A system of principles, practices, techniques, procedures, and rules used by those who manage projects.

Project Performance Domains

A project performance domain is a group of related activities that are critical for the effective delivery of project outcomes. Project performance domains are interactive, interrelated, and interdependent areas of focus that work in unison to achieve desired project outcomes. There are eight project performance domains:

- Stakeholders
- Team
- Development Approach and Life Cycle
- Planning
- Project Work
- Delivery
- Measurement
- Uncertainty

Project Phase

A collection of logically related project activities that culminates in the completion of one or more deliverables. A phase has a set of goals and objectives, and the attainment of these goals/objectives triggers a milestone.

Project Plan

Defines project goals and objectives, specifies tasks, and methodology. The plan identifies the resources required, associated budgets, and timelines for completion. A project plan is expected to define all works in a project, the human resources and other resources required to execute the plan in its entirety.

Project Requirements

For a project, these are the agreed-upon conditions or capabilities of a product, service, or outcome that a project is designed to satisfy. See also "*Requirements*".

Project Schedule Network Diagram

A graphical representation of the logical relationships among the project schedule activities. An output of a schedule model that presents linked activities with planned dates, durations, milestones, and resources. See also "*Network Diagram*".

Project Scope

The features, functions, and works that characterize the delivery of a product, service, and/or result.

Project Scope Statement

The description of the project scope, major deliverables, assumptions, and constraints.

Project Sponsor

A person or group who provides resources and support for a project, program, or portfolio and is accountable for enabling success. See also "*Sponsor*".

Project Team

A set of individuals performing the work of the project to achieve its objectives.

Projectized Organization

A structure in which a project manager and a core project team operate as a separate organizational unit within the parent organization.

Prompt List

A checklist for a specific category of risk. This tool is a simple series of broad risks, for example environmental or legal, rather than specific risks, such as flooding or regulatory changes. The idea is to push (prompt) the team to think and brainstorm the risks in groups and eventually prioritize the same.

Prototypes

A method of obtaining early feedback on user requirements by building a working model of the expected product. Prototypes can be used to solicit aesthetics, functionalities etc. Several iterations may be displayed.

Psychological Safety

Being able to show and employ oneself without fear of negative consequences of status, career, or self-worth—we should be comfortable being ourselves in our work setting.

Pull Communications

Messages that require the interested people to access the information based on their own initiative.

Push Communications

Messages that are sent out to people who need to receive the information.

Qualified Vendors

The vendors who are approved to deliver the products, services, or results based on the procurement requirements identified for a project.

Qualified Vendors List

Contains details regarding vendors who meet the organization's requirements and to whom requests can be sent.

Qualitative Risk Analysis

A technique used to determine the probability of occurrence and the impact of identified risk.

Quality

The degree to which a set of inherent characteristics fulfills requirements.

Quality Audit

A structured, independent process to determine if project activities comply with organizational and project policies, processes, and procedures.

Quality Function Deployment (QFD)

Workshops that are commonly used in the manufacturing field to determine new product development requirements.

Quality Gate

A special type of gate located before a phase that is strongly dependent upon the outcome of a previous phase. The quality gate process is a formal way of specifying and recording the transition between stages in the project life cycle.

Quality Management Plan

A component of the project or program management plan that describes how applicable policies, procedures, and guidelines will be implemented to achieve the quality objectives.

Quality Metric

A description of a project or product attribute and how to measure it.

Quality Policy

The basic principles that should govern the organization's actions as it implements its system for quality management.

Quality Report

A project document that includes quality management issues, recommendations for corrective actions, and a summary of findings from quality control activities and may include recommendations for process, project, and product improvements.

Quantitative Risk Analysis

Technique used to assess the risk exposure events to overall project objectives and determine the confidence levels of achieving the project objectives.

Questionnaires

Written sets of questions designed to quickly gather information from many respondents.

RACI Chart

Stands for **R**esponsible, **A**ccountable, **C**onsulted, and **I**nformed. A common type of responsibility assignment matrix (RAM) that uses responsible, accountable, consult, and inform statuses to define the involvement of stakeholders in project activities.

Recognition

A more personalized, intangible, and experiential event that focuses on behavior rather than outcome.

Refactoring

Refers to software development. Improving the design of the code so that it is easier to test, debug, and maintain.

Referent Power

Refers to establishing trust, respect, and credibility with people in work or personal life contexts.

Regulations

Requirements imposed by a governmental body. These requirements can establish product, process, or service characteristics, including applicable administrative provisions that have government-mandated compliance.

Relative Authority

The project manager's authority relative to the functional manager's authority over the project and the project team.

Relative Estimating

Also called sizing. The process of estimating stories or backlog tasks in relation to each other instead of in units of time.

Release Plan

The plan that sets expectations for the dates, features, and/or outcomes a project expects to deliver over the course of several iterations.

Release Planning

The process of identifying a high-level plan for releasing or transitioning a product, deliverable, or increment of value to the customer.

Reports

A formal record or summary of information.

Request for Information (RFI)

A type of procurement document whereby the buyer requests a potential seller to provide various pieces of information related to a product or service or seller capability.

Request for Proposal (RFP)

A type of procurement document used to request proposals from prospective sellers of products or services. In some application areas, it may have a narrower or more specific meaning.

Request for Quotation (RFQ)

A type of procurement document used to request price quotations from prospective sellers of common or standard products or services. Sometimes used in place of request for proposal and, in some application areas, it may have a narrower or more specific meaning.

Requirement

A measurable condition or capability that must be present in a product, service, or result to satisfy a business need.

Requirements Documentation

A description of how individual requirements meet the business need for the project.

Requirements Management Plan

A component of the project or program management plan that describes how requirements will be analyzed, documented, and managed.

Requirements Traceability Matrix

A grid that links product requirements from their origin to the deliverables that satisfy them.

Reserve

A provision in the project management plan to mitigate cost and/or schedule risk, often used with a modifier (e.g., management reserve, contingency reserve) to provide further detail on what types of risks are meant to be mitigated. See also *"Buffer"*.

Reserve Analysis

A method used to evaluate the amount of risk on the project and the amount of schedule and budget reserve to determine whether the reserve is sufficient for the remaining risk.

Residual Risk

The risk that remains after risk responses have been implemented.

Resource

A skilled individual or team, equipment, services, supplies, commodities, materials, budgets, or funds required to accomplish the defined work.

Resource Breakdown Structure

A hierarchical representation of resources by category and type.

Resource Calendar

A calendar that identifies the working days and shifts for which each specific resource is available.

Resource Histogram

A bar chart that represents when a resource will be needed in the project.

Resource Levelling

A resource optimization technique in which adjustments are made to the project schedule to optimize the allocation of resources and which may affect the critical path.

Resource Management Plan

A component of the project management plan that describes how project resources are acquired, allocated, monitored, and controlled.

Resource Optimization Techniques

A technique in which activity start and finish dates are adjusted to balance demand for resources with the available supply. See also *"Resource Levelling"* and *"Resource Smoothing"*.

Resource requirements

The types and quantities of resources required for each activity in a work package.

Resource Smoothing

A resource optimization technique in which free and total float are used without affecting the critical path. See also *"Resource Levelling"* and *"Resource Optimization Technique"*.

Responsibility Assignment Matrix (RAM)

A grid that shows the project resources assigned to each work package.

Retrospective

Agile meeting held after the iteration/sprint/increment for the team to review the process and results to identify what went well and what can be done differently. Closely tied to continuous improvement. The process is the same as lessons learned.

Return on Investment (ROI)

A financial metric of profitability that measures the gain or loss from an investment relative to the amount of money invested.

Reward

A tangible, consumable item that is given to a person based on a specific outcome or an achievement.

Reward and Recognition Plan

A formalized way to reinforce performance or behavior.

Rework

Action taken to bring a defective or nonconforming component into compliance with requirements or specifications.

Risk

An event or condition of uncertainty that, if it occurs, has a positive or negative effect on one or more project objectives.

Risk Acceptance

A risk response strategy whereby the project team decides to acknowledge the risk and not take any action unless the risk occurs.

Risk Appetite

The degree of uncertainty an organization or individual is willing to accept in anticipation of a reward.

Risk Avoidance

A risk response strategy whereby the project team acts to eliminate the threat or protect the project from its impact.

Risk Breakdown Structure

A hierarchical representation of potential sources of risk.

Risk Breakdown Structure (RBS)

A hierarchical representation of potential sources of risk.

Risk Categorization

Organization by sources of risk (e.g., using the RBS), the area of the project affected (e.g., using the WBS), or other useful category (e.g., project phase) to determine the areas of the project most exposed to the effects of uncertainty.

Risk Category

A group of potential causes of risk.

Risk Enhancement

A risk response strategy whereby the project team acts to increase the probability of occurrence or impact of an opportunity.

Risk Exploiting

A risk response strategy whereby the project team acts to ensure that an opportunity occurs.

Risk Exposure

An aggregate measure of the potential impact of all risks at any given point in time in a project, program, or portfolio.

Risk Impact

The likely effect on project objectives if a risk event occurs.

Risk Management Plan

A component of the project, program, or portfolio management plan that describes how risk management activities will be structured and performed.

Risk Mitigation

A risk response strategy whereby the project team acts to decrease the probability of occurrence or impact of a threat.

Risk Owner

The person responsible for monitoring the risk and for selecting and implementing an appropriate risk response strategy.

Risk Probability

The likelihood that a risk event will occur or prove true during the project.

Risk Register

A repository in which outputs of risk management processes are recorded. As the central planning document for project risk analysis and control, the risk register contains a list of the most important risks to the project's completion. For each risk, it identifies the likelihood of occurrence, the impact to the project, the priority, and the applicable response plans.

Risk Response Plan

This plan involves reducing and eliminating risks and their potential impacts through appropriate mitigation techniques.

Risk Sharing

A risk response strategy whereby the project team allocates ownership of an opportunity to a third party who is best able to capture the benefit for the project.

Risk Threshold

The level of risk exposure above which risks are addressed and below which risks may be accepted.

Risk Transference

A risk response strategy whereby the project team shifts the impact of a threat to a third party, together with ownership of the response.

Risk Workshop

A technique that uses a special meeting conducted for the purpose of identifying project risks. In addition to the project team members, this workshop might also include the project sponsor, SMEs, customer representatives, and other stakeholders, depending on the size of the project.

Role

Refers to a human-driven function in a work setting.

Rolling Wave Planning

An iterative planning technique in which the work to be accomplished in the near term is planned in detail, while the work in the future is planned at a higher level.

Root Cause Analysis

An analytical technique used to determine the basic underlying reason that causes a variance or a defect or a risk. A root cause may underlie more than one variance or defect or risk.

SAFe® (Scaled Agile Framework)

A knowledge base of integrated patterns for enterprise-scale lean-agile development. A framework that implements Scrum at an enterprise level.

Salience Model

A classification model that groups stakeholders according to level of authority, immediate needs, and how appropriate their involvement is in terms of the project.

Schedule Baseline

The approved version of a schedule model that can be changed using formal change control procedures and is used as the basis of comparison to actual results. It is one of the main project documents that should be created before the project starts.

Schedule Compression

A method used to shorten the schedule duration without reducing the project scope.

Schedule Forecast

Estimates or predictions of conditions and events in the project's future based on information and knowledge available at the time the schedule is calculated.

Schedule Management Plan

A component of the project or program management plan that establishes the criteria and the activities for developing, monitoring, and controlling the schedule.

Schedule Performance Index (SPI)

A measure of schedule efficiency, expressed as the ratio of earned value to planned value.

Schedule Variance (SV)

A measure of schedule performance is expressed as the difference between the earned value and the planned value.

Scope Baseline

The approved version of a scope statement, Work Breakdown Structure (WBS) and its associated WBS dictionary can be changed using formal change control procedures and is used as a basis for comparison to actual results.

Scope Creep

The uncontrolled expansion of project scope without adjustments to time, cost, and resources.

Scope Management Plan

A component of the project or program management plan that describes how the scope will be defined, developed, monitored, controlled, and validated.

Scope Statement

Details about project deliverables and the major objectives of a project, including measurable outcomes.

Scrum

An agile framework for developing and sustaining complex products, with specific roles, events, and artifacts.

Scrum Master

The coach of the development team and process owner in the Scrum framework. Removes obstacles, facilitates productive events, and protects the team from disruptions.

Scrum of Scrums (SoS)

A technique to operate Scrum at scale for several teams working on the same product, coordinating discussions of progress on their interdependencies, and focusing on how to integrate the delivery of software, especially in areas of overlap.

Scrum Team

Dedicated, self-managing, cross-functional, fully empowered individuals who deliver the finished work required by the customer.

Secondary Risk

A risk that arises as a direct result of implementing a risk response.

Self-Organizing Team

A cross-functional team in which people fluidly assume leadership as needed to achieve the team's objectives. See also "cross-functional team."

Sensitivity Analysis

An analysis technique to determine which individual project risks or other sources of uncertainty have the most potential impact on project outcomes, by correlating variations in project outcomes with variations in elements of a quantitative risk analysis model.

Sequential Relationships

Refers to a consecutive relationship between phases; phases occur in procession and without overlap.

Servant Leadership

The practice of leading the team by focusing on understanding and addressing the needs and development of team members in order to enable the highest possible team performance.

Service-Level Agreement (SLA)

A contract between a service provider (either internal or external) and the end user that defines the level of service expected from the service provider.

Share

A strategy for managing positive risks or opportunities that involves allocating some or all the ownership of the opportunity to a third party.

Silo

See "*Organizational Silo*".

Simulation

An analytical technique that models the combined effect of uncertainties to evaluate their potential impact on objectives.

Six Sigma

See *"Lean Six Sigma"*.

Skills List

The skills list provides details of all the skills the team possesses. This includes interpersonal skills needed to establish and maintain relationships with other people. Some of the skills may be irrelevant to the project team, while some are highly relevant to project goals.

Slack

Used in the critical path method. Amount of time that a task can be delayed without affecting the deadlines of other subsequent tasks.

Smoothing

See *"Resource Smoothing"*.

SoS

See *"Scrum of Scrums"*.

Source Selection Criteria

A set of attributes, desired by the buyer, which a seller is required to meet or exceed to be selected for a contract.

Source-Based Risk Classification

A method of analyzing risk in terms of its origins.

Special Cause

Refers to a system in project management. Also called an assignable cause. Any factor or factors which may affect a system either in progress or outcome. See also *"Common Cause"*.

Special Interval

A period during a project when normal work may be suspended for some or all team members. See also *"Hardening Iteration/Iteration H"*

Spike

An agile term emerging from Extreme Programming (XP). Refers to timeboxed work for the purpose of answering a question or gathering information, rather than producing a viable product.

Sprint

Used in Scrum. A short time interval during which a usable and potentially releasable increment of the product is created. See also "**Iteration**".

Sprint Backlog

A list of work items identified by the Scrum team to be completed during the Scrum sprint.

Sprint Planning

A collaborative event in Scrum in which the Scrum team plans the work for the current sprint.

Sprint Retrospective

This critical part of the Scrum process is attended by the product owner, Scrum Master, and the Scrum team to analyze from a process perspective what is working well and what is not and to agree upon changes to implement.

Sprint Review

A review at the end of each iteration with the product owner and other customer stakeholders to review the progress of the product, get early feedback, and review an acceptance from the product owner of the stories delivered in the iteration. See also "**Demo**".

Sprint Velocity

A descriptive metric used by agile and hybrid teams. It describes the volume of work that a team performs during a sprint. Use this metric to understand the rate of your team's work during an average sprint.

Stakeholder

An individual, group, or organization that may affect, be affected by, or perceive itself to be affected by a decision, activity, or outcome of a project, program, or portfolio.

Stakeholder Analysis

A technique of systematically gathering and analyzing quantitative and qualitative information to determine whose interests should be considered throughout the project.

Stakeholder Cube

A three-dimensional classification model that builds on the previous two-dimensional grids to group stakeholders.

Stakeholder Engagement Assessment Matrix

A matrix that compares current and desired stakeholder engagement levels.

Stakeholder Engagement Plan

A component of the project management plan that identifies the strategies and actions required to promote productive involvement of stakeholders in project or program decision-making and execution. Used to understand stakeholder communication requirements and the level of stakeholder engagement in order to assess and adapt to the level of stakeholder participation in requirements activities.

Stakeholder Register

A project document including the identification, assessment, and classification of project stakeholders.

Stakeholder Requirement

A description of the needs of a particular stakeholder or category of stakeholders that must be met to achieve the business requirements. They may serve as a bridge between business requirements and the various categories of solution requirements.

Standard

A document established by an authority, custom or general consent as a model or example.

Standard Deviation (SD)

Statistical concept that gives a measure of the duration uncertainty and risk in project time estimation. SD represented by the Greek letter sigma (σ). A low value for the SD indicates that that data points are close to the mean or the expected value of the set, while a high value indicates that the data points are spread out over a wider range.

Start-to-Finish (SF)

A logical relationship in which a predecessor activity cannot finish until a successor activity has started.

Start-to-Start (SS)

A logical relationship in which a successor activity cannot start until a predecessor activity has started.

Statement of Work (SoW)

A document used to describe project work. The SoW identifies requirements, deliverables, scope, project details, and timelines for delivery.

Statistical Sampling

Choosing part of a population of interest for inspection. Used when more thorough data analysis methods are not suitable.

Statistical Sampling Process

A process that involves dividing sampling data into two categories—attribute and variable— each of which is gathered according to sampling plans. As corrective actions are taken in response to analysis of statistical sampling and other quality control activities, and as trend analysis is performed, defects and process variability should be reduced.

Strategic Plan

A high-level business document that explains an organization's vision and mission plus the approach that will be adopted to achieve this mission and vision, including the specific goals and objectives to be achieved during the period covered by the document.

Story

Describes the smallest unit of work in an agile framework. An informal, general explanation of a product, service, or software feature written from the end-user's perspective. Its purpose is to articulate how the feature will provide value to the customer. See also "*User Story*".

Story Card

One unit of delivery for an agile team.

Story Map

A visual model of all the features and functionality desired for a given product, created to give the team a holistic view of what they are building and why.

Story Points

Used in agile practice to estimate the amount of time it will take to complete a story item from the project backlog.

Storyboarding

The prototyping method that uses visuals or images to illustrate a process or represent a project outcome. Storyboards are useful to illustrate how a product, service, or application will function or operate when it is complete.

Supportive PMO

The type of PMO that provides a consultative role to projects by supplying templates, best practices, training, access to information, and lessons learned from other projects.

Sustainability

The planning, monitoring, and controlling of project delivery and support processes with consideration to environmental, economic, and social aspects of project-based working to meet the current needs of the stakeholders without compromising future generations.

Swarming

Act of all development team members working on only one requirement at a time during the sprint. Team members focus collectively to resolve a specific problem.

SWOT Analysis

A grid used to assess the strengths, weaknesses, opportunities, and threats of an organization, project, or option.

System

The rules, processes, procedures, people, and other elements that support an outcome or process. A project can have one or many systems, for example, a work authorization system, change control system, information system, etc.

System Development Life Cycle (SDLC)

Typically used with software development projects, SDLC depicts the group of phases which encompass the entire project life cycle from start to finish. How the project is executed is defined by the methodology—waterfall, agile, iterative, incremental, etc.

Tacit Knowledge

Personal knowledge that can be difficult to articulate and share such as beliefs, experience, and insights.

Tailoring

The mindful selection and adjustment of multiple factors. Determining the appropriate combination of processes, inputs, tools, techniques, outputs, and life cycle phases to manage a project.

Task

An activity to be accomplished with a specific purpose within a defined period of time. See also "**Activity**".

Task Board

Used to visualize the work and enable the team and stakeholders to track their progress as work is performed during an iteration. Examples of task boards include Kanban boards, to-do lists, procedure checklists, and Scrum boards.

Team

Group of people responsible for executing project tasks and producing deliverables outlined in the project plan and schedule.

Team Building

The process of continually supporting and working collaboratively with team members to enable a team to work together to solve problems, diffuse interpersonal issues, share information, and tackle project objectives as a unified force.

Team Charter

A document that records the team values, agreements, and operating guidelines as well as establishes clear expectations regarding acceptable behavior by project team members.

Team Management Plan

A component of the resource management plan that describes when and how team members will be acquired and how long they will be needed.

Team Resource Management

The processes necessary to organize, manage, and lead the people on the project team as well as the processes needed to procure and manage physical resources for a project.

Team-Building Activities

The specific functions or actions taken to help the team to develop into a mature, productive team. They can be formal or informal, brief, or extended, and facilitated by the project manager or a group facilitator.

Teaming Agreement

A legal contractual agreement between two or more parties to form a joint venture or any other arrangement as defined by the parties to meet the requirements of a business opportunity. The parties can be internal or external to the organization executing the project.

Technique

See *"Tool"*.

Template

A partially complete document in a predefined format that provides a defined structure for collecting, organizing, and presenting information and data.

Term Contract

A type of contract that engages the vendor to deliver a set amount of service— measured in staff-hours or a similar unit—over a set period of time.

Test-Driven Development (TDD)/Test-First Development

Derived from a software development practice, TDD helps in the design process by using repeated short development cycles. First the developer writes an (initially failing) automated test case that defines a desired improvement or new function. The team then produces the minimum amount of code to pass that test before finally refactoring the new code to acceptable standards.

Theme

Agile term. Refers to groupings of epics or stories.

Theory X

Refers to Theory X by Douglas McGregor which proposes that managers micro-manage their employees or team members because they assume their workers are unmotivated and dislike work.

Theory Y

Refers to Theory Y by Douglas McGregor which proposes that managers have an optimistic and positive opinion of their employees or team members, so this type of manager encourages a more collaborative, trust-based relationship between employees.

Threat

A risk that would have a negative effect on one or more project objectives.

Three-Point Estimating

A technique used to estimate cost or duration by applying an average or weighted average of optimistic, pessimistic, and most likely estimates when there is uncertainty with the individual activity estimates. Also called "triangular estimating".

Threshold

A predetermined value of a measurable project variable that represents a limit that requires action to be taken if it is reached.

Throughput

A key agile metric used to determine how many finished work items a process produces over a given time frame.

Time and Material (T&M) Contract

A type of contract that is a hybrid contractual arrangement containing aspects of both cost-reimbursable and fixed-price contracts.

Timebox

A fixed period of time to provide duration limits for an activity, a piece of work, or a meeting—for example, 1 week, 2 weeks, 3 weeks, or 1 month.

To Complete Performance Index (TCPI)

The estimate of the future cost performance that may be needed to complete the project within the approved budget.

Tolerance

The quantified description of acceptable variation for a quality, risk, budget, or other project requirement.

Tool

The applied function, action, procedure, or routine defined for a process to produce the desired output.

Tornado Diagram.

A special type of bar chart used in sensitivity analysis for comparing the relative importance of the variables.

Total Float

The amount of time that a schedule activity can be delayed or extended from its early start date without delaying the project finish date or violating a schedule constraint.

Total Quality Management (TQM)

An approach to improve business results through an emphasis on customer satisfaction, employee development, and processes rather than on functions.

Training

An activity in which team members acquire new or enhanced skills, knowledge, or attitudes.

Transfer

A strategy for managing negative risks or threats that involves shifting the impact and ownership of the risk to a third party and paying a risk premium to the party taking on the liability of the risk.

Transparency

One of the three pillars of empirical process (transparency, inspection, and adaptability) that promotes real-time, accurate progress on every aspect of the project. See also *"Visibility"*.

Trend Analysis

An analytical technique that uses mathematical models to forecast future outcomes based on historical results.

Trigger Condition

An event or situation that indicates that a risk is about to occur.

Triple Constraint

Refers to the factors of time, cost, and scope which can be adjusted when managing projects. Often called the project management triangle.

T-Shaped

Refers to a person whose skill set comprises one area of specialization and broad ability in other skills required by the team.

Unanimity

Agreement by everyone in the group on a single course of action.

Unique Identification Code

A specific configuration of a code of accounts that assigns a particular alphanumeric sequence of characters to each element of a WBS.

User Story

An informal, general explanation of a product, service, or software feature written from the perspective of the end user. Its purpose is to articulate how the feature will provide value to the customer. See also *"Story"*.

Validate Scope

The project management process of formalizing acceptance of the completed project deliverables.

Validation

The assurance that a product, service, or result meets the needs of the customer and other identified stakeholders. See also *"Verification"*.

Value

The worth that a project delivers to the business.

Value Analysis

The process of examining each of the components of business value and understanding the cost of each one. The goal is to cost effectively improve the components to increase the overall business value.

Value Delivery System

The combined and systematic effort by leadership, portfolio, and program and project management to create value in and for an organization.

Value Engineering

Systematic, organized approach to providing necessary functions in a project at the lowest cost.

Value Stream

An organizational construct that focuses on the flow of value to customers through the delivery of specific products or services.

Value Stream Mapping

A Lean enterprise technique used to document, analyze, and improve the flow of information or materials required to produce a product or service for a customer.

Variability Control Charts

Used to analyze and communicate the variability of a process or project activity over time. See also "*Control Charts*".

Variable Sampling Data

Data from a sample that is measured on a continuous scale such as time, temperature, or weight.

Variance

A quantifiable deviation, departure, or divergence away from a known baseline or expected value.

Variance Analysis

A technique for determining the cause and degree of difference between the baseline and the actual performance.

Variance at Completion (VAC)

A formula that measures a project's actual cost, compared with the budgeted amount. It is the difference between the budget at completion (BAC) and the estimate at completion (EAC). The formula is VAC = BAC – EAC.

Velocity

A measure of a team's productivity rate at which the deliverables are produced, validated, and accepted within a predefined interval.

Vendor Bid Analysis

A cost estimation technique used to understand what a product/service should cost.

Verification

The evaluation of whether a product, service, or result complies with a regulation, requirement, specification, or imposed condition. See also "*Validation*".

Verified Deliverable

Deliverables that have been compared to the scope/requirements and specifications to ensure they are correct.

Version Control

A system that records changes to a file, in a way that allows users to retrieve previous changes made to it.

Virtual Team

A group of people with a shared goal who fulfill their roles with little or no time spent meeting face-to-face.

Visibility

See "*Transparency*".

Vision Statement

A stated direction for the project established and communicated by the project sponsor.

Waiver

A legally binding provision in which one party in a contract agrees to forfeit a claim without the other party becoming liable, even inadvertently.

War Room

Refers to a physical space where project team members and stakeholders plan strategy and run a project.

Warranty

A promise, explicit or implied, that goods or services will meet a predetermined standard. Usually limited to a specific period of time.

Waterfall

An informal name for predictive project management approach. This term is no longer used by PMI. See "*Predictive Life Cycle*".

WBS Dictionary

A document that provides detailed deliverable, activity, and scheduling information about each component in the work breakdown structure (WBS).

What-If Scenario

Used in the Develop Schedule process, this technique evaluates different scenarios to predict their effects–both positive and negative–on the project objectives.

Wideband Delphi Estimating

Consensus-based estimation technique for estimating effort.

Wireframe

A non-functional interface design (not written in code) that shows the key elements and how they would interact to give the user an idea of how the system would function.

Withdrawal

Refusal to deal with a conflict.

Work Authorization System

Used to ensure that work gets performed at the right time, in the right sequence, and with the right resources. This can be formal or informal.

Work Breakdown Structure (WBS)

A hierarchical decomposition of the total scope of work to be carried out by the project team to accomplish the project objectives and create the required deliverables.

Work in Progress (WIP)

Work that has been started but not yet completed.

Work Package

The work defined at the lowest level of the work breakdown structure (WBS) for which cost, and duration are estimated and managed.

Work Performance Data

The raw observations and measurements identified during activities being performed to carry out the project work. They can be recorded in the PMIS and project documents.

Work Performance Information

The raw performance data collected from controlling processes, analyzed in comparison with project management plan components, project documents, and other work performance information.

Work Performance Report

The physical or electronic representation of work performance information compiled in project documents, intended to generate decisions, actions, or awareness.

Work Shadowing

An on-the-job technique that enables someone to learn about and perform a job while observing and working with another, more experienced person.

Workaround

A suitable, unplanned alternative action used to complete work.

Workflow

Carefully planned sequence of the tasks and activities that need to be done to complete the project.

XP Metaphor

A common Extreme Programming (XP) technique that describes a common vision of how a program works.

Index

ABOUT THE AUTHORS

The authors of this book were contributors to the 5th, 6th, and 7th editions of the PMBOK Guide and are PMI Authorized Training Partners (ATP) and authorized PMP instructors. We have also participated in updating the initial versions of the PMI PMP Prep Boot Camp course and were selected as a key developer of the v3.1 release of the PMI-authorized PMP course materials and practice questions.

Greta Blash, PgMP, PMP, PMI-ACP, DASSM, PMI-PBA, CDAI, PMI-RMP, CBAP, AAC, Agile Hybrid Project Pro

Greta Blash is a certified Program Management Professional (PgMP) and Project Manager Professional (PMP) with extensive experience as an executive and consulting IT professional, both domestically and internationally. Her areas of expertise include program management, project management, Agile scrum and kanban approaches, customer relationship management, data warehousing/business intelligence, and systems development. She also holds Agile certifications (PMI-ACP, DASSM, and CDAI), business analysis certification (PMI-PBA), and risk management certification (PMI-RMP) from Project Management Institute (PMI), the world's leading professional association for the project management profession. She also holds several business analysis certifications (CBAP, AAC, and POBA) from the International Institute for Business Analysis (IIBA).

Greta has taught project and program management, Agile, and business analysis certification courses worldwide, held various positions at the PMI chapter and regional levels, and given many presentations.

Greta is also the author of two top-rated courses on LinkedIn Learning: Foundations of Business Analysis and Business Analysis for Project Managers.

Steve Blash, PMP, PMI-ACP, DASSM, Agile Hybrid Project Pro

Steve is the cofounder of Facilitated Methods and a senior instructor with Facilitated Methods and is a certified Project Management Professional (PMP®), an Agile Certified Practitioner (PMI-ACP®), and a certified Disciplined Senior Scrum Master (DASSM®) with exceptional Information Technology knowledge and project management experience managing all aspects of large complex projects. His areas of expertise include strategic business alignment, business requirements analysis, business re-engineering, business intelligence, and system development methods.

He is a PMI® Authorized ATP Instructor for PMP®, CAPM®, and Disciplined Agile courses.

Steve is a past president of the PMI® chapter in Las Vegas (PMI-SNC).

He has written numerous articles for ProjectTimes.com, BATimes.com, and AllPM.com, as well as for the PMI® chapter's newsletter. He has spoken on project management for various PMI® chapters and organizations including the PMI® Congress 2015 - North America Conference and the Art of Projects in Budapest, Hungary, in 2022.

Made in United States
Troutdale, OR
04/07/2024